Palgrave Studies in Democracy, Innovation, and Entrepreneurship for Growth

Series Editor
Elias G. Carayannis, The George Washington University, Washington, DC, USA

The central theme of this series is to explore why some areas grow and others stagnate, and to measure the effects and implications in a trans-disciplinary context that takes both historical evolution and geographical location into account. In other words, when, how and why does the nature and dynamics of a political regime inform and shape the drivers of growth and especially innovation and entrepreneurship? In this socio-economic and socio-technical context, how could we best achieve growth, financially and environmentally?

This series aims to address such issues as:

- How does technological advance occur, and what are the strategic processes and institutions involved?
- How are new businesses created? To what extent is intellectual property protected?
- Which cultural characteristics serve to promote or impede innovation? In what ways is wealth distributed or concentrated?

These are among the key questions framing policy and strategic decision-making at firm, industry, national, and regional levels.

A primary feature of the series is to consider the dynamics of innovation and entrepreneurship in the context of globalization, with particular respect to emerging markets, such as China, India, Russia, and Latin America. (For example, what are the implications of China's rapid transition from providing low-cost manufacturing and services to becoming an innovation powerhouse? How do the perspectives of history and geography explain this phenomenon?)

Contributions from researchers in a wide variety of fields will connect and relate the relationships and inter-dependencies among (1) Innovation, (2) Political Regime, and (3) Economic and Social Development. We will consider whether innovation is demonstrated differently across sectors (e.g., health, education, technology) and disciplines (e.g., social sciences, physical sciences), with an emphasis on discovering emerging patterns, factors, triggers, catalysts, and accelerators to innovation, and their impact on future research, practice, and policy.

This series will delve into what are the sustainable and sufficient growth mechanisms for the foreseeable future for developed, knowledge-based economies and societies (such as the EU and the US) in the context of multiple, concurrent and interconnected "tipping-point" effects with short (MENA) as well as long (China, India) term effects from a geo-strategic, geo-economic, geo-political and geo-technological set of perspectives.

This conceptualization lies at the heart of the series, and offers to explore the correlation between democracy, innovation and growth.

More information about this series at
http://www.palgrave.com/gp/series/14635

Luis Antonio Orozco ·
Gonzalo Ordóñez-Matamoros ·
Jaime Humberto Sierra-González ·
Javier García-Estévez · Isabel Bortagaray
Editors

Science, Technology, and Higher Education

Governance Approaches on Social Inclusion and Sustainability in Latin America

palgrave
macmillan

Editors
Luis Antonio Orozco
School of Management
Universidad Externado de Colombia
Bogota, Colombia

Jaime Humberto Sierra-González
Pontificia Universidad Javeriana
Bogota, Colombia

Isabel Bortagaray
Universidad de la República
Montevideo, Uruguay

Gonzalo Ordóñez-Matamoros
Universidad Externado de Colombia
Bogota, Colombia

Javier García-Estévez
Universidad de Los Andes
Bogota, Colombia

ISSN 2662-3641 ISSN 2662-365X (electronic)
Palgrave Studies in Democracy, Innovation, and Entrepreneurship for Growth
ISBN 978-3-030-80719-1 ISBN 978-3-030-80720-7 (eBook)
https://doi.org/10.1007/978-3-030-80720-7

This Palgrave Macmillan imprint is published by the registered company Springer Nature Switzerland AG
The registered company address is: Gewerbestrasse 11, 6330 Cham, Switzerland

Contents

Notes on Contributors

Cristian Alister Sanhueza is a Ph.D. candidate in intercultural studies at the Catholic University of Temuco. He is a computer engineer and sociologist. His areas of research are sociology of science and technology, sociology of development and sociology of work. He is currently working on the development of his Ph.D. research on the processes of indigenous consultations as devices for approaching socio-technical controversies and strategies of ethnogovernance.

Alejandra Boni is professor at Universitat Politècnica de València (Spain) and deputy director of Ingenio (CSIC-UPV). She is honorary professor at the University of the Free State in South Africa. Her research interest focus on human development, higher education, global citizenship and transformative innovation. She is leading the formative evaluation component of the Transformative Innovation Policy Consortium.

Kleinsy Bonilla is an Associate Researcher, Department of Science and Technology DPCT, University of Campinas UNICAMP—Brazil. Her areas of interest are: Science and Technology Policy, International Cooperation, Science Diplomacy, S&T Capacity Building.

Ricardo Bonilla is a Professor at Corporación Universitaria Minuto de Dios UNIMINUTO, Bogotá—Colombia. He is an expert in quantitative modelling for decision-making in complex social systems. He is a Physicist with Master of Science, and a Doctor of Engineering with application in Operations Research, Complexity Sciences and Information Theories.

He is a consultant in visual, predictive and prescriptive analytics, and a Leader in data quality management projects, conceptual and quantitative updating of indicators, models for prospective. He is a Teacher of Complex Thinking, Operations Research and Business Analytics, and a Researcher with publications on applied probabilistic models.

Isabel Bortagaray is a sociologist, who holds a Ph.D. in Public Policy, with a focus on Science, Technology and Innovation Policy from the Georgia Institute of Technology. She is Professor at the University of the Republic in Uruguay; and Honorary Research Fellow at the Center for Science, Technology and Innovation Indicators (CeSTII), of the Human Sciences Research Council of South Africa.

Felipe Bustos Mg (c) on the Social Science Department of the Universidad de la Frontera, Chile. He graduated as Sociologist in The University of the Frontera. His theoretical–methodological developments are inscribed in the general field of social studies of science and technology, especially in science and technology policies, bibliometrics and political economy of science.

Ronald Cancino Salas is an anthropologist, a Lecturer at Social Sciences Department and Researcher at Centro de Investigaciones Sociológicas (CIS), Universidad de la Frontera, Chile. He is a Ph.D. in Social Sciences from the University of Chile. His main area of research is contemporary science from the perspective of Complex Adaptive Systems, especially regarding the relationship between the structure and evolution of lines of research as emerging phenomena and the forms of collaboration and regulation of scientific activity. Along with this, he works on the modelling of science, technology and innovation systems, the analysis of conflicts and socio-technical controversies, and science, technology and innovation policies in Latin America. Methodologically, he employs Agent-based models, bibliometrics and network analysis, and qualitative and ethnographic research in science and technology studies. Member at the board of ESOCITE Latin American Association of Social Studies in Science and Technology.

Alexander Castillo Garcés is a Political scientist, Mg. in Public Policies. Professor at the Faculty of Law, Political and Social Sciences of the Cauca University, and a member of the Social Sciences and Humanities Interdisciplinary Research Group—GIISCH. He is Professor of the Faculty of Law, Social and Political Sciences of the Cauca Autonomous University

Corporation, a member of GIICSH. He is a postgraduate professor at the School of Social Work and the Administration Sciences Faculty of the Universidad del Valle. He is also a Consultant for UNDP, Transparency Secretariat of the Presidency of the Republic, Ministry of Justice and Law, National Planning Department.

José Coloma Zapata is a Ph.D. candidate in Sociology from the Alberto Hurtado University, Chile. He graduated as a Master in Applied Social Sciences and also graduated in Sociology at Universidad de la Frontera. He is working for more than eight years in bibliometrics and social studies of science. He has recently started working on the role of technological mediators in solidarity economy companies.

Salim Chalela Naffah is Ph.D. in Education at the Autonomous University of Barcelona from the Applied Pedagogy Department. He is the Chief of Research Promotion at Universidad del Rosario—Colombia. His research field is research management in Higher Education Institutions. He was Vice-Chancellor for Research at the Autonomous Latin American University—UNAULA, and the Administrative Coordinator of the Latin American and Caribbean HUB for Transformative Innovation linked to Transformative Innovation Policy Consortium—TPC.

William Chará Ordoñez is a political scientist, with a master's degree in Sociology. He is Professor of the Faculty of Law, Social and Political Sciences of the Cauca Autonomous University Corporation, and a member of the Social Sciences and Humanities Interdisciplinary Research Group—GIISCH. He is a Consultant at the National Planning Department, Save The Children, Transparency Secretariat of the Presidency of the Republic, UNDP, Ministry of Justice and Law and Verification Mechanism FF.MM.

Nohora Galvis is a marine biologist who has dedicated her 30-year career to study how to improve coral reefs conservation effectiveness. Her multidisciplinary background reaches Ph.D. Studies from ecological sciences towards the social involvement and economic valuations of coral reefs.

Rosa Helena Galvis has her Doctorate studies in Social and Environmental Psychology and an expertise working with fishers communities.

Mauricio García Ojeda is Lecturer at Department of Social Sciences and Researcher at Centro de Investigaciones Sociológicas (CIS), Universidad de la Frontera, Chile. He is currently completing his Ph.D. at Department of Sociology at the Universitat Autònoma de Barcelona. His main area of research is the governance of public policy enforcement at local and regional level. He is mainly interested in the role of trust, reputation, social networks and formal institutions, and their effect on expected outcomes in public policy, specifically those having to do with efficiency, citizens' participation, citizens' control and technological innovation. Mauricio Garcia Ojeda specializes in behaviourally enriched rational choice theory, principal-agent theory, social capital theory, institutional design theory, social network theory, new institutional economics and new economic sociology. Methodologically, he employs social networks analysis, game theory and analytic narratives.

Javier García-Estévez is an Associate Professor in planning and territorial development at the Interdisciplinary Centre of Development Studies at the University of Los Andes. His area of research is regional and local economic development with particular emphasis in science, technology and innovation. He is the principal investigator of the "Contribution of Universities to Regional Development" project, participates in the "Transformative Innovation Policy in Colombia" project led by the University of Sussex's Science Policy Research (SPRU), and is a researcher on the "Regional Development Index - Latin America" Project in collaboration with researchers from the Autonomous University of Chile, the Inter-American Development Bank and the University of the Republic of Uruguay. He is an economist from the Industrial University of Santander (Colombia) and has a master's degree and a doctorate in economics from the University of Barcelona (Spain).

Javier Medina is Doctor of Social Sciences, Gregorian University. He is a Coordinator of the Confederation of Latin American and Caribbean Foresight Networks, CYTED Program. Full Professor, Universidad del Valle, Cali, Colombia. He has designed and executed around 50 prospective exercises since 1989. He has published 134 texts, including books, articles and institutional documents as author, co-author and editor. Author of the "Prospective and Strategic Decision Manual", published by ECLAC, Santiago de Chile (2006), "Prospective and Public Policy for structural change in Latin America and the Caribbean (ECLAC, 2014)" and "Opening paths in the prospect of Latin America" (Universidad del Valle - Usach, 2020).

Paula Andrea Mora Pedreros holds a Degree in Philosophy and Letters and Master in Etnoliteratura, University of Nariño; is a Specialist in Pedagogy of Autonomous Learning and specialist in Higher Education, UNAD; has a Master's Degree in Educational Technology Tecnológico de Monterrey; is a Candidate for Doctor of Philosophy, Universidad Pontificia Bolivariana. He is also a Teacher Researcher of the Corporación Autónoma del Cauca. GIICSH group.

Gonzalo Ordóñez-Matamoros is a Ph.D. in Public Policy of the Georgia Institute of Technology and the Georgia State University, USA. He is an Assistant Professor at the Faculty of Behavioural, Management and Social Sciences at the University of Twente, The Netherlands, and Dean at the Faculty of Finance, Government and International Relations at the Universidad Externado de Colombia in Bogotá.

Luis Antonio Orozco is a Ph.D. in management at Universidad de los Andes and business administrator at Pontificia Universidad Javeriana. He is a Full Professor in the School of Management at Universidad Externado de Colombia and senior researcher at Colombian Ministry of Science, Technology and Innovation. He is a member at Asociación Colombiana para el Avance de la Ciencia—Avanciencia. He is an editorial advisory board member at the *Journal of Management History* and a member at the scientific committee at the International Conference on Scientometrics and Infometrics. He was adjoined researcher at University of Twente (The Netherlands), University of Massachusetts (United States) and Observatorio Colombiano de Ciencia y Tecnología—OCyT.

Cristhian Fabián Ruiz Ramos is a Ph.D. candidate in Universidad Católica de Perú. He is a Mechanical and environmental engineer. He is the author of different books and articles in scientific journals on planning, knowledge management, and data and information analysis. His areas of research are data analysis of science, technology and innovation Systems. He is the Director of Organizational Development in Governorate of Cundinamarca.

Carlos Eugenio Ramos-Pérez is an Adjunct Professor at the Business Department, School of Business and Economics—Pontificia Universidad

Javeriana (Col). He is a Ph.D. in Business and Management, The University of Manchester (UK); and a Master in Economics and Innovation Management, Universidad Autónoma Metropolitana—Xochimilco (Mex); with a B.Sc. in Management, Universidad del Pedregal (Mex).

Juan David Reina Rozo is an Industrial Engineer, is a Magister in Environment and Development, and a Candidate to Doctorate in Engineering—Industry and Organizations at Universidad Nacional de Colombia. He is also a Researcher of the Technologies and Innovation for Community Development Research Group. He had participated in co-design processes of technologies in Brazil, Peru, Colombia, Uganda and Nepal. He is editor of the International Journal of Engineering, Social Justice and Peace. His main topics of interest are community innovation, socio-technical change, community-based innovation ecosystems, popular engineering and peacebuilding.

Hector Heraldo Rojas Jiménez is a Researcher and lecturer at the Faculty of Finance, Government and International Relations of the Universidad Externado de Colombia, also a Professional in Finance and International Relations from the same university; a lawyer, he holds a M.Sc. in Economic Development in Latin America, M.Sc. sciences politiques spécialité idées politiques et intelligence du monde contemporain, and Ph D. in sciences politiques of the Université Sorbonne Nouvelle, Paris III. Under the auspices of the Externado University of Colombia and the Rutherford Scholarship, he advanced a postdoctoral research stay at the Manchester Institute of Innovation Research of the University of Manchester researching about Bioeconomy.

John Sanabria is a Ph.D. candidate at School of Management—Universidad Externado de Colombia. He has a master's in industrial engineering (Universidad de los Andes—Colombia), and is a business administrator (UNIMIMUTO). He is a Teacher, Researcher and Consultant in management, strategy, entrepreneurial and business networks. He is the Director of the Business Administration program at Universidad de la Salle—Bogotá, Colombia.

Milena Serafim is Assistant Professor in the School of Applied Sciences FCA—University of Campinas UNICAMP—Brazil. Her areas of interest are: Analysis of Public Policies and Institutions; Actor, Governance and Decision Process; and Higher Education.

Jaime Humberto Sierra-González is Associate Professor at the Business Department, School of Business and Economics—Pontificia Universidad Javeriana (Col). He is a Ph.D. in Business and Management, The University of Manchester (UK); He has Master's in economics of the Internationalization of Business and Finance, Università di Roma "Tor Vergata", Rome (Ita); a Master in Economics, Pontificia Universidad Javeriana; Diploma in International Relations, Academia Diplomática (Col); B.A. in Education, Universidad Distrital (Col). He is Professor at the Master in Economics, Master in Strategy, Innovation and Competitiveness, Diploma in Technology Management, and the Diploma in Management of Social and Solidarity Enterprises at PUJ.

Diana Velasco is adjunct professor of the Universidad de Ibagué in Colombia and research fellow in Ingenio (CSIC-UPV), Spain. She is a Ph.D. in innovation studies from Edinburgh University and an active member of the Transformative Innovation Policy Consortium with field work in Sweden, Colombia, South Africa and Catalonia. Her research interest focus on human development, higher education and transformative innovation.

List of Figures

List of Tables

CHAPTER 1

Science, Technology, and Innovation Governance for Social Inclusion and Sustainable Development in Latin America

Luis Antonio Orozco, Gonzalo Ordóñez-Matamoros, Javier García-Estévez, Jaime Humberto Sierra-González, and Isabel Bortagaray

1.1 Introduction

Latin America and the Caribbean (LAC) is a plural and diverse region endowed with wide munificence of natural resources, peoples, and

L. A. Orozco (✉)
School of Management, Universidad Externado de Colombia, Bogotá, Colombia
e-mail: luis.orozco@uexternado.edu.co

G. Ordóñez-Matamoros
Universidad Externado de Colombia, University of Twente, Bogotá, Colombia
e-mail: gonzalo.ordonez@uexternado.edu.co

L. A. Orozco et al. (eds.), *Science, Technology, and Higher Education*, Palgrave Studies in Democracy, Innovation, and Entrepreneurship for Growth,
https://doi.org/10.1007/978-3-030-80720-7_1

culture. This involves high heterogeneity across countries and several differences in terms of policy orientations, the capacity to create economic growth, and the way to meet social and environmental needs. The region has been improving in terms of GDP growth since 2016 but without substantially improving the existing income gap, poverty rate, and Gini coefficient (ECLAC et al., 2019).

Latin America is one of the most unequal regions in the world, as ascertained by several indicators concerning education, health, and social security services, as well as income and wealth distribution (ECLAC, 2019). The Inter-American Development Bank Research Network project on social exclusion in Latin American and the Caribbean has long stated that inequalities are associated with the absence of opportunities (Behrman et al., 2002).

Several initiatives like those led by the Economic Commission for Latin America and the Caribbean (ECLAC) regard projects intended to defeat poverty and enhance social inclusion (Cepal, 2006) in an effort to boost the region into the route to Agenda 2030 for sustainable development (Sustainable Development Goals—SDGs[1]). Such initiatives have promoted the enactment of better policies for social development through inclusive economic growth that includes social protection and the creation of work opportunities with dignifying jobs (Cepal, 2016). Likewise, the OECD LAC Regional Program (LACRP) has tried to enhance social inclusion through efforts to strengthen institutions, improve governance, and increase productivity (OCDE, 2017).

J. García-Estévez
Universidad de Los Andes, Bogotá, Colombia
e-mail: jh.garcia@uniandes.edu.co

J. H. Sierra-González
Pontificia Universidad Javeriana, Bogotá, Colombia
e-mail: jhsierra@javeriana.edu.co

I. Bortagaray
Universidad de La República, Montevideo, Uruguay

[1] See SDG #10 goal 10.2 that stated "by 2030 empower and promote the social, economic and political inclusion of all irrespective of age, sex, disability, race, ethnicity, origin, religion or economic or other status".

The concept of governance began to be used in the neoliberal rationale to refer to the bargaining process and agreements between public and private organizations in the realm of issues that governments cannot face alone (Bevir, 2008). The concept appeared in New Institutional Economics' frame to mean the agreements that infuse order, mitigate the conflict, and realize mutual gains in the contractual or hybrid forms between markets and hierarchies (Williamson, 1996, 2005). Rhodes (1996, p. 652) extends this vision claiming that "governance refers to 'self-organizing interorganizational networks' (that) complement markets and hierarchies as governing structures for authoritatively allocating resources and exercising control and coordination".

Governance includes not only a bargaining process and agreements between public and private actors, but also civil society and different regions and jurisdictions as happening in the European Union. In the realm of multilateral agencies like the United Nations, the World Bank, or the OCDE emerged the idea of global governance, promoting the coordination of policies among countries to pursue common goals like social and environmental development and sustainability. Then, awareness about poverty eradication for improving social inclusion and justice has been embedded in the concept of governance or good governance (Bevir, 2008).

Governance for social inclusion means that public policy does not exclusively belong to the State. Instead, several if not all actors belonging to civil society can participate in the definition of problems and the ways to solve them. Thus, governance implies hybrid structures that organize multiple stakeholders' participation in a multi-jurisdictional and multiregional scenario in which formal and informal spaces and mechanisms of relationships and accountability can be performed (Bevir, 2008).

The idea of governance was introduced in Latin America by multilateral agencies like The World Bank, The United Nations Development Programme (UNDP), and the Inter-American Development Bank based on their interest to improve the management of international aid and funding across the region (Zurbriggen, 2011). The aid programs that want to alleviate poverty have been one of the most important efforts to introduce governance as a means to coordinate public, private, and civil organizations for social inclusion.

Here it is valuable to remember the ideas of Zygmunt Bauman about the social exclusion. He stated that "Uncertainty, insecurity's principal cause, is by far the most decisive tool of power—indeed, its very substance" (Bauman, 2011, p. 42). In fact "Human vulnerability and uncertainty is the foundation of all political power" (Bauman, 2011, p. 122). Then, the manipulation of uncertainty is an instrument for discrimination between us and them. Bauman understands that "The fear which democracy and its offspring, the social state, promised to uproot has returned with a vengeance. Most of us, from the bottom to the top, nowadays fear the threat, however unspecified and vague, of being excluded, proved inadequate to the challenge, snubbed, refused dignity and humiliated... On the diffuse and misty fears that saturate present-day society, politicians as much as the consumer markets are eager to capitalize". And continues "The risks to which democracies are currently exposed are only partly due to the way state governments desperately seek to legitimize their right to rule and to demand discipline by flexing their muscles and showing their determination to stand firm in the face of the endless, genuine or putative, threats to human bodies – instead of (as they did before) protecting their citizens' social usefulness, respected places in society, and insurance against exclusion, the denial of dignity and humiliation". (Bauman, 2011, pp. 18–20). Finally, he proposed the alternative in terms of provision of security and safety using fear as a channel to engage voters and costumers. He saw "That alternative seems to have been recently located (...) in the issue of personal safety: current or portending, overt or hidden, genuine or putative fears of the threats to human bodies, possessions and habitats—whether arising from pandemics and unhealthy diets or lifestyle regimes, or from criminal activities, anti-social conduct by the 'underclass', or most recently global terrorism" (Bauman, 2011, p. 54).

In LAC countries, several initiatives began to provide support to vulnerable families to alleviate poverty and exclusion. The management of fears and uncertainty with the discourse of governance as a tool to promote democracy with social inclusion began to monger the policy and its social programs. However, the creation of collateral damages, as Bauman (2011) conceptualized the unintended consequences of policies, emerged in the region. As Zurbriggen (2011) pointed out, programs such as *Familias por la Inclusión Social* in Argentina; *Puente-Chile Solidario*; *Bolsa Família* in Brazil; *Panes* in Uruguay; *Red de Protección Social* in Nicaragua; *Familias en Acción* in Colombia; *Programa de Asignación Familiar* in Honduras, and *Bono Solidario* in Ecuador do not contribute to improve governance and democracy with the empowerment of citizenship and social capital. These programs just created a market for

Non-Governmental Organizations (NGOs) to deliver social assistance and allowed private organizations to become providers of social services such as health care and food supply.

With the governance discourse, the first case of privatization in Latin America was the infrastructure development and public services as water and sanitary issues. The State was in charge of coordinating several actors' efforts to warranty the quality and efficiency in social services provided by privates and controlled by civil organizations. In Colombia, a group of contractors began to centralize the water services due to their capacity to sell the idea that they will be able to provide a more efficient administration. However, the entrepreneurs began to be corrupt and civil society and unions were not taken into account. The losses for mismanagement created more and more profound problems, showing that private interest could lead to more trouble for social and economic development (Ardila, 2013; Colmenares, 2013), damaging not only public services, also, in this case, the financial markets (Orozco et al., 2018). In Argentina, private multinational corporations faced several shortcomings in terms of the lack of previous studies, badly designed biddings, and deficient contracts in an inadequate regulatory framework that finalized in international judiciary tribunals and expensive lawsuits. In Honduras and Peru there is not an organized market, the tanks cars abuse with their power, the quality of the liquid is not trustworthy and the water became an expensive good (Zurbriggen, 2011). The decentralization also carried out more challenges in terms of controls and disputes for the access and management of resources, widening the gap in the concentration of wealth.

The STI policies in LAC have disjunctives between social and environmental needs and economic growth with scarce resources for creating opportunities with science, technology, and innovation (STI). It is not easy for policymakers to go beyond statistics and create with the available information new meanings to foster the decision-making that encompasses the restrictions and limitations in productivity and industrial evolution with the problems around poverty and environmental degradation. With scare resources, dilemmas like investing in STI for the oil industry that assure several jobs instead to recover a river damaged by oil extraction, a river that in the long term assure survival, surround the policymakers that need more insight to understand ways to improve governance and straight institutions to assure social justice, environmental protection, reduce corruption and create opportunities for enhancing the quality of life.

The ideology that STI is a tool to achieve competitiveness for the nations created more damages than benefits. As the Nobel Price Paul Krugman noted many years ago, "competitiveness is a meaningless word when applied to national economies. And the obsession with competitiveness is both wrong and dangerous" (Krugman, 1994, p. 44). The ideology was developed mainly by Michael Porter in which the US's neoliberal interest spread a model that nations must be managed as a private corporation instead of creating conditions for welfare (Aktouf, 2008). Aktouf et al., (2005, p. 184) stated that "For Habermas, the morality of a given utterance depends on the dialogical exchange made up of a claim to validity by a speaker, objections to this claim by other speakers, and arguments by the speaker in response to these objections, all of which occurs within the framework of a space of free speech. The problem here is that Porter's positivism imposes the number and nature of competitive forces and the result of the ensuing analysis of industries as scientific and therefore non-debatable truths. It is in this sense that Porter's model is a formidable instrument of domination". Then, Aktouf (2008, p. 170) questioned "*¿Se puede impunemente transformar de esta manera a los Estados en comités de gestión de los intereses financieros transnacionales, y a las naciones en espacios dedicados únicamente a la competencia entre gigantes empresariales obstinados en acaparar el único resultado presentado como deseable en todo lo que hacen: la multiplicación más rápida posible del dinero por el dinero mismo?*" Porter's framework cannot explain the reality of market dynamics and, instead, provided simplistic toolkits for managers—diamonds, forces, and chains—to promote the creation of profits in a struggle between firms and countries in wild capitalism (Aktouf, 2004).[2] Aktouf (2008, p. 177) concludes that "*Al convertir al planeta en un gran campo de batalla para la competitividad infinita, bajo el sólo apremio de la maximización de los beneficios y los dividendos, Porter nos conduce tan simplemente a hacer depender lo macroeconómico de lo microeconómico y las políticas nacionales*

[2] "The determinants in the diamond model are a necessary reduction to enable the continuity of Porter's reasoning, in that he attempts to compare different economies without having to concern himself with their differences. It is not easy to compare the maximalist financial logic of the self-regulated, American-styled capitalist market (which in recent times has moved towards unimaginable and irrational summits of speculation since the heady rush engendered and maintained by Internet businesses and the Enron and Worldcom scandals) to the kinds of 'stale-regulated, social-market' industrial capitalism found in Germany and Japan" (Aktouf, 2004, p. 28).

de las decisiones del mundo de los negocios. El tratamiento de la economía sólo se concibe en un muy corto plazo, agravando exponencialmente los desequilibrios, ya desastrosos, entre el Norte y el Sur, y entre los factores de producción mismos (capital, trabajo y naturaleza)".

The movement of competitiveness and public policies' orientation includes STI as a key tool to achieve better indicators in terms of market shares and corporative profits, instead of addressing social and environmental challenges such as poverty, social inclusion, and climate change. The movement of automation and the application of management science and operation research in the name of the advancement of science has been helping entrepreneurs to cut costs in re-engineering process and low wages (as the gospel of Porter instigates), firing people in downsized hierarchies and replaced humans with machines and algorithms. The damage created with the promotion of this ideology sells more than others the belief that competitiveness through STI is the main goal for countries, and the wealth created is distributed around the nation (Gough, 1996). However, the analysis of the crisis of capitalism reveals that the concentration of wealth has been increasing with income inequality (Goda et al., 2017). As Dutrénit and Sutz (2014) show, there is no linear correlation between innovation and international competitiveness, growth, and equal income distribution. The governance of STI between public policy and private corporations with the proposal to make profits and pay more taxes did not improve human development. We agree with the distinguished professor Deirdre McCloskey that "Competitiveness is not a word that a serious economist ever uses" (McCloskey, 2019, p. 2) and the fact that the Sustainable Development Goals (SDGs) does not include the term competitiveness in their discourse.[3]

The United Nations stated that "social inclusion is defined as the process of improving the terms of participation in society, particularly for people who are disadvantaged, through enhancing opportunities, access to resources, voice and respect for rights" (UN, 2016, p. 17). There are several issues in the field of STI to discuss to better understand the process of social inclusion due to the advancement of scientific knowledge. Knorringa et al. (2016) present the debate around frugal innovation. This concept emerged to refer to the new product and services created to solve problems or attending needs for a lot of poor people at the bottom of the

[3] https://www.undp.org/content/undp/en/home/sustainable-development-goals/background/.

pyramid, creating a "win–win" business in which companies contribute to poverty alleviation at the same time that creates profits, instead of that "frugal innovation will merely exacerbate capitalist exploitation and inequality" (Knorringa et al., 2016, p. 143). Kuhlmann and Ordonez-Matamoros (2017) edited a Handbook that addressed a well-known critique of the questionable links between economic growth and social welfare. This might be well known and discussed by this research community but much less popular to a significant part of the science and policy community, especially those involved in developing and governing emerging technologies. For example, do social inclusion results from the transfer of new technologies that communities cannot control? Developing the concept of social value as a result of the creation and use knowledge to develop communities with their own capacities to solve their problems and improve their possibilities to enjoy welfare with dignity, Orozco and Chavarro (2011) showed that solutions imposed in a top-down scheme by the government failed in the case of Chagas disease in Colombia. The scientific solutions supported in the co-design with the community using a bottom-up schema emerged and showed how shared governance of STI could promote welfare and social inclusion. Another example shows how the integration of techno-economic networks in which government, researchers from public and private institutions, not-for-profit organizations, and local communities translate the advancements in biotechnologies to improvements in productivity, increasing the social inclusion for peasant families to the potatoes corps in Colombia (Orozco et al., 2007). Analyzing national innovation systems and social inclusion, Dutrénit and Sutz (2014) evidenced that clear incentive is needed to introduce social inclusion research in research centres and universities and concludes that greater involvement of the innovation beneficiaries is crucial to the success of any social policy. Then the research founded that a multidisciplinary and beneficiary participatory approach to design effective inclusive innovation policies is needed to improve results. In this way, Bortagaray and Gras (2014) show the cases from Bolivia, Colombia, Ecuador, and Peru in the light of the general discussion of STI for inclusive development. The chapter highlights how traditional knowledge and know-how toward searching for solutions for national and local problems are at the center of the discussion. These shifts in STI policy frameworks are still in the planning phases, but deliberation and participation seem crucial for building capabilities and expanding the choices about STI policies for development goals.

Another example is provided by the different points of view for policies that promote social inclusion. For example, formalizing employment for public agencies means the dignification of work and access to social security and statal support and protection. For informal vendors, it means the loss of dignity due to new conditions of schedules, accountabilities, and less freedom to perform work by their own will. Another issue in STI is the differentiation between users and beneficiaries of scientific and technological advancements. Researchers in molecular biology and biotechnologies could develop new techniques to produce milk with more nutritional compounds. The users are the enterprises in the business of breeding and growing cows, and the beneficiaries could be the children who receive, probably in public dietary programs, the new milk.

The governance and management of STI (GMSTI) and their role in explaining both economic development and social transformation is a growing topic of interest in the international literature, attracting academic, policy, and practitioners' attention alike. In this field, questions increasingly arise regarding GMSTI main features, challenges, and positive and negative effects in Latin America as a developing region that has some valuable lessons to offer. We claim that Latin American scholarly work on the topic has been dramatically underexploited, while its relevance is acknowledged for a better understanding of GMSTI challenges and opportunities in the global north.

Efforts in the investment and promotion of STI, which can create opportunities to overcome social exclusion and advance in sustainability, are modest in Latin American countries. According to the RICyT (2019), the investment in STI, which means just 3% of the world, reach 0,64% of the GDP in 2017 and is characterized by the high concentration. Brazil, Argentina, and Mexico represent 86% of LAC investment. In terms of human capacity, the LAC countries present 1,73 researchers for every one thousand economically active populations, while countries like Spain are near 10 (RICyT, 2019). In terms of education, only 1% of students belonging to LAC countries presents results at the highest levels of proficiency in mathematics, according to the Program for International Student Assessment (PISA) (ECLAC et al., 2019). Between 2009 and 2015, the mean PISA score in science performance increased from 406 to 412, almost 100 points below OCDE countries. In general, the enrolment in STI is low, and it is clear the mismatch between the professional skills with the technical requirements that have been reframing in the context of the fourth industrial revolution (Ordoñez-Matamoros et al., 2021).

The governance between policy networks defined by law that steer guidelines to create cross-agency collaboration between several actors—government, scientists, universities, firms, able to invest and perform R&D, and the evaluation and accountability in online social networks has been one of the key advancements in understanding national innovation systems (Orozco et al., 2019). The main question is how STI governance has been developed to include sustainability with social inclusion regarding the silenced voice of those that contribute to STI governance. Governance as a means of shared administration in which the State must assure the stability of justice and force, and private organizations must attend the rest of the affairs like social services (health, education among others) using the market mechanisms, respond to the neoliberal interest of making more efficient public policy in the division of tasks in which law enforcement and incentives prevent and punish corruption and promote transparency and democracy. However, this top-down approach can be discussed with several cases in the field of STI studies. The way to overcome the social exclusion, understood as a collateral damage that takes advantage of the fears and risks, as Bauman (2011) pointed out, is to develop governance mechanisms in which STI lead to opportunities that dignify the work with the creation of social value that empowers the community to solve their own problems and attend their needs (Orozco & Chavarro, 2011).

One of the most valuable contributions to advance in critical thinking to imagine and create new governance models is with cases, explanations, and theoretical insights that allow studying the efforts to steer governance toward social inclusion and sustainability. Policymakers and practitioners, in general, need to learn from more cases and experiences to figure out how to rethink their own systems. Thus, this book is a tool to find theoretical approaches and empirical analyses that shed light on broad and specific features in several topics such as sustainability, higher education policy, and institutional models, and funding experiences and challenges, among others. Furthermore, scholars will find some novel methodological approaches and theoretical debates that help improve future research while learning from experiences in the Latin American context. Scholars can also find academic material to support their teaching activities, using cases to enrich their approaches on GMSTI.

This work is a product of the Network on Governance and Management of Science, Technology, and Innovation—(Red GCTI) from a congress "Governance of science, technology and innovation for inclusive and sustainable development in Latin America" organized in 2019 by Universidad Externado de Colombia, Universidad de los Andes, Pontificia Universidad Javeriana, and the Colombian Association for Scientific Advancement (ACAC), with the support of Colombian Observatory of Science and Technology (OCyT), ACUA Foundation and Fondo Internacional de Desarrollo Agrícola (FIDA).

In October 2014 professors Gonzalo Ordoñez-Matamoros and Luis Antonio Orozco understood that there was a time to give a name of an informal research team that has worked 12 years ago, led by one of the most influential scientists in Colombia, José Luis Villaveces, in the topics of STI in policy, sociology, management, and scientometrics. They organized using the name of Thinking Center for STI Governance, with the PhD program's support in public policy from the Universidad Externado de Colombia, the forum: Science, technology, and innovation as a tool for development. The main idea was to enhance the relationships between Universidad Externado de Colombia and the University of Twente. With the visit of Stefan Kuhlmann, president at that time of EU-SPRI Forum, the idea was to invite the people, not only researchers, interested in STI governance to promote the creation of a community for sharing knowledge, experiences, ideas, and alliances to work together. Also, the idea was to create a space like EU-SPRI in Latin America. The suggestion of an open network began to operate with the support of Diego Andrés Chavarro and María Alejandra Tejada that steered a space for PhD students to show their results in the field of STI. Between January and March 2015 began the discussion about PhD research. The first presentation was Diego Chavarro thesis at SPRU—Sussex University in UK; followed by María Alejandra Tejada and Ernesto Andrade from Twente University in The Netherlands. In April 2015 María Piedad Villaveces contributed to open a space to invite people to plan the Network's activities. Then, several scholars such as Astrid Jaimes, Mónica Salazar, Alejandro Balanzó, Iván Montenegro, Galo Tovar, and Jaime Sierra, among others, began to interact with the idea to perform several activities to promote the research and public discussion of governance and management of STI.

After five years with the interaction of more than 100 persons, in summer 2019 the Red GCTI, integrated by members from academia, government, and Civil Society Organizations in Colombia, organized the first conference on this subject in Latin America. More than 700 persons were inscribed for the conference, with 282 attendants. Near 90 papers were submitted from more than 15 countries, including Argentina, Chile, Uruguay, Mexico, Peru, Ecuador, Costa Rica, Panama, Spain, Canada, United Kingdom, United States, Switzerland, and The Netherlands. We selected 20 works that offer an original reflection and results, highlighting in one way or another current trend, challenges and opportunities characterizing STI governance in terms of social inclusion and sustainable development in Latin America.

This effort is organized in two books according to the orientation of the chapters. In this compilation, several researchers bring an academic perspective of institutional arrangements and goal definitions around sustainable development in the context of Latin American countries and the challenges of developing absorptive STI capacities for social inclusion. Chapters tackle the important role of citizen science, science diplomacy, peace building, mission-oriented policies, public innovation, institutional entrepreneurs, and policy networks. In the second volume "Policy and Governance of Science, Technology, and Innovation Social Inclusion and Sustainable Development in Latin América", the chapters show specific features of innovation policies in the framework of Latin American contexts, analyzing the barriers and opportunities for STI governance in the region. In so doing, the books cover both novel and studied topics, but from renewed perspectives that address issues related with the role of institutions, innovation funding, technological trajectories, regional innovation policies, innovation ecosystems, universities, knowledge appropriation, and markets with insights that deal with a new STI framework called the Transformative Innovation Policy, which are approached from both a top-down and bottom-up perspectives.

Thus, the chapters that make up this volume offer a varied and conceptually rich landscape in which cases, contexts, actors, and relationships are used to broaden and deepen relevant discussions. The chapters incorporate new elements and views to renew traditional stances, offer fertile insights about relevant realities, and propose new research and action avenues to face the challenges that Latin American communities confront daily.

The chapters cover two main topics. The first part shows cases that illustrated the STI governance in diplomacy, ecosystems conservation, peace, agricultural production, and sharing economy in which civil society and triple-helix interactions are the main issues analyzed in the section. The second part focuses on higher education institutions as the main actor in STI governance for social inclusion. Some works advance in methodological proposals as well as cases in which the STI governance is shown in the frame of transformative innovation and their contribution to peace and social inclusion.

In chapter two Bonilla and Serafim's "*Relevance of Science, Technology and Innovation Diplomacy for STI Capacity Building in Central America: the cases of Guatemala, El Salvador and Honduras*" text illustrates how latecomers to science, technology, and innovation diplomacy (STID) discussions and analyses in peripheral regions, such as Central America, are, however, taking important steps to build STI capacities for inclusive development. This also provides evidence on the relevance of STID to strengthen capacity building in such a particular context and draws some relevant policy implications for the roads that lay ahead.

In the next chapter, Galvis and Galvis discuss how an effective governance model to protect coral reefs in Colombia was developed bottom-up during the past decade, thanks to the joint efforts and trust of government, civil society, and communities. In fact, "*Transdisciplinary Citizen Science connect Caribbean Hope Spots of Colombia to improve Coral Reefs Governance*" showcases a citizen's science program associated with scuba diving operators, fishermen, and other volunteer observers, which helped gather massive data based on geo-referenced reports of observations and semi-structured interviews with videos and photos. As a direct outcome of such coordinated effort, the target geographical regions boast substantially higher healthy coral cover and more frequent sightings of vulnerable species listed on the IUCN Red List, higher fishermen's community stewardship, more effective bottom-up schemes of protection, and less visitors in contrast with the Park. This talks loudly about the positive scheme results and the ensuing need to connect case studies within effective protection frameworks to increase governance that guarantees ecological connectivity.

Reina's chapter forwards a conceptual proposal related to Community-Based Innovation Ecosystems, which he deems an appropriate framework to study processes of communal and transformative innovation in territories affected by heavy social conflict. Thus, "*Community-Based Innovation Ecosystems in Peace-building and Resilience Contexts*" challenges the notion of innovation "*as a transactional process to open new markets in capitalism*" and pivots around a socio-technical process of collective transformation linked to actions carried out by grassroots organizations and communities. This proposal is embodied by the case study of a community located in a South-Western region (Guapi, Cauca) where diverse social actors, that have been usually excluded, build collaborative interactions in post-conflict/post-agreement contexts.

Likewise, Rojas analyzes the main challenges faced by a developing country such as Colombia in an attempt to organically link local economic development strategies to the manifold opportunities arising from a richly endowed bioeconomy expressed in several regions within the same country. Thus, "*Local economic development and the Colombian strategy for a sustainable and inclusive bioeconomy*" explores the traits of triple-helix actors related to the progress of development supported by a bioeconomy-based strategy and offers a stance based on local territories and bottom-up participation.

The chapter by Sanabria and Orozco, "*Sharing economies and digital platforms: Between access and social inclusion in Colombia*", analyzes several cases, performed in collaboration with Connecting the Dots and Sharecollab, the dilemma of platforms that could generate social inclusion and may help disrupt traditional non-inclusive dynamics for market mechanisms, or creating new forms of mega-corporations that exert power and dominance with the new digital technologies in a new wave of capitalism. The cases help to understand the technology as a mediated agent in the frame of Actor Network Theory, to be analyzed by its capacity to traduce the new business models into practices for social inclusion or marginalization. This research extends a previous analysis of the transformation of capitalism with the discourse of sharing economy (Sanabria & Orozco, 2021).

In the second part of the book, chapter six presents universities as key actors in Chalela, Boni, and Velasco's "*Developing transformative innovation through policy experimentation in two Colombian Universities*", in which two experiences are examined under the light of transformative innovation. The cases of two regional, privately owned universities are brought forward to illustrate "*inclusive and participatory processes that have taken into account voices that are usually excluded in the formulation of university policies*". Although the two processes examined are still unfinished, the authors trust that such an approach can offer useful alternatives to improve university governance.

Along the same line, in "*The STI contribution of higher education institutions of Cauca to peace building and social inclusion*", Castillo and co-authors analyze the implementation of territorial peace conceived as the return of the State to territories (e.g., Cauca state) where governmental institutional presence is neglected. The study uses quantitative and qualitative analysis to establish how, despite understandable shortcomings, Caucan universities do develop joint STI initiatives that foster social inclusion with/of social organizations through knowledge diffusion to counter specific problems (e.g., digital divide) and by supporting the design, implementation, and assessment of public policies aimed at boosting human talent in the region.

The next two chapters cover the advancements in methodological issues. "*A classification model to analyze inclusion in higher education systems: an approximation from contingency theory*" by Ruiz and co-authors examines Colombia's national science, technology, and innovation system plans to include more students in the higher education system as a condition to create the human capital needed to boost socio-economic development. Their concern regards a supply–demand imbalance that creates a governance problem by pressing the inclusion of human capital in higher education organizations, which adds to regional inequalities. Ruiz et al. propose a model to study such a problem and present results showing that shifts in inclusion depend on the development level of regions.

Another case scenario is presented by Cancino et al. in "*Methodology for the governance and management of the university as a complex adaptive system based on the three missions: research, education and connecting with its surroundings*". The authors propose to examine the sustainability and governance of university-based capacities by redefining the very notion of science, technology, and innovation capabilities in terms of the heterogeneity that characterizes the different types of universities' scientific and technological activities. That is achieved by examining the case of a high-standing public university in Colombia and putting forward a proposal to strengthen the governance and management of its mission.

In the last chapter, Sierra and Ramos' "Science, Technology, Innovation and inclusive development: A country comparison between Colombia and Mexico" discusses the key historical elements that have produced the current situation in both nations and the, consequently, long way to go to for the two countries to build strong knowledge-based economies where opportunities and performance help drive a change in equality and wealth concentration into greater and better distributed resources, opportunities, and social welfare in general. Universities and their relationships are showed as an important factor in both cases, giving a framework to understand the governance for STI in the inclusive development.

The books convey original reflections from the science, technology, and innovation policy and governance studies and those related to the development studies field with an approach to social inclusion and sustainability. Social inclusion and sustainable development supported by STI governance have been an essential topic in Latin America, though understudied so far. Then, more than an academic discussion about the conception of governance, in Latin America, the term tends to be more a fashion than a scientific construction using evidence about the changes in the way to understand the relationships between several actors to define and control policies. The books produced by the Red GCTI are an effort to contribute to the academic and practical vision about STI governance.

References

Aktouf, O. (2004). The false expectations of Michael Porter's strategic management framework. *Revista Universidad & Empresa, 6*(6), 9–41.

Aktouf, O. (2008). Gobernancia y pensamiento estratégico: Una crítica a Michael Porter. *Administración y Organizaciones, 11*(21), 157–183.

Aktouf, O., Chenoufi, M., & Holford, W. D. (2005). The false expectations of Michael Porter's strategic management framework. *Problems and Perspectives in Management, 4*, 181–200.

Ardila, E. (2013). *Prácticas ilegítimas en la gestión pública colombiana—Estudio del caso: grupo Nule. (Tesis de Maestría)*. Universidad Nacional de Colombia.

Bauman, Z. (2011). *Collateral damage: Social inequalities in a global age*. Polity Press.

Behrman, J. R., Gaviria, A., & Székely, M. (2002). Social exclusion in Latin America: Introduction and overview. *SSRN Electronic Journal*. https://doi.org/10.2139/ssrn.1814705.

Bevir, M. (2008). *Key concepts in governance*. Sage.

Bortagaray, I., & Gras, N. (2014). Science, technology, and innovation policies for inclusive development: Shifting trends in south America. In G. Crespi & G. Dutrénit (Eds.), *Science, technology and innovation policies for development* (pp. 255–285). Springer.

Cepal. (2006). *Defeating poverty through social inclusion*. ECLAC. Santiago de Chile.

Colmenares, Rafael. (2013). *¿Gobernanza del agua o justicia del agua?* Available at http://viva.org.co/cajavirtual/svc0342/articulo12.html.

Comisión Económica para América Latina y el Caribe—CEPAL. (2016). *Desarrollo social inclusivo: una nueva generación de políticas para superar la pobreza y reducir la desigualdad en América Latina y el Caribe*. Santiago de Chile.

De Ferranti, D., Perry, G. E., Ferreira, F., & Walton, M. (2004). *Inequality in Latin America: Breaking with history?* The World Bank.

Dutrénit, G., & Sutz, J. (Eds.). (2014). *National innovation systems, social inclusion and development: The Latin American experience*. Edward Elgar.

Economic Commission for Latin America and the Caribbean (ECLAC). (2019). *Social panorama of Latin America (LC/PUB.2019/22-P/Rev.1)*. Santiago

ECLAC, CAF and OCDE. (2019). *Latin American economic outlook 2019: Development in transition*. OECD, CAF, ECLAC. Santiago de Chile.

Goda, T., Onaran, Ö., & Stockhammer, E. (2017). Income inequality and wealth concentration in the recent crisis. *Development and Change, 48*(1), 3–27.

Gough, I. (1996). Social welfare and competitiveness. *New Political Economy, 1*(2), 209–232.

Knorringa, P., Peša, I., Leliveld, A., & Van Beers, C. (2016). Frugal innovation and development: Aides or adversaries? *The European Journal of Development Research, 28*(2), 143–153.

Krugman, P. (1994). Competitiveness: A dangerous obsession. *Foreign Affairs, 73*, 28–44.

Kuhlmann, S., & Ordonez-Matamoros, G. (Eds.). (2017). *Research handbook on innovation governance in emerging economies*. Edward Elgar.

McCloskey. D (2019). I*nterview for a Colombian Newspaper*, January 2019. Available at: https://www.deirdremccloskey.com/docs/pdf/McCloskey_ColombiaInterviewJan2019.pdf.

OECD. (2017). *Enhancing social inclusion in Latin America: Key issues and the role of social protection systems*. OCDE.

Ordoñez-Matamoros, G., Centeno, J. P., & Orozco, L. A. (2021). Las ciencias sociales y humanidades en la cuarta revolución industrial. Retos y oportunidades. *Colección Así Habla el Externado*. Tomo II Tecnologías Regulación y Políticas Públicas. Universidad Externado de Colombia.

Orozco, L. A., & Chavarro, D. A. (2011). *El programa de investigación del CIMPAT—Centro de investigaciones en microbiología y parasitología tropical de la Universidad de los Andes*. Ediciones Uniandes.

Orozco, L. A., Chavarro-Bohórquez, D. A., Olaya, D. L., & Villaveces, J. L. (2007). Methodology for measuring the socio-economic impacts of biotechnology: A case study of potatoes in Colombia. *Research Evaluation, 16*(2), 107–122.

Orozco, L. A., Villaveces, J. L., Ordoñez-Matamoros, G., & Moreno, G. (2019). Innovation policy and governance networks on national innovation systems. In G. Catalano, C. Daraio, M. Gregory, H. Moed & G.

Ruocco (Eds.), *17th International Conference on Scientometrics & Informetrics, ISSI 2019—Proceedings* (Vol 1, pp. 541–553). Sapienza University. Available at: http://www.issi-society.org/publications/issi-conference-proceedings/proceedings-of-issi-2019/.

Orozco, L. A, Beltrán, C, Vargas, C, García, L. F., & Ruiz, M. (2018). El fraude en Interbolsa y Fondo Premium en el caso Fabricato. In J. C. Henao & C. E. Ruiz-López (Eds.), *Corrupción en Colombia*. Tomo 3. Corrupción privada. Colección así habla el Externado. Universidad Externado de Colombia.

Sanabria, J., & Orozco, L. A. (2021). *Del capitalismo liberal a la economía colaborativa, nuevos modelos de negocio y retos para el marco institucional*. Colección Así Habla el Externado. Tomo IV "Tecnologías Negocios y Gestión". Universidad Externado de Colombia.

Rhodes, R. A. W. (1996). The new governance: Governing without government. *Political Studies, 44*(4), 652–667.

RICyT. (2019). El estado de la ciencia. *Principales Indicadores de Ciencia y Tecnología Iberoamericanos/Interamericanos*. Buenos Aires.

UN. (2016). *Identifying social inclusion and exclusion*. United Nations. http://www.un.org/esa/socdev/rwss/2016/chapter1.pdf.

Williamson, O. E. (1996). *The mechanisms of governance*. Oxford University Press.

Williamson, O. E. (2005). Transaction cost economics: The process of theory development. *Great minds in management: The process of theory development* (pp. 485–508).

Zurbriggen, C. (2011). Gobernanza: Una mirada desde América Latina. *Perfiles Latinoamericanos, 19*(38), 39–64.

PART I

Cases on STI Capacities for Inclusion and Sustainable Development

CHAPTER 2

Relevance of Science, Technology and Innovation Diplomacy for STI Capacity Building in Central America: The Cases of Guatemala, El Salvador and Honduras

Kleinsy Bonilla and Milena Serafim

2.1 Introduction

In the world of today international science entails a double-edge approach. In one hand, scientific knowledge has become an important factor for the growth of economies, leading to an increasing competition among countries based on innovation (Gilpin, 2001). On the other

K. Bonilla (✉)
Group for Studies of Organization of Research and Innovation GEOPI, Department of Science and Technology Policy DPCT, Institute of Geosciences IG, University of Campinas UNICAMP, São Paulo, Brazil

M. Serafim
School of Applied Sciences—FCA, University of Campinas, UNICAMP, Campinas, SP, Brazil
e-mail: milenaps@unicamp.br

L. A. Orozco et al. (eds.), *Science, Technology, and Higher Education*, Palgrave Studies in Democracy, Innovation, and Entrepreneurship for Growth,
https://doi.org/10.1007/978-3-030-80720-7_2

hand, science is a common ground in which nations can work together to solve global problems, such as climate change, migration flows, transnational diseases, and threats to security, among others. Economic growth is not enough for a society to progress, instead inclusive development requires that knowledge and innovation should enable environmentally sound prosperity in due respect of human labor rights and social protection. Moreover, in societies with the levels of poverty, inequality and exclusionary structures (based on gender, territory, ethnic, wealth) such as Guatemala, El Salvador and Honduras, the generation and impact of scientific, technological and innovation activities have to be interpreted accordingly. In addition, the international engagement of these nations is also affected by the indicated elements present in their population. The processes toward development should be integral and inclusive.

Due to the importance of science in global affairs, theorists and practitioners of International Relations and Science, Technology and Innovation studies have been building an emerging field in the intersection between foreign policy and science. In this interface, two types of diplomacy are proposed: Science Diplomacy and Innovation Diplomacy. The first is understood as a mechanism in which science is used to foster scientific collaborations among nations with the explicit goal of addressing common challenges and with the implicit goal of leveraging influence through soft power (Fedoroff, 2009). The American Association for the Advancement of Science (AAAS, 2010: 34) proposed breaking out Science Diplomacy into three types of practice resulting in a seminal taxonomy: scientists offering advice in the design of foreign policies (science in diplomacy); the diplomatic apparatus promoting scientific cooperation (diplomacy for science); and scientific cooperation to better relations among countries (science for diplomacy). On the other hand, Innovation Diplomacy is understood as a set of diplomatic strategies and tools to defend national interests in the international arena and streamline innovation systems through international cooperation (Leijten, 2017).

The concept and practices of Innovation Diplomacy are still under construction; however, according to Bound (2016) nations use diplomatic bodies to attract human resources, ideas and investments; establish pre-commercial or commercial cooperation between home companies with foreign firms and universities; actively participate in the formulation of frameworks that crosscut innovation (e.g. intellectual property regime or migration rules); and foster collaboration among different actors to solve global challenges. Currently, most of the discussions of science and innovation diplomacy are taking place in European countries and the United States, while scholars from regions such as Latin America are joining the building of this emerging field at a slower pace. In the context of Latin America rather than considering separately Science Diplomacy and Innovation Diplomacy, the literature refers to the field in general as Science Diplomacy (Fecyt, 2017; Fernández-Poluch, 2015), or to a more comprehensive terminology including Science, Technology and Innovation Diplomacy (Barañao, 2016; SENACYT-MINEX Panamá, 2019).

Barañao (2016) sustains that science can be a helpful platform to facilitate integration among Latin American countries, particularly through interdisciplinary collaboration and mobility among scientists and researchers. His scope, though is mainly focused on the southern part of the continent. This perspective is also shared by Soler (2014) who emphasizes the role that inter-governmental scientific networks can play in the regional integration of the Latin American continent. Fernández-Poluch (2015) calls the attention to relying on science diplomacy activities to strengthen capacities in countries with wider gaps in terms of scientific and technological progress of Latin America, although he emphasizes the challenges in the STI governance experienced in the region. Once again, the geographic focus of his work refers to experiences in major countries and blocks within Latin America such as MERCOSUR (Southern Common Market, for the initials in Spanish), and Central America is once again absent from this discussion.

From this perspective, Brazil is probably the Latin American country where further scholars and practitioners are discussing the relevance of science, technology and innovation (STI) in its foreign policy as well as in its participation in international engagement (da Silva, 2018). In the case of Central America few discussions can be found, mostly in Panamá (SENACYT-MINEX Panamá, 2019) and Costa Rica (Castro, 2018; Soler, 2014). As a matter of fact, Panamá is among the few countries in the world with a published national strategy in science, technology and innovation diplomacy (SENACYT-MINEX Panamá, 2019). Otherwise, as it was stated before, Central American countries are often absent from studies related to the state of science, technology and innovation in Latin America. This occurs more markedly with the three countries included in this work, which are located in the northern part of the isthmus: Guatemala, El Salvador and Honduras. The commonalities among Guatemala, El Salvador and Honduras in their STI general contexts and their similar policy trajectory justify the delimitation of this work, leaving Nicaragua, Costa Rica and Panamá as subjects for a separate analysis.

Guatemala, El Salvador and Honduras share common features that place them as scientific and technologically lagging behind countries (Wagner et al., 2001). These features include the precariousness of their higher education systems (and education in general), the institutional weakness of public bodies and governance relevant to science, technology and innovation and a private (industrial) sector disconnected from the greater national development project. These elements among other characteristics have resulted in fragmented national innovation systems showing fragile (often nearly nonexistent) science, technology and innovation capacities. This context implies that, while other regions in the world are advancing rapidly in their integration into the global knowledge economy, the gap between these three Central American countries and the more advanced countries continues to widen. Moreover, the low priority given to scientific research in the public agendas of these three nations as well as the limited investment in science and technology (both historically and as a current trend) results in a perpetuation of STI backwardness.

One of the mechanisms followed by the governments of these countries to narrow down such gaps and to foster advancement of the building of their STI capacities has been international cooperation. For decades, Guatemala, El Salvador and Honduras have received cooperation from partner countries and the international community in different modalities such as multilateral, bilateral and triangular cooperation, as well as official development assistance and technical cooperation.

In terms of STI international cooperation initiatives (design, implementation, results and impact) have been difficult to be systematized as data is often not available. Moreover, political volatility and the lack of stable and long-term national development plans have made it extremely complex to organize STI capacity building efforts with the support of international cooperation. In this scenario, the emergence of a new field of knowledge in the interface of international relations and science, technology and innovation (Weiss, 2005, 2015) may offer new possibilities for these Central American societies to engage with more advanced countries, and foster their STI capacity building processes.

This framework is still under construction, known with different terminologies and approaches such as Science Diplomacy, Innovation

Diplomacy, Diplomacy of Science, Scientific Diplomacy, and others. For the purpose of this text we will use STID, understood as initiatives aimed at promoting the advancement of these areas involving actors from different countries, including governments, scientific communities, universities, research centers, and a wider variety of stakeholders. The literature suggests that STID can play a meaningful role in response to the challenges faced by Central American societies in their process of building their STI capacities (human, institutional, organizational, societal), particularly in the cases of Guatemala, El Salvador and Honduras confronting common challenges with shared socio-economic developing context (Bonilla & Serafim, 2019).

This work presents findings of an ongoing investigation on the relevance of STID in the building of STI capacity in Guatemala, El Salvador and Honduras. Through a qualitative research methodology, the research focused on systematizing the perspectives of local actors from the scientific and research communities of these three Central American countries. Complementarily, the study of a practical experience of STID from the Guatemala foreign policy implement in their Embassy involving a bilateral relation with the Republic of Korea provides relevant inputs to enhance the analysis. From the study of the collected data and the sustained discussions with relevant actors in the Central American region, evidence suggest that STID might be relevant in the process of construction of STI capacities for inclusive development. On the other hand, challenges and obstacles for the successful international engagement of Guatemala, El Salvador and Honduras have been also identified. The construction of research agendas of these three countries deserves special attention, in which the absence of evidence-based decision-making, the limited production of data and good quality indicators, as well as the lack of intersector interactions have made it difficult to establish common grounds that could allow greater efficiency and impact in STID practices. International STI engagement with scientifically more advanced countries, both within Latin America and with extra-regional partner countries, has proven to be puzzling. The framework is complex and has multiple edges; therefore, further discussions and studies are critical to advance the field.

2.2 STI Context in Central America

Latin America as a region shows significant gaps in terms of STI capacities when compared to other blocks in the globe such as Western Europe, North-East Asia, the United States and Canada. Admittedly, this regards the use of conventional science and technology standards and main stream metrics (as opposed to traditional knowledge from native populations, for example). Wagner et al. (2001), using a composite index of science and technology assessment, propose a categorization of countries based on their scientific and technological capacity. This index classifies countries into four categories: Scientifically Advanced, Scientifically Competent, Scientifically Developing and Scientifically Lagging. In the Latin American region, there is no single country in the first category. The most STI advanced countries comprise 22 nations responsible for 86% of all scientific articles published internationally, and finance between 85 and 90% of all research and development activities (R&D) of the world. The second category includes two Latin American countries: Cuba and Brazil (out of 24). Countries in this category are considered competent from the scientific point of view since some of their index values of scientific and technological capacity are above the international average, while in others they may fall below the average. In addition, Brazil and Cuba show world class standards in particular areas or sub-fields of science. In particular, in the case of Brazil, investments in infrastructure and investment in R&D have increased, which has generated accumulated improvement in its STI context over time.

The third category is composed of 24 countries classified as scientifically developing. In this group some nations have made certain investments in science and technology. However, their general scientific capacity is below the world average. Here are found six Latin American countries: Argentina, Mexico, Colombia, Venezuela, Costa Rica and Bolivia. It is relevant to call attention to the inclusion of Costa Rica in this category, the best positioned Central American country. Finally, all the rest of the Central American countries are included in the fourth category—the scientific lagging behind. According to Wagner et al. (2001: 15) "These countries have little or no ability to conduct science at the international level which offer opportunities for building STI capacity". These countries are: Uruguay, Peru, Ecuador, Panama, Paraguay, Nicaragua and the three Central American countries that are the object of the present analysis: Guatemala, El Salvador and Honduras.

Different measures and indicators in the latter three countries lead to believe they share a dismissive attitude toward science, technology and innovation; in other words, the level of investment, the quality and scope of its science and technology policies, the participation of the government, the private sector and the organized civil society in STI activities demonstrate that science and technology do not hold a priority position in their agendas. This helps to explain their limited performance and poor STI indicators.

2.2.1 STI Context in Guatemala

In Guatemala, the number of full-time researchers is 27 per million inhabitants, a Figure 16 times lower than the average for Latin America and 262 times lower than the average in developed nations (UNESCO, 2017). It is widely accepted that economies in developing countries require more research and innovation activities. Nevertheless, in the case of Guatemala, the size of the scientific community should be at least 45 times larger (between 1,000 and 1,200 full-time researchers). As for the investment in science and technology, it becomes another limitation that negatively affects the scientific and technological progress. Guatemala dedicates only 0.029% of its GDP to R&D activities. This is 14 times lower than the investment in Sub-Saharan Africa, 25 times less than the average for Latin America and the Caribbean, 85 times less than the average in Western Europe and almost 200 times less than what is invested in Korea or Israel. As a consequence of the minimum investment, scientific production in terms of international specialized journals indicate Guatemala produced 11 articles per million inhabitants. The same figure in Chile, a relatively more advanced Latin American country, is 45 times higher.

This complicated scenario is also evident in the formation and accumulation of highly educated human resources. According to Bonilla and Kwak (2014), up to 96.5% of the population in Guatemala lacks complete tertiary education. Furthermore, from those few who manage to complete tertiary education, an overwhelming majority concentrate in undergraduate and technical programs, with restricted access to graduate programs. Few specializations and master's programs are available in Guatemala, and only a handful of doctoral programs are offered by local institutions. Regarding the field of study, a generalized emphasis in activities exclusively oriented to teaching (without research) perpetuates the reproduction of knowledge rather than the generation of new knowledge. Research, science and technology are fields not yet explored or prioritized in higher education institutions in the country. Guatemala desperately needs to double its efforts to accumulate a trained and well-trained workforce, capable of responding to the increasing pressures of globalization and changing productive paradigms. It is worrying that the national higher education system in Guatemala has proved insufficient to produce the workforce with advanced education to meet the market demand (Bonilla & Kwak, 2014). And beyond the market, inclusive development remains elusive in this context in which enormous disparities are observed between men and women, between the indigenous population and the European descendants, and between the rural and the urban areas.

2.2.2 STI Context in El Salvador

In El Salvador, the number of full-time researchers is 65 per million inhabitants, which is higher than in the case of Guatemala, yet significantly lower than the average of 547 observed in Latin America. From the small group of full-time researchers, a great concentration can be found in the social sciences (CONACYT, 2017). Up to 55% of researchers have full tertiary education only at the bachelor's level, while 38% have a master's degree and 7% have a doctorate. This Central American country in 2016 allocated 0, 14% of its GDP to R&D activities, which considering the expenditure on scientific and technological activities at 1.18% of GDP remains insufficient to generate relevant improvements in the development process of local capacities of STI. Regarding the production of highly educated human resources, while Brazil has five Ph.D. graduates per 100,000 inhabitants, El Salvador does not reach one. According to Duriez (2016: 28), the adult population that has access to higher education is estimated at 5.7%. Of this figure, a very small portion of undergraduate studies, with a minimum number of Salvadorian completing masters or doctorate programs. More strikingly, the areas of knowledge that dominate the spectrum belong to the social sciences, particularly Law, Administration and Commerce. In terms of academic production, in 2014 Salvador produced 5.4 scientific articles per million inhabitants. As for the governance and the strength in the STI institutional configuration, El Salvador showed certain progress compared to Guatemala and Honduras by elevating to vice-ministerial level the mandate for science and technology public policies (under the Ministry of Education); however, the constant changes and reorganization process according to the replacement in the leadership of the country make it difficult to successfully achieve long-term goals.

2.2.3 STI Context in Honduras

The case of Honduras presents an even more complicated STI context because accessing up-to-date information and indicators has proven problematic. A systematic practice of keeping records and good quality registries has not been observed in nearly every aspect of the public agenda, and science occupying a marginal position in the national agenda offers no exception. Frequently regional and sub-regional reports published by UNESCO, The United Nations Economic Commission for Latin America and the Caribbean (ECLAC) and the Inter-American Development Bank (IDB), for example, leave the space of Honduras empty when analyzing science, technology and innovation indicators. With a population of almost 8.5 million, the number of full-time researchers in this country in Central America is 24 per million people. The government's investment in science and technology is almost negligible, approximately 0.04% of GDP and the R&D figure in 0.02%, one of the lowest in the Latin American region. The responsibility for scientific research has traditionally been assigned to higher education institutions, especially the National Autonomous University of Honduras. According to Duriez, Lopez and Moncada (2016) until 2014, of the adult population in Honduras, 3.8% completed at least one level of higher education. However, without clear records, most of them remain at the technical or bachelor's level, while a small number do master's or doctoral studies. Higher education is still considered elitist in terms of coverage and accessibility. Regarding academic production, Honduras shows a figure of three scientific articles per million inhabitants.

The preparation of the research process that resulted in the present work offers an illustrative example of the precariousness of the Honduras STI scenario. While Guatemala and El Salvador presented registries with national coverage of communities of researchers and scientists, in Honduras such data bases were not possible to locate. Universities and research centers keep isolated registries or catalogs and the main body with the mandate of public policies in STI, the Honduras Institute of Science and Technology, does not produce such information.

2.3 Methodology

This exploratory and qualitative research was structured following a methodological approach of triangulation[1] applying a survey and a case

[1] Methodological triangulation involves using more than one mechanism/instrument to collect data, such as interviews, observations, questionnaires and desk review.

study. The survey[2] was filled by members of the research communities in the three Central American countries—Guatemala, El Salvador and Honduras—who provided information on their perspective about their country's international engagement in STI projects, processes or initiatives. Complementarily, a case study was carried out involving science diplomacy already implemented by the Guatemalan Ministry of Foreign Affairs. This case study provided in-depth details on a practical initiative that involved concrete foreign policy actions addressing science, technology and research collaboration within a bilateral agenda between Guatemala and the Republic of Korea. In addition, a permanent corroborating exercise took place through the use of secondary data and alternative sources.

In order to implement the survey, the first step consisted in identifying databases with information of the researchers in the three countries. In this process it was found that, while Guatemala and El Salvador have registries of researchers with nationwide coverage, Honduras has only partial catalogs of researchers such as the one maintained by the National Autonomous University of Honduras—UNAH.[3] Once the mapping of researchers was completed, the survey was sent to the members of such research communities including the following question:

> How can the international engagement of your country in science, technology and innovation (STID)contribute to the building of STI capacities? [Please consider the diversity of actors including those from the government, universities and research organizations, private sector or civil society]

In the case of Guatemala, the survey was sent to the members of two public registries: The National Directory of Researchers[4] (DNI acronym in Spanish) and the Guatemala Science and Technology Network[5] (RedCTI). In the case of El Salvador, the survey was sent to the Network

[2] The design and application of the research instruments followed all the recommendations of the ethics council, regarding anonymity, free and informed consent, and the prospect of withdrawal from the data collection exercise at any time.

[3] See https://dicu.unah.edu.hn/inveS&Tgacion-cientifica/publicacion-comunicacion-y-difusion/inveS&Tgadores-unah/catalogo-de-inveS&Tgadores/.

[4] See https://nis.senacyt.gob.gt/portal/index.php/inveS&Tgadores.

[5] See https://redcti.senacyt.gob.gt/portal/index.php/inveS&Tgadores/directoriocti.

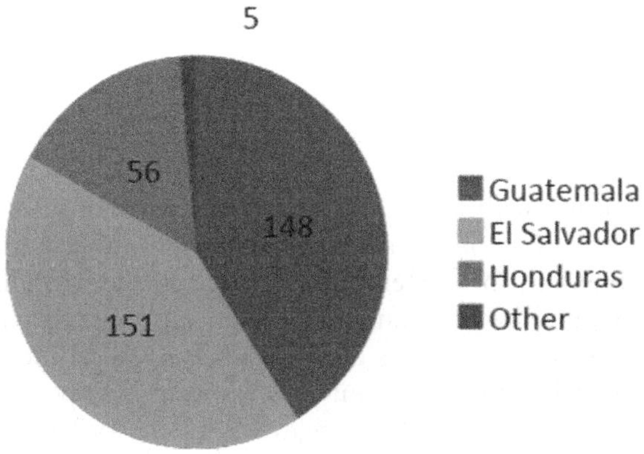

Fig. 2.1 Online survey respondents by country

of Researchers of El Salvador[6] (Redisal). In the case of Honduras, the survey was shared with the members of the UNAH catalog and was also sent to the members of the National Directory for Scientific and Technological Research in Higher Education[7] (SICES) which includes participants at a national level.

The number of responses to the online survey varied as multiple obstacles were encountered. In the case of the DNI of Guatemala, and Redisal of El Salvador a significant number of members did not have an email address available; therefore, it was not possible to send them the instrument through an email communication. On the other hand, an important number of the registries had outdated email addresses which resulted in the bouncing back of the electronic communication. In view of this, a complementary search was done to reach the highest possible number of updated email addresses, particularly searching in public repositories of published academic articles which included contact information. In the case of Honduras, a similar exercise was implemented.

As observed in Fig. 2.1, the online respondents achieved a total number of 360, which based on their country of origin amounted to 148 from Guatemala, 151 from El Salvador and 56 from Honduras; all of them active researchers in different fields of knowledge. Five reported

[6] See https://www.redisal.org.sv/directorio.php.

[7] Seehttps://des.unah.edu.hn/sistema-de-educacion-superior/sices/.

being from other nationalities, yet engaged in research activities located in the three studied Central American countries.

Researchers shared their perspectives on the role of international engagement of Guatemala, El Salvador and Honduras in science, technology and innovation initiatives with actors from STI advanced countries, either located within the Latin America region or in other parts of the planet. For the sake of organization, we present the relevance of STID for capacity building in Guatemala, El Salvador and Honduras in four categories: relevance to governments, relevance to scientific and research communities, relevance to firms and relevance to social movements and the organized civil society. Relevant answers were incorporated based on their elaboration and completion regardless of the order in which they were registered.

As for the selection of the case study, an exploratory consultation was carried out in order to identify cases of foreign policy guidelines or foreign policy actions already implemented in any of the three Central American countries involving STID. Three regional organizations were also contacted: The Secretariat for Central American Economic Integration (SIECA), the Central America Council for Higher Education (CSUCA) and the Commission for Education, Sports, Culture, Science and Technology of the Central American Parliament (PARLACEN). At the same time, consultations were done with the Ministry of Foreign Affairs of the three countries. As a result of this exploratory exercise, only one case was identified in the Ministry of Foreign Affairs of Guatemala, more precisely in the diplomatic representation of Guatemala before the Government of the Republic of Korea. Therefore, the case study was based on the study of the pilot program: Appointment of a Knowledge Transfer and Education, Science and Technology Officer in the Guatemala Diplomatic Mission in the Republic of Korea. Details of the case study are presented in Sect. 2.5.

2.4 Relevance of STI Diplomacy for STI Capacity Building in Guatemala, El Salvador and Honduras from the perspective of their Research Communities

In this section, following the organization suggested in FECYT (2017), we present findings from the primary data in four categories: a. Relevance of STID to the governments, b. Relevance of STID to the academic sector and scientific communities, c. Relevance of STID at the firm level (private/industrial sector), and d. Relevance of STID to the organized civil society. Some of the most relevant responses from the researchers are presented throughout these categories in order to illustrate the shared arguments. The answers are identified only with the number of the respondent, implying no level of importance, rank or priority.

2.4.1 *Relevance of STI Diplomacy to the Governments*

The STID framework aims at placing science, technology and innovation among the priorities of the countries′ agenda as well as the diversification of their interest promoted within their international relations with the inclusion of scientific and research endeavors. In addition, for STID it is a fundamental element to ensure the design of public policies and the making of political decisions considering the scientific evidence (Fernández-Poluch, 2015; Selleslaghs, 2017). In this sense, it is imperative to consider STID as a collaborative interaction of multiple agents (governmental and non-governmental, public and private) with governments and political representatives called to engage in leading roles. That is why, according to the members of the surveyed research communities, the governments of Guatemala, El Salvador and Honduras have to first recognize the value of research, knowledge production and innovation as key elements that contribute to the prosperity of their societies; otherwise the worrisome STI indicators discussed previously would remain unchanged and the gaps with advanced countries and regions will continue widening. Below, in these excerpts, we can see how the respondents elaborated in their answers.

A first group related their responses to the significance of moving STI capacity building to a higher priority in the social and institutional setting in order to achieve better results

> It is important that the government provides all the necessary support and show interest in knowing the progress and development of the research carried out in the country and that it is not only reflected in a document, it is important to look for alternative solutions to measure the social impact. (Respondent No. 18)

> All of the government policies must have a STI component. Professionals and civil servants should have among their profiles the abilities to identify strategic alliances, external partners and international networks with expertise in STI. In general, public institutions, but also the Ministry of Foreign

Affairs should, improve the capacities of their officers and staff who are involved in STI affairs to become less bureaucratic institutions with better results. (Respondent No. 20)

Allocate the state budget to enhance research cooperation efforts with countries with shared interests but higher research standards. (Respondent No. 65)

STID could facilitate the reduction of bureaucracy and the simplification of procedures, in addition to the improvement of inter-institutional interactions. (Respondent No. 70)

Another fundamental issue in the case of governments is their role as responsible for the foreign policy shaping international relations. Various respondents expressed their concerns about the structural weaknesses in the organization of the foreign services in the three countries.

Institutional shortcomings, misconceived incentives in the recruitment of diplomats and inexistence of a stable and evolving career in Foreign Service have allowed administrations to appoint family members, political party aids and other inadequate representatives in high, middle and lower positions in foreign missions. This is consistent with documented experiences of nepotism (Gavarrete, 2019), incompetence and poor practices in the Ministries of Foreign Affairs in Guatemala, El Salvador and Honduras (Alpirez, 2014; ECLAC, 1995). In order to advance STI initiatives in international collaboration, diplomats and the staff in foreign missions are required to meet high qualifications and clear understanding of the value of science and technology projects involving a diversity of actors in their society. It is necessary to "provide official training [advise] to the President of the Republic and his/her ministers on STI issues" (Respondent No. 231) and also "the Ministry of Foreign Affairs should work closer with public and private universities" (Respondent No. 288).

A deeper involvement of relevant public institutions with actors from the industrial sector for the advancement of science, technological development and innovation is mandatory. Coordinated efforts with Ministries of Economy, Trade and Production and their equivalents are to meet their peers in Ministries of Education and Official Bodies in the governance of STI. It is important to prioritize R & D policies at national and regional level by providing such initiatives with appropriate and timely resources and budgets, for the development of activities in the scientific field.

Governments are responsible to facilitate formal and informal mechanisms to foster linkages between scientists, politicians, firm managers and the society in general so that the scientific knowledge enriches public administration and decision-making based on evidence. Governments should facilitate the contribution of society during the entire cycle of the research (definition of problems and priorities, design, exploitation of results, evaluation, etc.).

Governments can also facilitate the mobility and integration of scientists in administration and advising positions of public organizations. "The Government is responsible for having a database of researchers and their research strengths and skills in areas of knowledge, invite them to participate in national and international research, conduct it and invite researchers" (Respondent No. 122). Collaborate with associations of national scientists in each country, promoting open communication channels so that your experience and advice can reverse in the national system of science, technology and innovation. "A collaborative agenda based on initiatives of the Central American isthmus should be prioritized by the government" (Respondent No. 245). Encourage the Ministries of Foreign Affairs, the need of universities and research centers in the formation of their influence and in the public policies of its competition.

Below, in these excerpts, it can be seen how the respondents elaborated in their replies:

> I think it is of greater benefit for science, technology and innovation that collective efforts can take place between universities, firms and non-governmental organization assuming that the government is fully committed through its Science and Technology Council. (Respondent No. 87)

> Our governments should establish clear programs and make it available their counterpart contribution (financial resources, human capital, infrastructure, equipment) proportional to STI international initiatives. (Respondent No. 131)

Also in this cooperation, horizontal and equitable cooperation relations are important and reinforces the government's need to prioritize these relations. "Decolonize North–South cooperation relations. Establish horizontal and equitable cooperation relationships. Diversify our foreign relations traditionally focused on Europe and North America. Think of Asia with the impressive stories of STI catching up…" (Respondent No. 348).

2.4.2 Relevance of STI Diplomacy to the Academic Sector and the Scientific Communities

The communities of researchers are scattered, fragmented and there is lack of systemic and cohesive collaborations. International collaborations are scarce among researchers from Guatemala, El Salvador and Honduras. Monge-Nájera and Ho (2018: 315) point out that in cases such as Guatemala a more optimistic outcome is expected as "collaboration with foreign institution is on the rise, particularly with collaborators from the United States, Mexico and the United Kingdom". It is important to visualize the value of this indicator, whether it is relevant to promote the authors of a country to engage in co-authorship with researchers and institutions of other countries and consider the risk of neglecting the quantity and quality of the national publications. By not only concentrating efforts in promoting international co-authorship, but also contributing to the expansion of knowledge, considering the quality of journals and quantity and quality of national publications to promote the inclusion of national production in regional and comprehensive databases with high visibility. Institutional collaboration can also occur; however, the patterns shown in Central America indicate that quality research is dependent on particular individual researchers rather than on institutions. However, "In the case of El Salvador, there is only one public university; there are over 50 private universities. Many programs, especially the Europeans, do not allow the participation of private HEIs [Higher Education Institutions]. It is very important that this is changed" (Respondent No. 29).

Another aspect pointed out, in relation to the structuring of capacity generation in STD, refers to the mechanisms of mobility (students, professors, scholars, decision-makers in academia, leaders). Respondent No. 33 highlights the need to "encouraging mechanisms for mobility of scholars on systematic and regular basis". Corroborating this aspect, respondent No. 41 also reinforces the inclusion of "researchers who are [living] outside of their countries of origin and who perform research activities in international institutions", in other words the Central American scientific diaspora engaging with the international scientific diaspora would facilitate the strengthening of international and national networks of scientists and national science academies in proposing technical solutions for common problems in Latin America and the Caribbean. However, it is worth emphasizing here the need of reinforcing the role of the STI Policy in each country, integral approach in their design and implementation with other specific policies (health, environment, education policy, etc.). Thus, politicians and policy-makers need, in addition to having this clarity, to direct demands and projects to the STI Policy (Serafim & Dagnino, 2011). Otherwise, the scientific community, imbued with its intrinsic logic to its academic ethos, can align itself much more with the social problems of the central countries than with the local problems of its countries. The phenomenon of the emulation of the research agenda of the central countries has been present consistently in the countries of Latin America. In fact, this phenomenon—of the colonization of the global south—is quite common in Latin American countries, causing anomaly and atypical science and technology policy (Dagnino, 2014).

Expanding the training of students, scientists and researchers beyond technical–scientific skills, including communication, management, leadership, multidisciplinary teamwork, negotiation, emotional intelligence and other qualities, could be areas in which STID would provide an adequate structure. Promoting the exchange of experiences and training practices between scientists and public managers is essential so that the anomaly and atypicality of the Science, Technology and Innovation Policy do not occur. This aspect is important for the creation and strengthening of scientific capacities that support the governance and scientific diplomacy of the Central American countries in a horizontal cooperation with developing or developed countries.

Along with this, another aspect concerning the generation of scientific and technological capacities involves strengthening international and national networks of scientists and national science academies to propose technical and scientific solutions to common problems in Latin America and the Caribbean to politicians and policy-makers. Thus, the involvement of scientists in strengthening national systems of science and technology and in the governance of universities and research centers, through flexible formulas, is necessary.

Besides that, it is desirable to promote the association university and research organizations, with industry and private firms throughout the Central American region, to develop research processes that allow producing, disseminating and transferring scientific and technological knowledge. Disseminate research results (knowledge management), emphasizing the evidence, to elicit the engagement and support of decision-makers as strengthening and promoting contact and exchange programs between scientists and political and diplomatic authorities are important measures.

The academic sector could engage in the curricular design and content of disciplines, academic events, courses and specialties on scientific diplomacy in university, and university policies research centers would be valuable to encourage research, teaching and extension initiatives in this new field. Advance the idea of Central America Research initiative that allows free circulation of scientific talent in the region and greater scientific collaboration between countries. A mechanism highly successful in international experiences consists in promoting scientific collaboration. Through collaboration between researchers from different countries, interdisciplinary research and a complex approach to common problems of equally wide complexity can be enhanced.

The opportunities to pursue a career in research (which in Central America is still incipient) and complete dedication to these activities are considered as factors that influence negatively the prospects for national and international collaborations and scientific productivity. Some of the most relevant responses in this category from surveyed researchers are placed below:

> Create instruments for cooperation between different sectors so that research has an impact and benefit to society university-university and international networks of researchers. Although it would help a lot that in the agendas of international cooperation agencies they consider the local capacity to do research and do not consider a non-approach issue in cooperation, since the assistance approach predominates which favors underdevelopment and dependence; an opportunity is needed for local talents to generate knowledge and evidence that can influence politically in each country. (Respondent No. 45)

> Explore opportunities to reach out networks of Guatemalan [Salvadorian and Honduran] scientists living abroad or engaged in research activities in other countries interested in collaborating with scientists residing in their home countries. Some may have the ability to contribute applying for grants and getting funding, some others leading research projects. We

can procure the transfer of capacities among researchers. (Respondent No. 194)

At the Central American level, networks should be formed between universities that have equal or related areas of knowledge to strengthen research and exchange of research. (Respondent No. 197)

In terms of language for the publication of scientific works and influential scientific research is still English, and communication technologies are easier to access and at lower cost. The command of English language also impacts chances of mobility and generates additional channels of scientific collaboration. It is undeniable that science is global and that the formation of knowledge networks at the sub-regional level could strengthen integration efforts with researchers from Guatemala, El Salvador and Honduras having stronger English language skills. The prevalent trend is still the use of Spanish which certainly could be the language to communicate and disseminate findings from research; also, it is useful in research collaboration with other countries in the Latin American region and Spain; however, the importance of English language is critical for the advancement of STID initiatives.

2.4.3 Relevance of STI Diplomacy at the Firm Level (Private Sector)

The economic sector of Guatemala, El Salvador and Honduras still rely on conservative structures based on agribusinesses with extremely limited number of new firms being created. Most of the production in the three countries come from large companies that perform few activities in research and innovation. At the same time, Small and Medium Enterprises (SMEs) are the largest source of employment, many of them micro-enterprises or small traditional businesses. There is an incipient new business sector, with motivated young entrepreneurs who are willing to engage in activities to transform their economies (using science and technology); however, their activities face obstacles due to several factors: there are still few emerging companies that inject new ideas and opportunities into the sector; existing companies that lack local and international connections with specialized research, services and financing; companies with connections that can find bureaucratic processes that slow down the speed of doing business which could benefit from STID-oriented networks and after being exposed to better practices, update their processes and systems.

It is worthy to remark that responses in the survey incorporated significantly fewer mentions to firms, private sector or actors from the industry compared to those referring to the role of governments, research communities (universities or research organizations) and civil society (social movements, activism). Some mentions could be seen in these two excerpts: "Promote the triad of R&D systems: Government + Companies + Universities. Leaving the trenches that confront the sectors, focus on collaborative activities" (Respondent No. 9) and "Closer interactions between private firms, government and higher education institutions" (Respondent No. 144).

Private firms could improve by investing in sustainable and steady R&D initiatives considering both aspects of financial return as social impact. One constructive action would be the incorporation of graduates from graduate education programs (master/doctors) who have been left out with restricted access to professional development opportunities in the industrial structures of the country. "Provide employment opportunities to highly educated human resources (masters/Ph.D.) in the industry and avoid the common excuse: you are overqualified" (Respondent No. 154).

STID could be relevant to the private sector in the creation and strengthening of business networks with science and technology intensive counterparties at the country, region level and international levels. A recurrent mention by respondents is not only considering the business integration among Central American countries, but expand relations with firms located in non-traditional country partners in other regions of the world.

Fostering public–private cooperation alliances to promote R&D projects would facilitate dialogue between industry, public administration and actors from the academia, to achieve cooperation and mutual benefit through the education and training. Some successful, although isolated cases of good practices in the interaction of research and industry are: the Guatemalan Center for Sugarcane Research and Training (CENGICAÑA), the National Association of Coffee ANACAFE in Guatemala, the Foundation for the Research about Coffee in El Salvador PROCAFE and the Honduras Foundation for Agriculture Research FHIA in Honduras (Stads et al., 2008). One suggestion from the survey respondent could be addressed: "Use instruments to promote participation of researchers in multinationals based in Central American territory. With this approach we can achieve transfer of knowledge and access to know how from local researchers to advanced technological capacities" (Respondent No. 357).

Fostering interactions between the industry and universities could be pursued along with international engagement mechanisms. Further interactions between these sectors could decrease the gaps in terms of technical training and the existence of capabilities required in the labor market. It is critical for representatives of the private sector to participate in the public policy debate and become key agents of the society to contribute to prosperity and social welfare through the promotion of R&D. Finally, the engagement of organizations of actors from the industry in the three countries such as the Chamber of Industry (Guatemala) and the Chamber of Industry and Commerce (El Salvador and Honduras) could also be meaningful to promote STID projects and processes.

2.4.4 Relevance of STI Diplomacy to Social Movements and Organized Civil Societies

Common cultural roots and shared historical and economic history along with unstable democracies and weak institutions in the three countries have resulted in a significant number of organized groups from the civil society and social movements playing significant roles in the development process. Non-government organizations (NGOs) have for decades occupied institutional vacuums left unattended by the public and private sectors, and they have also acted in STI activities. The presence and activities of these type of organizations have even frequently involved in the provision of public services, activism in human rights, poverty alleviation and promoted incipient exercises of citizenry. In some cases, NGOs have shown higher scientific productivity compared to universities and research organizations, such as the case of the Center for Studies of Sensory Impairment (CeSSIAM), an NGO with steady production about food and health sciences (Monge-Nájera & Ho, 2018). Fields of critical relevance such as climate change, biodiversity, conservationism, environment, public health have also involved active participation of NGO in research activities.

Social organizations could play a role in the STI capacity building process as there are concrete examples of their contribution tending bridges between society and actors from the national innovation systems.

The Institute for the Development of Higher Education in Guatemala (INDESGUA)[8] founded in 2007 offers evidence on an active role in providing counseling and mentoring to excluded groups from the Guatemalan population to access to training and education programs with scholarships and various schemes of financial aid. According to public registries, over 1,000 of beneficiaries from Guatemala and its neighbors have been able to engage in educational and training programs mostly supported by international cooperation resources. Here is the summary of the results achieved by INDESGUA between June 2007 and June 2020 (INDESGUA, 2020):

- 1,025 Guatemalan beneficiaries from the 22 provinces of the country and 76 people from other countries.
- 451 are men and 650 are women.
- Of the total, 903 consider themselves having mixed Spanish-native ethnic origins, and 198 from other ethnic backgrounds.
- As for the level of education 24 processes have supported technical secondary education, 286 specialization short courses, 240 undergraduate or bachelor's degrees, 505 in masters, and 22 in doctorates.
- The orientation process has benefited applicants obtaining scholarships and financial aid to 240 to education/training programs taking place in Guatemalan educational institutions and 604 abroad (in 52 countries, 5 continents) and 52 remotely (on line).

Various other NGOs have participated actively in the promotion of scientific evidence for activism such as data observatories and record keeping organizations, filling gaps left unattended by responsible public institutions. NGOs have assumed co-responsibility both in the identification of problems, as well as their causes as possible solutions. Respondents of the survey indicated their perspectives:

> I think it is a priority for the country to have a prospective vision of what it wants to do, not only do what the economic system has to do, we need democratic governments, governance, respect for human rights, more

[8] See http://www.indesgua.org.gt/.

funds for education and health and to restrict the military expenses that are unproductive. (Respondent No. 239)

Develop processes to encourage mission-oriented applied research for its results to be meaningful for the entire society. I mean, countries at the current stage of socio-economic development of Honduras cannot afford to invest already meager available resources to attempt science discoveries at the frontier...we need first to promote problem-solving research and this demands collaborative work between activists from the organized civil society and the academy. (Respondent No. 271)

Civil society can also participate in the creation of a scientific and research-oriented culture through philanthropy. The respondent No. 42 points out the importance to "generate an inclusive training center for researchers from the most unprotected social sectors". Having regular citizens interested in science and research, who eventually co-sponsor STI activities result in social awakening toward scientific and technological vocations. It is important for the entire society to participate broadly in STI activities in the form of civil associations, foundations and laboratories that connect local knowledge with their community reality. This is particularly relevant in cases such as Guatemala in which indigenous population's traditional peoples have been excluded. In the cases of El Salvador and Honduras it also regards contrasting participation between urban and rural civil society. Of course, we have to understand that "the results of the investigations are not an immediate solution, but that you have to allow time to obtain an immediate response to the needs demanded by society" (Respondent No. 47).

All sectors, especially the public sector, need to realize that in addition to time and maturation of research and development, the scientific community needs to establish.

inter-institutional, regional and national research networks to propose comprehensive solutions to serious national problems. Engagement with communities at the local level, not only national level, but more focused on smaller units of social organization. (Respondent No. 92)

That is, the power of Central American countries is derived from the plurality of social actors involved not only in the process of diagnosing social demands/problems, but also in the process of building scientific knowledge applied in the context in which it is produced. Traditional knowledge can be better exploited.

2.5 Case study: Appointment of the Knowledge Transfer and Education, Science and Technology Officer in the Guatemala Diplomatic Mission in the Republic of Korea

The Guatemala National Development Plan K´atun 2032 (SEGEPLAN, 2015: 12) highlights the need to "guarantee the coverage and quality of education, as well as the stimulation of science and technology as generators of knowledge and bases for the development of people". This policy instrument has provided the frame for the National Science and Technology National Policy Development (SENACYT, 2017).

In this scenario the Government of Guatemala through the Ministry of Foreign Affairs (MINEX) designed and implemented a pilot STID initiative creating the position of "Coordinator of Cooperation and Knowledge Transfer" in the Embassy of Guatemala to the Republic of Korea. This initiative was designed and implemented by the then Ambassador Herbert Estuardo Meneses Coronado (Meneses, 2020) who built up over the bases laid by former Ambassador Rafael Salazar Galvez. From March 2017 to August 2019, the person in charge of the referred position would devote specific efforts to promote cooperation projects in science, technology, higher education and innovation within the bilateral relation between both countries. The definition of the profile required for the position, the establishment of indicators of performance and the monitoring and constant evaluation of results were clearly separated from the conventional (and more traditional) forms of bilateral agendas such as the commercial and cultural diplomacy.

Some of the duties of the referred position included: "...search, management and promotion of scholarships at the undergraduate and graduate level as a priority within the activities of diplomatic mission in order to foster joint cooperative efforts between Korea and Guatemala in this area and support the country's [Guatemala] progress in technology, innovation and competitiveness" (Villagran, 2017). From 2005 to 2017, at least 180 Guatemalan nationals engaged in long-term scholarships in 48 specializations, which involved three large areas of knowledge: Natural Sciences and Engineering, Political, Administrative and

Economic Sciences, Humanistic and Social Sciences. This precedent justified the action taken by the MINEX in devoting specific human power in its Embassy of Guatemala before the government of Korea. In this context the newly appointed person would be in charge of promoting academic exchange between scholars in the two countries, participation of Guatemalans in relevant scientific networks, pursuing Guatemala–Korea joint research projects, among others.

Most of the cooperation projects in STI between Korea and Guatemala corresponded to higher education programs taught by 27 universities located within the Korean territory and received funding from 15 public and private partner institutions, among which were: The Korea International Development Agency (KOICA), The National Institute of International Education (NIIED), and the agreements signed between the Guatemala National Secretariat Science and Technology (SENACYT) and Kyung Hee and Chonbuk universities. This cooperation has been estimated at nearly 10 million US dollars within a range of 12 years. In the STI cooperation experience between Guatemala and Korea it is worthy highlighting that 53% of the funding was provided by sources from the public sector while 46% came from sources of the private sector.

The STI cooperation initiatives between Guatemala and Korea experienced a considerable increase between 2014 and 2015, in view of which the Embassy of Guatemala in Korea created the position equivalent to a Science attaché as part of its personnel. According to Villagrán (2017: 3), some of the challenges faced by the officer in this this position while in functions included:

- Dispersion of information related to STI cooperation between Korea and Guatemala;
- Limited effort of dissemination of the available information;
- Lack of follow up on behalf of the Guatemalan government in the implementation of STI cooperation initiatives;
- Limited knowledge and reduced understanding about the operation of mechanisms such as: scholarships, fellowships, joint research initiatives, other forms of scholar mobility among the higher education institutions, their authorities;
- Poor data collection and production of statistics;
- Limited promotion of two-way cooperation programs;
- Difficulties in nominating suitable candidates: student as well as scientist/researchers mobility (lack of command of English or Korean language, insufficient number of interested candidates);

- Insufficient understanding of the culture, language and potential win-win opportunities offer by the partner country (success in STI policies and indicators in Korea are not fully grasped in Guatemala, still Europe and North America are seen as prevalent or ideal);
- Prevailing of the vertical concept of international STI engagement as 'assistance' instead of a horizontal cooperation between equals (in Guatemala we tend to expect the partner will provide the human, financial and technical resources without a counterpart.

Part of these limitations were pointed out by the survey respondents. Anyway, they are not exclusive to a difficulty in Central American countries. There may be particularities, but issues about gap implementation, poor data collection, prevailing of vertical cooperation (instead horizontal cooperation), etc. are very common in different countries in Latin America.

The prevailing idea in the Guatemalan side (public institutions, researchers, students), by which as a less advanced STI country there dominates the "recipient" attitude rather than "a partner" attitude, was highlighted as a major hindrance for STID initiatives to succeed. In order for the country to engage in meaningful exchange, a shift in the mindset of authorities and individuals as well as the existence of basic STI capacities become conditions.

As for achievements, the appointment of a Science attaché in the Diplomatic Mission in Guatemala resulted, among others, in the following positive outcomes (Villagrán, 2017: 21):

> The production of relevant databases and building of statistics and good quality indicators: including relevant information about the fellows, details on their study programs, universities, donor entities, updated status of their programs... For the first time in more than a decade of STI cooperation in the form of scholarships between Korea and Guatemala, a consistent estimation of costs of each and every one of the types of scholarships offered by the 15 donor institutions becomes available. Having a clear idea of the amount and quality of cooperation is of vital importance, in order to evaluate each of the programs offered and prioritize outreach efforts...Thanks to the work done by the appointed specific attaché discussions about cooperation and decisions are made based on good quality information and evidence. Evaluation exercises are being proposed on the cooperation instruments framing the STI cooperation initiatives...Communication and dissemination of opportunities arising from STI cooperation initiatives is relevant in order to reach those interested parties and other potential

participants, even before the calls have been officially opened. This was achieved thanks to the collection of early information through universities, and thanks to the scheduling that has been defined keeping records of discussions and agreements.

An extremely important measure was "*the appointment of a science attaché fostered interactions and fluent communication between different parties from the two countries including public institutions, universities, higher education students and researchers, and even firms from the private sector*" (Villagrán, 2017: 21). The person was responsible to promote STI International Cooperation approach experienced in Guatemala and the structure minimum basis for a new approach in the perspective of STID.

It is insightful to emphasize on some of the key differences between STI International Cooperation approach experienced in the Guatemala for the past few decades to a new approach enabled by STID (Table 2.1).

The Guatemala Diplomatic Mission in South Korea also presented to the Korean Ministry of Foreign Affairs the initiative of a project called "Educational, Scientific and Technological Center" (Meneses, 2020), which was intended to be developed with the cooperation of Korean business consortiums and the universities of that country. They would interact with their counterparties in Guatemala, with the possible extension to the rest of Central American countries. Such initiatives had several components that ranged from research (Guatemala biodiversity is one of the natural reserves in the world), the exchange and mobility of professors

Table 2.1 STI international cooperation vs STID

STI international cooperation	*STID*
– Vertical relations of cooperation	– Horizontal relations of cooperation
– Isolated and fragmented interventions	– Integrative role of science and research
– Aid-oriented approach	– Empowering approach
– Absence of basic local STI capacities in less developed parties	– Requirement of basic local STI capacities in all parties
– Receiving–giving logic	– Win–win logic
– Predominance of government– government cooperation	– Diversity of participants involved: universities, individuals and organized researchers, official institutions, private firms

Source Based on Villagran (2018)

and young scholars engaging with companies and R&D and the provision of fiscal incentives (free zones) for investments aiming at building industrial plants for the production of medicines, laboratories and clinics working with social health services and universities. Certainly, property rights would be negotiated in a later stage. In principle, the San Carlos of Guatemala University (USAC) agreed to host the Center offering as counterparty their Technological Institute locating in Palín and in that place the Center could be built, which was promising as it is located close to the major logistic maritime facilities in the shores of the Pacific Ocean. However, the change in authorities of USAC resulted in the discontinuation of the negotiation, ultimately bringing the initiative to a termination.

The rotation of authorities, the lack of long-term planning and the inability to maintain sound STI initiatives for extended periods were pointed out as significant obstacles to promote successful STID initiatives in the case of Guatemala. Notwithstanding, with the incorporation of STID discussions in the Guatemalan Foreign Service through the work of the Diplomatic Academy (Meneses, 2020) further understanding will be enabled, consequently engaging in meaningful international STI projects is foreseeable.

The experience of the case study—Diplomatic Mission of Guatemala in the Republic of Korea—and also the researchers' perceptions, through applied research, made it possible to raise questions and address some learnings about STID dynamics within the particular contexts of the nations located in northern Central America.

2.6 Conclusions

The analyzed evidence suggests that STID framework could provide a helpful structure to organize STI capacity building projects in the three Central American countries—Guatemala, El Salvador and Honduras on the grounds that such nations have strategies or country development plans; otherwise, the shortcomings experienced with the implementation of the conventional STI international cooperation approach would persist. In addition, the limitations of the conventional STI international cooperation approach may result in isolated and fragmented interventions with limited results, instead of meaningful impacts in the reduction of STI capacities. STI diplomacy incorporates more complexity and diversity in the origins, characteristics and interests of a variety of participating actors. Promoting the interactions of a more diverse range of stakeholders could enhance the possibilities of addressing specific inclusive development challenges through a more integrated perspective.

In the traditional approach of STI international cooperation, the prevalence of government-to-government assistance has tended to limit the incorporation of other parties from the civil society, as well as, the private sector (firms) and the academia. A systemic approach and coordinated efforts among official institutions with an explicit mandate in STI could enable further achievements. Yet, efforts from the governments are to be accompanied by active engagement from the academia, the private sector and the organized civil society. It is also noteworthy how actors of great relevance have had limited interactions and showed a dismissive in their attitudes toward STI activities. An example of this involves the media and its responsibility to communicate science. Communicating scientific advances to society and the importance of science and technology in solving everyday problems is of critical importance to increase public awareness. It is also worthwhile calling for attention to the scarce participation of companies and private firms in these discussions. In sum, specific efforts ought to be devoted to the promotion of constant interactions between all these actors considering the separated paths the stakeholders have taken, instead of converging in common interests within the STI context in their societies.

Strong and sound public policies that involve the governments of Guatemala, El Salvador and Honduras and the different international cooperation platforms (bilateral, multilateral, sub-regional and triangular) can enable accelerated steps to be taken in the pursuit of STID projects aiming at building STI capacities. Therefore, it is important to work on integration throughout a variety of channels and mechanisms simultaneously. Governments must establish priorities and ensure that their STI systems are diversified and decentralized, resources provided to centers of excellence with large-, medium- and small-scale stimuli are dispersed and which in turn make it difficult to measure the research or achievements. Central America must reach out and engage with its already formed scientific diaspora and connect scientists who live within the borders of their countries with the research human power scattered around the globe. In addition, regional integration efforts could build closer collaborative bonds among different scientific communities across Central America. One natural partnership that should be explored involves the Central America System for Regional Integration—SICA.

The case study of STID practice between Guatemala and Korea provides evidence of the benefits arising from devoting separate and specific diplomatic efforts to advance STI cooperation ties based on a win–win perspective. While Guatemala greatly benefited from different mechanisms of engagement between local actors (graduate students, higher education institutions, public officers and entrepreneurs) and their Korean counterparties. Likewise, the mobility to Korea and the interactions achieved between such actors enriched possibilities to be exposed to better practices. Admittedly, the pilot STID program faced numerous obstacles which diminished the opportunities of obtaining greater results and at the same time precipitated its termination. The institutionalization of innovative practices in diplomacy requires a greater period of time and resources which require clear foreign policy guidelines and protocols yet to be designed. Meneses (2020) acknowledged "resistance from the established organizational structures against innovative STID practices, with the prevalence of more conventional and conservative approaches" which increases the value of increasing the exposure to different thinking and better global practices.

The STI gaps clearly observed in the depicted Central American national contexts require of assertive international engagement strategies in order to reduce their extent. Admittedly, the support provided by international cooperation efforts has been helpful in the process of building STI capacities in Guatemala, El Salvador and Honduras; notwithstanding, the impact in the inclusive development in these countries has been limited due to different characteristics and structural impediments for social progress experience by extended groups of their societies.

In summary, STID offers a helpful framework for countries with challenging STI context such as Guatemala, El Salvador and Honduras. These societies can use these constructs and logics to promote further engagement in international STI initiatives. The involvement of a wider diversity of actors from multiple sectors represents an enhancement compared with the traditional STI international cooperation approach, which offered a more restrictive framework. Understanding STID as a set of strategies and diplomatic tools to promote the national interest in the global sphere and to rationalize innovation systems through international cooperation, its application for STI capacity building and capacity development is relevant for the three Central American nations.

References

AAAS American Association for the Advancement of Science. (2010). *New frontiers in science diplomacy: Navigating the changing balance of power.* Royal Society.

Alpirez, A. C. (2014, January 7). *Los chicos buenos viajan al extranjero.* In P. Publica (Ed.). https://www.plazapublica.com.gt/content/los-chicos-buenos-viajan-al-extranjero.

Barañao, L. (2016). Educación Científica Regional e Integración de América Latina. *Science & Diplomacy, 5*(4), 1–8.

Bonilla, K., & Kwak, J. S. (2014), Challenges of highly educated human resources in Guatemala. *Asian Journal of Latin American Studies, 27*(3), 17–43.

Bonilla, K., & Kwak, J. S. (2015). Effectiveness of donor support for capacity development in Guatemala: A study of scholarship provision for overseas postgraduate education. *Iberoamerica, 17*(1), 293–344.

Bonilla, K., Salles-Filho, S., & Bin, A. (2018). Building science, technology, and research capacity in developing countries: Evidence from student mobility and international cooperation between Korea and Guatemala. *STI Policy Review, 9*(1), 99–132.

Bonilla, K., & Serafim, M. (2019). Atlanta Conference on Science and Innovation Policy. Georgia Institute of Technology—Scientific Work Force "Human Capacity Building in Central America: Challenges and Opportunities for Guatemala, El Salvador, Honduras", Poster session.

Bound, K. (2016). Innovating together? The age of innovation diplomacy. En W. W. Organization, *2016 Global Innovation Index* (pp. 91–95). Cornell University.

Caroline S. W., Brahmakulam, I., Jackson, B., Wong, A., & Yoda, T. (2001). *Science and technology collaboration: Building capacity in developing countries.* RAND.

Castro, E. F. (2018, August). *La Estrella.* Retrieved September 15, 2019, from Diplomacia de la Ciencia: https://www.researchgate.net/publication/327118487_Diplomacia_Para_La_Ciencia.

CONACYT. (2017). *Indicadores de Ciencia y Tecnología El Salvador [Science and Technology Indicators, El Salvador].* Ministry of Education.

Dagnino, Renato Peixoto. (2014). A anomalia da política de Ciência e Tecnologia. *RBCS, 29*(86). Outubro.

Duriez G., M. & Zamora, A. B. (2016). *Educacion Superior en iberoamerica informe 2016: Informe Nacional El Salvador.* CINDA.

Duriez, M., Lopez, B., & Moncada, G. (2016). *Educacion Superior en iberoamerica: Informe Nacional Honduras.* CINDA.

ECLAC UN Economic Commision for Latin America and the Caribbean. (1995). *Propuesta Programa y Estructura de la Academia Diplomatica de Guatemala*. CEPAL.

FECYT Fundación Española para la Ciencia y la Tecnología. (2017). *Recomendaciones para Fomentar la Diplomacia Científica en la Región de América Latina y el Caribe*. AECID.

Fedoroff, N. (2009). Science diplomacy in the 21st century. *Cell*, *136*(1), 9–11.

Fernández-Polcuch, E. (2015). *Ciencia y Diplomacia en América Latina: la perspectiva de la UNESCO*. Oficina Regional de Ciencias de la UNESCO para América Latina y el Caribe.

Gavarrete, J. (2019, February 28). *El FMLN hizo del servicio exterior un nicho familiar*. https://gatoencerrado.news/2019/02/28/los-apellidos-que-pesan-en-el-exterior/.

Gilpin, R. (2001). *Global political economy: Understanding the international economic order*. Princeton University Press.

INDESGUA, Institute for the Development of Higher Education in Guatemala. (2020). *Resultados del Trabajo de Gestión de INDESGUA*. Retrieved September 15 from http://www.indesgua.org.gt/sobre-nosotros/.

Leijten, J. (2017). Exploring the future of innovation diplomacy. *European Journal of Futures Research*, 5–20.

Meneses, C. H. E. (2020, January 22). Former Ambassador of Guatemala in the Republic of Korea, and current Director of the Guatemala diplomatic academy (K. Bonilla interviewer).

Monje-Nájera, J., & Ho, Y. S. (2018). Guatemala articles in the science citation index expanded: Bibliometry of subjects, collaboration, institutions and authors. *Biología Tropical*, *66*(1), 312–320.

SEGEPLAN Guatemala National Secretariat for Planning and Programming. (2015, May 5). *K'atun our Guatemala national plan 2032*. Retrieved August 20, 2019, from https://www.undp.org/content/dam/guatemala/docs/publications/undp_gt_PND_Katun2032.pdf.

Selleslaghs, J. (2017). *EU-Latin American*. Institute for European Studies.

SENACYT Guatemala National Secretariat for Science and Technology. (2017). *Política Nacional de Desarrollo Científico y Tecnológico 2015–2032*. Available at: http://ecursos.segeplan.gob.gt/CAPP/documentos/70/PoliticaNacionaldeDesarrollo%20C%20y%20T%20(21062017).pdf.

SENACYT-MINEX Panamá. (2019). *LIneamientos de la estrategia de diplomacia científica, tecnológica y de innovación*. Panama City.

Serafim, M. P., & Dagnino, R. (2011). A polícia científica e tecnológica e as demandas da inclusão social no Governo Lula (2003–2006), *en Revista Organizões e Sociedade*, 18(58), 403–427.

Silva, P. I. F. (2018). Fundamentos teóricos e práticos para uma Diplomacia da Inovação. (IPRI, Ed.). *Cadernos de Política Exterior*, 4(7), 307–330.

Soler, M. G. (2014). El Papel de las Redes Científicas Intergubernamentales en las Relaciones Regionales y la Integración de América Latina. *Science & Diplomacy, 3*(4), 1–18.

Stads, G., Hartwich, F., Rodriguez, D., & Enciso, F. (2008). *I & D Agropecuaria en América Central: Políticas, Inversiones y Perfil Institucional.* IICA Instituto Interamericano de Cooperación para la Agricultura.

UNESCO United Nations Educational, Scientific and Cultural Organization. (2017). *Relevamiento de la Investigación y la Innovación en la República de Guatemala [Survey of research and innovation in Guatemala].* Paris: Lemarchand. Available at: https://unesdoc.unesco.org/ark:/48223/pf0000248067.

Villagrán, A. L. (2018, March 1). STI capacity building in Guatemala, mobility of graduate students. (K. Bonilla, Interviewer).

Villagran, A. L. (2017). *Reporte sobre el aprovechamiento de los programas de becas de estudios superiores ofrecidos por la República de Corea por parte de estudiantes y profesionales guatemaltecos.* Reporte Anual Oficina de Cooperación y Transferencia de Conocimiento, Misión Diplomática de Guatemala en la República de Corea, Seul.

Weiss, C. (2005). Science, technology and international relations. *Technology in Society, 27*, 295–313.

Weiss, C. (2015). How do science and technology affect international affairs? *Minerva, 53*, 411–430.

CHAPTER 3

Transdisciplinary Citizen Science Connects Caribbean Hope Spots of Colombia to Improve Coral Reefs Governance

Nohora Galvis and Rosa Helena Galvis

3.1 Introduction

The United Nations (UN) has called on governments, the private sector, academia, civil society and the public to join forces for achieving sustainable development as "the development that meets the needs of the present, without compromising the ability of future generations to meet their own needs" (WCED, 1987: 8). UN members alongside civil society, stakeholders and major groups can help the implementation of Sustainable Development Goals (SDGs). Sustainability considers the ecological, social and economic systems searching for mathematical theory embodying these concepts to integrated perspectives comprising humans

N. Galvis (✉) · R. H. Galvis
International Coral Reefs Observatory, Fundacion ICRI Colombia, Bogota, Colombia

L. A. Orozco et al. (eds.), *Science, Technology, and Higher Education*, Palgrave Studies in Democracy, Innovation, and Entrepreneurship for Growth,
https://doi.org/10.1007/978-3-030-80720-7_3

and the natural ecosystem trophic linkages, biodiversity and biogeochemical cycles (Cabezas et al., 2004). Mauser et al. (2013) clarifies that scientific disciplines from natural and social science will collaborate with relevant societal groups based on transdisciplinary and integrated research concepts to achieve the three different dimensions of the integration of ecological, social and economic sciences to explore together successful pathways toward global sustainability. In agreement with Tress et al. (2004), the strength of integration varies across research concepts, from low (participatory, multidisciplinary) to fully integrated (interdisciplinary, transdisciplinary), stresses that transdisciplinary, in comparison to interdisciplinary, is also characterized by the involvement of non-academic actors in the research process. For Nicolescu (2002) the prefix "trans" from transdisciplinarity means working between the disciplines, across the different disciplines and beyond all disciplines. Lang et al. (2012) defines transdisciplinarity as a reflexive principle that aims at the solution or transition of societal problems by differentiating and integrating knowledge from various scientific and societal bodies of knowledge. Mauser et al. (2013) focus on integration as an iterative process that involves reflection among all stakeholders based on three stages: co-design, co-production and co-dissemination. In order to solve scientific ecological problems associated to global change and sustainability it is necessary to ensure collaboration and a "wise and efficient coordination" of a broad range of disciplines from the natural science and humanities.

The Sustainable Development Goal 14 refers to the protection of Life Below Water. Millions of species depend on the ecosystem integrity of coral reefs—including human beings. However, coral reefs face degradation in all the regions of the world. According to Anthony et al. (2011) and Burke et al. (2011), approximately 75% of coral reefs worldwide are currently threatened by a combination of local and global stressors. Without actions taken to minimize local stressors, this figure will increase to 90% by 2030 and close to 100% by 2050. Ocean acidification and warming will lower coral reef resilience and local stressors reduce coral resilience to bleaching (Carilli et al., 2009). Thus, effective local-scale stressors management is critical to keep reefs healthy in the trend of increasing global stressors.

Two international studies (Hocking, et al., 2000; Pomeroy et al., 2004) have attempted to develop tools for assessing coral reef management effectiveness, although to date such measures have only been applied to a few sites. Most focus is given to Marine Protected Areas

(MPAs), coastal or oceanic management areas designed to conserve ecosystems together with their functions and resources. Specifically, coral reefs are the mega-diversity areas of the ocean targeted for protection from land-based sources of pollution, with use restrictions and regulation of resources use to ensure sustainability (Fontaubert et al., 1996: 47–48). Site level data with adequate detail would be ideal to evaluate MPA performance and provide information on potentially explanatory variables but it is not yet available at the global level, as the cost and effort would be prohibitive (Hargreaves-Allen et al., 2017). Many MPAs are failing to meet their aims, and the majority of reefs, including those inside MPAs, remain threatened (Christie & White, 2007; Jameson et al., 2002). Dalton et al. (2015) in the wider Caribbean, analyzed social and ecological data from rapid assessments in thirty-one MPAs associated to human communities to investigate the extent to which MPAs are making progress toward their stated social and ecological objectives. Despite the UN focus to implement SDGs, there is still a gap of understanding assertive communication based on scientific facts to reach decision-makers, who do not have the political will to consider them. Assessing coral reef resilience and effective conservation is an increasingly important component of coral reef management. Bachtiar et al. (2019) selected for the resilience indicators: coral functional group, coral habitat quality, sand-silt cover, coral cover, coral small-size number and algae-other-fauna cover using line-intercept-transect (LIT). Colding and Barthel (2019) noticed that in the twenty years' course of existence, the Social-Ecological System SES concept has a descriptive focus or diagnostic focus that still lacks a more unifying definition to facilitate communication to a broader multidisciplinary audience.

In Colombia, most coral reefs are included in a governmental protection framework as it is a mandate to protect coral reefs. However, most coral reef areas have become deteriorated in the last decades, which make us wonder why and how the governance should be improved. The only way to improve governance is to evaluate their effectiveness identifying what needs to be improved and with whom. Thus, we evaluate the conservation effectiveness by involving the local communities as a process to improve the governance. The official monitoring performed by INVEMAR (Government Marine Research Institution) through its monitoring program SIMAC (Camargo et al., 2008; Galvis, 1989a, 1998, 2002 and 2006), have evaluated and monitored the effectiveness of coral reef management with managers, scientists, divers and fishers. According to Bunce and Galvis (2002), socioeconomic assessments are relevant to identify all the perspectives about the performance of ecological indicators to improve governance for planning improvements in effectiveness of management. Citizen science is relevant to diminish costs and to consider reports of hidden international, national and local anthropogenic causes of coral reef deterioration from their observations on isolated coral reef areas that do not have permanent surveillance (Galvis & Galvis, 2016; Shein et al., 2016). The ecosystem integrity in coral reef areas may change according to the effective management of anthropogenic threats and the consideration of environmental conditions that may benefit the resilience of less visited places.

We review the nature of the complex system including its ecological, social and economic aspects, and propose an approach to assess conservation effectiveness based on information theory that bridges the natural and human systems. These principles are illustrated using a model system with the identification of indicators, evaluation and monitoring of their performance. Indicators of Pressure, State, Impact and Management clarified causes, effects and extent of threats in order to apply assertive conservation measures (Galvis, 1996, 1998, 2001 and 2002). From the start of the ability to monitor permanently, all the indicators in all areas are constrained by cost, and it requires inter-institutional and expert multidisciplinary coordination with the involvement of the stakeholders and volunteer reporters to assure transdisciplinarity and governance. Our participatory research is based on the conceptual approach of citizen science combined with transdisciplinarity. We develop specific communication means for citizen science projects to create and maintain active and participatory communities to improve coral reef conservation. Shein et al. (2016) defined as relevant the implementation of citizen science programs in the planning of improvements of coral reef conservation effectiveness. Citizen science permanently monitors Colombian coral reefs by online communication, allowing public participation in scientific research to increase the public's understanding of science and engagement with the potential solutions to the environmental problems.

3.2 Methodologies

The performance of ecological, social and economic indicators was compared between one protected coral reef area and two non-protected coral reef areas for twelve years. Monitoring indicators of pressure, state, impact and management looking for potential causes, effects and extent of threats in order to apply assertive conservation measures were used (Galvis, 1996, 1998, 2001 and 2002). We received 1958 verified reports with videos and photos, GPS locations, depths, currents, turbidity, date and time. Reports were sent through the network of volunteer observers of the reefs, RENOVOs, within the citizen science program of the Coral Reefs Observatory created by the Foundation ICRI Colombia in 2008. All the reporters of observations are committing to do transdisciplinary science together. Thus, integrated processes of co-designing research were relevant to co-producing knowledge with researchers, decision-makers and stakeholders for addressing challenges to implement Sustainable Development Goal 14 to protect Life below Water on the Colombian coral reefs. For Galvis and Galvis (2016) to evaluate the coral reef governance effectiveness, the total area of Colombian coral reefs should include the 1421.92 Km^2 protected deep coral formations. The total area to consider for effective protection is 4281.92 km^2 from which only 15 km^2 are in the Pacific, the rest being in the Caribbean Sea (Fig. 3.1). Three Caribbean case studies were compared to identify differences to improve coral reef protection. The Natural National Park Corales del Rosario and San Bernardo has an area of 1200 km^2 that is located between the two Caribbean Hope Spots of Colombia. The thirty-two Rosario Islands are within 167 km^2; at 52 km of the north of the park, is the south of Cartagena Bay (Fig. 3.2), where is situated the Coral Reef Varadero that is not protected by the government. However, it is protected by civil society and the community within an international framework of Mission Blue[1] and is approximately 1.12 km^2 from which Pizarro et al. (2017) characterized the well-developed coral reef of 0.44 km^2. At the south of the Park is located the other Caribbean Hope Spot with the coral reefs between Capurganá and Cabo Tiburón. It has 400 km^2 of open sea.[2] We are implementing collaborative forms of governance including environmental education and involvement in citizen science for the Hope Spots that are not protected by the government. In accordance with Clement et al. (2019), these forms of governance are

[1] See https://mission-blue.org/2018/10/capurgana-and-cabo-tiburon-declared-a-hope-spot-in-support-of-leatherback-sea-turtles/.

[2] See https://mission-blue.org/2018/04/corales-de-varadero-varaderos-coral-reef-off-the-colombian-coast-at-cartagena-is-designated-a-hope-spot/.

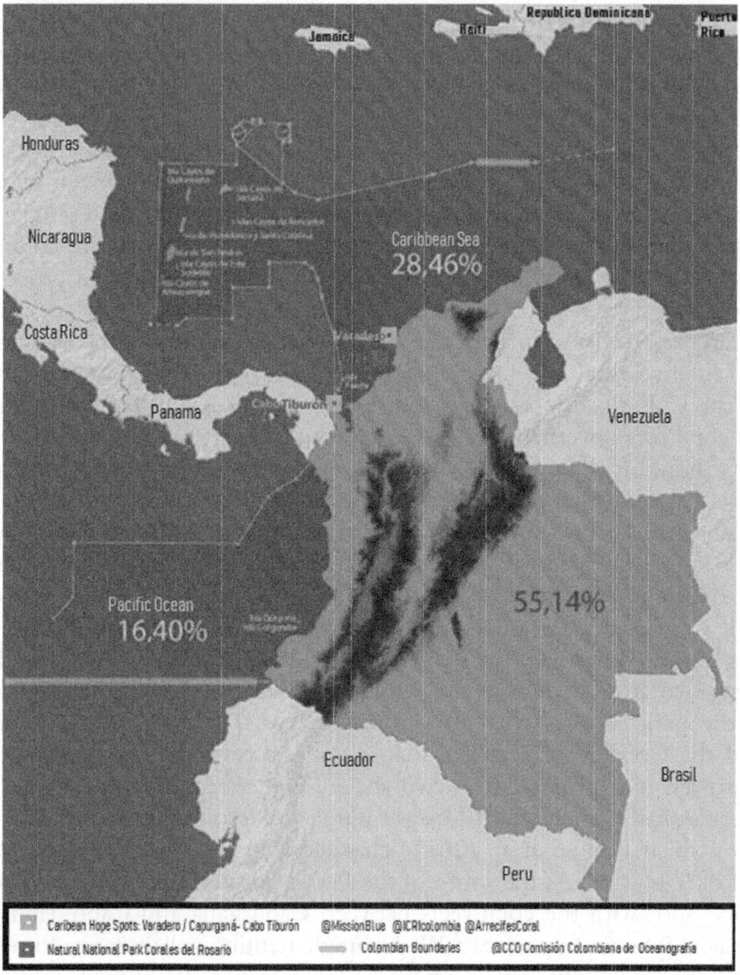

Fig. 3.1 Map of Colombian case studies

increasingly favored in conservation and potentially offer a range of practical and outcome-based benefits. Stakeholders' analysis in each case study and characterization of the Coral Reef Ecosystem Integrity by evaluation and monitoring ecological indicators of the ecosystem dynamic processes

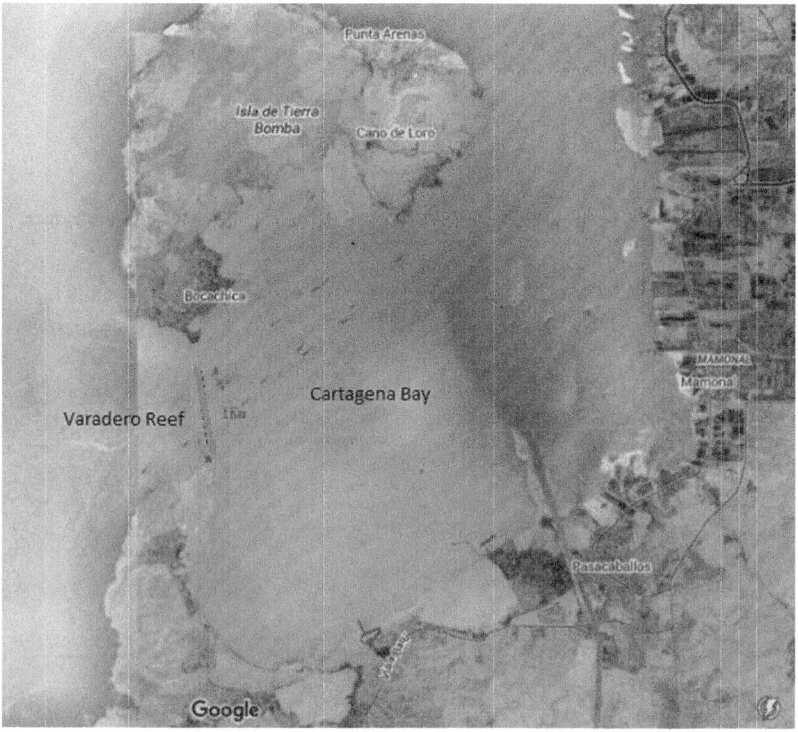

Fig. 3.2 Map of the case studies Corales del Rosario and Varadero

assist in the identification of potential changes in function, structure, and composition (Galvis, 2001).

Healthy coral cover, diseases incidence, predation, herbivory, biodiversity, presence of IUCN listed species measured per hour in geo-referenced transects at Corales del Rosario Park are compared with others at the Hope Spot areas: Capurganá-Cabo-Tiburón and Varadero, identifying local threats, management and social arrangements. The means of communication were direct messages through the social media (Twitter @ArrecifesCoral @ICRIcolombia, Google-blog ICRI-Colombia and Facebook ICRI.Colombia), email, WhatsApp, skype and smart phones. The data was reported systematically per geo-referenced diving and fishing sites, e.g., Figs. 3.2 and 3.3. These records become scientific evidence

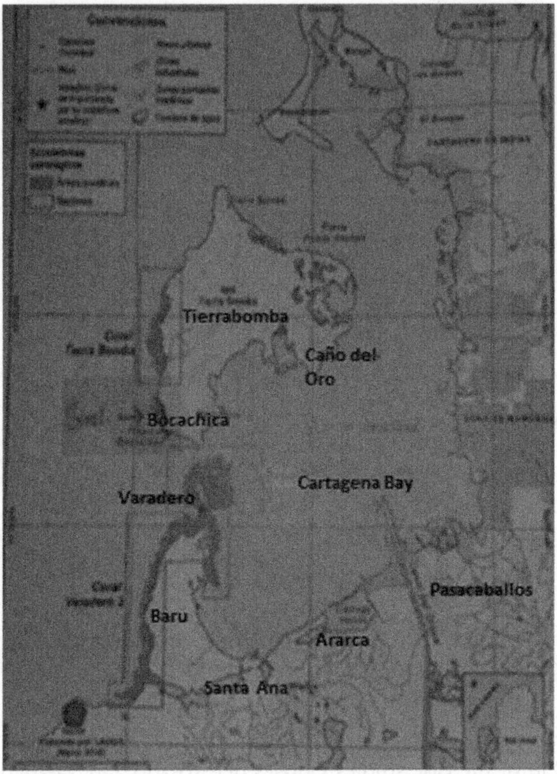

Fig. 3.3 Map of the fishers´communities of Varadero Coral Reef

verified by the scientists in situ within geo-referenced line-transects (verifications performed in 2009, 2010, 2012, 2014, 2016, 2017, 2018 and 2019).

3.3 Case Studies

3.3.1 Corales Del Rosario Park

Corales del Rosario Park is connected to the coral reefs of San Bernardo within the same framework of National Parks. However, it has been protected longer as an underwater area with low enforcement, surrounded by non-protected private islands where crowd activities produce littering, sewage pollution, construction on coastline with coral rubble as construction material, and on boats (fishing, littering, oil pollution, anchoring). There is freshwater and large sediment charge coming from the Dique Channel. The protection framework has diminished dynamite fishing since 1977. The coral cover average for the massive coral colonies is 18, 83% ±2,47. The fleshy macroalgae cover is >50%. Low herbivory and high dominance of the fleshy algae, mainly *Dictyota dichotoma* (Hudson) J.V. Lamouroux 1809: 42 and *Pockiella variegate*, has covered large portions of the dead coral colonies in Corales del Rosario Park. These two last algae species are not edible, besides that it is low herbivory at the Park. *Acropora cervicornis* and *Acropora palmata* are critically endangered species in the IUCN-Red-listed and threatened in Colombia by the Ministry of Environment and Sustainable Development. Acropora species have 95% of mortality in the Park (Gutiérrez-Moreno, et al., 2011). According to Rogers (1990), sedimentation from run-off and dredging is one of the major sources of reef degradation in the Caribbean. Due to anthropogenic impact, the protected coral reefs in the Park have deteriorated. Species in the IUCN Red List were scarce in the Park. Gutiérrez-Moreno et al. (2011) and Henao (2013) reported high temperatures, nutrient enrichment and high sedimentation rates. The sedimentation threshold in coral reefs is 10 mg/cm^2 which besides limiting the survival of coral colonies, decreases fertilization success and inhibits larval settlement of coral species (Erftemeijer et al., 2012). A combination of high temperatures and high concentrations of nutrients (e.g., >20 μM NH4) can alter the duration of coral larval competence time and decrease the dispersal capacity (Bassim & Sammarco, 2003). As expected from prolonged ocean temperatures of 2°C above the range of usual coral experience, this has led in the last three decades to the breakdown of the algal/corals symbiosis, to widespread episodes of coral bleaching and to mass coral mortality (Norström et al., 2016) during a period of rapid climate change. Coral reef ecosystems are further impacted by increasing diverse anthropogenic impacts, that in combination with climate change drivers, inflict a wide range of profound damages on the coral reef ecosystems (Norström et al., 2016), with multiple conjoined effects (Eddy et al., 2018).

The spatial collaborative multicriteria analysis of Corales del Rosario Park is a participatory decision-making process based on semi-structured interviews about value judgments indicators weights per perspectives to evaluate the state of health and use of geo-referenced diving sites. The evaluation of conservation effectiveness was calculated with equations for multicriteria analysis (adapted from Winterfeldt & Edwards, 1986 in Galvis, 2002) for the systematic selection of relevant indicators as recommended by Galvis (2001). The equations for accumulative evaluations of the performance indicators per perspective of the governance in the implementation of the SDG14: Coral Reefs Protection. Few sightings of species of the IUCN Red List, reported only one to three per month. The perspectives of managers, fishers, divers and ecologists identified common indicators per mandate or interest of use. The low performance is shown in red, and high in green letters under all perspectives as shown in Fig. 3.2. The closer dive site of the Corales del Rosario National Park to the Hope Spot Varadero Reef is Pendales (A). It has the higher performance indicator under all the perspectives. Thus, Pendales is the evidence of the ecological connection between the protected coral reefs (Park) and the resilient coral reef Varadero. However, the two Hope Spots, despite being resilient, have other threats from dredging plans in Varadero and also industrial fishing in Capurgana-Cabo Tiburón.

3.3.2 Varadero Coral Reef Hope Spot

The coral reef has grown over the course of 500 million years on the leeward region of the Draga and Abanico Islands close to Barú with influence of open sea currents at the bottom and turbid waters at the surface. Varadero was founded over one hundred years ago for fishers and has appeared in the government fisheries reports since 1989 (Galvis 1989b). In fact, fishers have defended the coral reef from dredging plans since 1990 (LA APERTURA NECESITA A EL VARADERO, Archivo EL TIEMPO, ANA LUCIA DUQUE SALAZAR 09 September 1991, 12:00 a.m.).[3] The promoters of dredging wanted to create a coral reef baseline as already negative impacted, at the south of the Abanico and Draga islands, in order to get the dredging license (Procanal, 2011). However, Varadero is a resilient coral reef at the north-east of the Park Corales del Rosario (Figs. 3.2 and 3.3). It is not an "improbable or a paradoxical" coral reef as described by Pizarro et al. (2017) and López et al. (2015) when invited by AQUA&TERRA, the firm contracted by Instituto Nacional de Vias (INVIAS) to favor the Environmental Impact

[3] see https://www.eltiempo.com/archivo/documento/MAM-151349.

Assessment (EIA) to dredge on Varadero. These scientists learned then about its existence, arguing before the media, that they cannot be against development. That wrong nomination favors the unsustainable developers interested in destroying the coral reef by allowing dredging on it. In fact, the Bocachica Channel was enlarged without paying attention to the strikes of fishers in 2014, who blocked the entrance to Cartagena Bay. The enlargement was based on the technical support of AQUA&TERRA affecting at least 100 m^2 at the western part of Varadero. Our verification evidenced the total mortality of large *Orbicella* colonies that took 500 years to grow, close to the enlargement area.

The Financiera de Desarrollo Nacional in 2016 again hired AQUA&TERRA with US$1.5 million for a positive EIA that would allow for dredging and thus destroy the remaining coral reef. This project is not necessary as megaships are already entering the area by the recently enlarged Bocachica Channel. The government was considering as an "environmental cost" only the US$1.5 million paid to hire that confidential environmental study to support dredging on Varadero Reef for the Autoridad Nacional de Licencias Ambientales (ANLA). Nevertheless, the environmental costs are larger in comparison to other alternatives as explained by Galvis and Galvis (2016).

According to the valuation of the opportunity cost for the two mutually exclusive decisions for the resilient Varadero Reef: Dredging vs. Protecting the 1km^2, this is even higher the environmental cost. Considering the ecosystem integrity within its natural dynamics functioning within time and spaces scales, the environmental cost will increase, as a minimum, to the equivalent to the conservative estimate of ecosystem services loss: US$244 million/Km 2+ >10%/year. If added to the cost of dredging (US$50 million), the minimum is US$294 million, being the most expensive alternative in comparison with the cost of other alternatives. Therefore, the best option for the public treasury is the effective governmental protection of the resilient Varadero Coral Reef. The benefits of effective governance favor present and future generations for the annual production of coral reefs ecosystem services (Galvis, 1999). The cost of potential real time needed for recovery (*500 years) cost was estimated after Spurgeon and Lindahl (2000).

The developers applied the strategy of not asking for a new license, but using instead the old license of the enlargement of the Bocachica Channel to argue that it was still valid. Under the previous license they were allowed to destroy 50% of the Varadero Reef, but they think that they only destroyed 10% of it, so they go for the rest. To confuse the public, they now call the same project "Variante" in relation to the Bocachica Channel. About a thousand fishers joined a legal petition to the government to stop the dredging plan, and to protect the coral reef which is their food security and also enjoyment for the present and future generations on behalf of their right to a healthy environment. A popular action from the community is requiring the government to allow a previous consultation with the seven communities of fishers in Varadero: Ararca, Santa Ana, Pasacaballos, Bocachica, Tierrabomba, Caño Del Oro and Barú. However, the government only acknowledges two communities to negotiate the compensations for Bocachica and Caño de Loro, as these were the only communities consulted for the enlargement of the Bocachica Channel.

Restoration projects that support dredging, but are based on breaking fragments of coral colonies are fake promises to "save" Varadero, as they have a low survival rate and coral growth is very slow in replacing each $5m^2$ of dead coral colonies. The special conditions of Varadero that made it a resilient coral reef were the "shadow coral colonies" on the surface formed by turbid current from the Dique Channel and plenty of nutrients from the bottom open sea currents (Fig. 3.2) that do not allow sedimentation to affect the health of coral colonies. However, the current impact in Varadero is the frequent navigation of large ships through the enlarged Bocachica Channel. This may increase the abundance of fine particles (<125 μm in diameter) that may decrease coral fertilisation rates due to gamete abrasion (Gilmour, 1999) or obstruction of egg micro piles (Galbraith et al., 2006; Humprey et al., 2008). Dredging causes resuspended particles <63 μm) with nutrients affecting coral colonies and the whole ecosystem (Erftemeijer et al., 2012).

Until now, due to the opposition from fishers' communities and support from NGOs (including Foundation ICRI Colombia) and academia, the plans have been delayed. The civil society requested the government to stop the dredging plan and include Varadero within the Colombian Coral Reefs Atlas of INVEMAR and the National Parks System, during the International Year of the Reef, when declared a Hope Spot by Mission Blue.

Mejia et al. (2018) found species richness at Varadero Coral Reef: 120 species of thirty-six families in eleven orders. This reef that can serve as a refuge against climate change is thus at risk due to potential threats of unsustainable development by dredging plans. The reef has open water currents at the bottom and at the surface run-off, which protects the reef from over-heating in the dry season. Mejia et al. (2018) reported higher temperatures measured at 29.5°C and particulate organic nutrients that could be causing heterotrophy in the coral community waters, nowadays usually look cloudy due to the high content of suspended material and for being inland waters that reach the bay through the Canal del Dique. The presence and abundance of herbivores *Echinometra viridis* and *Diadema antillarum* have the important function of grazing to prevent macroalgae overgrowth. According to Galvis (1989a), the dominant algae was a natural indicator found in healthy coral reefs: *Halimeda spp*, (Lamouroux, 1812).

We confirmed these findings by monitoring that the flow of bottom currents that enter from the open sea to the Cartagena Bay support its healthy existence. Its massive structure is formed by coral colonies as big as $5m^2$ (*Orbicella* sp. among forty-four other species of corals) on the leeward of the Islands Draga and Abanico close to Barú. The turbidity from the Dique Channel most of the year goes toward north, or at the rainy season flows toward south of Cartagena Bay, but always at the surface on the coral reefs without producing sedimentation. The trade winds create the turbidity at the first meters of the water column; in Varadero this may be associated as natural shade to the resilient coral-algal symbiosis, resembling the characteristics of a climate change refuge. The healthy coral cover in Varadero is 80%, due to its low incidence of diseases as reported in other areas of the Caribbean, even in the Park. These verifications were made in 2017 and 2019. It has low algal cover (<5%) due to abundant herbivory (58–71 urchins) *Diademaantillarum* (Philippi, 1845) and 33–46 parrotfishes (Scaridae) per one-hour line-transect. Other inhabitants of this resilient reef are large carnivores e.g., sharks *Ginglymostoma cirratum* (Bonnaterre, 1788) and lobsters (*Panulirus Argus*; Latreille 1804); as well as endangered species within IUCN Red List (1–3 per week), e.g. Green Turtle (*Chelonia mydas* Linnaeus, 1758). In 2019, the Foundation ICRI Colombia requested the government to nominate Varadero Coral Reef and the following Hope Spot (Capurganá-Cabo Tiburón Coral Reef) as World Heritage Sites because they accomplish UNESCO´s universal criteria.

3.3.3 *Hope Spot Capurganá-Cabo Tiburón Coral Reef*

The community of fishers in Capurganá, Caribbean Choco (Fig. 3.4), contacted the Foundation ICRI Colombia in 2008 to request support to avoid industrial fishing in the area. The Foundation officially requested the Fisheries Authority, AUTORIDAD NACIONAL DE ACUICULTURA Y PESCA AUNAP, the Navy and the Association of National Industries (ANDI) about the situation. They communicated with industries and the same industries decided to stop their activities in the area by complaining about the poor fisheries resources in that year. On their report, the industrial fisheries representatives confess it was convenient for them to go from Cartagena through the Panama Channel to fish in the Pacific rather than to stay on the coral reefs.

The Artisanal Fishers Association of Capurganá, PESCAPUR in agreement with the Foundation, started in 2009 to report their fisheries statistics to the Coral Reefs Observatory of the Foundation ICRI Colombia, before the lionfish appeared in 2010. The evaluation of the state of the coral reefs from Capurganá-Cabo Tiburón includes written reports from scientists of Antioquia University, confirming low coral disease incidence and 70% healthy coral cover as well as photos and videos from our permanent monitoring with scuba diving operators.

This Hope Spot has an area of 400 km^2. The area was established according to the boundaries of the Sanctuary Playona, Acandi. The Director of the National Parks plans to include this coral reef area within

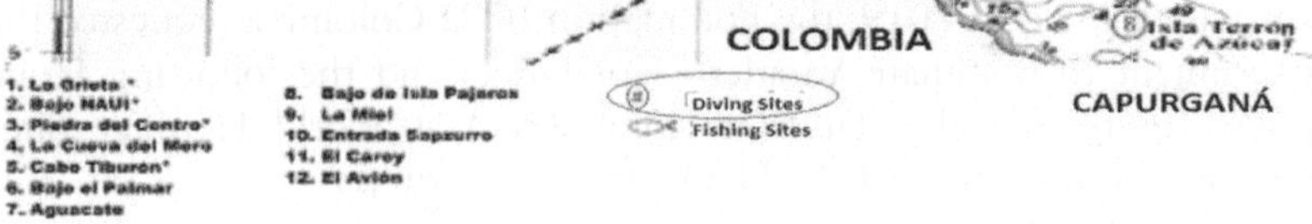

Fig. 3.4 Fishing and diving sites in the non-protected area declared Hope Spot Coral Reef Capurganá and Cabo Tiburón

the system including the same distance of 20 km from the coast, on the way of the world's main nesting sea turtle sites. The IUCN International Union for Conservation of Nature's Red List of Threatened Species marks out as vulnerable the leatherback turtle, *Dermochelys coriacea* (Vandelli, 1761) with only 250 reports per season. Also frequently seen is the critically endangered Hawksbill turtle, *Eretmochelys imbricata*[4] (Linnaeus, 1766), the endangered Green turtle i (Linnaeus, 1758), and Loggerhead turtle *Caretta caretta* (Linnaeus, 1758). The reports of sightings of endangered species within the IUCN Red List are seven to ten per week, for example, Hawksbill turtles[4] located per diving or fishing site of the map (Fig. 3.3). Herbivory include *Diadema antillarum* (Philippi, 1845), *Mithrax spinosissimus* (Lamarck, 1818), parrotfishes (Scaridae) and butterflyfishes (Chaetodontidae). There are also sightings of dolphins *Sotalia guianensis* (van Bénéden, 1864), *Tursiops truncatus* (George Montagu 1821), and carnivores, e.g., sharks *Ginglymostoma cirratum* Bonnaterre 1788) and lobsters *Panulirus Argus* (Latreille 1804). There was a pattern of depletion of native fisheries after industrial fishing and from the appearance of the invasive lionfish, *Pterois volitans* since October of 2010. The Foundation ICRI Colombia promoted lionfish fishing through environmental campaigns and consumption, since the invasive species was common in the catches from line fishing, and has to be enhanced for the interests of fishers for its consumption, and thus a local and national market was stimulated. This strategy was successful in controlling the invasive species, nominated with its family Scorpaenidae in Fig. 3.5.

The strategy of the government to control the invasive species before 2012 was not to involve fishers, only divers with spearguns. However, due to the progression of the invasion in the Caribbean Sea, it was understood that any kind of hunting / fishing was allowed in coral reefs to control lionfishes. Reports show direct destruction of coral colonies from the use of spear guns and illegal lobster collection during the lionfish derbies with scuba. The lionfish invasive population moved deeper after 2013 to the fishing grounds. Therefore, we continued working with the local association of artisanal fishers to control lionfishes in the deeper areas where it was also controlled naturally by the retrieval native fish stocks of the family Lutjanidae or snappers and Scombridae or tuna after stopping

[4] See https://youtu.be/IzN0FqOKKFg and and https://www.facebook.com/ICRI.COLOMBIA/videos/969552076764370/.

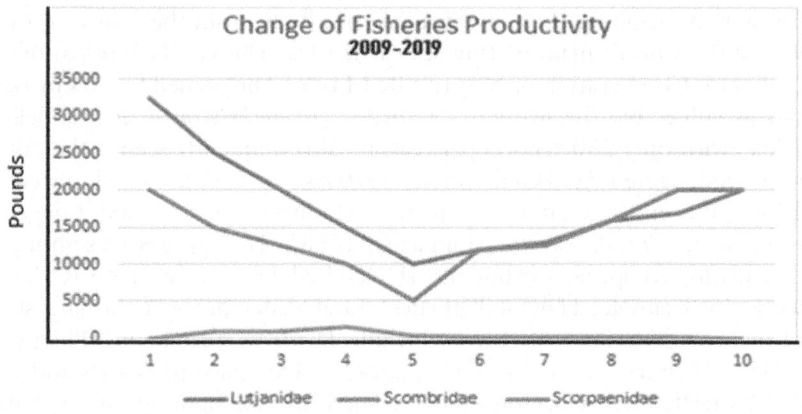

Fig. 3.5 Change of fisheries productivity of main commercial and invasive species in Capurganá between 2009 and 2019

industrial fisheries as it is evidenced in Fig. 3.5. Reports of groupers and snappers with lionfishes found in the stomach contents are evidence of biological control. After 2013, also evident was the positive impact of the bankruptcy of industrial fisheries enterprises that had stopped activities in the area due to overfishing and non-profitable activities in 2008–2009. Gradual retrieval of native species was reported in the following years while the catches of lionfishes by line fishing, scuba diving operators and volunteer scuba divers was constant and added to the biological and social control of the invasive species. We studied the change in fisheries productivity before and after the appearance of the lionfish *Pterois volitans*. A decade of quantitative statistical reports from anglers on pounds as reflected as catches per effort unit (CPEU) in Capurganá were analyzed for possible *P. volitans* impact on the reef fisheries. A separate analysis considered in detail quantitative reports from divers with their catches after 2010 when the invasion started in this last Colombian coral reef area in the Caribbean border with Panama (Galvis & Galvis, 2016).

3.3.4 Comparison to Identify Probable Climate Change Refugia

The two Caribbean Hope Spots of Colombia fulfill criteria as climate change refugia. According to Morelli et al. (2020) climate change refugia are areas that remain relatively buffered from contemporary climate change over time and enable the persistence of valued physical, ecological, and sociocultural resources. The key attribute of refugia is their relative persistence, despite changes in the climate; they have shaded coral reefs caused by turbidity that provides protection from long-term environmental change, such as warming oceans. Also long-term buffering; environmental changes in refugia are not ruled by regional trends from the rest of the Caribbean Coral Reefs of Colombia. Stability is an extreme form of decoupling and refers to refugia maintaining near-constant environmental conditions in the face of regional change. Both Hope Spots have complex food webs, healthy coral recruitment and healthy coral cover that resembles the coral reefs described for the 1980s with controlled biological threats such as diseases, invaders, eroders and competitors. Successful recruitment has been observed in both refugia, and coral larvae will need to survive, settle and grow when conditions surrounding the refugia become inhospitable. For microclimatic heterogeneity, we have identified internal currents and deeper parts of coral reefs with the lower temperatures and subsequent lower bleaching rates of coral reefs. Also geographical, hydrological and biological barriers and availability of suitable substrates for coral larval settlement. Action to identify and protect the Hope Spots will most likely facilitate the survival of coral reefs in rapidly changing oceans.

The good performance indicators in the non-protected areas are related to the higher natural coral recruitment, resilient reef growth and low macroalgal cover in the Hope Spots as the indicators of healthy coral reefs, mostly *Halimeda spp*, (J.V. Lamouroux, 1812), with high herbivory and ecosystem integrity and composition. Low-intensity diving and constant turbidity with freshwater enrichment from local rivers in the first meters of the water column combining with permanent flow from open sea at the bottom, may be beneficial and the key explanation variables for the good coral health and large massive coral colonies. Tomascik and Sander (1985) explained that sizes of coral colonies might increase at sites with moderate increments of suspended particulate matter in the water column, because they are a significant source of additional food for the polyps. Sediment levels affect coral species according to their capability to remove sediments (Rogers, 1990). According to Galvis (1989a) *Diploria labyrinthiformis* (Linnaeus, 1758) and *Diploria strigosa* (Dana, 1846) have shown better capability to remove sediments than *Montastrea annularis* (previous nomination; now *Orbicella annularis*)

(Ellis & Solander, 1786) and (*Orbicella cavernosa* var. hirta Verrill, 1901 *Montastraea cavernosa* (Linnaeus, 1767).

In Varadero there are large live coral colonies (diameter 3–5 m) specifically *Orbicella spp.* (López et al., 2015). Also at the Hope Spot Capurganá-Cabo Tiburón are large colonies that correspond with the structure, composition and function of highly resilient healthy coral reef integrity and climate change refugia. Cacciapaglia & Woesik (2016) describe the characteristics of coral reef climate change refugia as turbid environments that shade bleaching resilient corals. Furthermore, they are the living natural nurseries for the Corales del Rosario Park. Therefore, they should be included urgently within an effective protection framework, in accordance with the global strategy to assure coral reef persistence under the current scenario of climate change.

The contrast of reports without lethal coral bleaching in the Hope Spots (non-protected areas), and frequent signs of diseases and mortality in the Park related to coral bleaching, favors the nomination of the resilient coral reefs in the Hope Spots as refugia for climate change. The key attribute of refugia is their relative persistence, despite changes in the climate in the surrounding landscape. Morelli et al. (2020) propose considering refugia in the context of a multifaceted, long-term, network-based approach, as temporal and spatial gradients of ecological persistence that can act as "slow lanes" rather than areas of stasis.

The extreme conditions of turbid waters at the surface provide shadow to the coral reefs of the Hope Spots with low sedimentation rates. The live coral cover for the Hope Spots (non-protected areas) has been resilient since 2008, while for the Park it has declined over the past three decades. According to Eddy et al., (2018), most of the experts in the Caribbean Sea estimated a good coral cover% for the Caribbean Sea of between 25–50%. Galvis (1989a) measured in the Park a total coral cover of 34.43% within a completely mapped Pavitos Island at the south-west of Rosario Park. In contrast, the environmental conditions of turbid waters caused by rain and run-off at the surface and low sedimentation produces natural shadow on the resilient coral reefs of the Hope Spots without lethal coral bleaching events, which may characterize them as refugia against climate change.

There is a contrast between healthy coral covers in non-protected areas (>70%) and the protected area (<30%). Coral species in the IUCN Red List were scarce in the park, while they are frequently reported at the Hope Spots. Reef Check Colombia reported for Varadero in August

2019 42% general coral cover average, 10% algae cover and abundance of butterflyfishes, grunts and parrotfishes at 33.33% each. The most exuberant population of Acropora cervicornis (Lamarck, 1816) of the Caribbean was found in Capurganá[5].

The land use threats have not been controlled in the Park, therefore, the Foundation ICRI Colombia do not recommended the restoration projects based only in breaking coral colonies. It may be a source of further stress for coral reefs that have already deteriorated. Coral fragments are likely to be covered by fleshy algae as indicators of reefs undertaken a natural shift. Mainly *Dictyota dichotoma* (Hudson) (Lamouroux 1809: 42) and *Pockiella variegata* covered large portions of the dead coral colonies in Corales del Rosario Park. Although fleshy macroalgae cover is low in the Hope Spot areas, these restoration projects should be forbidden in the resilient coral reefs to keep them as control sites for the rest of the Caribbean region, were most of the private sector and governments to promote breaking colonies to justify unsustainable development. Besides, current restoration projects do not have permanent monitoring for the survival of original coral colonies from which fragments are removed. The focus of restoration projects is the survival of fragments that have a maximum 60% survival rate. The mortality of fragments is higher in other sites different from the original natural coral reef distribution of the species, different depths, windward/leeward zones, etc. Colombian Caribbean Hope Spots should be set aside as coral reef areas without experimenting with restoration projects. In the Caribbean Sea, there is no need to manually break coral colonies. Hurricanes produce the corals of Hope Spots to be used as fragments in mitigation instead of restoration projects.

The non-protected vs. protected schemes differ, besides the extreme conditions, in the number of visitors in the rank of hundreds and thousands per week in the Park to less than one hundred per month in the Hope Spots. The Foundation ICRI Colombia has nominated these Hope Spots as World Heritage Sites to the UNESCO through the Committee of the Colombian Government. The National Parks Authority is acknowledging the importance of protecting both Hope Spots within the System of Marine Protected Areas of Colombia for their high biodiversity and

[5] (Sistema Información Biodiversidad de Colombia, SIB, Report Number 158B2349043, Garcia, R., 2016-11-29). https://ipt.biodiversidad.co/cr-sib/pdf.do?r=11_conectividadacroporas_20161129&n=158B2349043.

for larval connectivity with the parks. Both coral reef areas accomplished the United Nations Educational, Scientific, and Cultural Organization, UNESCO criteria for selection of World Heritage Sites, as they are natural marine resilient coral reef areas with universal values.

3.4 Discussion

Mixed methodologies are required to monitor governance effectiveness, as the main objective is to protect coral reef areas. According to Clement, Guerrero and Wyborn, (2019) there will inevitably be trade-offs between depth and breadth with issues of cause-and-effect relationships between governance and outcomes, but complemented by case study data, and systematic reviews. The characterization of the coral reef ecosystem integrity of our three case studies provides evidence about the current health state of these coral reef areas and contrasts the general belief that protected areas are in better condition. The protected case study complies with the findings of Bruno, Côté and Toth (2019); marine areas protected from fishing and pollution did not reduce how much coral was killed by extreme temperatures or how quickly coral populations recovered from coral disease, bleaching and large storms. However, our case studies in non-government protected areas or Hope Spots, challenge their results that coral reefs in areas with fishing and pollution regulations had the same level of decline as the coral reefs in unprotected areas. We found the opposite: better coral reefs ecosystem integrity in the Hope Spots. The real governance by the communities, by not allowing unsustainable development, may explain the more effective protection in Hope Spots. In contrast, the coral reef areas managed by the government depend on decisions from land developers and higher political interests. Case studies contradict generalizations by Bruno and Valdivia (2016) that coral reef degradation is not correlated with local human population density. The community protection was effective to avoid unsustainable development in the Hope Spots.

The government should protect resilient coral reefs at the Hope Spots as they may act as coral reef refugia against climate change effect. Resilient coral reefs act as natural laboratories. Local effective protection is needed to allow coral reef resilience to the regional shifts in ecosystem functioning (Hughes et al., 2007). Strengthening the local effective protection is worthy while the actions to reduce carbon emissions are also needed. The coral reef refugia represent a baseline for pristine conditions allowing scientists to study climate change impacts separately from human impacts, thus providing fundamental insights for conservation. Natural shadow on coral reefs may keep temperatures within ranges that do not place extreme stress on coral reefs. Refugia can facilitate the persistence of biodiversity under changing environmental conditions, such as anthropogenic climate change, and their effective protection is the best chance of survival for many coral species in the wild. According to Kavousi and Keppel (2018) refugia have the capacity to facilitate species persistence, including long-term buffering, protection from multiple climatic stressors, accessibility, microclimatic heterogeneity, size, and low exposure to non-climate disturbances. A healthy self-sustaining ecosystem requires essential structural (species, habitats) and functional components (Hughes et al., 2005). Therefore, understanding and protecting the role of local adaptation and acclimatization will be crucial for evaluating coral accessibility and persistence. Connecting the Hope Spot Varadero with Corales del Rosario and the Hope Spot Capurganá Cabo-Tiburón forms a larger refuge that can support more species, larger populations and more genetic variation due to low exposure to other disturbances. Stressors not caused by climate change, such as habitat degradation, can have severe impacts. Habitats constituting refugia for multiple species are likely to be of higher conservation value. The climate change refugia might be the larvae suppliers of the Caribbean coastal MPAs.

The intrinsic value of coral reefs is indeed priceless. Economic valuations are in fact very poor estimates of the real benefit of effectively protecting coral reefs. Nevertheless, decision-makers should be provided with conservative monetary indicators of the high environmental costs for which they should be responsible when favoring unsustainable development. Values are within the hundreds of millions range/Km^2. Galvis (1999) estimate the first total value of the ecosystem services for Colombian coral reefs. Indonesia could lose US$1.9 billion over twenty years due to overfishing (Burke et al., 2002). Burke and Maidens (2004) discussed a Caribbean study that projected degradation of Caribbean reefs from human activities such as overfishing and pollution estimating annual losses of US$95 million to US$140 million in net revenues from coral reef-associated fisheries, and US$100 million to US$300 million in reduced tourism revenue. In addition, degradation of reefs could lead to annual losses of US$140 million to US$420 million from reduced coastal protection within the next fifty years. Burke et al. (2011) described the yield of between 5 and 15 tons/Km^2/year of seafood for a healthy, well-managed reef. That was the start of fisheries production at Capurganá when the study of Galvis and Galvis (2016) began in 2008. After the appearance of the lionfish in 2010, the decline was obvious. The retrieval ocurred when lionfish was fished and consumed as promoted by the Foundation ICRI Colombia. Galvis and Galvis (2016) calculated the cost of dredging on Varadero Reef at US$131million. Maldonado and Cuervo (2016) estimated the economic valuation of the Corales de Profundidad National Natural Park (1490Km^2) with contingent valuation of US$95 million annually (178 billion COP per year) based on the 2014 exchange rate COP/USD: 1878. For them, the lack of resources assigned to this area becomes evident as well as the need to identify and implement alternative funding sources to ensure financial sustainability of the Park. The most recent valuation in the world was the Deloitte report that estimated for the Great Barrier Reef a value of US$120.76 million/km^2 + >10%/year (Perry et al., 2017). According to the perspectives of the community of divers, fishers and other stakeholders, researchers and managers are interested in improving coral reef conservation effectiveness in all coral reef areas.

The results make evident that the enforcement in the Park does not target causes of local damage as unsustainable development that is now also threating the Hope Spots of the Caribbean Sea of Colombia. Our collaborative decision-support system to evaluate management effectiveness in the Park shows good robustness, due to the ability to adapt to changes over time to reach objectives in a constructive focus that provides insight into how processes and patterns of collaboration influences actors' abilities to address conservation problems. Structure is important because certain structural characteristics facilitate processes such as learning and coordination across governance levels. Morrison (2017) defines effectiveness as the authority and ability of key actors and instruments to respond to emergent problems. According to Clement et al. (2019) frameworks that capture administrative competence and adaptive capacity are essential to achieving conservation objectives in complex social-ecological systems. For Morrison (2017) frameworks should capture endogenous factors to the governance system that impact on environmental outcomes. The need for collaboration varies depending on the stage of the process (e.g., setting of shared goals, trust formation stage), resourcing and political priorities (McAllister & Taylor, 2015). The protection for the Park should be improved, and government should protect the Hope Spots according to their high value and resilient coral reefs within the National Parks system. Currently, the communities are requesting the government to officially support the nomination of the Foundation ICRI Colombia to declare both Caribbean Hope Spots as World Heritage Natural Marine Sites by UNESCO.

3.5 Conclusions

Currently, 100% of coral reef areas are within a framework of protection. Corales del Rosario Park is managed from a top-down management approach; however, the Hope Spots are a bottom-up management scheme. For effective governance, all economic, social and ecological objectives should be considered in decision-making and participative evaluations of sustainable development. The first case explained the relevance of perspectives in the evaluation to improve governance; the second one focuses on the economic valuation of protecting or destroying a coral reef; and the third case evaluates the improvement of fisheries productivity when overfishing ends and governance improves. In the implementation of the Sustainable Development Goals, specifically the number 14 or SDG14 and the coral reefs protection, it is necessary to increase participation with government, civil society, academia and communities in decision-making for an effective governance.

The efforts to include diving operators and fishers' communities in decision-making have been helpful in declaring and protecting Colombian Caribbean Hope Spots. Researchers gained these people's trust and thus benefited from their observations; while the divers and fishers controlled among themselves their economic activities and requested the researchers to inform the authorities to act accordingly on the need to improve the protection of their coral reefs. After twelve years of receiving and analyzing reports of scuba-diving operators and fishers who participate in the collection of data (contributory projects), within the citizen science program of the Observatory of the Foundation ICRI Colombia, we found improvement of citizen participation and governance. By becoming involved in the evaluation of conservation effectiveness, citizens improved their empowerment for protection within a bottom-up scheme for the Colombian Caribbean Hope Spots.

The resilient coral reefs in the Hope Spots accomplish universal criteria to be included as World Heritage Marine Sites for UNESCO with the connotation of potential climate change refugia. The reefs remain relatively buffered from climate change over time, and enable the persistence of valuable physical, ecological and sociocultural resources due to their endurance, despite changes in the climate in the surrounding coral reefs. We studied the Hope Spots in the Colombian Caribbean of in the context of a multifaceted, long-term, network-based approach, as temporal and spatial gradients of ecological persistence that can act as "slow lanes" rather than areas of stasis. At present, researchers and resource managers are now working together to put refugia conservation into practice, looking for appropriate conservation frameworks within the national and international concern about saving coral reefs.

Citizens' messages were transferred from "bottom to top" using communication technologies such as social media, phone and e-communications putting citizens in contact with top decision-makers, managers and researchers. Related implications go beyond the purely technological; they constitute a de facto increase in the power of society, and in the governance of knowledge that can lead to changes in governance models, especially in the scope of environmental policies. We have experienced that citizen science can develop early-warning systems, environmental management systems, or even collaboratively produce climate change adaptation strategies. Citizen science measures governance effectiveness in Colombian coral reefs, precisely because collaborative processes and patterns influence the capacities of actors to contribute to improve conservation by identifying and solving problems. It is a fact that Hope Spots are in better ecological condition than government-protected ones, and their direct relationship between scientists and fishers' communities and diving operators favors a permanent monitoring program to improve governance as a collaborative process that requires appropriate communication tools, institutional arrangements and tailored funding possibilities. Successful governance welcomes critical and ethical reflection among researchers, stakeholders, funders and policy-makers to improve coral reef conservation effectiveness.

Bibliography

Anthony, K. R. N., Maynard, J. A., Diaz-Pulido, G., Mumby, P. J., Marshall, P. A., Cao, L., & Hoegh-Guldberg, O. (2011). Ocean acidification and warming will lower coral reef resilience. *Global Change Biology, 17*, 1798–1808. https://doi.org/10.1111/j.1365-2486.2010.02364.x.

Bachtiar, I., Suharsono, Damar, A. et al. (2019). Practical resilience index for coral reef assessment. *Ocean Sci. J. 54*, 117–127. https://doi.org/10.1007/s12601-019-0002-1.

Bassim, K.. & Sammarco, P. (2003) Effects of temperature and ammonium on larval development and survivorship in a scleractinian coral (Diploria strigosa). *Marine Biology, 142*(2), 241–252. https://doi.org/10.1007/s00227-002-0953-z.

Bruno, J. F., & Valdivia, A. (2016). Coral reef degradation is not correlated with local human population density. *Scientific Report, 6*, 297–728.

Bruno, J., Côté, I. M., & Toth, L. T. (2019). Climate change, coral loss, and the curious case of the parrot fish paradigm: Why don't marine protected areas improve reef resilience? *Annual Review Marine Science, 11*, 307–334. The Annual Review of Marine Science. https://marxiv.org/ugk4v.

Bunce, L., & Galvis, N. H. (2002). Hows and whys of socioeconomic assessments. In B. Best, R. Pomeroy & C. Balboa (Eds.), *Implications for coral reef management and policy* (p. 61). Relevant Findings from the 9th Int Coral Reef Symp, Bali, Indonesia. http://pdf.usaid.gov/pdf_docs/Pnada629.pdf.

Burke, L., & Maidens, J. (2004). *Reefs at risk in the Caribbean*. World Resources Institute.

Burke, L., Reytar, K., Spalding, M., & Perry, A. (2011). *Reefs at risk revisited* (p. 115.). World Resources Institute. ISBN: 978-1-56973-762-0.

Burke, L., Selig, E., Spalding, M. (2002). *Reefs at risk in Southeast Asia* (p. 72). World Resources Institute. ISBN: 1-56973-490-9.

Cabezas, H., Pawlowski, C. W., Mayer, A. L., & Hoagland, N. T. (2004). Sustainability: Ecological, social, economic, technological, and systems perspectives. In S. K. Sikdar & P. Glavič Jain R. (Eds.), *Technological choices for sustainability*. https://doi.org/10.1007/978-3-662-10270-1_3 . Print ISBN: 978–3–642–05934–6, Online ISBN: 978–3–662–10270–1.

Cacciapaglia, C, van Woesik, R. (2016, March). Climate-change refugia: Shading reef corals by turbidity. *Change Biology, 22*(3), 1145–1154. https://doi.org/10.1111/gcb.13166. Epub 2015, December 22.

Camargo, C., Maldonado, J. H., Alvarado, E., Moreno-Sánchez, R., Mendoza, S., Manrique, N., ... Sánchez, J. A. (2008). Community involvement in management for maintaining coral reef resilience and biodiversity in southern Caribbean marine protected areas. *Biodiversity and Conservation April 2009*, 8(4), 935–956.

Carilli, J. E., Norris, R. D., Black, B. A., Walsh, S. M., & McField, M. (2009). Local stressors reduce coral resilience to bleaching. *PLoS ONE, 4*, 6324.

Christie, P., & White, A. T. (2007). Best practices for improved governance of coral reef marine protected areas. *Coral Reefs, 26*(4), 1047–1056.

Clement, S., Guerrero, A., & Wyborn, C. (2019). Understanding effectiveness in its broader context: Assessing case study methodologies for evaluating collaborative conservation governance. *Journal Society & Natural Resources, 33*(4), 462–483. https://doi.org/10.1080/08941920.2018.1556761.

Colding, J., & Barthel, S. (2019). Exploring the social-ecological systems discourse 20 years later. *Ecology and Society, 24*(1), 2. https://doi.org/10.5751/ES-10598-240102.

Dalton, T., Forrester, G. E., & Pollnac, R. (2015). Are Caribbean MPAs making progress toward their goals and objectives? *Marine Policy, 54*, 69–76.

Eddy, T. D., Cheung, W. W., & Bruno, J. F. (2018). Historical baselines of coral cover on tropical reefs as estimated by expert opinion. Peer J, 6, e4308. https://doi.org/10.7717/peerj.4308.

Erftemeijer, P. L., Riegl, B., Hoeksema, B. W., & Todd, P. A. (2012). Environmental impacts of dredging and other sediment disturbances on corals: A review, marine pollution bulletin. 64(9), 1737–1765. ISSN: 0025-326X. https://doi.org/10.1016/j.marpolbul.2012.05.008.

Fenner, D. (2012). Review: Challenges for managing fisheries on diverse coral Reefs. *Diversity, 4*(1), 105–160.

Fontaubert, C., Downes, D., & Agardy, T. (1996). Biodiversity in the Seas: Protecting marine and coastal biodiversity and living resources under the convention on biological diversity. *Georgetown International Environmental Law Review, 10*, 796.

Galbraith, R. V., MacIsaac, E. A., MacDonald, J. S., & Farrell, A. P. (2006). The effect of suspended sediment on fertilization success in sockeye (Oncorhynchus nerka) and coho (Oncorhynchus kisutch) salmon. *Canadian Journal of Fish and Aquatic Science, 63*, 2487–2494.

Galvis, N. H. (1989a). Evaluación Cuantitativa de las Llanuras Arrecifales de Pavitos, Parque Nacional Natural Corales Del Rosario, Cartagena, Col. *Boletín ECOTRÓPICA, Museo Del Mar, Universidad Jorge Tadeo Lozano, 19*, 27–54.

Galvis, N. H. (1989b). Análisis socio-económico de las comunidades pesqueras de la Boquilla, Tierra Bomba, Barú y Ararca. *Revista Recursos Hidrobiológicos, INDERENA, 2*, 70–84.

Galvis, N. H. (1996). Monitoreo de arrecifes coralinos en Colombia. *Colombia Revista GEOTRÓPICA. U. J. T. L. del Área de los Recursos Naturales. 10*, 14–21. ISSN: 0122-8579.

Galvis, N. H. (1998, October). Creación de la Contabilidad Ambiental de los Arrecifes Coralinos como instrumento de manejo. *Memorias del Seminario Nacional de Política, Ciencias y Tecnologías del Mar* (pp. 26–30), CD-ROM. CCO-COLCIENCIAS.

Galvis, N. H. (1999). Valoración Económica de los arrecifes coralinos en Colombia. *Revista GEOTRÓPICA, 69*(2), 847–859. Área Recursos Naturales, Universidad Jorge Tadeo Lozano. ISSN: 0122-8579.

Galvis, N. H. (2001). Monitoring ecological and socioeconomic indicators for management of coral reefs in Colombia. Proceedings of the International Conference on Scientific Aspects of Coral Reef Assessment, Monitoring, and Restoration. *Bull. Marine Sciences, 69*(2), 847–859(13). ISSN 0007–4977 http://www.ingentaconnect.com/content/umrsmas/bullmar/2001/00000069/00000002/art00047.

Galvis, N. H. (2002). *Análisis de Multicriterios para la concertación, formulación, gerencia, seguimiento y monitoreo de Proyectos Ambiéntales Complejos* (p. 150). Colombian Book Ed: Javergrafics.

Galvis, N. H. (2006). Implementing collaborative decision-making in latin america to improve coral reef management. *084 Oral Presentation at the First International Marine Protected Areas Congress* (p. 370). Geelong: Australia Proceedings.

Galvis, N. H., & Galvis, R. H. (2016). *Colombian citizen science to improve coral reef conservation—13th ICRS*, SESSION 88–83: Nohora H. 606–619. http://coralreefs.org/wp-content/uploads/2019/01/Session-88-3-Galvis-and-Galvis.pdf.

Gilmour, J. (1999). Experimental investigation into the effects of suspended sediment on fertilisation, larval survival and settlement in a scleractinian coral. *Marine Biology, 135*, 451–456.

Gutiérrez-Moreno, C., Marrugo, M., Lozano-Rivera, P., Sierra, P., & Andrade, C. (2011). Clima marino. In Zarza-González, Esteban (Ed.), *El entorno ambiental del Parque Nacional Natural Corales del Rosario y de San Bernardo. Parques Nacionales Naturales de Colombia* (pp. 39–47), dirección territorial Caribe. Cartagena de Indias.

Hargreaves-Allen, V. A., Mourato, S., & Milner-Gulland, E. J. (2017). Drivers of coral reef marine protected area performance. *PLoS One, 12*(6), e0179394. https://doi.org/10.1371/journal.pone.0179394.

Henao, H. A., (2013). *Efectos de los aportes de Canal del Dique sobre reclutamiento de especies de coral en los arrecifes del Archipiélago Nuestra Señora del Rosario, área Marina Protegida* (p. 125). Master's Thesis. Universidad Jorge Tadeo Lozano.

Hocking, M., Stolton, S., Leverington, F., Dudley, N., & Courrau, J. (2000). *Evaluating effectiveness: A framework for assessing the management of protected areas* (Vol. 2, pp. 121). IUCN-World Edition No. 6. https://portals.iucn.org/library/efiles/documents/pag-014.pdf.

Humphrey, C., Weber, M., Lott, C. et al. (2008). Effects of suspended sediments, dissolved inorganic nutrients and salinity on fertilisation and embryo development in the coral Acropora millepora (Ehrenberg, 1834). *Coral Reefs, 27*, 837–850. https://doi.org/10.1007/s00338-008-0408-1.

Hughes, T. P., Bellwood, D. R., Folke, C., Steneck, R. S., & Wilson, J. (2005). New paradigms for supporting the resilience of marine ecosystems. *Trends in Ecology and Evolution, 20*, 380–386.

Hughes, T. P., Rodrigues, M. J., Bellwood, D. R., Ceccarelli, D., Hoegh-Guldberg, O., McCook, L., et al. (2007). Phase shifts, herbivory, and the resilience of coral reefs to climate change. *Current Biology, 17*, 360–365.

Jameson, S. C., Tupper, M. H, Ridley, J. M. (2002, November). The three screen doors: Can marine "protected" areas be effective? *Marine Pollution Bulletin, 44*(11), 1177–1183.

Kavousi, J., & Keppel, G. (2018, January/February). Clarifying the concept of climate change refugia for coral reefs ICES. *Journal of Marine Science, 75*(1), 43–49. https://doi.org/10.1093/icesjms/fsx124.

Lang, D. J, Wiek, A, Bergmann, M, Stauffacher, M, Martens, P, Moll, P, Swilling, M, Thomas, C. J. (2012). Transdisciplinary research in sustainability science: Practice, principles, and challenges. *Sustainability Science, 7*. https://doi.org/10.1007/s11625-011-0149-x.

López-Victoria, M., Rodríguez-Moreno, M., & Zapata, F. A. (2015, March). A paradoxical reef from Varadero, Cartagena Bay, Colombia. *Coral Reefs, 34*(1), 231. https://doi.org/10.1007/s00338-014-1246-y.

Maldonado, J. H., & Cuervo, R. (2016). Economic valuation of the Corales de Profundidad National Natural Park. *Bulletin Investigation Marine Costeras, 45*(1), 99–121. ISSN 0122–9761.

Mauser, W., Klepper, G., Rice, M., Schmalzbauer, B. S., Hackmann, H., Leemans, R., & Moore, H. (2013). Transdisciplinary global change research: The co-creation of knowledge for sustainability. *Current Opinion in Environmental Sustainability, 5*, 420–431. https://doi.org/10.1016/j.cosust.2013.07.001.

McAllister, R., & Taylor, B. M. (2015). Partnerships for sustainability governance: A synthesis of key themes. *Current Opinion in Environmental Sustainability, 12*, 86–90. https://doi.org/10.1016/j.cosust.2015.01.001.

Mejía-Quintero, K., Rincón-Díaz, N., Parrado, M., Chasqui, L., Vanegas, J., & Alonso, D. (2018). Línea base de biodiversidad del arrecife coralino de Varadero. Anexo 2.5.2. In *invemarminambiente. Cuarto informe técnico. Convenio Interadministrativo 659 de 2017* (p. 374). + anexos.

Meyers, D. G. 2010. The Bystander Effect. *Social psychology* (10th Ed). McGraw-Hill. ISBN 978–0–07–337066–8.

Morrison, T. H., Adger, W. N, Brown, K., Lemos, M. C., Huitema, D., Hughes, T. P. (2017). Mitigation and adaptation in polycentric systems: Sources of power in the pursuit of collective goals. *Wiley Interdisciplinary Reviews: Climate Change, 8*(5). Ed. John Wiley & Sons, Inc.

Morelli, T. L., Barrows, C. W., Ramirez, A. R., Cartwright, J. M., Ackerly, D. D., Eaves, T. D., ...Thorne, J. H. (2020, June). Climate-change refugia: Biodiversity in the slow lane. *Frontiers in Ecological Society of America, 18*(5), 228–234 Climate-Change Refugia. https://doi.org/10.1002/fee.2189.

Morgan, P. B., Sutton, P., Taschini, L., Gregory, J., Collins, A., Leach, M., Stark, J., Aldy, J., Livermore, M. A., & Knight-Lenihan, S. (2017). *What's the economic value of the great barrier Reef? It's priceless.* The Conversation Articles on Environmental economics. Academic rigor, journalistic flair. Copyright © 2010–2021, The Conversation US, Inc. https://theconversation.com/whats-the-economic-value-of-the-great-barrier-reef-its-priceless-80061.

Nicolescu, B. (2002). *Manifesto of transdisciplinarity.* State University of New York Press.

Norström, A. V., Nyström, M., Jouffray, J. B., Folke, C., Graham, A. J. G., Moberg, F. ... Williams, G. J. (2016). Guiding coral reef futures in the Anthropocene. *Frontiers in Ecology and the Environment*, 14(9), 490–498. https://doi.org/10.1002/fee.1427.

Pizarro, V, Rodríguez, S. C., López-Victoria, M., Zapata, F. A., Zea, S., Galindo-Martínez, C. T., Iglesias-Prieto, R., Pollock, J., & Medina, M. (2017). *Unraveling the structure and composition of Varadero Reef, an improbable and imperiled coral reef in the Colombian Caribbean.* Peer J 5:e4119 https://doi.org/10.7717/peerj.4119.

Pomeroy, R. S., Parks, J. E.,& Watson, L. M. (2004). *How is you MPA doing? A guidebook of natural and social indicators for evaluating marine protected areas management effectiveness.* IUCN-WWF-NOAA. https://portals.iucn.org/library/efiles/documents/pag-014.pdf.

Pomeroy, R., Mascia, M., & Pollnac, R. (2007). Marine protected areas: The social dimension. *FAO Fisheries Report, 825*, 149–181.

Procanal, corporación promotora canal el varadero. (2011). estudio de impacto ambiental. *Construcción nuevo canal de acceso a la bahía de Cartagena* (p. 70). El Varadero. https://www.commissiemer.nl/docs/mer/diversen/tomo_i_executive_summary_from_eia_rapport_varadero.pdf.

Rogers, C. (1990). Responses of coral reefs and reef organisms to sedimentation. *Marine Ecology Progress Series, 62*, 185–202. https://doi.org/10.3354/meps062185.

Shein, K, Loder, J., Bourne, D. G., & Galvis, N. H. (2016). Citizen science: The next big leap, ICRS Town Hall Meeting. Proceedings of the 13th International Coral Reef Symposium, 88–81 (Overview): 591–598 http://coralreefs.org/wp-content/uploads/2019/01/Session-88-1-summary-CitizenScienceTownHall-ICRSproceedings-final-NS-1.pdf.

Spurgeon, J. P. G., & Lindahl, U. (2000). Economics of coral reef restoration. In H. S. J. Cesar (Ed.), *Collected essays on the economics of coral reefs* (pp. 125–136). Coral Reef Degradation in the Indian Ocean (CORDIO), University of Kalmar.

Tomascik, T., & Sander, F. (1985). Effects of eutrophication on reef-building corals. *Marine Biology, 87*(2), 143–155. https://doi.org/10.1007/BF00539422.

Tress, B., Tress, G., & Fry, G. (2004). Clarifying integrative research concepts in landscape ecology. *Landscape Ecology*. https://doi.org/10.1007/s10980-004-3290-4.

World Commission On Environment And Development. (WCED) (1987). *Our common future* (p. 383). The Brundtland Report. Oxford University Press.

Winterfeldt, D., & Edwards, W. (1986). *Decision analysis and behavioral research*. Cambridge University Press.

CHAPTER 4

Community-Based Innovation Ecosystems in Peace-Building and Resilience Contexts

Juan David Reina-Rozo

4.1 Introduction

Innovation has become a space in conceptual dispute. Different definitions and opposing visions of change gain space in a society of information, knowledge, and consumption. In the face of this, authors such as Leary (2019) maintain that we live in an era of the cult of innovation. That is, the human being is called (only) to generate innovation to energize the market machinery, and therefore to sustain capitalism. A system that seeks to grow indefinitely in a finite world. In this way, questions emerge such as: Why and for whom is innovation made? Who participates in innovation processes? Are innovation processes inclusive? Are communities considered only as informants in participatory innovation processes? And, do communities have power over decisions and resources in innovation processes?

J. D. Reina-Rozo (✉)
Universidad Nacional de Colombia, Bogotá, Colombia
e-mail: jdreinar@unal.edu.co

L. A. Orozco et al. (eds.), *Science, Technology, and Higher Education*, Palgrave Studies in Democracy, Innovation, and Entrepreneurship for Growth,
https://doi.org/10.1007/978-3-030-80720-7_4

Innovation must be re-examined and integrated frameworks sought in order to generate transformations in the challenges faced by human groups and natural systems, especially marginalized communities and ecosystems at risk. Challenging inherited and hegemonic concepts are therefore necessary to create novel ways of approaching innovation, i.e. sociotechnical change from, with, and for society as a whole. In addition to the above, reflections on ideas to decolonize innovation as a phenomenon that has colonized our thinking and action around neoliberal capitalism has recently emerged in the academic literature (Jimenez & Roberts, 2019). These ideas outside of the hegemonic path are gestated from autonomous and historical processes of the social movements of peasants, indigenous people, afro-descendants, and urban groups, and are closely linked to alternatives to development such as Sumak Kawsay (buen vivir) in Latin America, Ubuntu in Sub-Saharan Africa, Swaaj in India, among others.

The relationship between community and innovation is not clear, even more from an alternative perspective to economic growth. The literature around processes of communal or community innovation is scarce. However, even though processes of basic innovation are not sufficiently visible in the academic field, communities seek to transform their realities and materialize their aspirations and desires from their territories. That is to say, they generate transitions or transformations from their reality towards states of collective well-being beyond the development narrative using techno-science and traditional knowledge. According to Shiva (2005), the keys to transitions are relocation strategies, for example, building organic food distribution and energy systems based on the local environment and biodiversity. These systems are managed based on ecological integrity, soil conservation, biodiversity, local economies, and grassroots democracy. Transitions to other forms of living and social relations are key to solving the present cultural, ecological, and civilization crises.

Consequently, reflecting on the democratization of innovation is a priority. That is, access, visibility, and the strengthening of innovations created by people, communities, or social movements that have historically been excluded from governance processes within science, technology, and innovation (STI). This serves to allow for the collective the enjoyment of its benefits. Therefore, the inquiry question focuses on: how and why do community-based organizations in post-conflict/post-agreement territories collaborate to generate innovations? This is because not much attention is paid to the innovation processes of grassroots organizations in the literature, particularly the way they collaborate. Thus, by understanding how grassroots organizations are the managers of sociotechnical change at the local level, democratization can be enhanced, especially with the use of advances in information and communication technologies (ICTs) in key transitions, in this case, in transition to peaceful communities.

Hence, in many of these transitions, the place of the local in the conceptions of future is central. For communities that have been victims of social and armed conflicts, the generation of alternatives to inhabit the territory based on science, technology, and innovation is key. The local involves people's relationships with their environment, culture, and others in their community. In addition, the role of the place in the processes of community-centred innovation is definitive, to the extent that it is the cradle of their experiences, knowledge, social relations, and territory. Therefore, the main objective of this research is to describe the main implications of collaboration between community-based organizations at the local level in post-agreement/post-conflict contexts in Colombia. In this particular case, through the perspective of community-based innovation ecosystems and their contribution to grassroots processes.

This chapter is primarily comprised of the conceptual and theoretical framework through which a critique of the conventional concept of innovation is carried out and a proposal of communal innovation as an element of collective transformation in the territory. In addition, the theory of innovation ecology and innovation ecosystems is used as a framework of analysis for the present investigation and in particular, the concept of the community-based innovation ecosystem is used. The third section describes the methodological framework, which is composed of the techniques and tools used for fieldwork development and the analysis of the information is described. The fourth section presents the results of the research, particularly the analysis of the case study of the Guajuí River Innovation Ecosystem in the Department of Cauca, Southwestern Colombia. Finally, the fifth part shares the discussion of the results and conclusions of the present study, accompanied by some future lines of action.

4.2 Conceptual and Theoretical Framework

The conceptual and theoretical framework used for the present text has its origins in recent discussions on innovation that have emerged, especially around grassroots innovation, the inclusion of other actors (traditionally excluded from innovation practices and policies), and their relationship to peacebuilding. Similarly, the theory of innovation ecosystems is used to understand the collaborative relationships between collections of diverse actors. In particular, the community-based innovation ecosystems approach is used to determine the environments where collaborative relationships and co-created innovations among various actors occur.

4.2.1 Innovation, Territory, and Peace-building

According to the previous discussion on the conventional conception of innovation, in this part, it is proposed that innovation is a sociotechnical change generated by communities themselves, settled in a particular territory, and mainly, that it aims to strengthen the social fabric, the collective welfare and therefore the peacebuilding. In this way, the communal innovation approach emerges as a construct to conceptualize the processes of collective sociotechnical change. These processes allow for transforming communities' futures towards alternatives beyond development. Communal innovation is focused on strengthening the social fabric (Fig. 4.1).

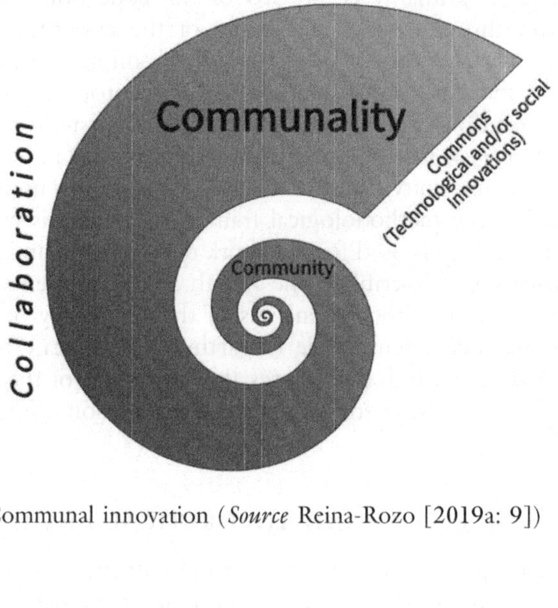

Fig. 4.1 Communal innovation (*Source* Reina-Rozo [2019a: 9])

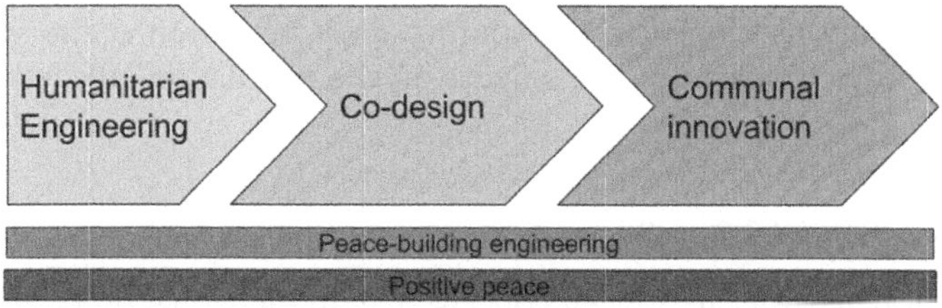

Fig. 4.2 STI co-design spaces (*Source* Reina-Rozo [2019b: 4])

Communal innovation is the iterative process of creating new transformative practices by excluded communities, to appropriate them to their places and strengthen the collective social fabric. It allows for the autonomous design and creation of relevant, contextual, and collective solutions to their challenges, opportunities, and aspirations to generate a common good and, therefore, move towards a future of well-being. Similarly, this process is mediated by the collaboration of community members, communities, and organizations in the territory (Reina-Rozo, 2019a). In this way, a series of emerging qualities in the practice of communal innovation are freedom, disruption, and autonomy, which operate as key pieces in redefining these sociotechnical processes. These qualities are intended to transform the structures of innovation processes and the people themselves.

In terms of the processes of generating STI in post-agreement and peacebuilding scenarios, the proposal of Reina-Rozo et al. (2018), regarding spaces of co-design of STI, especially in a Territorial Space for Training and Reincorporation of former guerrillas, stands out. These authors propose STI co-design spaces as a complement to traditional peacebuilding interventions, especially in Colombia. Therefore, these spaces are based on the concepts of Positive Peace by Galtung (1996), Humanitarian Engineering (Reina-Rozo & León, 2017), and Peacebuilding Engineering (Kleba & Reina-Rozo, 2021; Reina-Rozo, 2020; Vesilind, 2010). Fig. 4.2 describes the elements of co-design spaces and their flow of action.

However, these dynamics have not yet been consolidated in Colombia due to the instability that the peace agreement has generated and the difficulties in reaching these territories where the state and its services are not yet present. Additionally, the articulation of this experience with other grassroots initiatives is necessary but full of challenges. The various efforts that are being developed in the country must be woven at the systemic level in order to increase their impact on the population affected by the conflict.

4.2.2 *Towards an Innovation Ecology*

Innovation activities have been conceived as an individual process, typical of an entrepreneur, traditionally isolated from surrounding organizations and cultural, social, political, and environmental factors. In this way, an ecosystem approach and one that is oriented towards the interrelations of human and non-human actors is necessary to understand the innovation processes situated within the context. From this point of view, these phenomena can be studied from various perspectives. National innovation systems have been particularly predominant in the investigation of innovation processes and articulation of actors in Latin America (Arocena & Sutz, 2001; Dutrénit & Sutz, 2014).

This framework of analysis, according to Fagerberg (2003) has two main aspects to determine the dynamics of the actors in the territory. The first has been to study innovation systems according to technological, industrial, or sectorial factors. In this framework, varying the level of analysis, other key elements are included such as institutions, political processes, public research infrastructure, financial institutions, and skills. The second approach has focused on the spatial aspect. It uses national and regional boundaries to distinguish between different systems. The terms national innovation systems (Lundvall, 1992; Nelson, 1993), regional innovation systems (Asheim & Gertler, 2004), and local innovation systems (Martin & Simmie, 2008) are often used in the literature to understand these processes from a geographical point of view. The main characteristic of this approach is that they are analysed from an administrative scale perspective.

However, its main limitations are found in the conceptualization and inclusion of non-formal actors, that is, the participation of these historically marginalized actors, such as neighbourhood associations and indigenous, peasant or afro-descendant communities on the innovation processes. It is necessary to consider that the relationships of the actors, especially the informal ones, are complex, dynamic, and adaptive, to the extent that organizations of various kinds participate and emerge as active actors in their territories, with different interests and political dynamics. Therefore, the rigid structures of traditional innovation systems fall short of these new emerging relationships, especially in peacebuilding contexts where there is a fragmentation of the social fabric and mistrust of state institutions and other communities.

Since the first decade of the twenty-first century, many criticisms and alternatives have been generated to overcome national innovation systems. These use the ecological analogy taken from the biological sciences to understand the complex interrelations between actors. Among the first people who proposed using this type of analogy for the business sector was Moore (2005). Likewise, Landry et al. (2002), point to the transition from the classic notion of innovation towards a relationship of interdependent creation among actors and the importance of their interactions. In the face of the above, the concept of innovation ecology emerges from understanding the interactions of each one of the actors, which may be institutional or not. In this way, Wulf (2007: 1253) defines innovation ecology as *"the collection of interdependent and interactive policies and activities that support innovation.."*.

The above perspectives on innovation ecologies are oriented towards understanding them from the point of view of commercial or productive innovation, in other words, from visions linked to the search for profit by companies and government entities. Therefore, alternatives are needed that seek other ends beyond accumulation and economic growth.

4.2.3 Community-Based Innovation Ecosystems

Innovation from a systemic perspective has encompassed the term systems to understand the relationships of different actors that interact in the innovation processes. However, this concept falls short of identifying successful strategies for local public policy, culture, natural environments, and tacit knowledge that drive innovation beyond its own boundaries, as well as understanding the role of collaboration and value co-creation (Smorodinskaya et al., 2017). In this sense, the term innovation ecosystem combines perspectives of open innovation, crowd-sourcing, digitalization, differential roles or niches, strategic management, co-evolution, interdependence (Adner & Kapoor, 2010; Martinez et al., 2017) and structural theories of the biological metaphor, particularly in various organizational exercises (Montoya etal., 2012).

On the other hand, there are criticisms of the use of the ecological metaphor in these collections of actors and innovation relations. In response, Oh et al., (2016: 4) states that although Moore was consistent in applying the metaphor to the business world, "*he did not establish rigorous rules of correspondence between business and natural ecosystems...*" and they end by remarking "*natural ecosystems have no policies*". Therefore, this concept is a dynamic and current discussion within academic literature. Thus, the study of innovation ecosystems is observed as the continuation of the line of research on the relationships of various actors in processes of creation of sociotechnical change using the ecological perspective and analogies (Shaw & Allen, 2018; Tsujimoto et al., 2018).

However, being an area in consolidation in the literature, a unanimous definition of this construct had not been yet found (Oh et al., 2016). The literature finds that innovation ecosystems are hybrid and interdependent systems with a multiplicity of actors and relationships, i.e., they are complex adaptive systems (Russell & Smorodinskaya, 2018). In this sense, as it integrally embraces the phenomenon of collaborative innovation and focuses on two elements: co-creation of value and co-evolution. Table 4.1 shows the main characteristics of innovation ecosystems:

However, Durst and Poutanen (2013) argue that for innovation to occur properly in an innovation ecosystem, it must overcome several conditions, as it must address environmental, structural, organizational, and cultural factors. The development of the field of innovation ecosystems has been under discussion since its creation about a decade ago. Finally, Ritala (2017: 41) suggests that the innovation ecosystem concept "*should ideally be used with respect to systems that focus on innovation activities (goal/purpose), that involve the logic of actor interdependence within a particular context (spatial dimension) and address the inherent co-evolution*

Table 4.1 Characteristics of innovation ecosystems

- It is composed of a network of interconnected and interdependent actors, which include a complementary focal organization, customers, suppliers, and innovators
- Some roles of the actors are initiator, specialist, and adopter
- It is sometimes led by a key stakeholder, who provides a common platform, a set of goals and is responsible for the health of the ecosystem
- They are built on a platform which is composed of tools, services, and technologies
- Members face cooperation and competition
- It has a life cycle which follows a process of co-evolution. In this case, Moore (1993) proposes four phases: birth, expansion, leadership, and self-renewal

Source Based on Gomes et al. (2018)

of actors (temporal dimension)". In this case, it is observed that the debate still continues in the literature, generating greater elements for the integral construction of a more complex conceptual model in the future at both the local and community levels.

Using the previous contributions and focusing them on social dynamics, the local innovation ecosystems (LIE) seek to understand the dynamics, actors, and environments to transform the reality of local contexts. These generate elements to guide future transformation actions, such as the creation of local alliances and the generation of strategies oriented to collective well-being. In this sense, for Hoffecker, a local innovation ecosystem is made up of "*local communities of actors that interact and are committed to the production of innovation and the support of innovation processes. In addition to the infrastructure, resources and enabling environment that allows them to create, adopt and disseminate more effective ways of doing things*" (2019: 4). For the International Development Innovation Network (2017), there are four main characteristics of this type of innovation ecosystem: Enabling environment, Broad commitment to innovation, Development of solutions, and Delivery of solutions.

Taking into account the previous framework, the Community-Based Innovation Ecosystems (CBIE) construct is used as a particular analytical perspective within the LIEs with a particular focus on community contexts, which are key to re-establishing social, economic, and environmental relationships. CBIE is defined as the interactive collection of community-based and local actors who engage in certain activities and direct their interests towards a communal purpose. These actors are exposed to contextual environments for the development of communal innovation activities and, through co-creation and co-evolution, use various elements to enhance the processes of co-creation of social and economic value, and thus strengthen the social fabric and collective welfare (Reina-Rozo, 2019b).

This conceptual framework is focused on visualizing and understanding the dynamics of the environment, the relationships among the actors, their roles, and the collective purpose, that is, the processes of communal innovation in the territories. The CBIE seeks to foster processes of co-creation of the value of community actors related to sociotechnical changes through collaboration and co-evolution. In this way, the focal organizations of the ecosystem are community-based organizations related to other public, private, or third sector organizations such as NGOs. Figure 4.3 presents the conceptual model around the interactions

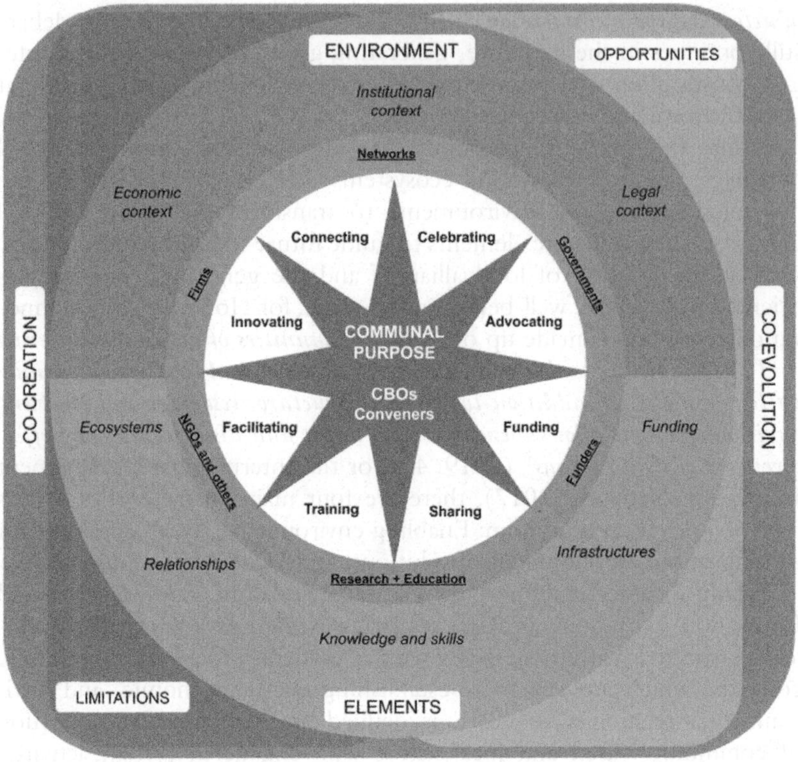

Fig. 4.3 Community-based innovation ecosystem (*Source* Based on Hoffecker [2019])

of community actors that strengthen collective welfare and peacebuilding initiatives through processes of community innovation.

At the heart of the proposal is the communal purpose, which is the objective of the innovation ecosystem as a whole, i.e. where the interests of community-based organizations and other stakeholders converge. Then, there are the roles or actions identified to facilitate co-creation, which are innovate, convene and facilitate, train, share knowledge, finance, advocate, celebrate, and finally connect. In other words, these actions enable the various actors to achieve the communal purpose. In terms of actors, the general categories identified are Businesses, NGOs and CBOs, Research and Education Institutions, Financial Institutions,

Government Institutions, and stakeholder networks. Thus, it is necessary to mention that actors can perform multiple actions or only one. On the other hand, the environment where these dynamics of communal and transformative innovation take place is characterized by two scenarios:

1. The physical environment, in the lower part, composed of five elements: natural environments, where actions are carried out, these can be transformed or even without transformation; previously generated relations, that is, the social capital; the knowledge, wisdom, and skills of the organizations and people; the infrastructures used by the actors, whether these are of private or public use; and finally, the financial resources, which make many of the innovation processes viable in the sense that they allow sustaining transport activities, payments for tasks or purchase of materials.
2. The sociocultural environment, at the top, composed of the economic context, in which social relations are established by a particular economic model; in addition, there is the institutional and cultural context, where the various formal or non-formal institutions have their place, as well as values, traditions, and other cultural aspects; and finally, the legal and regulatory context composed of public policies of various kinds, which can favour or limit the innovation processes.

Now, this notion of innovation ecosystems places relevance on community actors and the relations between them. This is an open, dynamic, co-evolving ecosystem that can be understood, oriented towards promoting innovation based on territories that allow the co-creation of social value from grassroots organizations. Additionally, it is crucial to explicitly state the limitations and opportunities of the environment, given that these are elements that can make innovation in the territory viable or hinder its impact. Therefore, this concept of CBIE is used to describe and analyse the processes of communal innovation in the territory of the Guajuí River Community Council in Colombia, as a case study.

4.3 Methodology

This research was carried out using a methodological design based on the case study as a qualitative approach, in turn, accompanied by a review of systematic literature and non-participating observation in the territory of the Guajuí River. The case study as a research method is an intense examination of an issue in action, i.e. one that is currently being developed and is beyond the control of the researcher. The main questions that this tool aims to work with are how and why, as they allow the analysis of contemporary events.

This research strategy is used in many situations to contribute to the understanding of social phenomena. In this particular case, it is used to describe and analyse the processes of communal innovation of community-based organizations. This originates in the fact that it allows researchers to retain the characteristics, qualities, and meanings of real-life events, for example, individual life cycles, organizational and management processes, change in neighbourhood dynamics, international relations, and the maturation of industries (Yin, 2009). Hence, the case study is used, since it is intended to describe reality and to generalize some conclusions.

The fieldwork was carried out in June 2018 in the municipality of Guapi, in the territory of the Guajuí River Community Council (GRCC), and the cities of Popayán and Bogotá in Colombia. For this, the main information collection techniques were semi-structured interviews based on understanding the phenomenon of collaboration between grassroots organizations identified in the territory of the Guajuí River. Table 4.2 describes the 14 semi-structured interviews conducted.

The data was also triangulated with internal and external documents, non-participating observation, visual information such as videos and photographs, and finally field notes. Table 4.3 shows the methods, the treatment of the collected data, and the concepts studied.

The information was analysed with the Nvivo 10 software. Finally, the analysis strategy consisted of validating an analysis proposal from the concordance of evidence around the governance of the community innovation processes. This establishes community governance as a process which community-based organizations collaborate based on joint decision-making (Gates, 1999): Participants who wish to collaborate must understand how to make decisions jointly about the rules that will govern their behaviour and relationships. Collaboration is about creating structures that enable participants to make decisions about how to solve collective action problems.

Table 4.2 Semi-structured interview information

ID	*Age*	*Gender*	*Occupation*	*Place*	*Organization*
OBC1	40–50	Female	Fisherwoman	Quiroga	Asociación construyendo sueños
OBC2	40–50	Male	Fisherman	Quiroga	Asoagropesqui
GOV1	40–50	Male	Public servant	Guapi	Local government
CCA1	70–80	Male	Board member	San Antonio	Guajuí River Community Council
OBC3	30–40	Male	Technologist	San Antonio	Telecomunicaciones RYV
OBC4	20–30	Male	Youth leader	San Antonio	Centinelas de la mañana
COM1		Collective	Inhabitants	Concepción	Community
CCA2	50–60	Male	Leader	Santa Rosa	Guajuí River Community Council
OBC5	20–30	Male	Youth leader	San Antonio	Cimarrones
INV1	30–40	Female	Researcher	Guapi	Pacific Environmental Research Institute
OBC6	50–60	Female	Community organizer	Guapi	Fundación Chiyangua
CCA3	40–50	Female	Advisor	Guapi	
INV2	50–60	Male	Researcher	Popayán	University of Cauca
INV3	20–30	Female	Researcher	Bogotá	Pontifical Xaverian University, Bogotá

4.4 Community-Based Innovation Ecosystem of the Guajuí River Territory

This section describes the CBIE case study for the territory of the Rio Guajuí Community Council. Hence a brief local and conflict context is provided, and then the main actors, their relationships, and innovations studied are highlighted. Finally, some results and implications for local well-being are shared.

The municipality of Guapi is located on the Pacific coast of Colombia and is one of the three coastal municipalities of the department of Cauca, Colombia. According to the Characterization Plan of the Guajuí River Community Council, the municipality of Guapi has an area of 2,688 km^2

Table 4.3 Methods used and data collected

Method	*Data collected*	*Concepts*
Observations	Work meetings, production activities, such as fishing and agriculture	Collaborative relationships
Field Notes	Relations between various actors and activities	Community-based innovation ecosystems
Semi-structured interviews with CBOs	Main activities of the organizations, effects of the armed conflict, communal innovations, and relations with other actors	Collaboration and its dimensions. Process of Governance
Semi-structured interviews with Local Government	Main activities of the organizations, effects of the armed conflict, site-based innovations, and relations with CBOs	Welfare. Community-based innovation ecosystems
Semi-structured interviews with Research Institutions	Main activities of organizations, effects of the armed conflict, place-based innovations, and relations with CBOs	Community-based innovation ecosystems
Documentary evidence	Publications of the processes carried out among various actors	Community-based innovation ecosystems Collaboration

(Ministerio del Interior, 2017). The GRCC is made up of eight communities which, according to their organizational structure, are: Concepción, Santa Rosa, San Antonio, San José, Carmelo, Limones, Quiroga, and Joanico. The department of Cauca has been one of the departments most affected by the armed conflict. This has been due to several factors, such as its geographical location, ecosystems, high rates of unmet basic needs, land tenure and ownership processes, and social conflict, among others.

This has led to the presence of illegal armed actors and the reconfiguration of new illegal actors, the presence of illicit economies, and the impact on the rights of the Caucan population (Ministerio del Interior, 2017). Specifically, there are three historical dimensions that are currently having an impact on the Pacific Coast zone, generating risk and a humanitarian crisis at the regional level: (i) Loss of the territory's production capacity and detriment to food security due to degradation and over-exploitation of nature, (ii) Unsustainability of economic processes in the face of the

Fig. 4.4 San Antonio township (*Source* Author)

contradictions and consequences of national economic models, and (iii) Incomplete development initiatives on the Caucan coast (Defensoría del Pueblo, 2016).

The fieldwork was carried out in the towns of Quiroga, Concepción, Santa Rosa, and San Antonio (See Fig. 4.4) and in the cities of Popayán and Bogotá. There, meetings, visits, and interviews were held with key actors from the various community-based organizations with the aim of determining the elements of the innovation ecosystem and the relationships of the various grassroots organizations identified for the study.

4.4.1 Dynamics of the Community-Based Innovation Ecosystem

Based on the information gathered through interviews, documentation, and observation, this subsection describes the organizations that are part of the Guajuí River innovation ecosystem. First, the identified actors and their roles are characterized. In this sense, nine local actors are found in the CBIE that are mainly focused around agricultural, fishing, and territorial activities. One local non-governmental organization and the community council (convening organizations), four community-based organizations, two governmental organizations, one local private organization, and one national non-governmental organization were identified.

It should be noted that the role of the focal organization is carried out, on the one hand, by the Fundación Chiyangua, which coordinates the other community-based organizations and relates to governmental and non-governmental organizations. On the other hand, the role is performed by the GRCC as the territorial ethnic authority. Additionally, there are other local and external actors that do not participate directly in the processes of sociotechnical change in the territory. The nine actors are described below:

- Fundación Chiyangua (Convenor/Innovating, Facilitating): is a local NGO. It is dedicated to working towards the vindication of the rights of Afro-Colombian women living in the rural area.
- Guajuí River Community Council (Convenor/Advocating): It is the ethnic territorial authority of the lower Guajuí River basin. It was created in 1994 thanks to Law 70 of 1993.
- Asoagropesqui (No specific role): Association of farmers and fishermen from the townships of Quiroga and Limones at the mouth of the Guajuí River.
- Construyendo sueños (Innovating): Association of Afro-Colombian women in the municipality of Guapi. It is dedicated to the trade of Pianguar.
- Women Community Council (Connecting and Facilitating): A space for women's political organization in the municipality of Guapi, it is not part of the municipality's institutional framework.
- Comunicaciones pacifico RyV (Innovating, Facilitating, Training): Non-formal organization that provides Internet communication services through wifi technology.
- Fundación ACUA (Funding, Connecting): National non-governmental organization that works with Afro-Colombian communities in Colombia.
- Pacific Environmental Research Institute (Sharing): Created by law 99 of 1993, where the environmental research centres of the Republic of Colombia are generated. In this case, its work is focused on the Colombian Pacific coast.
- Matamba Guasá Women Network (Connecting): The network comprises Afro-Colombian women from the municipalities of Timbiquí, López de Micay, and Guapi, on the coast of the Department of Cauca.

From the semi-structured interviews and based on the snowball technique, a series of relationships between diverse actors are identified in order to map the ecosystem (Fig. 4.5). Firstly, the convening actors are identified, which are the organizations that lead and energize the innovation ecosystem. Here, we find on one side the Guajuí River Community Council, and on the other, the Fundación Chiyangua (Black background). Additionally, there are other direct actors, who are immersed in the dynamics of the community innovation processes (Grey background) and indirect actors, who have previously worked with the community-based organizations studied (White background). The following figure shows the relationships between the actors and also the three innovations studied, which are marked with a dark line.

To understand the dynamics of the community-based innovation ecosystem, it is necessary to recognize the communal innovations created collaboratively by the organizations. These allow us to understand the processes of sociotechnical change at the local level, through the effects on the population and the opportunities that the territories have. Table 4.4 and photographs describe the innovation processes based on the territory that has been generated from the collaborations between the base organizations.

The above elements can enhance resilience, peacebuilding, and trust between communities through the organizational and ethnic diversity of

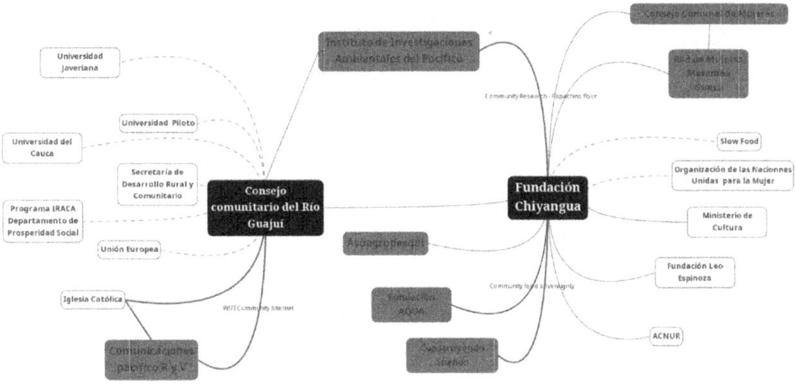

Fig. 4.5 Relations between actors in the Guajuí river innovation ecosystem (*Source* Author)

Table 4.4 Communal innovations of the CBIE Rio Guajuí—Colombia

Sector	*Communications*	*Agriculture*	*Nutrition*
Actors	Comunicaciones pacífico RYV, Parish and Guajuí River Community Council	Fundación Chiyangua and Pacific Environmental Research Institute	Fundación Chiyangua, Construyendo sueños and Fundación ACUA
Problem	Absence of radio, cellular, and Internet communication signal in the territory	Food and nutritional insecurity in the territory	Loss of cultural traditions linked to gastronomy and biodiversity
Solution	Point to point wifi network, through repeaters from Popayán (Fig. 4.6)	Production of Papachina flour as a replacement for exogenous products	Recovery of gastronomic traditions related to biodiversity and culture, through agriculture based on Azoteas
Use of the solution	A point was established in the village of San Antonio. A daily pin is sold at 3,000 pesos Col	Bromatological research on the nutritional properties of Papachina (Colocasia esculenta)	Use of the rooftop method for family farming, in particular, traditional herbs such as Chiyangua (Eryngium foetidum)
Scaling up	It will be extended to other towns in the territory. They are already in Timbiquí and López de Micay	The Chiyangua Foundation has started to produce, pack, and sell Papachina flour for distribution, especially in kindergartens	Publication of several books with Guapi's experiences and traditional knowledge

the region with Afro-descendant and indigenous groups. These groups maintain traditional forms of social organization, as well as generating alternatives for communication, food sovereignty, and the generation of knowledge of their own traditional foods. These are essential elements for creating alternatives for collective environment and peacebuilding in the territory.

Figure 4.7 presents a model where communal purpose is found at the centre of the ecosystem, moving to the developed roles, relevant actors, contexts where they are developed, and finally, the opportunities

Fig. 4.6 Point to point wifi network maintenance (*Source* Author)

and limitations. At the description level, the communal purpose of this ecosystem is cantered on resilience, given that the innovation processes in the territory seek to adapt to the new conditions of the political reality and of peacebuilding. Through novel strategies of communications, food sovereignty, and community research, community-based organizations transform their conditions to generate new futures of collective welfare. In this way, the two organizations that convene within the ecosystem energize the innovation processes by connecting dissimilar actors, such as international cooperation organizations, public institutions at national, regional, or local level, and public and private universities. However, they mainly weave a network of community actors around the main challenges in the territory.

Meanwhile, at the level of the activities carried out by the actors of the ecosystem, we find that the main ones (yellow) are: connecting, as many of the organizations maintain or generate new relationships with other organizations regardless of their nature; innovating, since several of them have generated new products, services, or knowledge with others in a collaborative manner when facing a local challenge; advocating, as some of these organizations facilitate dialogue between the population and government institutions; financing, since several organizations, especially the Non-Governmental ones, finance some of the innovation activities studied; sharing knowledge, for example, some organizations in particular

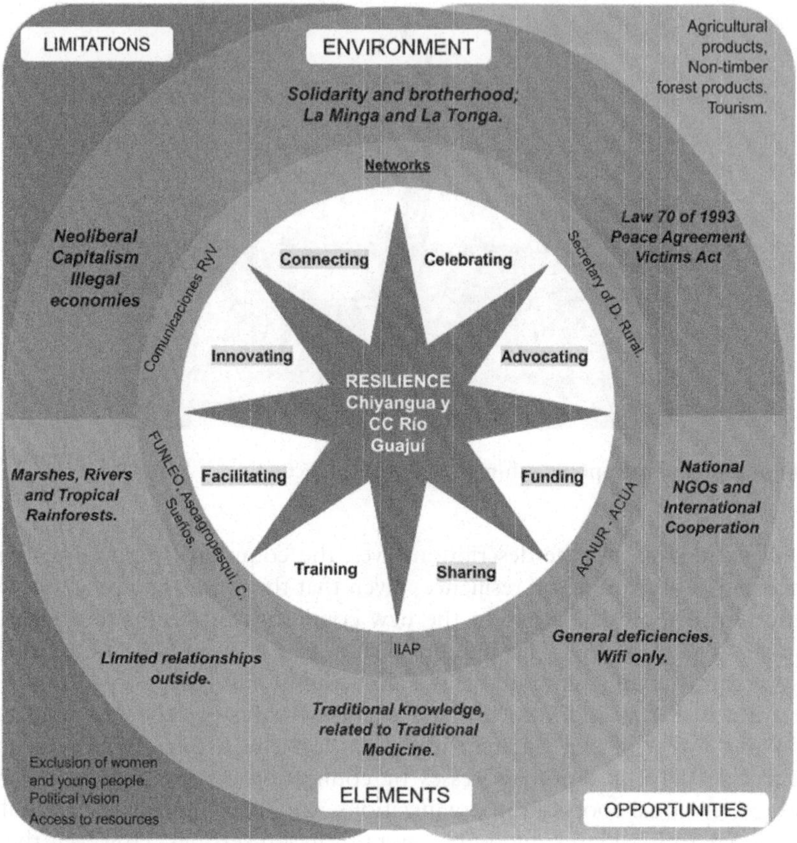

Fig. 4.7 Guajuí river community-based innovation ecosystem (*Source* Reina-Rozo [2019b])

like Fundación Chiyangua share their knowledge by means of publications such as booklets or books and; to mediate and facilitate, since the organizations mediate in the innovation processes by allowing close contact between financing entities, the knowledge generated, and the dialogue with the population in general.

The environment and the elements can be observed in the blue and green circles, respectively. As for the first, the economic environment is governed by a neoliberal model, where illegal economies such as unregulated gold-mining and, the cultivation and trafficking of drugs still continue to be activities in the territory. The cultural context is related to values such as solidarity, community, brotherhood, and identity. Meanwhile, at the level of non-formal institutions at the local level, the highlights are La Mano Cambiada, which is the exchange of work, La Minga, which is collective work, and La Tonga, which is the division of individual non-transactional tasks. The regulatory context is governed mainly by Law 70 of 1993, which is the law of Afro-Colombian communities, Law 99 of 1993, which regulates the national environmental system, Law 1448 of 2011, which is the law of victims, and the Acto legislativo 01 de 2016, which is the Peace Agreement between Presidencia de la República and FARC-EP.

The main elements where these activities are developed are provided by a diversity of ecosystems from tropical rainforests, lentic ecosystems such as rivers, to estuaries, mangroves, and the Pacific Ocean. Relations with other actors outside the territory are limited and the capacity to communicate the actions of the grassroots organizations is focused on the convenors, which have the greatest number of networks. At the knowledge level, according to the interviews, traditional knowledge, midwives, healers, sobanderos, traditional medicine, alabaos, as well as biocultural knowledge associated with biodiversity, stand out. As for infrastructure, the territory has some communication methods, such as the limited cellular network and local wifi. However, the only means of transport within the territory is by river, and the educational and health infrastructure is lacking. Finally, the financial resources for these communal innovation activities are mostly provided by international cooperation and national NGOs which promote these processes.

4.4.2 *Constraints and Opportunities of the Community-Based Innovation Ecosystem*

Regarding limitations or barriers to the processes of sociotechnical change, especially in the post-agreement context of the GRCC territory, the following are to be found:

- Illegal economies: Faced with this, there is the presence of illegal economies such as gold-mining and drug trafficking in the territory, which generate a series of threats to the population in terms

of contamination of water sources and ecosystems, in addition to the generation of violence related to alkaloid production.
- Speculation in the market of products (marine, agricultural, and forestry): Production chains in this part of the country are being monopolized by organizations and individuals. Such is the case of forest products such as wood, marine products such as Piangua, or agricultural products such as bananas, where there is already a pre-established structure of intermediaries and buyers who speculate with prices in consumer centres such as Guapi, Buenaventura, or Cali.
- Exclusion of women and young people: Women and young people have been excluded from decision-making and participation spaces in various scenarios, from the municipal spaces to community councils and grassroots organizations. Therefore, it is necessary to create strategies to generate equal opportunities for equal access to these spaces and their support.

In turn, opportunities in the territory are manifested from various perspectives, some of which are:

- Tourism: At the economic sectors, tourism is becoming a growth sector of the national economy in growth. In this sense, tourism in the municipality has been limited to the Gorgona National Natural Park. However, several people identify other places with the capacity to generate such initiatives like the river's mouth and upstream in the tropical forest. Therefore, tourism and essentially community-managed ecotourism is an opportunity for the Guajuí River territory. In this way, it can coordinate and link the initiatives that have been generated in the territory around gastronomy, food, and technological sovereignty.
- Non-timber forest products: Another opportunity is the research and creation of new environmental knowledge, particularly around non-timber forest products, that is, regarding the various benefits of fauna and flora, such as health, food, and products such as handicrafts.
- Agriculture and fisheries: As regards agriculture and fisheries, products identified as Papachina, Achiote, Naidí (known elsewhere as Azaí), and molluscs have market potential especially at the national and international level. To this end, experiences such as the Papachina flour have been developed.

4.4.3 *Governance in the Collaborative Process Within the Innovation Ecosystem*

The governance of collaborative relationships in the community is one of the most contested dimensions at the inter-organizational level, that is, between organizations in the territory and at the intra-organizational level; in other words, within the organizations. To exemplify this, OBC1 states, "*the community councils have viewed the organizations like flies in milk, practically. That is, they have not agreed with the organizations. It is the first council that now comes to interact with the organizations, because the others have not*". In other words, the relationship between Community Councils and community-based organizations has been tense according to the place. OBC1 suggests that the reason may be "*that the organizations pull some resources and those resources that the organizations pull, they practically need*". This denotes that there is no coordination between the Community Councils and the organizations, based on the issue of funding.

At the intra-organizational level, several of the people interviewed expressed criticism of the internal governance, especially of the community council. In this sense, CCA2 states that "*the townships, what they are looking for more than anything else is a union. Why? Because, most of the young people, talking about the youth, do not have participation in the townvillage*". And he continues, "*what they are looking for, more than anything else now, is for the youth to participate*". In the face of this, OBC5 backs him up by saying "E*h, in all of them. In other words, young people are practically excluded*". In the face of this, one of the directors of the Community Council maintains that "*a strategy must be developed to reach these populations*".

Additionally, other spaces of alternative governance have been generated in the territory. In response, OBC6 explains, "*the creation of women's organizations in the municipality of Guapi has helped to make us visible as women and to empower us*". She continues, "*the organization has been a strategy of collective protection; women alone are defenceless, 10, 20 women together are a force that not everyone can bring down*". Finally, "*meeting again among women and recovering practices and knowledge has made us strengthen our ethnic identity, it has made us empower ourselves as black women*". However, there are also critical voices about social organization in the territory, COM1 maintains that "*community organization here is very weak, we are working on that, to see if we can convince them where to walk, but it is not that easy*".

4.5 Discussion and Conclusions

The Colombian Pacific region has been a place not only forgotten but excluded from the dynamics of the Colombian State. The Afro-Colombian and indigenous populations settled here have generated their own ways and plans of life motivated by their own traditions, epistemologies, and ontologies. However, a milestone was the 1991 constitution and its progressive promise. In the face of this, among many of its advances was transitional article number 55, which protected the rights of rural and riverine communities that had been occupying vacant lands in the Pacific basin by implementing regulations. Law 70 of 1993 and Decree 1475 of 1995 were created to regulate the right to the land of these communities and their ethnic authorities. However, in spite of the fact that the second decade of the twenty-first century is coming to an end, only three of the seven chapters of the law have been regulated, and many promises remain unfulfilled.

To add to this, this region has been a scenario of armed conflict between various subversive groups, paramilitaries, and state forces since the 1990s. The effects in terms of violence, dispossession, threats, and environmental damage have been considerable. In this dead-end context, a peace dialogue emerged that resulted in the Colón Theatre Peace Agreement signed in November 2016, which generated hope and desire for change in the region. However, today it is not possible to speak of post-conflict in that territory; it must be considered as post-agreement. The conflicts have been transformed by illegal economic activities such as illicit crops and mechanized gold mining, which have changed the social relations of the population and therefore its materiality.

Thus, from a conventional perspective, it can be understood that this scenario does not produce science, technology, and innovation in an autonomous and free way, and in fact, public policy around these elements does not have a determined focus on these processes of communal innovation. This conception is wrong, since it has been demonstrated that community-based organizations generate situated innovation initiatives through collaboration. In other words, sociotechnical changes are generated from collaboration between different organizations. Experiences of food and nutritional sovereignty, such as the case of Papachina flour and the recovery of gastronomy linked to biodiversity, and the initiative of technological sovereignty in the case of the point-to-point wifi network, provide evidence of the re-signification of innovation in terms of who creates it, for whom it is created, how it is created, and for what purpose. The above, from a vision of sociotechnical change towards the strengthening of the communal social fabric in the territory, in particular, to strengthen resilience and with this the construction of peace through changing conditions of communication, food, and agriculture.

Resilience has been identified as the central purpose of this CBIE. In this sense, Fundación Chiyangua as convener and initiator of this CBIE, plays a fundamental role in articulating the diverse actors and interests of some of the organizations in the territory to co-create social value. Meanwhile, the GRCC, as a local ethnic authority, plays a role of political and social legitimacy, energizing the ecosystem. However, it is found that the life cycle of this CBIE is in its early stages, where there are no major relationships between the actors, so it is necessary to generate more relationships based on the opportunities and limitations of the context. In this way, organizations such as Asoagropesqui, the IIAP, Construyendo Sueños, and Comunicaciones RyV must diversify their collaborations with other organizations to make the social fabric stronger. Although there are relationships with organizations outside the territory, they are still singular experiences, rather than plural.

In particular, this CBIE is in a post-agreement context where the main constraints are the emerging conflicts around illegal economies in general, and the exclusion of women and youth from decision-making processes and access to resources. Meanwhile, local knowledge related to biodiversity, non-timber forest resources, and ecotourism are all found at the level of opportunities. The above allows us to establish the environment where communal innovation activities are developed within the framework of solidarity as a fundamental value, and the collaborative practices of Minga, Tonga, and Mano Cambiada as potentials, threatened by the hegemonic notion of monetary exchange within the capitalist economic model.

Since the peace process, Legislative Act number 1 of 2016 and law 1448, provide a legal framework for the victims of the conflict and the population in these territories. However, the communities are still waiting for the benefits of this legislation in the territory. An additional element of analysis is that this legislation is not articulated with laws related to science, technology, and innovation. Therefore, no state programmes or interventions were found to be working with these communities around innovation and peacebuilding. On the other hand, the conditions of the natural environment provide a scenario to enhance the dynamics of sociotechnical change, given its complexity, such as the tropical rainforest. However, the infrastructure to support these processes is lacking in all its dimensions.

At the level of the epistemologies reproduced by the Afro-Colombian communities orally in the Guajuí River, traditional medicine (midwives, sobanderos, and snakebite cure) is observed as fundamental for the local culture of resistance and resilience for overcoming the effects of the armed conflict. Regarding the implications of collaboration in innovation processes and analysed dimensions from a qualitative perspective, it is concluded that governance, collective norms, and administration of the collaboration processes are weak. This is because there is no inclusion or diversity in the decision-making process, given that decision spaces in the innovations studied are mostly composed of men in adulthood.

Additionally, there are no clear rules generated from the collaborations and very few organizations create formal agreements to determine the management of the collaboration. In the face of local collective welfare, there is a critical perspective around the idea of development imposed by a discourse of progress and economic growth. In this way, the idea of autonomy becomes more relevant when looking at the futures that this population can generate if supported within a perspective of innovation centred on the community, and where sense is found in the resilience of this population with serious economic and social threats. In this sense, the futures of the population must take into account the notions of collective welfare of the population settled there for generations, their relationship with the territory, and their sociocultural traditions.

Considering knowledge, values, and non-formal institutions as potentialities for generating these futures far from the developmentalist notion is more necessary than ever. Thus, the relationships that have been woven between the various actors during the armed conflict are evidence of the essential organizational processes within the dynamics of the Afro-Colombian people, such as the processes of community research where the experience of community members and researchers is taken into account, including several of these directed at the gender and biodiversity approach.

Furthermore, comprehensive research can be done related to the emerging paradigms of community-based innovation. In this same sense, to promote the use of participating methodologies to co-create knowledge and form co-research in the communities, so that these can be researched in the future from a perspective of cognitive sovereignty. Finally, this enables researchers to open the theoretical perspective to the literature in decolonial studies of innovation, in order to understand the implications of reflections and actions from a position of power in the research activities.

Bibliography

Acto Legislativo 01. (2016). *Acuerdo final para la terminación del conflicto y la construcción de una paz estable y duradera.*

Adner, R., & Kapoor, R. (2010). Value creation in innovation ecosystems: How the structure of technological interdependence affects firm performance in new technology generations. *Strategic Management Journal, 31*, 306–333. https://doi.org/10.1002/smj.821.

Arocena, R., & Sutz, J. (2001). *Sistemas de innovación y paises en desarrollo.* SUDESCA Research Papers No. 30 (2002), Department of Business Studies, Aalborg University, Denmark.

Asheim, B., & Gertler, M. (2004). The geography of innovation: Regional innovation system. In *The Oxford handbook of innovation* (pp. 291–317). Oxford University Press.

de Gomes, L. A., & V., Facin, A. L. F., Salerno, M. S., & Ikenami, R. K. . (2018). Unpacking the innovation ecosystem construct: Evolution, gaps and trends. *Technological Forecasting and Social Change, 136*, 30–48. https://doi.org/10.1016/j.techfore.2016.11.009.

Defensoría del Pueblo. (2016). *Problemática humanitaria en la Región Pacífica colombiana—Subregión Cauca.* Bogotá, Colombia.

Dutrénit, G., & Sutz, J. (Eds.). (2014). *National innovation systems, social inclusion and development the Latin American experience.* London: Edward Elgar Pubilishing. https://doi.org/10.4337/9781782548683.

Durst, S., & Poutanen, P. (2013). Success factors of innovation ecosystems—Initial insights from a literature review *. *CO-CREATE 2013: The boundary-crossing conference on co-design in innovation* (pp. 27–38).

Fagerberg, J. (2003). Innovation: A guide to the literature. In J. Fagerberg, D. Mowery & R. Nelson (Eds.), *Oxford handbook of innovation* (pp. 1–26). Oxford University Press.

Galtung, J. (1996). *Peace by peaceful means: peace and conflict, development and civilization.* Oslo: International Peace Research Institute.

Gates, C. (1999). Community governance. *Futures, 31*, 519–525. https://doi.org/10.1016/S0016-3287(99)00011-7.

Hoffecker, E. (2019). *Understanding innovation ecosystems framework for joint analysis and action*. D-Lab MIT Working Paper. Cambridge Mass.

IDIN. (2017). *What is a local innovation ecosystem?* Retrieved August 31, 2018, from http://www.idin.org/blog-news-events/blog/what-local-innovation-ecosystem.

Jimenez, A., & Roberts, T. (2019). Decolonising neo-liberal innovation: Using the Andean philosophy of ' buen vivir ' to reimagine innovation hubs. In P. Nielsen & H. Kimaro (Eds.), *2019 International Conference on social implications of computers in developing countries* (Vol. 1, pp. 180–191). Springer International Publishing. https://doi.org/10.1007/978-3-030-19115-3.

Kleba, J., & Reina-Rozo, J. D. (2021). Fostering peace engineering and rethinking development—A Latin American view. *Technological Forecasting y Social Change, 167*, 120711. https://doi.org/10.1016/j.techfore.2021.120711.

Landry, R., Amara, N., & Lamari, M. (2002). Does social capital determine innovation ? To What extent ? *Technological Forecasting and Social Change, 69*, 1–25.

Leary, J. P. (2019). The innovation cult. *Jacobin Magazine*. Retrieved from https://jacobinmag.com/2019/04/innovation-language-of-capitalism-ideology-disruption.

Ley 70. (1993). *Por la cual se desarrolla el artículo transitorio 55 de la Constitución Política*. 27 de Agosto de 1993.

Ley 99. (1993). Por la cual se crea el Ministerio del Medio Ambiente, se reordena el Sector Público encargado de la gestión y conservación del medio ambiente y los recursos naturales renovables, se organiza el Sistema Nacional Ambiental, SINA, y se dictan otras disposiciones. 22 de Diciembre de 1993. *Diario Oficial*.

Ley 115. (1994). Por la cual se dictan medidas de atención, asistencia y reparación integral a las víctimas del conflicto armado interno y se dictan otras disposiciones. *Diario Oficial*.

Ley 1448. (2011). Por la cual se dictan medidas de atención, asistencia y reparación integral a las víctimas del conflicto armado interno y se dictan otras disposiciones. 11 de Junio de 2011. *Diario Oficial*.

Lundvall, B. (1992). *National innovation system: Towards a theory of innovation and interactive learning*. Pinter.

Martin, R., & Simmie, J. (2008). Path dependence and local innovation systems in city-regions. *Innovation: Management, Policy and Practice, 10*(2–3), 183–196. https://doi.org/10.5172/impp.453.10.2-3.183.

Martinez, M., Serrano, A., Montoya, L., & Montoya, I. (2017). La metáfora biológica como metodología de aprendizaje organizacional. El caso de los ecosistemas de innovación. *Espacios, 38*(43), 18.

Ministerio del Interior. (2017). *Plan de caracterización del Consejo Comunitario Rio Guajuí—Guapi*. Bogotá, Colombia.
Montoya, I., Montoya, L., & Muñoz, G. (2012). Aplicación metafórica de elementos de la sociobiología en la formación comunitaria de la identidad territorial. In L. Montoya & I. Montoya (Eds.), *Metáforas biológicas aplicadas a las organizaciones* (Vol. 1, p. 252). Universidad Nacional de Colombia.
Moore, J. (2005). Business ecosystems and the view from the firm. *Business, 51*(1), 31–75.
Nelson, R. (1993). *National innovation system: A comparative study*. In R. Nelson (Ed.). Oxford University Press.
Oh, D. S., Phillips, F., Park, S., & Lee, E. (2016). Innovation ecosystems: A critical examination. *Technovation, 54*, 1–6. https://doi.org/10.1016/j.technovation.2016.02.004.
Reina-Rozo, J. D. (2019a). *Communal innovation: Collective creation towards wellbeing* (New Directions In Innovation Research No. 2). https://doi.org/10.2139/ssrn.3639564.
Reina-Rozo, J. D. (2019b). Ingeniería, innovación y construcción de paz: caso en el pacífico colombiano. In *Anales do I Encontro Latino-americano de engenharia e sociedade* (p. 11). Universidade do Sao Paulo.
Reina-Rozo, J. D. (2020). Ingeniería para la construcción de paz: Una reflexión preliminar para procesos tecno-científicos de resiliencia territorial. *OPERA*, (27), 141–162. https://doi.org/10.18601/16578651.n27.07.
Reina-Rozo, J. D., Thompson, M., & Leal, D. (2018). Co-design spaces for peace-building in Colombia: A preliminary conceptualization. In *2018 World engineering education forum—Global Engineering deans council* (pp. 1–9). Albuquerque, IEEE. https://doi.org/10.1109/weef-gedc.2018.8629673.
Reina-Rozo, J. D., & León, L. (2017). Ingeniería Humanitaria desde/ para el sur global. In M. B. Albornoz, J. Jímenez & J. Rojas (Eds.), *Ingeniería, innovación y tecnología social* (p. 308). Universidad Nacional de Colombia - FLACSO.
Ritala, P., & Almpanopoulou, A. (2017, February). In defense of 'eco' in innovation ecosystem. *Technovation, 60–61*, 39–42. https://doi.org/10.1016/j.technovation.2017.01.004.
Russell, M. G., & Smorodinskaya, N. V. (2018). Leveraging complexity for ecosystemic innovation. *Technological Forecasting and Social Change, 136*(January 2016), 114–131. https://doi.org/10.1016/j.techfore.2017.11.024.
Shaw, D. R., & Allen, T. (2018). Studying innovation ecosystems using ecology theory. *Technological Forecasting and Social Change, 136*, 88–102. https://doi.org/10.1016/j.techfore.2016.11.030.
Shiva, V. (2005). *Earth democracy: Justice, sustainability, and peace*. South End Press.

Smorodinskaya, N., Russell, M., Katukov, D., and Still, K. (2017). Innovation ecosystems vs. innovation systems in terms of collaboration and co-creation of value. In *50th Hawaii international conference on system sciences* (pp. 5245–5254). https://doi.org/10.24251/HICSS.2017.636.

Tsujimoto, M., Kajikawa, Y., Tomita, J., & Matsumoto, Y. (2018). A review of the ecosystem concept—Towards coherent ecosystem design. *Technological Forecasting and Social Change*, *136*, 49–58. https://doi.org/10.1016/j.techfore.2017.06.032.

Vesilind, A. (2010). *Engineering peace and justice (First).* Springer books.

Wulf, W. (2007). Changes in innovation ecology. *Science, 316*(5829), 1253. https://doi.org/10.1126/science.1145598.

Yin, R. K. (2009). *Case study research design and methods* (Vol. 5). SAGE.

CHAPTER 5

Local Economic Development and the Colombian Strategy for a Sustainable and Inclusive Bioeconomy

Hector Heraldo Rojas-Jimenez

5.1 Introduction

A particularity in this paper is the translation not from Spanish to English, but from *Pure Sciences* to *Social Science*. In a meeting with the colleagues of the Manchester Institute of Biotechnology, the feeling was that even when everyone was talking English, we all were speaking different languages. Although all disciplines offer different approaches the interaction among them, when trying to solve some new problems, is certainly part of the novelty. Bioeconomy is a novel language for social science, even if social science has been working on the challenges of society, as well as pure science, there is an important gap in the knowledge of terminology.

H. H. Rojas-Jimenez (✉)
Universidad Externado de Colombia, Bogotá, Colombia
e-mail: hector.rojas@uexternado.edu.co

L. A. Orozco et al. (eds.), *Science, Technology, and Higher Education*, Palgrave Studies in Democracy, Innovation, and Entrepreneurship for Growth,
https://doi.org/10.1007/978-3-030-80720-7_5

Ever since coming down from the trees, man has faced the problem of survival, not only as an individual but also as a member of a social group. His continued existence is a logical testimony to the fact that he has succeeded in solving the problem; but the continued existence of want and misery, even in the richest of nations, is evidence that his solution has been, at best, a partial one (Heilbroner, 2000, p. 18).

In survival, the learning has included manipulating organisms to improve processes, which resulted in bread, wine, cheese, yogurt, and even coffee. Thus, humanity has been close to practices in the field of bioeconomy. Coffee is one of the several products Colombians feel proud of. On the contrary, there is no pride in the Netflix series about cartels, drugs, or similar. Coffee is not an American native. It comes from Africa and came to America with colonization, just as chocolate, avocado, tomato, and many others arrived in Europe. Probably Jesuit missionaries were who entered the grain to Nueva Granada in the eighteenth century.

At the end of nineteenth century, coffee was already a representative source of income for Colombia. By the beginning of the twentieth century, in 1927, the National Federation of Coffee Growers (FNC) was created as an entity that recognizes itself as the largest rural NGO in the world, which would lead the grain collection process, generating support mechanisms for the small coffee farmer throughout the country. However, by having a monopoly of production, distribution, and other elements linked to the value chain, it became a very powerful entity, where benefits would soon be delivered to those closest to the governing bodies, leaving less coverage for small coffee growers. Due to the criticism and the new realities of coffee at the international level, the FNC has become now a more efficient entity close to the local coffee grower. Currently, several other companies and cooperatives of producers have started to improve their species, production processes, and distribution chains in such a way that they have achieved market segments important enough to attract the attention of models of social innovation such as *fair trade*.

This document searches for an answer whether bioeconomy could have the capacity to generate economic development in the local environments in Colombia, acknowledging the case of coffee as a significant element in the country's bioeconomic potential. To answer the above, the bottom-up model will be followed, considering the local spaces as the beginning point to move towards how the bioeconomy could contribute to the LED.

Bioeconomy has existed since the beginning of humanity and today arises as an academic concept in the pursuit of efficiency. Given the growth of the population, lack of resources, and search for alternatives to the use of fossil fuels, bioeconomy, as mechanisms that generate LED in Colombia, can be an alternative, keeping in mind its important limitations when looking to apply it in local environments.

The document offers in the first part an approach to (i) the Colombian context. Afterwards, to frame the understanding of the research trouble in the bottom-up model suggests some proximity with the (ii) LED focus. In the next part of the document, (iii) some of the characteristics that accompany the TH actors of the industry, government, and universities in Colombia in relation to the bioeconomy. Subsequently, it discusses (iv) a possible definition of bioeconomy to Colombia, to finalize with (v) a close up to the case of incorporation of knowledge and innovation in the local coffee production process in the country.

5.2 Context

With 62,829 registered species in the Biological Information System of Colombia (SiB, 2018), Colombia is the second country with the highest biodiversity in the world, surpassed only by Brazil according to Andres Hurtado (2006), and the most biodiverse of the world in proportion to its extension. This represents significant opportunities, not only in terms of preservation and conservation initiatives, but also for the bioeconomy sector, which promotes the efficient and sustainable use of the natural resources and biodiversity of the territory.

In Colombia, a public policy definition of bioeconomy is something new, but the opportunity to generate new growth channels for the country is recognized, with qualified employment, attracting and retaining international talent, new knowledge-based companies, valuing and making sustainable use of the biodiversity, as well as, incorporating modern biotechnology, among others (Aristizabal, 2017).

According to the System of Information on the Colombian Biodiversity, more than 50% of the country is protected and it is considered a megadiverse country. Likewise, Colombia has a part and contains two of the bioregions with the mayor biodiversity of the world: Amazon (with more than 6 million km^2) shared between Brazil, Peru, Colombia, Venezuela, Ecuador, Guyana, Suriname, French Guyana, and the Pacific bioregion, which is 99% of Colombia; and the rest is shared with Ecuador and Panama (Biointropic, Eafit, Silo, 2018, p. 1).

On the other hand, is a country with more than 60 years of armed conflict that arrived at a peace treaty signed with the more ancient guerrilla of the world, FARC (Revolutionary Armed Force of Colombia), a treaty that has been the most important event for Colombians and for a country in the last 200 years. On the last 30 of May 2018, Colombia begins to be part of the OECD. On the last 14 of June the DNP,[1] Colciencias[2] was launching the Green Book as the manual to address sustainability in Colombia oriented to the SDGs 2030, and on the last 10 of July, the new public policy of bioeconomy was published in the document CONPES 3934.[3]

Even when Colombia began to be a member of the OECD last May 2018, the social conditions of the country in terms of poverty are still regrettable (see Fig. 5.1). According to the National Department of Statistics (DANE, 2017) in 2017 in the distant rural zones, the monetary poverty index was 36%. Quibdo, Riohacha, and Florencia registered the higher monetary poverty index 47.9, 46.9 y 33.7% respectively, while the lower monetary poverty index was in Bucaramanga, Bogota, and Pereira with 12, 12.4 y 12.7%, in its order (Portafolio.co, 2018).

[1] Colombia is a democratic Republic, with a separation of power model, where the Executive includes the President, its ministries and in the level of ministries are the Departments; the DNP is the National Planning Department in charge of building the public policies at the national level.

[2] Colciencias is the Colombian institution that leads the areas of science, innovation, and development. However, it is under the Ministry of Education, so it is like a son condemned to walk hand in hand with his mother. Currently, has been transformed in the Science, technology, and innovation Ministry of Colombia.

[3] The National Council for Economic and Social Policy, CONPES is the highest national planning and performance authority as an advisory body to the Government in all aspects related to the country's economic and social development. The council produces policy papers also called CONPES.

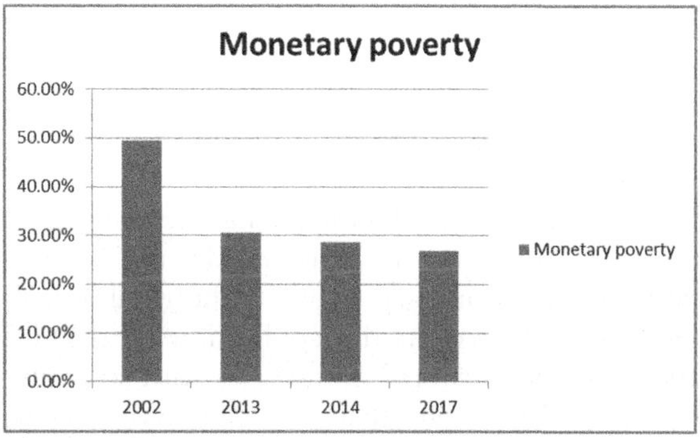

Fig. 5.1 Monetary poverty (Based on DANE [2017])

5.3 Local Economic Development (LED)[4]

When talking about economic development strategies, the conventional approach tends to visualize, for the most part, sequential processes linked to industrialization, outsourcing, and urbanization, which are assimilated to the advance of "modernization". In this way, the development strategy "from above", of a concentrating nature and based on a large company is considered (as a great "idea-force") as the way fundamental for achieving it. (…) Generally, this type of **LED**, based on the use of endogenous resources and carried out by small companies, has been emerging without too much or no political-administrative support from the central instances of the public administration. The emergence of such LED initiatives has essentially depended on territorial agents, through concerted efforts diverse (Vázquez Barquero, 1988 in Alburquerque, 2004).

In this sense, the concept of "local development" arises from the combination of two controversial terms, which have been the subject of scientific discussion and have generated disparate positions. Various contributions have been made to offer a unanimous and accepted definition that has not yet been achieved. The concept of development has been used in most cases with qualitative significance. In common parlance, it

[4] Based in working papers and discussions from the board of the public policy of the National Planning Department of Colombia, Local Economic Development Agencies in Colombia Red ADELCO, and University Externado de Colombia from which the author has been part.

is used as a synonym for growth, and generally, economic increase. On the other hand, the notion of "local" refers to a part of the space, small and encompassed or referenced in a broader structure. Both are closely related concepts and have had a growing role in the scientific body of the twenty-first century (Juarez, 2013).

Particularly, in Colombia in a national frame the concept local might be understood as rural. The local is the countryside, and as it was mentioned before, there is an important gap between the rural and the urban. It is evident the disarticulation in the application of the different planning instruments in the territorial entities. As with so many concepts in the social sciences, LED is one that does not have a single definition. However, its practice provides fundamental and unanimously accepted and recognized elements such as (Ascoli, 2006; Gallicchio, 2004):

- Involves an intentional action and social construction.
- Value existing resources in a given territory.
- Incorporates different economic, social, and institutional actors; the cooperation and negotiation between these actors are oriented.
- Although it is a process that arises from the community itself, it is not an isolated process, but on the contrary, it implies inter-jurisdictional articulations (local, departmental, and national) that empower it. Hence, it is necessary that local development is planned also taking into consideration the guidelines established by departmental and national policies.
- Involves the construction of a medium- and long-term vision, which establishes the point of arrival and the horizon that determines and gives meaning to short-term actions and allows gradual progress.
- Recognizes that reality is diverse, so that the value of particularities, potentialities, and territorial identities is recovered.

Supporting LED seems to be nonsense in an increasingly globalized world. However, "it has its logic in noticing that integrating into global dynamics, from a peripheral or disadvantaged position, is only possible from the strengthening of the resources available to each territory, especially those that may offer some unique feature and identified with a specific area that is, adding value to production through its cultural features" (Hevia, 2003). This is what, in synthesis, proposes LED.

The main advantages of LED can be summarized as follows (Aghón et al., 2001):

a. Strengthens the processes of productive adjustment, because, as economies become more international and more competitive, territorial governments are increasingly faced with the need to provide solutions to increasing unemployment and adapt the productive system to the context changes.
b. It contributes to the improvement of productivity and competitiveness, not only in terms of prices, but also with the introduction of local products and their permanence in the markets, improvement in quality, design, marketing, timely delivery, continuity of supply, and after-sales service.
c. It encourages the participation of local society in the development processes, they increase their protagonism by having to actively participate in the definition and execution of the strategies defined.
d. It dynamizes the decentralization processes, as when granting competences to local and regional communities, local development strategies are strengthened.

The LED is relevant for Colombia improving governance at all levels because it puts government and power within the reach of the people; the LED is a tool for inclusive economic development and the generation of opportunities from the peripheral territories not focused exclusively on SMEs or value chains, but also in processes of formalization, associativity, and solidarity economy.

In providing a theoretical framework for thinking about the role of social networks within the economic development process, notions of social capital clearly link into ongoing debates upon the role of networks and relational assets within the LED process, not least in realizing external economies such as transaction costs (Evans & Syrett, 2007).

5.4 Characteristics That Accompany the Triple Helix Actors

In the introduction of the Triple Helix **TH** of innovation article, Etzkowitz and Leydesdorff suggest that:

> The TH model is formulated not at the level of the phenomena to be explained, but as a model for helping with the explanation. In this sense,

> it is a methodological tool: the focus on the recursive overlay of communications among universities, industries, and governments allows for the organization of research questions in relation to the various models and metaphors. (1998)

In the same way, Etzkowitz and Leydesdorff continue to develop one of the models that has allowed motivating interactions between TH actors and has contributed to strengthening relationships and results as a product of the dynamics proposed by the model in this sense:

> The network of university-industry-government relations continuously restructures the opportunity matrix of a complex system which itself is the result of the reconstruction from different angles by each of the participating instances. All agencies are embedded in discourses at different levels, that is, within their respective institutions, at the specific interfaces between the helices, and at generalized levels where third actors may come into play. The reflections are only partially synchronized by the network of relations, thus enabling the participants to find niches in the knowledge-based economy. (cf. Bruckner et al., 1994 in Etzkowitz & Leydesdorff, 1998)

The **TH** is a spiral innovation model that captures the multiple and reciprocal interactions between the university as the first helix, companies, and industries as the second helix and the administrations or governments as the third helix; at different points of the knowledge capitalization process (Herrera et al., 2015).

The university plays an important role in the socio-economic activities of a country. It's roles include teaching-learning and research and development, but he also participates in the creation of new companies (spin-offs) based on knowledge through incubation mechanisms. This dynamic proposes the growth of the institutions that make up this first propeller is achieved, but also of the companies involved in HT that are beneficiaries of the results of the research obtained at the university (Herrera et al., 2015). The companies represent the second helix of the model. They stimulate their growth and competitiveness through cooperation mechanisms with universities, financing R+D+ i processes that solve problems of their daily work, or generate new technologies to be commercialized (Herrera et al., 2015). The proper functioning of the model implies the active participation of the government, the third helix, through legislation, instruments, and fiscal incentives conducive to the

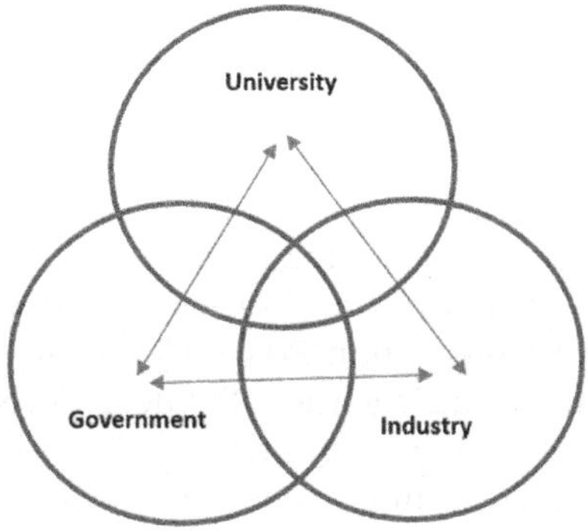

Fig. 5.2 "Laissez-faire". Model of government–industry–university relations (*Source* Etzkowitz and Leydesdorff 1996 in Piñeres [2016])

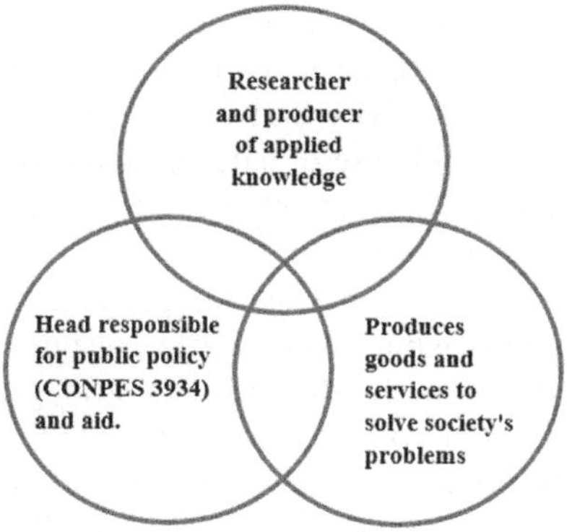

Fig. 5.3 Relations between the actors of the **TH**

promotion and dynamism of university–business relations (Herrera et al., 2015) (see Figs. 5.2 and 5.3).

5.4.1 *Some Characteristics of the Government*

Historically Colombia has had an extractive economy; the first row of the economy is petroleum extraction, normally in the second row were international remittances but more recently tourism came to be in the second position. In the transition frame to a post-conflict arena, some alternatives for social and economic growth are being studied. As stated before, bioeconomy has been somehow present in different spaces, since a decade from now, but just until 2018, there is a public policy to consider bioeconomy among the possibilities and change the point of view regarding the traditional extractive model. Enormous challenges have accompanied most of the different development planning approaches of the successive governments in Colombia. An interest has been to close the gap between the urban and the rural conditions.

Furthermore, Colciencias was a founder member of the Transformative Innovation Policy Consortium (TIPC). The consortium brings the following agencies: Sweden, (VINNOVA) Norway (National Research Council), South Africa (The National Research Foundation), Finland (Tekes), and Science Policy Research Unit from University of Sussex (SPRU) together to advance in a new policy of Science, Technology, and Innovation (CTeI, for its acronym in Spanish) that contributes to the solution of the most urgent problems of today (see Table 5.1).

The objective of the green growth policy is to stimulate an increase in productivity and economic competitiveness by 2030; while assuring sustainable use of natural capital and social inclusion in a manner compatible with climate change (NDP, 2018).

The purpose of the Green Growth Policy is to drive a national climate-compatible increase in productivity and economic competitiveness by 2030, while assuring the sustainable use of natural wealth and social inclusion. In this way, its strategies, actions, and goals, are attuned to the "Pacto por la Sostenibilidad" (Sustainability Pact) contained in the National Development Plan (2018–2022) called "Pacto por Colombia, pacto por la equidad" (Pact for Colombia, pact for equality) that seeks to consolidate actions to achieve an equilibrium between conservation and production in such a way that the natural wealth is assumed as a strategic asset of the nation (DNP, 2019).

The following table recognizes part of the path followed in the construction of public policy guidelines, until reaching the green growth policy. Biotechnology is related to biodiversity, productive development, comprehensive solid waste management, sustainable construction, and finally the green growth policy as a strategy that identifies the bioeconomy as one of its central axes.

Colombia has performed well at a regional level in terms of economic growth (see Table 5.2). Regardless, it has characterized itself for its low economic diversification, low productivity in resource utilization, and significant environmental impact associated with degradation and depletion of natural resources. Although the country possesses a robust

Table 5.1 Analysis summary by dimension

Dimension	*Findings*	*Gaps*
Technological	1. More than 1,500 research groups related to Bioeconomy, where more than 600 are related to areas of biodiversity and biotechnology 2. The first scientific community of Biotechnology is in Bogotá, the second in Medellín and the third in Cali 3. Programs such as Colombia BIO have promoted the development of 15 bioexpeditions identifying 131 endemic species and more than one and a half million new records for the Biodiversity Information System-SIB	1. Difficulty in converting the R&D results into innovation products, processes or services for the market. "Valley of death"
Regulatory	1. There is progress with the creation in 2012 of the Genetic Resources Group of Minambiente with the approval of 149 contracts, mostly for research purposes 2. Invima and ICA have made progress in health surveillance and quality control of medicines, food, biological products, biotechnology and agricultural inputs	1. Only 8 contracts for access to genetic resources for commercial purposes. Lack of clarity in management and application 2. Both the regulations and the capacities created serve traditional businesses and not the innovative and future activities of the bioeconomy 3. It is important to ratify the postulates in the Nagoya protocol

(continued)

Table 5.1 (continued)

Dimension	*Findings*	*Gaps*
Market	1. The international consumption of bio-products, biosolutions and bio-processes is increasing 2. Biotechnology is seeing global sales at the end of 2017 of USD 441.5 billion, with annual growth of more than 10% 3. Tractor agricultural sectors such as Palm and Sugar Cane with experience in bio-fuels could change to new models of the circular economy and bio-refineries 4. Miambiente has supported more than 900 green businesses through regional autonomous Corporations 5. Innpulsa has supported more than 50 companies with bio-based products 6. Colciencias has supported the development of 85 bio-products	1. Emergent demand in the national market for bio-based innovations 2. Absence of campaigns and specialized information to raise awareness about the consumption of bio-based products 3. International trade of bio-based products from Colombia is emergent and sectoral exports are not measured with adequate level of detail

Dimension	*Findings*	*Gaps*
Financing & investment	1. The country has experience in development, cooperation, financing and more recently in investment instruments in various sectors 2. In relation to calls for the promotion of R&D related to bio-based products, some of the projects by Colciencias, Innpulsa, Sena, SGR and Colombia Científica can be highlighted. Nevertheless, these calls are not permanent 3. Of 31 investment funds identified only 4 of have made investments in companies related to biotechnology 4. In credit, entities such as Bancoldex and Finagro have been developing agreements with territorial entities for special lines. However, there is not yet a line established in biotechnology or bio-economy	1. There is a deficit of specialized financing and investment instruments for each of the stages of the life cycle of biotechnology 2. There is a lack of a clear country portfolio of sophisticated businesses in the bio-economy and biotechnology to attract investment, as well as for the design of customized instruments

(continued)

Table 5.1 (continued)

Dimension	*Findings*	*Gaps*
Human talent	1. Undergraduate and graduate study programs in biotechnology were found: 3 undergraduate and 23 postgraduate programs exist in the country, with 19 currently active programs 2. At the level of Bio-economy, some universities begin to offer continuing education programs (such as diploma studies) or incorporate courses on bioeconomy into their curricula 3. The master's and doctorate students are majoring on agricultural disciplines mostly, followed by energy, chemicals, and food 4. The sectors with more doctors and master's hired by companies are health, food and energy	1. There is a lack of knowledge, personnel and business management methodologies based on biotechnology, technology transfer, market management, and international regulatory issues in bio-economy 2. There is a shortage of personnel for value added businesses in the bio-economy
Infrastructure	1. At the national level, there are robust infrastructures related to bio-economy such as: germplasm banks (CIAT, AGROSAVIA), genomic sequencing platforms (UDEA, CORPOGEN) tissue banks (IDCBIS, TISSUE BANK), bio-informatics (BIOS), phytochemical analysis (CENIVAM, UNAL, UDEA), bio-fuels production facilities (BIOD, Manuelita, Bioenergy), technology parks (GUATIVARA, BIOPACIFICO, UNAL) 2. There are leading biotechnology actors in several of the Colombian departments, that can be the main proponents of the bio-economy	1. Lack of coordination and institutional framework that would ensure leadership and development of the bio-economy, generating national guidelines and coordinating with the Colombian departments 2. Lack of institutional platforms for the measurement and monitoring of the bioeconomy 3. Deficit in infrastructures capable to bring the services required for bio-processes scale-up

Dimension	*Findings*	*Gaps*
Environment	1. In Colombia, 62,829 species have been identified in 2017 (SIB, 2017), which makes it a mega-diverse country 2. According to the Agricultural Census (DANE, 2014) there are 111.5 million hectares (ha) in the continental area of Colombia. 56.7% corresponding to forest (63.2 million ha), 38.6% dedicated to agricultural use (43.1 million ha) and 2.2% (2.5 million ha) destined to a different use 3. Only 7.1 million of the 43.1 million hectares suitable for agriculture are dedicated to planting crops and the remaining equivalent to 34.4 million hectares, are used for animal feed 4. The production of residual agricultural and livestock biomass is 279,333,596 tn/year (Ministry of Mines and Energy, 2010) from crops such as palm, cane, coffee, rice, banana, banana and cattle, pig and poultry 5. There is actual experience of companies focused on the sustainable use of biodiversity and ecosystem services	1. The availability of biodiversity and access to species can be affected by extractive pressures and deterioration of environmental conditions 2. Value chains interested in working with communities to value biodiversity face the difficulties of access permits, dispersion of biological resources, logistical difficulties and security problems in the rural zones

Source Based on Biointropic (2018).

Table 5.2 Antecedent of the initiative of Green growth

Year	*CONPES*	*Issue*
2011	3697	National policy about commercial development of biotechnology base on the sustainable use of biodiversity
2016	3866	National policy on productive development
2018	3874	National policy for the integral management of solid waste
	3918	National strategy for the implementation of the SDG
	3919	National policy on sustainable buildings
	3934	National strategy to organize the green initiatives as the Green Growth Policy where one of the central axe was the bioeconomy policy

[a]The Rural Agricultural Planning Unit (UPRA, 2018) publishes the Action Plan for the Development and Consolidation of Forest Plantations, which aims to consolidate a vision in which the Colombian forestry sector effectively promotes rural

[b]National Council for Economic and Social Policy, it produces policy papers also called document CONPES

political framework to address the challenges associated to sustainable development, it has not been able to efficiently integrate environmental sustainability aspects within sectorial policies and economic growth strategies. In addition, a road map had not been previously been defined to guide the long term and the transition process towards an economic model based on green growth (DNP, 2019) (Table 5.3).

Table 5.3 Why document CONPES 3934

The national economy had an average growth of 4.26% between 2000 and2015 (National Planning Department or DNP for its acronym in Spanish)	Petrol and coal represented 50%of exportations between 2002 and 2015
The costs of environmental degradation and social impacts related to economic growth, have been valued at 2.08% of the Gross Domestic Product (GDP) of 2015 (DNP, 2018)	CONPES 3934 defines that "greengrowth refers to those growth trajectories that ensure economic and social well-being of the population in the long term, assuring conservation of the natural capital and climate security"

Source Based on DNP (2019)

5.4.2 Some Characteristics of Universities

In Colombia, education is a fundamental right according to the Constitution. Despite this, according to the Ministry of Education, as of August 2015, out of 100 students who finished grade 11 (High School), only 48 entered the universities immediately the following year (Lenis, 2017). According to a report presented by the civil society organization *Niñez Ya* 62% of young people who finished high school did not achieve access to higher education, and 40% of children who do not attend school are in areas of armed conflict (El Espectador, 2018).

According to Susana Fiorentino, a researcher at the Javeriana University in an interview with Arbeláez "Unesco's report on knowledge generation in all countries confirms that Colombia will never have a knowledge-based economy in the current conditions of absence or limited investment in R+D+I" 2(...) Colombia allocated for science, technology and innovation in 2018 0.67%, when there are countries that allocate 7% of GDP or when the average investment among members of the OECD is 4% (2018).

In that sense, even if there are universities producing high levels of scientific discoveries, the gap between those who are able to go to the academy and those who cannot is representative. The distance between the rural and urban environment is even wider, but another important issue is the budget for research which generally is very limited against most of the members of the OECD, but in particular between the public and private education. In any case, even if in the universities the conditions are difficult especially about the budget, the academy is precisely the place where the importance of bioeconomy and its potential as a driver of development is clearer.

After a search through the websites of universities in Colombia and other regions, several masters were founded focused on the training of professionals in sustainable development, bioeconomy, and related topics. Below is the first systematization of its objectives. There is a master's degree in Biotechnology from the National University of Colombia, master's degree in Biotechnology from the ICESI University; the Medellin headquarters of the National University of Colombia offers the Master of Science in Biotechnology. This master's degree aims to train qualified human talent in foundations of cellular and molecular biology, biochemistry, biophysics, and statistics, with the aim of promoting development in the plant, microbial, animal, and industrial areas. The ICESI University located in Cali, Colombia, proposes its Graduate Program in Biotechnology, whose general objective is for professionals to acquire the interdisciplinary technical-scientific foundations to lead research–development–innovation (R+D+I) processes in biotechnology. The areas of concentration for research of the master's degree are agricultural, molecular, cellular, and organism biotechnology; environmental and bioindustrial biotechnology; pharmaceutical biotechnology and medical biotechnology (see Fig. 5.4).

There is a huge challenge for the universities. One of them is that the physical and budgetary conditions are present to be able to summon and support new generations of young researchers to advance in the creation of new knowledge in the field of bioeconomy. This also requires a paradigm shift in knowledge and procedure since the Colombian academic model is not created to motivate research. From the first years of training in schools and throughout the process, there is a significant distancing from research, which has been the engine of development for other countries, but in the Colombian case, it does not respond even to the call of one's own logic. On the contrary, by virtue of the lack of proper construction of an adequate educational model, results are projected based on models that do not correspond to a reading related to the education required. In that sense, scientific production is further diminished.

In this way, some records that show the limited production of bioeconomy issues in Colombia are suggested below. Through Scopus, 15 linked registers are recognized using the "bioeconomy" filter, selecting only those produced in "Colombia". However, in Web of science only two records are recognized (see Fig. 5.5).

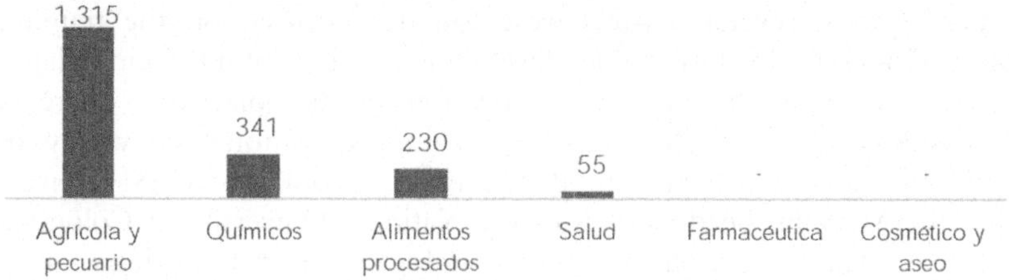

Fig. 5.4 Master's and doctoral students graduated in areas of bioeconomy (2006–2015) *Source* Observatorio Colombiano de Ciencia y Tecnología (2016)

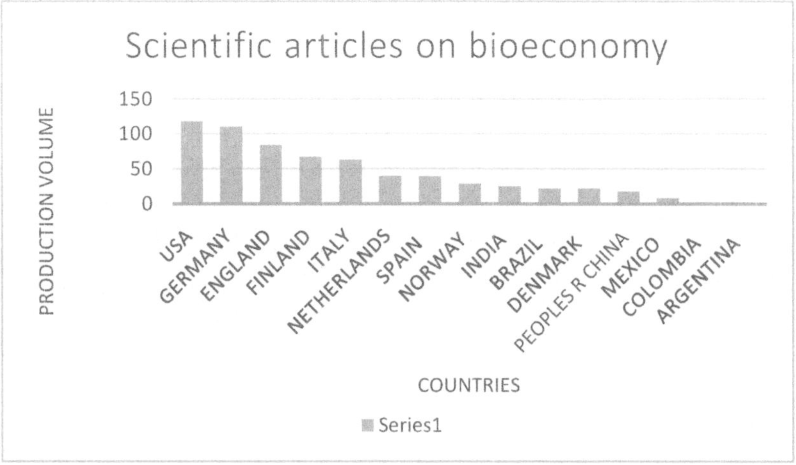

Fig. 5.5 Scientific articles on bioeconomy (*Source* Based on Web of Science [2018])

Finally, is worth mentioning the case of the Science, Technology, and Innovation for the Transformation Policy Factory project launched at the National University (Medellin) in conjunction with the University of Sussex and Colciencias, through the technology of transformative innovation raised great interest for its novelty and for putting the focus on innovation in the construction of a better society. Likewise, the importance of creating incentives for scientific, economic, political, and social production focused on transformative innovations stands out. The space thus opened contributed to the generation of new networks between the academic world, the business world, and the State (University of Sussex—COLCIENCIAS, 2018, p. 48) (see Table 5.4).

5.4.3 *Some Characteristics of Industries*

The Colombian BIO programme, carried out between 2015 and 2018, generated large efforts to position the bioeconomy in the country, carrying out 16 expeditions resulted in 151 possible new discovered species and the development of 84 bioproducts supported by means of calls (Colciencias, 2018). To date, only 305 companies have been consolidated in the country for the development of bio-innovation products,

Table 5.4 Main scientific universities and its research groups

Institution	*Research group in Colciencias*
Universidad Nacional de Colombia	Agricultural Science Medical and Health Science Natural Sciences Engineering and Technology
Universidad del Norte	Medical and Health Science Natural Sciences Engineering and Technology
Fund UnivKonrad Lorenz	Engineering and Technology
Escuela Colombiana de Ingeniería Julio Garavito	Natural Sciences Engineering and Technology
Escuela Naval de cadetes Almirante Padilla	Natural Sciences Engineering and Technology
Pontificia Universidad Javeriana	Agricultural Science Medical and Health Science Natural Sciences Engineering and Technology
Universidad de Los Andes	Medical and Health Science Natural Sciences Engineering and Technology
Universidad ICESI	Medical and Health Science Natural Sciences Engineering and Technology
Universidad CES	Medical and Health Science Natural Sciences Engineering and Technology

Source Based on Colciencias (2018)

which represent only 0.5% of companies in sectors with potential for bioeconomy (DNP, 2018, p. 30).

On the other hand, in the database of the National Trade Association Council, no record related to bioeconomy, biotechnology, or similar appears. However, consulting individually with those business groups that are possibly closer to bioeconomy and related, it was found that the National Association of Businessmen of Colombia ANDI has begun to recognize the concept more closely.

According to ANDI, taking the international context as a reference, Colombia has all the potential to enter the dynamics of the bioeconomy and the application of biotechnology to develop innovative processes, products, and services taking advantage of the benefits of biological and genetic resources and their derivatives, as well as the residual biomass, to incorporate knowledge and innovation and generate opportunities for new businesses and economic progress. In the country, there are more than 400 private research groups related to biodiversity and biotechnology (ANDI, s.f., p. 776).

While the Colombian Association of Medium and Small Industries ACOPI in its magazine My SME + Productive, not mentioning the subject of the bioeconomy in particular, however recognizes as a guild the potential that the country has in the agricultural industry. CAMACOL, the Colombian construction chamber, https://camacol.co/, in its internal search engine, mentions the issue of sustainable construction, but does not advance in the development of the concept or link it in particular to bioeconomy. For its part, the guild of flower growers ASOCOLFLORES (https://asocolflores.org/), does not openly offer information about its relationship with bioeconomy, although undoubtedly, since Colombia is the second producer of flowers in the world, there will be interventions on the matter that may occur and that have not yet been discussed by these producers or failing to be published on their website.

In the same way, FEDEGAN, the group of ranchers, milk and meat producers (http://www.fedegan.org.co/) that are a very influential group given their possession on important tracts of land, some even linked to paramilitarism, they do not have information readily available that they can access referring to bioeconomy. Nevertheless, there is enough information on biotechnology especially on the subjects of reproduction and fertilization. The association of farmers of Colombia, (https://www.sac.org.co/) that groups the largest volume of specialized associations, does not mention bioeconomy in any of its journals of the last five years; however, several of its affiliates refer to the subject of biotechnology and bioeconomy as follows.

The National Federation of Oil Palm Growers Fedepalma being much closer to the subject, in its official documents mentions that the potential for the guild is remarkable since only the current area planted with palm oil in the country in a few years will be able to produce two million tonnes of oil, some 3.8 million tonnes of solid biomass, and 211 million cubic metres of biogas. That is why, Fedepalma and Cenipalma have worked on creating and adapting technologies to optimize the use of biomass as a source of energy for the consumption of the plants and production units of the palm zones (Fedepalma, s.f.).

The association of sugarcane producers—Asocaña, in its 2017 Report, talks about bioethanol recognizing its importance, while considering that its business is the production of sugar and its demand in regions such as Asia and Africa and in general in emerging economies is still increasing. However, the objective is to continue to add value to biomass, transforming it into a wide variety of biocomposite products (food, chemical products, and bioplastics) and bioenergy (bioethanol and cogeneration) (Asocaña, 2018, p. 9).

The federation of rice producers http://www.fedearroz.com.co has a database of scientific documents related to rice production where no records on bioeconomy were found, however there are at least eight instances related to biotechnology although not all are linked to rice production.

Finally, neither the federation of producers of jaggery (http://www.fedepanela.org.co/) nor the federation of potato producers (http://fedepapa.com/home/) have any records related to bioeconomy or biotechnology in their search engines. .

In the next table, it is possible to recognize some interesting cases where bioeconomy is already a productive process in local environments base on small and medium-sized enterprises SMEs.

Below are some of the industrial production processes that incorporate the bioeconomy as input for its elaboration. Knowledge and innovation begin to be part of these processes. From research centres and business accelerators, to rural enterprises and small entrepreneurs (see Fig. 5.6).

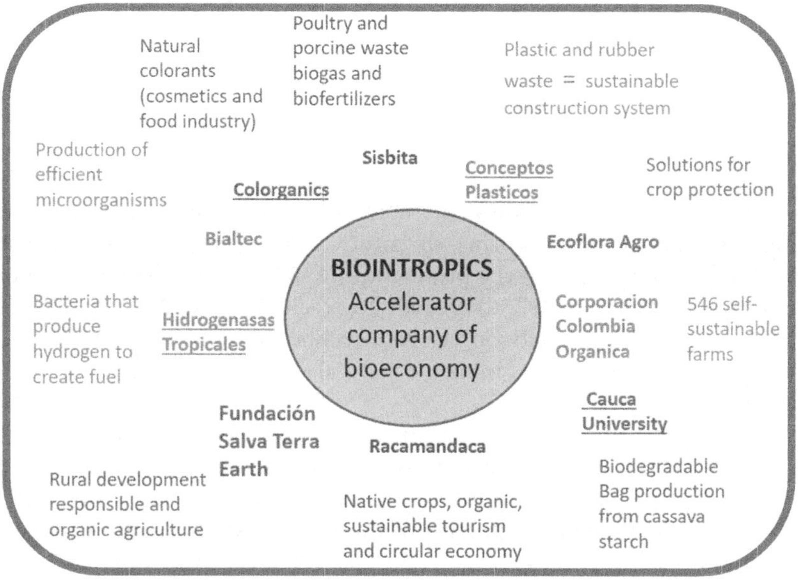

Fig. 5.6 Some production processes based on bioeconomy

5.5 A POSSIBLE DEFINITION OF BIOECONOMY FOR COLOMBIA

According to OECD, bioeconomy is "Transforming the knowledge of life sciences in new, sustainable, eco-efficient and competitive products. The application of biotechnology to primary production, health and industry could lead to an emerging bioeconomy contributing to economic production" (OCDE, 2009).

The manifesto with the pillars of the future economy for Europe defines bioeconomy as: "those parts of the economy that use renewable biological resources (biomass) of land and sea - such as crops, forests, fish, animals and microorganisms, as well as waste and waste of biological origin- to produce food, feed, materials, chemical products, fuels and energy in a sustainable manner». Bioeconomy is "as old as humanity", but a new approach to bioeconomy currently offers "characteristics and advantages, such as carbon neutrality, renewability, circularity and multifunctionality", according to the manifesto (Ec.europa.eu, 2016).

Colombia Bio Project, of Colciencias, has the Bio Expedition, which includes a total of 20 biological expeditions, ten of them in areas of the country that had not been possible to enter due to the conflict. The president highlighted the great opportunities that are opening up for Colombia and explained that "the end of the conflict implies the possibility of consolidating a new economy with greater use of our resources and to reclaim our environment". "He described the opportunities as immense and quoted tourism—of nature and science—, as well as the production of energy and the production of natural ingredients for food, cosmetics and medicines". "We want to reach the year 2025 converted into a bioeconomy based on science, technology and innovation, and that makes the most of its immense natural wealth" (Presidencia.gov.co, 2016).

The Bioeconomy is an area that encompasses a wide range of economic activities, which in turn benefit from new discoveries, products, and services, related and derived from biological sciences. Its implementation in each country involves a process of transition from production systems and traditional processing, towards processes that allow the optimal use of renewable resources and product generation of biological origin (OECD. 2009 in Gobierno de Colombia, 2019). In this sense, the bioeconomy is not identified as a sector in itself but as a group that interconnects different value chains and that is related to many existing sectors among which are: agriculture, food sector, forestry, wood industry, waste, industrial bioproducts, and energy (Gobierno de Colombia, 2019).

For the Colombian case, an economic growth strategy based on bioeconomy is one managed in an efficient and sustainable way, based on renewable biological resources and residual biomass to generate new products, processes, and value-added services grounded on knowledge that creates new levels for growth, development, and progress in the regions of Colombia (Betancur, 2017).

The analysis of prioritization of sectors started from the identification of 17 potential economic activities grouped in the primary sectors, the manufacturing industry, and services, for a final selection of six, prioritary for the analysis in the second phase of the bioeconomy study. Within the prioritized sectors, the following were considered: agricultural and livestock, processed foods and beverages, chemical, health, pharmaceutical, cosmetic, cleaning, and the energy sector (Biointropic et al., 2018).

Another definition: bioeconomy is one economy in which energy is managed efficiently and sustainably, using biodiversity and residual biomass to generate new products, processes, and services of added value, based on knowledge and innovation, that allow leveraging the growth, development, and progress in the regions of Colombia (Biointropic et al., 2018).

Finally, the bioeconomy definition of the last CONPES 3934 is: Economy that efficiently and sustainably manages biodiversity and biomass to generate new products, processes, and value services aggregate, based on knowledge and innovation (DNP, 2018, p. 26).

5.6 Close Up to the Case of Incorporation of Knowledge and Innovation in the Local Coffee Production Process in Colombia

Probably Jesuit missionaries were who entered the grain to Nueva Granada in the eighteenth century. At the end of the nineteenth century, coffee was already a representative source of income for Colombia, so that by the beginning of the twentieth century the FNC was created in 1927, as an entity that recognizes itself as the largest rural NGO in the world, which would lead the grain collection process, generating support mechanisms for the small coffee farmer throughout the country. However, by having a monopoly of production, distribution, and other elements linked to the value chain, it became a very powerful entity, where benefits would soon be delivered to those closest to the governing bodies, leaving less coverage for small coffee growers. Due to the criticism and the new realities of coffee at the international level, the FNC has become a more efficient entity close to the local coffee grower. Currently, several other companies and cooperatives of producers have started to improve their species, production processes, and distribution chains in such a way that they have achieved market segments important enough to attract the attention of models of social innovation such as *fair trade* (Rojas, 2015).

In 1938, the FNC created the National Coffee Research Center CENICAFE, since its foundation, it has received the support of the coffee growers and its challenge has been the development of appropriate technologies for the production of coffee in Colombia. In that sense, its economic relevance in the agricultural part of the country is the genetic improvement of coffee plants where they started knowing the genome of the plant and looking for genes for resistance to pests and diseases, through natural crosses. From all this research, varieties such as Colombia,

Castillo, Tabi, and Cenicafe 1, which are plants resistant to rust and CBD disease, have had economic importance because thanks to these varieties they have stopped using chemical products that, in addition to generating saving, contribute to human health. At this moment, around 70% of the Colombian coffee plantations have planted these varieties.

The coffee experience has specialized in different parts of the value chain, from the improvement of varieties, processes, and finished products, to associative, departmental, and regional processes, among others. Favouring the conditions of the environment to offer improvements at different moments of the process. The obtaining of varieties is technological innovation to achieve greater productivity and resistance to diseases situation that favours the coffee farmer or about 600 thousand Colombian coffee families, which constitute a social fabric that depends on this monoculture for their sustenance. On the other hand, since the broca is the main economic plague of coffee, although resistant varieties have not been obtained, there have also been strategies to control it through biological control by means of formulations of the *Beauveria bassiana* fungus that help control the insect. Another thing for the post-harvest and coffee collection have also obtained technological innovations, such as sleeves that facilitate the collection of manual coffee. For the benefit of coffee or coffee washing (pulping of coffee), an innovation is the use of Belcosub technology that reduces water consumption by up to 95% and control water pollution. There is also the transformation of the coffee product that is used by the Freeze Dried Coffee Plant with its Good Day brand products. These innovations favour the small coffee grower and the large coffee producers that contribute most of the coffee production. Colombia is behind in relation to other countries in innovation because it exports the raw product and the big roasters buy it, sell it and earn 90%. There are still many processes that can add value to the production chain, however, every time you are achieving greater social, environmental, and economic benefits in the production of coffee.

The success of the Colombian coffee industry in the twenty-first century has three names: quality, differentiation, and productivity. The Competitiveness Program and the Permanence, Sustainability and Future Plan guarantee us that the entire coffee industry will be renewed in the coming years. More importantly, the poorest coffee growers will benefit the most (Silva, 2009).

5.7 Conclusions

To answer the two questions proposed at the beginning of the article, the bottom-up model was followed, from (i) the Colombian context, the (ii) LED focus, considering the local spaces as the beginning point to recognize (iii) some of the characteristics that accompany the **TH** actors in Colombia in relation to the bioeconomy. After that, it was proposed (iv) a possible definition of bioeconomy for Colombia, to finalize with (v) a close up to the case of incorporation of knowledge and innovation in the local coffee production process in the country.

The two key questions that were explored are: What are the characteristics that describe **TH** actors in Colombia to motivate advances in bioeconomy? With the advances that exist in the production of the bioeconomy in Colombia, is it possible through bioeconomy strategies to generate LED? And to synthesize the answers to the main questions (see Table 5.5 and Fig. 5.7).

We do not have so much oil, nor good coal, we have rivers, trees, forests, genetic material to promote the future. Extraction depletes the

Table 5.5 To synthesize the answers to the main questions

(1) What are the characteristics that describe Triple Helix actors in Colombia to motivate advances in bioeconomy?
Nowadays, after the CONPES 3934/2018 the intention of the former government (Santos 2010–2018) is cleared when one addresses the bioeconomy as an engine to push development. However, it is not clear yet what will happen with the new government (Duque 2018–2022). The new president is closed to mining exploitation that is particularly opposite of sustainability in the Colombian case. Some universities are oriented to improve their standards and scientific production. Some industries recognize the importance of the sustainability and the opportunity of bioeconomy. There is a dialogue among them but the main actor is the government. The destiny of bioeconomy for the next 4 years depends on the new president and its real interest to develop local environments that is a very near topic of the agreements implementation of the peace treaty. The above it is not very close of the interest of president Duque
(2) With the advances that exist in the production of the bioeconomy in Colombia, is it possible through bioeconomy strategies to generate local economic development?
The technological advances are enough to motivate economic development, but the great challenge is to bring the knowledge, the tools, the budget and in general the conditions to the local environments
To turn the page of armed conflict, more opportunities are required especially for local environments. The first step is to build a new society that does not need technical tools from pure sciences but from social sciences. To advance in the rebirth of trust and re-create social capital as mainstay of the economy based on residual biomass

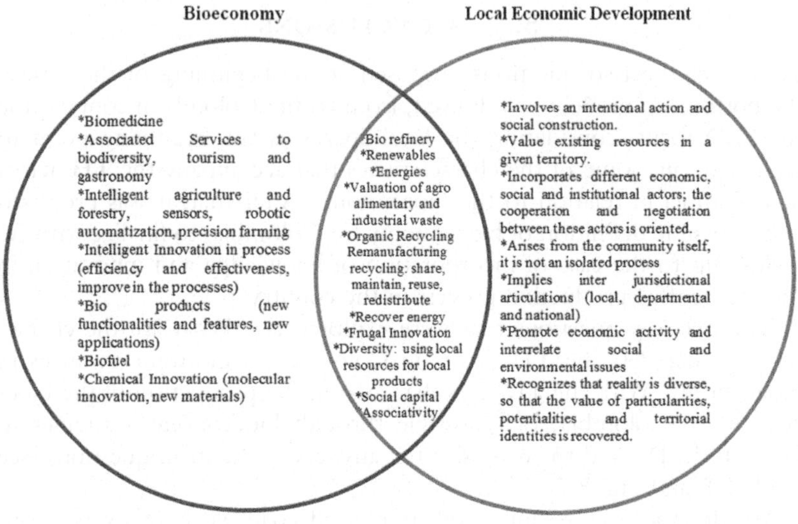

Fig. 5.7 Where the bioeconomy and the LED intersect

resources, the sciences must build the conditions to make good decisions. The economy based on the recovery of biomass is called to transform and integrate our views regarding the country.

Colombia has all the potential to enter the dynamics of bioeconomy and the application of biotechnology, to develop innovative processes, products, and services taking advantage of the benefits of biological and genetic resources and their derivatives, as well as residual biomass, to incorporate knowledge and innovation and generate opportunities for new business and economic progress (Biointropic et al., 2018, p. 22).

To have the enormous potential of bioeconomy in Colombia reaching the local environments, it is necessary to build bridges. The main one of them has to do with closing gaps, social, economic, and educational. It requires building the trust that an armed conflict of so much time has eroded. It is necessary to build bridges to consolidate associative models from social innovation, linked to models of financial innovation that facilitate access to economic resources in an environment of trust that allows this building of bridges and crossing to the other shore.

(i) The model of "frugal innovation or jugaad" propose by Navi Radjou is an interesting alternative that links social innovation with the market. Less value and high results. Master the art of doing more with less, the essence of frugal innovation, is about creating economic and social value using less resources. Not just, doing, but make it better.
(ii) Another interesting option is Cradle 2 Cradle C2C: Design, materials, and value, what materials. Just what could bring it back of Technical cycle: (i) Product use, (ii) Return, (iii) Disassemble, (iv) Manufacture.
(iii) It can be very important in the construction of bridges that in the local government programmes talk about the subject of bioeconomy and promote technical education in accordance with the context that facilitates the orientation towards this new outlook and way of understanding the social context, environmental, economic, productive, thinking about the possibility of appropriating local environments towards a new concept that recognizes the possible nuances of a tropical bioeconomy to enter more sophisticated market segments recognizing the particularities that bioeconomy "made in Colombia" can have.

Colombia suffers from lack of information in many of the indicators of bioeconomy; for example, the percentage of GDP affected, the number of projects financed, public spending on R and D, the number of communication strategies, the number of biotechnology companies operating in this sector, the number of patents and copyrights of the bioeconomic sector, the percentage of annual reduction of carbon emissions and the tons of biomass produced, among others. (...) it is important to build databases with up-to-date and pertinent information from the various aspects bioeconomy requires for future follow-ups (Biointropic et al., 2018, p. 30).

But taking into account Barkin "we cannot expect the experts to agree to define sustainable development or to commit Latin American nations to implement appropriate strategies. Facing the ecological contractions of the productive systems is an urgent need. Advances in our vision of sustainable development as an essential commitment to face the challenges of the survival of humanity have highlighted the importance of broad citizen participation in the improvement of democracy. The massive incorporation of grassroots social groups as an unavoidable step to establish economic strategies that include the conservation of the environment is one of the fundamental challenges of our time. For this reason, it is now essential to design policies that facilitate this incorporation as part of a work to reverse the growing polarization and promote sustainability" (Barkin, 2003, p. 169).

You will never have all the ideal conditions to start a change. At the beginning of this document, it was considered essential to recognize what were the necessary preconditions to achieve LED through bioeconomy, however, after broadening the perspective of the advances of bioeconomy in Colombia, recognizing it within the frame of LED, it can be considered that there is no time to wait, but many actions to undertake.

The path that should be taken to make bioeconomy a tool to generate LED starts from the local and should lead to the use of public resources for social benefit; the capture of political processes by hegemonic groups, in a Gramscian sense, so common in Latin America, diverts them to private ends at the expense of society and the planet, leading to a perverse resilience in which elites can continue with their devastating practices, as discussed in Barkin (2013). Collective action models (Ostrom, 2011) and cooperation offer mechanisms to counteract the betrayal of democratic discourse, but only apply to local societies, as demonstrated in numerous studies of these communities (e.g. Borrini-Feyerabend et al., 2007).

To end, it is important to say that the centralism and the concentration of power, investment, knowledge, and decisions are as well, one of the biggest challenges of the process to adapt bioeconomy to the regions and to make it able to drive LED. In that sense, according to Burbano (2018), there is a huge gap among the regions in Colombia. Bogota exceeds Boyacá Department by almost three times in S + T + I but there is a marked difference with respect to Vaupes Department. That is, Vaupes has a shortage, wherever you look for it, of postgraduate programmes, just as low coverage on the internet, among other indicators of the infrastructure dimension academic and research (...) 78.1% of the departments, making great efforts and focusing concrete actions to improve in S + T + I, it will be able to approach the current conditions of Bogotá, in a time approximate between 50 and 120 years.

An important step has already been taken. On July 10, 2018, the document CONPES 3934, Green Growth Policy, was approved, with five thematic axes: The first axis is aimed at generating new economic opportunities that allow diversifying the economy based on the production of goods and services grounded on the sustainable use of natural capital. The second axis seeks to improve the use of natural resources in economic sectors so that they are more efficient and productive, and reducing and minimizing the environmental and social impacts generated by the development of productive activities. The third axis promotes the generation and strengthening of human capital to face the new challenges of knowledge and experience generated by green growth. The fourth axis establishes strategic actions in science, technology, and innovation as a necessary tool to move towards changes in the productive sectors and find new processes, inputs, and more efficient technologies that generate added value to the national economy. The fifth axis outlines the actions to ensure coordination and interinstitutional articulation required for the implementation of this Policy, as well as the strengthening of the capacities for the generation of information necessary for decision-making in green growth and mechanisms for financing of sustainable projects.

Annex 1

Acronyms

ACOPI	Asociación Colombiana de Pequeños Industriales
AGROSAVIA	Corporación colombiana de investigación agropecuaria
ASOCAÑA	Association of sugarcane producers
ASOCOLFLORES	Colombian association of flower producers
BIOPACÍFICO	Parque Científico y Tecnológico
CAMACOL	Colombian Chamber of Construction
CENICAFE	National Coffee Research Center
CENIPALMA	Research center on palm
CENIVAM	Centro Nacional de Investigaciones para la Agroindustrialización de Especies Vegetales Aromáticas y Medicinas Tropicales
CIAT	Centro Internacional para la Agricultura Tropical
CONPES	Consejo Nacional de Política Económica y Social
CORPOGEN	Corporación CorpoGen
DANE	Departamento Administrativo Nacional de Estadística

DNP/NDP	Departamento Nacional de Planeación
FARC	Fuerzas Armadas Revolucionarias de Colombia
FEDEARROZ	Federation of rice producers
FEDEGAN	National federation of farmers
FEDEPALMA	National Federation of Oil Palm Growers
FEDEPANELA	Federation of producers of jaggery
FEDEPAPA	Federation of potato producers
FNC	Federación Nacional de Cafeteros
ICA	Instituto Colombiano Agropecuario
IDCBIS	Instituto Distrital de Ciencia, Biotecnología e Innovación en Salud
INVIMA	Instituto Nacional de Medicamentos y Alimentos
LED	Local Economic Development
OECD	Organisation for Economic Co-operation and Development
SAC	Colombian Farmers' Society
SiB	Biological Information System of Colombia
SPRU	Science Policy Research Unit from University of Sussex
TH	Triple Helix
TIPC	Transformative Innovation Policy Consortium
UDEA	Universidad de Antioquia
UNALUNAL	Universidad Nacional de Colombia
VINNOVA	Sweden's innovation agency

References

Aghón, G., Alburquerque, F., & Cortés, P. (2001). *Desarrollo económico local y descentralización en América Latina: análisis comparativo*. CEPAL/GTZ.

Alburquerque, F. (2004). *El Enfoque del Desarrollo Económico Local El Enfoque del Desarrollo Económico Local*. OIT.

Alonso, O. (2004). *La lógica de los actores y el desarrollo local*. http://www.scielo.org.ar/scielo.php?script=sci_arttext&pid=S1851-31232004000100004.

ANDI. (s.f.). *Cierre de brechas de innovación y tecnología*. http://www.andi.com.co/Uploads/Estudio%20Cierre%20de%20Brechas%20Innovacion%20y%20Tecnologia-ilovepdf-compressed.pdf.

Arbeláez, N. (2018). *Si Duque comprende que el conocimiento genera recursos, puede transformar el país*. http://lasillavacia.com/silla-academica/pontificia-universidad-javeriana/si-duque-comprende-que-el-conocimiento-genera#comment-210239.

Aristizabal, C. (2017). *Colombia Avanza hacia una política nacional de bioeconomia*. https://www.rutanmedellin.org/es/negocios/item/colombia-avanza-hacia-una-pol%C3%ADtica-nacional-de-bioeconom%C3%ADa.

Ascoli, C. (2006).*Reflexiones sobre el Desarrollo Local y Regional*. YRL-KFW.

Asocaña. (2018). *Informe Anual 2017–2018*. http://www.asocana.org/documentos/862018-E148DE81-00FF00,000A000,878787,C3C3C3,0F0F0F,B4B4B4,FF00FF,2D2D2D,A3C4B5.pdf.

Barkin, D. (2003). El desarrollo autónomo un camino a la sostenibilidad. en H. Alimonda (Ed.), *Ecología política Naturaleza, sociedad y utopía, Clacso, Primera reimpresión*. Buenos Aires.

Barkin, D. (2013). Viviendo el pacto fáustico. La resiliencia per- versa frente al cambio climático. *Veredas, 14*(27), 7–19.

Barkin, D., & Lemus, B. (2015). *Construyendo mundos pos-capitalistas*. Cultura y representaciones sociales, Año 10, núm. 19, México. http://www.scielo.org.mx/pdf/crs/v10n19/v10n19a2.pdf.

Betancur, C. (2017). *Bioeconomía y sectores potenciales en Colombia*. https://www.dnp.gov.co/Crecimiento-Verde/Documents/comite/sesion%206/BIOECONOM%C3%8DA%20Y%20SECTORES%20POTENCIALES%20EN%20COLOMBIA%2005122017.pdf.

Biointropic, (2018). *Bioeconomy as a source of new industries based on the natural capital of Colombia, phase II, Medellín*.

Biointropic, Silo, Eafit. (2018). *Estudio sobre la bioeconomia como fuente de nuevas industrias basadas en el capital natural de Colombia N.º 1240667, Fase I. Priorización de los sectores estratégicos de bioeconomia para Colombia*. https://www.dnp.gov.co/Crecimiento-Verde/Documents/ejes-tematicos/Bioeconomia/informe%201/1-INFORME%20BIOECONOMIA%20FASE%201%20FINAL%2024012018.pdf.

Bloomfield, G. (2018). *Schot delivers opening at colombia's unveiling of new national policy on transformative sti to meet the sdgs2018*. http://www.johanschot.com/news/colombia-unviels-transformative-innovation-policy-national-strategy-post-conflict-development/.

Borrini-Feyerabend, G., Pimbert, M., Farvar, T., Kothari, A., & Renard, Y. (2007). *Sharing power: Learning by doing in co-management of natural resources throughout the world. Sharing power: A global guide to collaborative management of natural resources*. IUCN and Earthscan.

Burbano, P. (2018). La incipiente influencia de la ciencia, tecnología e innovación,C+T+I, sobre el desarrollo territorial en Colombia. en *Apropiación, generación y uso edificador del conocimiento*. Cali, Ediciones REDIPE.

CEPAL. (2018). *Panorama social de América Latina*. https://repositorio.cepal.org/bitstream/handle/11362/42716/7/S1800002_es.pdf.

Colombia. (2016). *Acuerdo final para la terminación del conflicto y la construcción de una paz estable y duradera*. http://www.altocomisionadoparalapaz.gov.co/procesos-y-conversaciones/Documentos%20compartidos/24-11-2016NuevoAcuerdoFinal.pdf.

Colciencias. (2018). *Diagnóstico Programa Colombia Bio*. Colciencias.

DANE. (2017). *Información Pobreza monetaria 2017*. https://www.dane.gov.co/index.php/estadisticas-por-tema/pobreza-y-condiciones-de-vida/pobreza-y-desigualdad/pobreza-monetaria-y-multidimensional-en-colombia-2017.

DNP. (2018). *Documento Conpes 3934*. DNP.

DNP. (2019). Green Growth Policy Conpes Document 3934 of 2018 Executive Summary, Bogotá, DNP.

Ec.europa.eu. (2016). *Un manifiesto con los pilares de la bioeconomía del futuro para Europa*. disponible en: https://ec.europa.eu/environment/ecoap/about-eco-innovation/policies-matters/manifesto-maps-out-europes-future-bioeconomy_es.

El Espectador. (2018). *De cada 100 colombianos, 56 no completan la educación secundaria*. https://www.elespectador.com/noticias/educacion/de-cada-100-colombianos-56-no-completan-la-educacion-secundaria-articulo-740379.

Eltiempo.com. (2018). *En 2017 aumentó el abismo entre millonarios y pobres*. http://www.eltiempo.com/economia/sectores/desigualdad-aumento-en-el-2017-y-la-brecha-entre-ricos-y-pobres-175900.

Etzkowitz, H., & Leydesdorff, L. (1998, December). Triple Helix of innovation. *Science and Public Policy, 25*(6).

Evans, M., & Syrett, S. (2007). *Generating social capital?: The social economy and local economic development*. European Urban and Regional Studies

Fedepalma. (s.f.). *Innovación tecnológica: estrategias para la competitividad de la agroindustria de la palma de aceite en Colombia*. http://web.fedepalma.org/innovacion-tecnologica-estrategias-para-la-competitividad-de-la-agroindustria-de-la-palma-de-aceite-en-colombia.

Gallicchio, E. (2004). *El desarrollo local en América Latina. Estrategia Política basada en la construcción de capital social*. CLAEH.

Gallicchio, E. (2010). *El desarrollo local: ¿territorializar políticas o generar políticas territoriales? Reflexiones desde la práctica* (pp. 11–23). Eutopía.

German Bioeconomy Council. (2015). *Denmark*. https://biooekonomie.de/sites/default/files/danemark.pdf.

Gobierno de Colombia, (2019). *Misión de sabios*. https://minciencias.gov.co/sites/default/files/libro_mision_de_sabios_digital_1_2_0.pdf.

Heilbroner, R. (2000). *The worldly philosophers*. Penguin Books.

Herrera, J., Salas, L., Dominguez, G., & Torres, K. (2015, Julio–Diciembre) Parques científicos-tecnológicos y modelo triple-hélice. Situación del Caribe colombiano.*Entramado, 11*(2).

Hevia, E. (2003). *Planificación estratégica territorial y políticas públicas para el desarrollo local*. ILPES/CEPAL.

Hurtado, A. (2006). *Colombia: Estados Unidos con acceso a nuestros recursos genéticos*. http://www.biodiversidadla.org/Menu_Derecha/Prensa/Colombia_Estados_Unidos_con_acceso_a_nuestros_recursos_geneticos.

International Conference on Nanotechnology, *Renewable Materials Engineering & Environmental Engineering (ICNRMEEE) will be held in Berlin*, Germany during August 2nd, 2018.

Juarez, G. (2013). Revisión del concepto de desarrollo local desde una perspectiva territorial. *Revista Lider*, *23*, 9–28.

Lenis, D. (2017). *Educación colombiana más privada que pública*. https://www.las2orillas.co/educacion-colombiana-mas-privada-publica/.

NDP. (2018). Green growth policy CONPES document 3934 of 2018 executive summary.

Observatorio Colombiano de Ciencia y Tecnología. (2016). Línea base de indicadores I+D+i de TI : indicadores 2016. https://ocyt.org.co/wpcontent/uploads/2021/06/libro-indicadores-iditti.pdf.

OCDE. (2009). *The bioeconomy to 2030: Designing a policy agenda*.

Ostrom, E. (2011). *El gobierno de los bienes comunes. La evolución de las instituciones de acción colectiva*. Fondo de Cultura Económica.

OXFAM. (2018). *Informe anual 2016/2017 Latinoamérica y el caribe*. https://www.oxfam.org/es/peru-guatemala-honduras-ecuador-bolivia-colombia-el-salvador-republica-dominicana-haiti-mexico.

Piñeres, T. (2016). Paz y desarrollo rural: alianza entre universidad, Estado y sociedad (Vianí, Cundinamarca, Colombia). *Ingeciencia*, *1*(2).

PNUD. (2015). *Cómo le fue a Colombia con los Objetivos de Desarrollo del Milenio*. http://www.co.undp.org/content/colombia/es/home/presscenter/articles/2015/09/28/-c-mo-le-fue-a-colombia-con-los-odm-.html.

Portafolio.co. (2018). *La pobreza monetaria en Colombia bajo en 2017 a 26,9*. http://www.portafolio.co/economia/la-pobreza-en-colombia-bajo-en-2017-515460.

Presidencia.gov.co. (2016). *Colombia no fumigará más los cultivos ilícitos, anunció el Presidente Santos*. http://es.presidencia.gov.co/noticia/160914-Colombia-no-fumigara-mas-los-cultivos-ilicitos-anuncio-el-Presidente-Santos.

Radjou, N., & Prabhu, J. (2015). *Frugal innovation* (p. 15). Profile books Ltd.

Rojas, H. (2007). *Made in the world is better*. http://www.redalyc.org/pdf/909/90915105.pdf.

Rojas, H. (2015). Comercio no ayuda, Los retos del comercio justo en el escenario de la Cooperación Sur-Sur. en *Cuando el Sur piensa el Sur*. Universidad Externado de Colombia.

SiB. (2018). *Colombia*, SiB. Obtenido de https://www.sibcolombia.net.

Silva, G. (2009). *Palabras del gerente general de la Federación de Cafeteros de Colombia, Congreso Extraordinario.* Bogotá

Trigilia, C. (2001). *Social capital and local development. European Journal of Social Theory, 4* (4).

University of Sussex—COLCIENCIAS. (2018). *Orientaciones para la formulación de políticas regionales de innovación transformativa en Colombia.* http://tipconsortium.net/wp-content/uploads/2018/07/Orientaciones-formulacion-politicas_defweb.pdf.

UPRA. (2018). Plan de acción institucional versión 2. https://www.upra.gov.co/documents/10184/75586/Plan+de+Accion+2018+V3+%2815082018%29.pdf/b8603db4-a55c-47a0-a2dd-e351120c3401.

Vázquez, A. (2007). *Desarrollo endógeno. Teorías y políticas de desarrollo territorial Investigaciones Regionales,* núm. 11, pp. 183–210. Asociación Española de Ciencia Regional.

Villaveces, J., & Orozco, L. (2015). *Colombia,* En: Barro, S, La transferencia de I+D, la innovación y el emprendimiento en las universidades, Educación Superior en Iberoamérica, Informe 2015.

CHAPTER 6

Sharing Economies and Digital Platforms: Between Access and Social Inclusion in Colombia

John Alirio Sanabria and Luis Antonio Orozco

6.1 Introduction

Many policies have been promoted to increase access to ICT as a means of social inclusion that creates tension in the multilevel governance process, as shown in the case of the national-territorial coordination around the eLAC agenda (Orozco et al., 2019). Moreover, little progress has been made in terms of coordination between the national and territorial governments around ICT in science, technology, and innovation (Orozco et al., 2020). There is evidence of success cases where, relying on research and development processes, ICT have facilitated access to market

J. A. Sanabria (✉) · L. A. Orozco
School of Management, Universidad Externado de Colombia, Bogota, Colombia

L. A. Orozco
e-mail: luis.orozco@uexternado.edu.co

L. A. Orozco et al. (eds.), *Science, Technology, and Higher Education*, Palgrave Studies in Democracy, Innovation, and Entrepreneurship for Growth,
https://doi.org/10.1007/978-3-030-80720-7_6

mechanisms, thereby enabling social inclusion, as seen in scenarios that occur in the context of heterodox economics—such as sharing economies (Sanabria & Ruiz, 2018). ICT themselves do not lead to inclusion since access can be confused with the development of abilities—especially in science—for mastering technology in a way that creates inclusion. It is necessary to develop reflective abilities and attain lessons where the efforts of multiple social agents are centered on the exploration and exploitation of knowledge (March, 1991) to facilitate technological governance and the distribution of power. Thus, in the spirit of a sharing economy, it is possible to foster exchanges that empower communities through the joint use and development of technology, leading to its mastery and preventing the centralization of power and the emergence of new exclusion mechanisms.

This chapter presents a conceptual framework for social inclusion and to explain how ICT have been incorporated into the emergence, operations, and practices of organizations via the logic of collaboration to present a critical assessment of seven cases in Colombia based on interviews that were conducted as part of doctoral research on organizational growth in sharing economies by the first author with advice from the second author. The chapter ends with reflections on new opportunities and paths toward inclusion that do not depend on centralized governance processes but, instead, face the challenge of overcoming the kind of mere access to markets that do not promote the emergence of participatory citizens with the potential to grow and close the social gap.

6.2 Inclusion and Social Exclusion

Social exclusion is one of the greatest challenges faced by emergent—particularly Latin-American—economies and it translates into political, economic, social, and cultural issues (Puyana, 2018) marked by the lack of access to participation mechanisms. This leads not only to poverty but to a proliferation of illegal economies and organized crime. In Colombia, social exclusion is much more intense than in other neighboring countries, and it is not a historical problem, but an ongoing one. Even amid the pandemic, Transparency International raised alarm over the excessive concentration of power in the Presidency to the detriment of other democratic instances (Dinero, 2020).

In the context of political science, social exclusion refers to the situation where an individual living in a society cannot participate in normal citizen activities in terms of consumption, saving, production, political participation, and social interaction among groups of family, friends, and culturally related communities (Selwyn, 2002). From a sociological perspective, these people are what Bauman, (2011, p. 3) calls the underclass, "a congregation of individuals who, unlike the rest of the population, do not belong to any class – and so in fact do not belong to society." Technology constitutes a social exclusion mechanism insofar as it is monopolized by an elite that manages to exercise power above others through ideological domination (Habermas et al., 1984).

Social exclusion is seen in data handling because it coerces the decisions of economic actors within a society based on how limited their access to information is. Limited access to information hinders the ability of the governed to understand and evaluate the policies that are implemented by the governors; the state's ability to regulate dominating banks and corporations, protect the environment or manage innovation; and investors' control over the uses of their investments. It also posits challenges in managing interpersonal relationships and even our relationships with ourselves (Tirole, 2017). This leads to situations such as the concentration of power, lack of housing, insufficient or irrelevant education, social mobility stagnation, high education costs, pensions deficits, spikes in public debt, and environmental problems (Tirole, 2017) that especially affect the vulnerable population.[1]

According to Rivera and Calva (2015), the concept of inclusion emerged in the'90s. It was initially applied in education in the International UNESCO forum held in Thailand (in 1990) as a response to the different characteristics of the population in the search for social and individual well-being and within the formal system. It was later expanded to include the search for equity, the removal of differences, and the improvement in living conditions (Rivera & Calva, 2015). Thus, social inclusion can be defined as:

> The process of change that ensures that all people, families, communities, and even regions have the same real and effective opportunities to access, participation, relationships as well as the social, economic, political, and

[1] Vulnerable populations are groups of people (women, girls, farmers, ethnic groups, people with disabilities, people who have been displaced, victims of armed conflict, and frontier inhabitants) that are unsafe or incapable in the face of psychological, physical, mental, social, economic, political, and/or cultural threats (Muñoz, 2018, p. 287).

> cultural enjoyment together with the rest of citizens without limitation or restriction. (Muñoz, 2018, p. 286)

And social exclusion is defined as:

> A multidimensional phenomenon that expresses the situation of a fragmented, dual society characterized by the negation or inobservance of a group's social, economic, political, and cultural rights. This situation is rooted in the State's ineffectiveness in guaranteeing society's basic rights and reflects a rupture in social cohesion—which is a critical element in democracy and the development of citizenship. (Muñoz, 2018, p. 286)

Hence, inclusion is a multidimensional phenomenon that can have factual references of various kinds that go from access to labor, production, and educational systems to those that dignify citizens through the fulfillment of needs such as food and security (Acevedo & Martinez, 2016; Contreras et al., 2015; Domínguez & Rama, 2012; Maestre et al., 2019; Pérez & Titelman, 2018).

6.3 ICTs as Mechanisms of Social Inclusion

ICT are considered a viable option toward social inclusion since "multimedia and online environments can be adapted in a versatile, dynamic and interactive way to the needs of communities to mediatize knowledge in a scenario of information globalization" (Builes, 2016, p. 127). Thus, ICT help consolidates digital identities by overcoming geographic limits and allowing for the social and political construction of communities, and, as a result, facilitating communication in terms of time and process outreach, relating common interests, fostering values, cooperation, equity, and supporting the definition of priorities for community work (Builes, 2016).

ICT can be viewed as an actor able to reassemble the social relationships and mediated the power in the socioeconomic transactions (Latour, 2005). Then, in the frame of digital technologies that incorporated algorisms to create artificial intelligence capacities' to perform autonomous decisions, the platforms can define who is included or marginalized from the possibilities to work, for example. The platforms can act as a new boss, as Taylorism promoted by rigid supervisors, but without any human consideration to the people behind the algorisms (Sanabria & Orozco, 2021).

The rapid development of ICT has motivated political, economic, and social transformations on a planetary scale; and, though ICT were expected to close the digital gap,[2] in some cases they have widened it (Rueda & Franco-Avellaneda, 2018). Exclusive inclusion situations lead to greater coverage through technological tools but also to a decrease in permanence and failure in terms of learning adjustments to conduct processes and improve relationships with users (Cubillos, 2018; Yu et al., 2018).

This kind of digital inclusion is oriented toward fostering digital literacy, the development of information processing tools, the ability to identify, access, manage, integrate, evaluate, analyze and synthesize digital resources, develop a subcultural behavior and a personal attitude, gain access to bandwidth connections, hardware, software, and relevant content and services. It also comprises actions oriented toward learning how to use these tools and access jobs, education, public services for marginalized people, social and citizenship activities, and the ability to create media expressions and communicate with others in specific situations (Ramirez & Sepúlveda, 2018). The *e-inclusion* approach, as defined by the European community (the eEurope Initiative), posits that these skills allow people to fully participate in an information society—in all the knowledge-based social and economic dimensions through ICT—thereby controlling their destiny using resources and seizing opportunities that are amplified by technology (Yu et al., 2018).

Certainly, this form of inclusion has various challenges in terms of access, motivation, resources, and forces that have been identified and described by Yu et al. (2018) based on research regarding Chinese migrants. These challenges pertain to the material, cognitive, motivational, and social access that demand change to facilitate attainment (Turlea et al., 2011; Yu et al., 2018); said challenges depend on the availability of financial, material, cognitive, educational, psychological and

[2] The digital gap is a binary disparity between those who have physical access to the internet, digital devices, bandwidth connections and other information technologies and those who do not (Yu et al., 2018). This disparity is seen also in the consumption and production of content, interactions, information availability, as well as social differences in skills, abilities, population age, and gender that affect the desirable development that could be attained through an efficient use of ICT (Cabero-Almenara & Ruiz-Palmero, 2017; Cubillos, 2018).

interpersonal resources, as well as ideological, industrial, public administration, communal, and personal forces that are related to the interests of decisionmakers and institutions in charge of inclusion (Yu et al., 2018).

In inclusive education processes, ICT are recognized for their potential to improve the living conditions of historically marginalized groups (Cabero-Almenara & Ruiz-Palmero, 2017; Watts & Luz, 2017). According to UNESCO, "ICT contribute to universal access to education and equality in education, teaching, quality learning, the professional development of educators (…) and management, leadership and administration" (Rivera & Calva, 2015).

Regarding labor, ICT have been incorporated through alternative options such as telework—and the laws that promote it (Contreras et al., 2015)—whose presence has been massified during the COVID-19 crisis of 2020. In terms of financial inclusion, ICT allow for information access and more work and education opportunities (Rivera & Calva, 2015). Likewise, ICT are used to promote associativity, thereby fostering business inclusion (Arias & Rendón, 2015).

However, as a mechanism of inclusion, ICT have the important challenge of overcoming access gaps to foster the ability of communities to dominate technology and empower them in sharing activities to prevent an organization—such as Uber (Acquier, 2018)—from centralizing technology, thereby giving rise to new forms of exclusive inclusion via the monopolization of decisions regarding fees, prices, and employment conditions.

In a context where private property and exclusive models have been widely criticized for hindering innovation, new business models have arisen through the use of technological advances. These models are integrated into trends of open innovation and the development of digital platforms, based on the principles of collaboration and free access, gathering together enterprises, people, and organizations such as universities and laboratories that are voluntarily linked to complementary ecosystems to deal with common objectives and create value for users (Nambisan et al., 2018).

This process facilitates social inclusion, since the proposals that arise in it respond directly to the social, economic, and environmental needs of communities in various regions, allowing them to appropriate technologies to create and solve their problems, thus creating social value (Orozco et al., 2012). A clear example—aside from those that abound in poverty and social vulnerability scenarios—can be found in the media that have migrated to online platforms, creating a new business model that reaches a wider audience and has variable costs. This new model has enabled those who have been traditionally excluded by print media to access information and interact with other users through digital communities—as seen in the use and development of videoblogs (vlogs) (Crawford-Visbal et al., 2018).

There is a series of problems related to social inequality, inequity, unemployment, labor informality, irrelevant education, social mobility blockages, criticism of how power is used, the recognition of humankind's new visions, criticism of enterprise networks in terms of their impact on the alienation of communities, high levels of debt and wealth accumulation, excessive consumerism, as well as social, financial, value, and environmental crises brought about by the capitalist system (Buenadicha et al., 2017; Mendes & Giménez, 2015; Ostrom, 2000; Ramis, 2017; Tirole, 2017).

Various organizational initiatives have emerged to address these problems from a logic of the common good[3] while staying away from the public–private debate (Ramis, 2017). Such initiatives are framed within so-called sharing economies[4] (Buenadicha et al, 2017) that help create networks of small enterprises or individuals that capitalize on the transformation of local communities through the development of abilities to overcome market shortcomings using ICT, looking for socioeconomic inclusion, self-sufficiency, and the efficient use of scarce resources by reducing access costs to economic dynamics (Buenadicha et al., 2017).

These sharing economy organizations take up traditional community practices based on sharing and exchanging (Sundararajan, 2016),

[3] This line of thinking emerged in the face of various social movements in favor of justice and equity, such as the struggles and debates regarding the use of seeds in Mumbai (2004), the access to water in Cochabamba (2000), free and public education in Chile (2011), property rights in the United States (2011), the protection of natural parks in Istanbul (2013), and the defense of housing against commerce in Burgos, Spain (2014). These movements do not claim things, they call for rights, capabilities, and life choices. Uncared for by legal reason, they entail what Adela Cortina (1998) calls "appropriation of possibilities."

[4] "Sharing economy" is an umbrella term that groups terms as diverse as sharing consumption, the maker movement, peer production, participatory finance, capital distribution, open and sharing knowledge, the exchange of goods, services or productive assets, timeshare, gig economy, peer economy, new economy, sharing economy, access economy, on demand economy, and disaggregate economy (Bostman, 2019).

incorporating concepts such as innovation communities, practice communities, and mediation communities, as well as markets based on multiple segments and multiple ways of creating value, removing intermediaries and reducing operating costs through economies of scale in markets and providing access to historically marginalized groups (Castor, 2016).

They also include flexible and automatized production processes with organizational structures that comprise prosumers (consumers and producers) and self-control logics (Stępnicka & Wiączek, 2018), with little state intervention, where control is mediated by algorithms and technology (Acquier, 2018; Karatzogianni, 2018), bringing together social responsibility practices, sustainability principles, and energy efficiency (Bocken et al., 2014). Furthermore, they are oriented toward productive transformation processes and they dynamize social change (Goñi, 2012), expanding from the logic of network externalities with mid- and long-term investment returns (Cerro et al., 2005).

Due to rapid expansion, some of the organizations that emerged in the context of sharing economies have turned into global mega-corporations that, far from promoting social well-being, are accused of increasing inequality and work precarity. Such mega-corporations follow the logic of reducing costs and increasing profit for entrepreneurs and stakeholders, transferring their responsibility to third parties by taking advantage of anonymity and legal voids to create jobs that contribute to new forms of labor exploitation (Karatzogianni, 2018; Rinne, 2019). Organizations that create income opportunities for many people through the use of algorithms and ICT platforms are not necessarily bound to the logic of sharing economies where the property is shared, power is distributed and no corporation monopolizes technology or uses it as a means to dominate asymmetrical relationships between those involved in business activity. Such is the case of Uber (globally) and Rappi (in Latin-America), which, despite being created under the logic of sharing economies, have gradually turned to an excessive concentration of power while neglecting the wellbeing of their participants due to the way they handle hiring frameworks and civil responsibilities (Lendrys & Crawford-Visbal, 2018). These mega-corporations engage in labor exploitation and unfair competition. Thus, far from creating opportunities, they hinder social inclusion and shape the regulations that protect them from the masses that they recruit for their services following a logic of exclusion that removes access to the democratic development possibilities that lie in technologies (Ramis, 2017). Another risk arising from these platforms is that, given the growing number of workers that accept such business model, some chains that regulate the market without state intervention have emerged; and they resort to fear of being excluded from the system as a device of control, since, in cases where there is no physical structure—because everything is done through digital platforms—there is a risk of getting disconnected at any moment. Furthermore, those who are opportunistic can abuse others' assets (Karatzogianni, 2018).

However, it is interesting to note that even though those who participate in these models understand the inappropriate conditions and partake in them based on a logic of cash income, they already go by a logic of collaboration and have organized themselves in groups to defend their interests. Such is the case of organizations of workers on-demand as *Peers.org* and *Freelancers Union*, among others, who have undertaken the task of proposing inclusion alternatives as well as regulatory models that help new organizations and create good work practices, urging on-demand enterprises to make changes in the relationships with autonomous workers toward prioritizing stability, flexibility, transparency, fair wages, shared prosperity, inclusion, and access to supplies (Rohman, 2016).

This chapter intends to showcase the difference between access and inclusion from the perspective of sharing economy initiatives where diverse parties that intervene in the process of creating value participate in the development of capabilities and the attainment of technological control. Thus, we want to see how these cases overcome access problems and allow for inclusion, as seen in the following example. In the state of Texas, Uber shutdown its operations in 2016 due to disagreements with the local government. A community of 36,000 drivers moved their operations network to Facebook, thereby gaining not only control over the business model but also over the technology to operate it. This allowed them to bypass the barriers to access social inclusion. This community eventually developed its own decentralized, shared-ownership app called ArcadeCity, building innovation in the context of a sharing economy (Stocker & Stephens, 2019).

Case analysis serves the purpose of contributing to policy reflections to create regulations and governance systems that facilitate social inclusion and allow for the emergence of monopolizing corporations that dominate new markets. In this sense, countries with high rates of labor exploitation like China are working on social regulation to standardize new economies and tackle societal issues by capitalizing on the momentum gained by digital initiatives in the market to foster social inclusion—signaling a healthy market through a flexible regulatory environment (under the *regulatory sandbox* concept) (Yudong & Ying, 2019). In 2015, the European Union launched a committee to analyze the impact of sharing economies and called for the definition of a public policy agenda that does not hinder the development of sharing economies while fostering economic growth, job creation, and the development of the European Union (Pacheco, 2016). What follows is an outlook of sharing economies in Colombia.

6.4 The Emergence of Collaborative Economy Initiatives and Their Impact on Social Inclusion: Some Colombian Cases

In Colombia, inclusion has been sought through ICT as a means to repair the social fabric and promote the development of remote rural communities, towns, and villages that have little access to market systems and the institutionalized formalities of the economy through the creation of digital communities, virtual education, and social networks that boost connectivity and foster social development with equity (Builes, 2016). Some strategies for ICT-based social inclusion are included in Table 6.1.

One of the most successful strategies was the creation of "Vive Digital" kiosks, which are places that seek to "facilitate the means so that rural or remote populations (from towns and villages) have access to ICT" (Builes, 2016, p. 129). This strategy aimed to foster digital literacy and improve access to digital tools and was present in 100% of Colombia's municipalities through a network of 900 Vive Digital spots, 7,000 Vive Digital kiosks, and one thousand free wi-fi zones (Crawford-Visbal et al., 2018). However, even though the strategy improved connectivity, it has not had important results in community use and appropriation of ICT as a means to develop economic initiatives (Davila, 2017). In terms of educational inclusion, the key social barriers that have been identified are unemployment and low family income, overcrowding, sub-normal settlements, segregation of ethnic minorities, high cost of public utilities, child labor, insecurity, social, and domestic violence, gender inequality, low basic healthcare coverage, difficulty in owning their own homes, etc. (Domínguez & Rama, 2012). To face these obstacles, social responsibility has been promoted in schools through inclusive and virtual education programs—which constituted a key point in the peace agreement with

Table 6.1 ICT-related programs for social inclusion in Colombia

Year	*Program*
1994	National Science and Technology Policy for using ICT in education and science
1999	Compartel Program to provide community telephones in areas without basic phone service Computers for Education Program—within the "Vive Digital" initiative—where enterprises donate technological equipment for the Government to give it to public education institutions around the country
2000	Digital Connectivity Agenda within the National Council of Economic and Social Policy, with six implementation areas: (1) Access to information infrastructure; (2) Use of ICT in education and training programs; (3) Online enterprises; (4) Promotion of investment in the ICT sector; (5) Content creation; and (6) Electronic government Compartel Program to provide community internet services in areas without internet coverage
2002	Programs for reducing the digital gap through the social telecommunications policy
2006	Orientation toward social inclusion and recognition of ICT as crucial in the development of the country
2007	Bicentennial Colombia Plan: 2019, which proposes building adequate infrastructure for development
2008	National ICT Plan
2009	Creation of the Ministry of Information and Communications Technology (MinTIC) to promote the use of ICT and transform the National Science and Technology System by incorporating the element of innovation
2010	Outline of an inclusion policy Library Network with 1,329 areas that provide internet access and digital literacy The Connectivity Agenda was redefined to improve the relationship between citizens and government agencies
2012	Outline of the Online Government strategy Creation of open resources for digital education ICT become an education subject in the context of the Computers for Education Program
2013	Credits for technology transfers in basic and higher education ICT for education are strengthened

Source Adapted from Cubillos (2018)

Fuezas Armadas de Colombia—FARC—to engage a greater number of vulnerable population groups (Muñoz, 2018).

Virtual education programs have had an increasing demand. 426 programs in 2020 cover 7% of higher education students, up from 6,477 new students in 2011 to 82,688 in 2018 (Laboratorio de Economía de la Educación—LEE, 2020).

6.4.1 Case Analyzes

Sharing economies have grown in recent years in Colombia as a result of a series of actions led by entities such as Sharecollab, which, through the Connecting the Dots[5] program seeks to promote sharing culture as a viable development option for the country. This connection platform began its operations in Colombia in 2014 and—by 2020—has 300 registered organizations, of which 58 are sharing enterprises. Sharing entrepreneurs find in Sharecollab a place to meet and support one another by having a registry, but there is also room for support and acceleration that helps those who only have a business idea to materialize it.

In cities like Medellin, the sharing economy trend is spearheaded by citizens as a response to the need to save money, have an income source, find new jobs, gain social inclusion, or even as an environmental initiative—according to former mayor Federico Gutierrez. Medellin has one of the most salient sharing economy initiatives with state participation, the EnCicla program that was launched in 2011 as a public transportation system with bicycles for shared use. By 2016, EnCicla accounted for 52,000 monthly bicycle trips (BID, 2016).

6.4.2 Rappi

The most well-known sharing enterprise in Colombia, Rappi was created by Sebastian Mejia, Felipe Villamarin, Guillermo Plaza, and Simon Borrero—the current CEO. Rappi is known as the first Colombian unicorn because it received a billion-dollar investment from Scotiabank (Ojeda, 2018).

Rappi is an app that connects couriers and delivery persons with local businesses and end consumers. It offers people access—through technological means—to different ways of buying products, send items, make payments, run errands, and transfer money via a network of "rappitenderos" (Crawford-Visbal et al., 2018). Rappi works in the following way:

[5] A program led by ShareCollab to promote sharing economies in Colombia.

the app receives the user's order and creates a service offer for rappitenderos—which they can accept or reject—and then programs their routes using a georeferencing system that optimizes their work time, for which they receive payment. Local businesses and small enterprises are given options to work through e-commerce, thereby widening their business possibilities without having to invest in their own logistics and delivery workforce. Rappi is characterized by constant innovation and portfolio diversification, as evidenced by the fact that it currently offers financial services to users that have no credit history (Dinero, 2019).

Rappi has become a source of income for over 50,000 rappitenderos and constitutes an option that responds to Colombia's high unemployment rate and the high number of Venezuelan immigrants (Dinero, 2019) without requiring permanence contracts and promising a quick and efficient source of income, with no access restrictions, so it is a viable option for students and people who are looking for a side job (Crawford-Visbal et al., 2018). This kind of inclusion allowed Rappi to organize an informal market that already existed in Colombia and worked precariously with local businesses, receiving daily wages based on the number of delivered services (Dinero, 2019). This constitutes a potential contribution to the governance of said market since it could provide the government with key data to build a policy for helping vulnerable population groups that find in this activity a promise of social inclusion.

However, the employment conditions are precarious given that workers do not have employment contracts, the actual income does not match the promised amounts, couriers have to cover the initial cost of their work equipment and they are the ones who assume all of the operating risks—even though they are not insured—under penalty of being excluded from the app (Crawford-Visbal et al., 2018; Santos, 2017).

This business model allows for technological access—but no mastery of it—without promoting the development of capabilities and without offering fair employment conditions. Additionally, Rappi was the subject of over 750,000 complaints between 2017 and 2019 due to overcharges, delays, delivery failures, customer rights abuses, false advertising, abusive clauses, right of withdrawal violations, payment issues, and e-commerce quality controversies that have led to sanctions (Superintendencia de Sociedades, 2019).

In addition to the complaints, the core problem with Rappi has to do with value creation—which is absent in the use of the app since the conditions for the businesspeople that sold their products in person and now sell them through the application have not improved aside from reaching new markets. Rappi benefits from the way it captures and handles data from users and rappitenderos, exploiting the real economy but using technology that allows it to be more efficient than traditional production units in terms of time and response capabilities (Dinero, 2019). However, those benefits do not extend to the community. Rappi reported 238 million pesos in corporate losses (La República, 2019) which gave it tax benefits—while there is no clarity about the remuneration of its owners and executives.

In sum, though Rappi began its operations under the sharing economy model, it gradually turned into a corporation, not unlike Uber, which limits its offer of technological inclusive access to the environment's workforce and resources without offering distribution of benefits, while centralizing decision-making, price controls, and data handling. This evidences a process of exclusive inclusion that Mazucatto has described as "socializing the risk of innovation while privatizing rewards" (Dinero, 2019).

6.4.3 5Bogota[6]

5Bogota was created in 2013 as a result of the experience of cities where tourism is much more advanced than in Colombia. The goal of the enterprise is to do tourism with locals through applications that allow the tourist to know—through guided tours—the city's non-conventional places, led by a guide that helps penetrate the capital city's history and immaterial heritage, creating an experience with valuable memories. The current proposal includes tours for creating, learning, cooking, dancing, and appreciating architecture, graffiti, etc. Tours are adjusted to the tourists' tastes and expectations.

The team comprises two people and approximately 15 hosts that are hired for each tour. These hosts are natural people that have a history, are empathetic, and are interested in knowing and relating to people from other cultures. There are artists, dancers, and professionals among them. Through their personal history, they share their vision of the city with the tourists while catering to their interests. Hosts are required to be fluent in English to properly communicate with the tourists.

[6] August 6th of 2020 interview with the owner, Diana Zuluaga.

This opportunity allowed hosts to quit their former jobs and devote themselves to touring since they have a better income, tranquility, enjoyment, and the chance to know and interact with people from other cultures. Besides, they have work schedule freedom since they do not work more than thre days a week.

5Bogota is linked with five tourism agencies that share the same development vision and promote it around the world. They also use Airbnb as a promotional platform and their services can be accessed from Airbnb's website. By 2020, 5Bogota received on average 30–40 people a week, with the corresponding social effect that these visits can have since each tourist is estimated to visit around 10 businesses during a tour, which generates 400 impacts per week.

One of the company's main objectives is to benefit small and local businesses that are outside the tourist circuit and which would otherwise be unable to connect to the tourism chain. The guiding principles are fair prices and fair income distribution. This initiative represents a direct form of social inclusion in entrepreneurial and cultural terms.

6.4.4 *Agrapp*[7]

Agrapp is an online platform for financing the agriculture sector in Colombia. Created in 2018, it helps small and medium-sized agricultural enterprises to get in contact with individuals who can invest anywhere from one million pesos to support a farming business with up to 75% of the total required investment. This model allows people who have been traditionally excluded from the financial sector—due to not meeting the minimum access criteria—to be included in an alternate financial model. Likewise, this model allows people who are interested in investing—but have no experience or large sums—to join entrepreneurial processes only by providing financial means and have the opportunity to increase their income.

The enterprise's operations imply providing technical and financial support to farmers as well as professional assistance and guaranteed commercialization of their products. Investors have access through the platform, where the interested party selects a project and a rural businessperson to support. The investor confirms their choice and receives a

[7] June 9th of 2020 interview with owner David Duarte.

call from a business representative that explains in detail the investment conditions and arranges for the signing of the corresponding contracts. As to the trade routes, the business is connected to exports companies that handle this part of the business. In its first two years, Agrapp has secured investments of over 500 million pesos to support over 19 rural businesses while connecting over 72 investors.

In terms of inclusion, it is clear that Agrapp connects small rural entrepreneurs that have been traditionally excluded from business models, facilitates their growth, and improves their opportunities. The entry requirements are having at least half a hectare of land (owned or rented), experience in growing exotic fruits, not having a negative credit history—though it is not necessary to have a bank account. Farmers also need to provide some local references, receive a visit from Agrapp representatives for an assessment of the project, soil analysis, and improvement suggestions that are uploaded to the app as relevant information for investors. Agrapp allows agriculture businesses to access certain benefits since trade processes and client-supplier relationships are consolidated there. Thus, Agrapp represents farmers so they can access better prices per volume and increase their knowledge about techniques and processes. Likewise, Agrapp connects urban dwellers that wish to participate in rural processes without having to travel or having to rely on logistics capabilities. In the medium term, farmers are expected to be the ones to upload the information about their crops on the app—after receiving the advisors' approval—but it will take some time for them to learn how to do it properly.

The analyzes conducted through machine learning of data that have been gathered for over four years and 150 thousand records on regional behavior give access to specialized knowledge that is shared with federations, associations, and banks to support the use of Agrapp and improve the operations, which can inform governance processes in the territories. With this information, public sector actors and associations can identify the needs of agriculture businesses and communities, in general, to build policies and develop support initiatives.

6.4.5 *Amazoniko*[8]

Amazoniko is an online recycling sharing platform created in 2017 that operates in Bogota by connecting relevant actors in the recycling chain to give a new life to residues and mitigate environmental harm.

Households that are registered on the platform receive a recycling kit, two labeled bags, and a user manual; then they are connected to recyclers who sort through the recyclable items and evaluate their quality. Households are then given a score on the app based on the materials they give. This score translates into points that can be exchanged in a marketplace that gathers other connected actors which are businesses that have decided to support environmental care.

Aside from offering a more efficient way for recyclers to access valuable materials, the app makes their operations more efficient since critical routes are created based on the information entered by households on the platform—so recyclers get a notification when the bags are ready to be collected. The recyclable materials are then sorted out and taken to recycling industries.

In terms of inclusion, Amazoniko allows recyclers to dignify their work, since data analysis and the use of technology helps them refine their processes and create more efficient bonds with companies, creating trust-based relationships and strengthening the social fabric with households. There are currently 2,160 households and over 8,000 collections have been made. Amazoniko works with three recyclers associations, 14 partners in the marketplace, and over 60 tons of recyclable materials have been processed by recycling companies. Moreover, Amazoniko has taken up the role of sustainability advisor to companies that wish to implement recycling campaigns.

6.4.6 *Ecobot*[9]

Ecobot was created in 2016 as a green company—dealing with environmental issues—to promote responsible consumption habits through machines called "ecobots" where individuals can toss plastic bottles and receive in return a ticket with points that can be exchanged for groceries

[8] June 9th of 2020 interview with the founder, Daniel Rodriguez.

[9] August 5th interview with owner Lina Aramburo.

at sponsoring stores. Ecobot was created to incentivize recycling in Colombia—where only 17% of waste is recycled.

Its business model connects at least four actors: users who receive a discount when recycling; enterprises that function as "eco-partners" and contribute through advertising or renting ecobots, following a strategy of cause marketing; enterprises or institutions that provide space for ecobots in their premises; and communities of recyclers that receive the items recycled by the ecobots to be processed.

So far, 2 million plastic bottles have been collected using 70 machines that are located in highly crowded areas in 6 cities. The project has had an impact in terms of recycling culture on up to 148,000 people in shopping centers and institutions. The initiative has also been established as a social program in regions such as Tulua, where the community was given points that could be exchanged for rewards to promote the recycling culture. However, in such cases, there is a direct dependency on sponsors that is not sustainable.

In terms of inclusion, Ecobot promotes a social cause that is of community interest and connects users with recyclers and enterprises. It offers recyclers an organized way to access useful materials, given that the ecobots are linked to an app that shows a message notifying the right moment to collect the recyclable materials, thereby maximizing economic benefits, dignifying the work or recyclers, and promoting the development of technological capabilities as a means to improve their work and obtain better results.

6.4.7 *Entregalo.co*[10]

Entregalo.co is a logistics app that specializes in e-commerce using product storage technology and last-mile delivery with the promise of same-day delivery in domestic commerce.

The operations were focused on e-commerce enterprises. However, the national lockdown led Entregalo.co to work with small enterprises, thereby giving access to many business people who had been excluded from this business model due to lack of knowledge about how to use the tools or lack of interest in their implementation. As a result, a strategy was launched to help these businesspeople by contributing to their learning

[10] June 10th of 2020 interview with owner Andrés Triana.

and providing them with data analysis—since the app is designed to analyze trends, frequencies, and other market aspects.

Their data analysis shows that 80% of traditional e-commerce network users do not have entrepreneurial education, they only buy and sell products without knowing how to measure results. Moreover, when their operations increase, they tend to get scared because they do not know how to respond from a logistics perspective. Therefore, Entregalo.co offers its expertise so enterprises can consolidate their operations and measure their numbers, define their market targets according to their results, and avoid being excluded from efficient e-commerce business models, thereby empowering business people to develop managerial capabilities.

Entregalo.co operates in Bogota, Medellin, Bucaramanga, and Cali with logistics centers—but it has nationwide shipping coverage. Entregalo.co hires couriers that specialize in package pickup and delivery. These couriers, who act as messengers that participate in projects, are linked to the company through a contract or a closed sharing model. Projects involve delivering packages to a specific location within a specified time-frame, and couriers are only contacted upon demand so that they can spend their free time on other activities. Couriers are paid per each task they complete—and they can make more money than messengers that are hired directly by shipping companies. Entregalo.co has gathered together small enterprises of bicycle messengers that operated in other cities, effectively using their work capabilities and guaranteeing a minimum number of services as well as the technology transfer to enhance their processes.

Entregalo.co's financial statements show a monthly income of 400 million pesos. The company has 12 couriers who work as contract employees and three administrative staffers. There is no fixed number of sharing couriers, but it is growing. Entregalo's couriers have found a way to have an income source with work stability since, unlike at Rappi, they are given life and shipping insurance. The company takes couriers in as part of a family where they get a sense of belonging—thus social inclusion is reinforced.

6.4.8 *Travolution*[11]

Travolution was created in Chile in 2010 and it operates in Colombia since 2016. It is a social organization that provides support to communities involved in regional tourism to help them enhance their processes, increase the number of tourists, and access new markets through co-creation initiatives, the development of existing capabilities, and the efficient use of community resources. Travolution works with multidisciplinary teams that promote the growth of grassroots organizations involved in the tourism industry (either formally or not) to improve the living conditions in the territories where they operate.

Its model is based on the logic of local and rural development through tourism initiatives—that are nonetheless related to other activities within a territory—in search of collective growth. Small organizations that do not have the means to access international resources and projects receive support in terms of collective project presentations until they manage to develop this capability and learn to efficiently manage their resources in a business incubator model. Travolution charges a fee for each tourist that hires the organization as well as an annual support fee.

Work strategies include volunteering with payment to students and professionals on different wage scales, namely apprentices, senior consultants, and experts, whose fees are normally beyond the means of communities that can access their knowledge and advice thanks to Travolution.

Travolution has developed projects in various regions of Colombia such as Antioquia, Putumayo, Nariño, and Boyaca. Its operations gather together beneficiaries from the communities, tourism agencies that support the initiatives, and sometimes the state itself. So far, over 100 organizations have received support, six ongoing projects have an impact on 220 families in Putumayo, 20 in Choco, and more in different places around the country.

Travolution's principles have led the company to engage in reverse exclusion since organizations that affect the territories—such as mining and oil companies—are banned from joining the initiative. Likewise, Travolution protects organizations when working toward international cooperation by protecting the information and databases of participants—following security criteria—given that some participants are social leaders. Moreover, Travolution blocks illicit financial flows.

[11] August 10th of 2020 interview with Colombia Director Camilo Alvarado.

As a means to inclusion, Travolution teaches communities how to use e-commerce platforms, thereby allowing them to reach new markets and participate in the commercial dynamics of international tourism and empowering them so that they are not co-opted by large corporations—particularly from extractive industries.

6.4.9 Geofield[12]

Geocampo operates through an app that systematizes information about crops via mobile devices and analyzes it using satellite and sensor technology to perform tasks such as counting trees, evaluating the health of crops, keeping a record of plagues and diseases, monitoring soil humidity, and tracking farming machinery. These processes reduce the use of chemicals by up to 30% and improve the general management of crops to obtain organic produce without decreasing profit.

Basically, the project has modernized the data-entry processes that farmers used to carry out individually and manually, and groups the information to avoid human-caused damage that has an impact on crops to reduce risks related to the spread of plagues. Farmers formed alliances to measure common indicators such as the weather, as in a project involving 85 farms in three departments that are all measuring information following the same metrics and the same data technology to control the HLB bacteria in citrus fruits—a bacteria that is transmitted by the *Diaphorina citri* insect. This form of collective control facilitates governance in terms of plague control by the Colombian Agricultural Institute (ICA), providing valuable information for the development of its functions and helping build regional statistics for risk management. So far some 550 farms and roughly 800 workers have benefited from the project in the Eje Cafetero, Antioquia, Tolima, and other areas.

To enter a particular region, anchor companies are used. This allows for large-scale operations while promoting the inclusion of small agriculture businesses from the vicinity. At the same time, workers and small businesses receive training to understand the different kinds of plagues and learn how to use the app. The operations also involve the use of communication networks to foster contact with the community.

[12] August 12th of 2020 interview with the owner, Eduardo Llano.

Moreover, businesses pay a fee for each hectare of soil and each installed board. Thus, small businesses do not need to invest much, and the operations are subsidized by larger businesses that find in the initiative a way to prevent damages originated in a land that does not belong to them. Geocampo avoids working with state funds because this hinders the development of community capabilities and community empowerment. This model of collective work constitutes a real barrier against plagues since it fosters trust relationships within the territory.

The project promotes social inclusion in terms of developing farmers' abilities to analyze their terrains and use technology as a means to coordinate actions within their community and with specialized entities and government agencies, thereby improving results and attaining territories that are efficient in terms of production. This also facilitates the regional governance of agricultural production, especially when it comes to plague control. Farmers are thus empowered because they do not just provide personal information but also receive information with added value. In sum, the app has contributed to the creation of social capital within communities because it helps their members to get together for the common good and overcome personal differences.

6.5 Conclusions

Case analyzes show that, even though all the sharing economy initiatives profess inclusion processes, not all succeed. Rappi provides access to a source of income through technological means but it also brings about social exclusion—as in the case of Venezuelan immigrants. Thus, social inclusion is not attained since there are no fair employment conditions, and the population groups that join the platform—who are the real creators of value—are not allowed to develop capabilities that foster change. If the technological platform was the real source of value creation, the company would not be subject to the sanctions, losses, and corporate issues that were described in the case analysis.

On the other hand, initiatives such as 5Bogota, Agrapp, Travolution, and Geocampo go beyond mere technology to develop training processes, the use of knowledge, and the development of capabilities to create inclusion through changes that benefit the community and generate social value. 5Bogota shows that the knowledge and experience of hosts have allowed tourists to know the noncommercial side of Bogota with its culture and heritage, contributing to change the negative image of the city and motivating future relationships and trips among the international community. In turn, Agrapp and Geocampo take technology and knowledge to the Colombian countryside so that farmers can improve their production processes, coordinate tasks oriented toward developing social capital, and identify new ways to participate in market dynamics. Likewise, Travolution develops the ability of small organizations to enter international tourism dynamics facilitating their inclusion in new business models within the leisure and entertainment industry.

In the case of Amazoniko and Ecobot, technology is the key actor—following the actor-network theory (Latour, 2005)—that mediates the relationships between vulnerable population groups, large corporations, and citizens to foster active participation within a circular economy that has a positive impact on the environment. In turn, the technology developed by Geocampo and Agrapp has facilitated information sharing with government agencies such as ICA and department administrations to improve planning processes and provide efficient offers that include the communities while also favoring the governance of productive systems.

This chapter shows the power of sharing economies that rely on ICT platforms and other related technologies as a means to attain social inclusion following business models that promote an integrated form of social inclusion, ensure participation, empowerment, and the democratization of technology and property, thereby improving the individual and collective wellbeing of participants. This leads to material, cognitive, motivational, and social access as outlined by Turlea et al. (2011) and Yu et al. (2018). On the other hand, the chapter shows how corporations that operate within capitalist frameworks and promote exclusive inclusion practices can be mistaken for sharing economy initiatives.

Another key matter is how technology promotes governance in production systems, facilitating information management, and adding value to it so that it can be used for policymaking by government agencies. Likewise, technology enables the coordination of different actors in regional processes while providing models where the role of companies goes beyond the search for profit, focusing instead on promoting the development and well-being of participants. This constitutes an alternative to enterprise development that responds to the crises that have been caused by traditional models.

According to Yu et al. (2018), from a financial perspective, it is necessary to use the concept of exclusive inclusion to identify how initiatives can create access to income sources and financial alternatives within legal economies with fair employment conditions. The case of Rappi shows clearly that these conditions are not met, while Agrapp does create alternative solutions for farmers and develops knowledge for banks to offer more relevant products.

Lastly, inclusion in sharing economies depends on the leadership of social entrepreneurs that are focused on creating social value (Orozco et al., 2012) while preventing technology from becoming a domination device where work is restricted to the decisions of algorithms. Technology should be, instead, a means to create opportunities for gathering and sharing data with an added value to promote the freedom and dignity of population groups that have been excluded from market participation.

References

Acevedo, A., & Martinez, J. (2016). *La agricultura familiar en Colombia Estudios de caso desde la multifuncionalidad y su aporte a la paz* (E. U. C. de Colombia, Ed.) (Ediciones). Ediciones Universidad Cooperativa de Colombia. https://doi.org/10.16925/978-958-760-047-6

Acquier. (2018). Uberization meets organizational theory: Platform capitalism and the rebirth of the putting-out system. In *The Cambridge handbook of the law of the sharing economy* (pp. 13–26). https://doi.org/10.5465/amgblproc.surrey.2018.0077.abs

Arias, F., & Rendón, S. (2015). Modelos descentralizados de comercialización agropecuaria como estrategia para la inclusión social en Colombia: el caso Exofruit SAS. *Scientia Agropecuaria*, *6*(3), 201–209. https://doi.org/10.17268/sci.agropecu.2015.03.06

Bauman, Z. (2011). *Collateral damage: Social inequalities in a global age*. Polity Press. Cambridge.

BID. (2016). *Economía colaborativa En América Latina. IE Business School* (Vol. Abril). BID.

Bocken, N. M. P., Short, S. W., Rana, P., & Evans, S. (2014). A literature and practice review to develop sustainable business model archetypes. *Journal of Cleaner Production, 65*, 42–56. https://doi.org/10.1016/j.jclepro.2013.11.039

Botsman, R. (2019). *The sharing economy: Dictionary of commonly used terms*. https://rachelbotsman.com/blog/the-sharing-economy-dictionary-of-commonly-used-terms/

Buenadicha, C., Cañigueral, A., & De Leon, I. (2017). *Retos y posibilidades de la economía colaborativa en América Latina y el Caribe. Documento para discusión.*

Builes, C. (2016). "Kioscos Vive Digital": una estrategia digital y de conectividad para promover la inclusión social en comunidades rurales en Colombia. *International Journal of Psychological Research, 9*(1), 126–130.

Cabero-Almenara, J., & Ruiz-Palmero, J. (2017). Las Tecnologías de la Información y Comunicación para la inclusión: reformulando la brecha digital. *International Journal of Educational Research and Innovation, 9*, 16–30.

Castor, E. (2016, January). *Opportunities in the sharing economy*, 2. https://www.accenture.com/us-en/_acnmedia/Accenture/next-gen/insight-sharing-economy/documents/Accenture-Opportunities-In-The-Sharing-Economy-Transcript.pdf

Cerro, J. del, López, J., & Arroyo, J. (2005, January). Redes y efectos de Red . Una breve introducción a las externalidades. *Tecnología y Sociedad, 153.*

Clark, J., & Curl, A. (2016). Bicycle and car share schemes as inclusive modes of travel ? A socio-spatial analysis in Glasgow, UK. *Social Inclusion, 4*(3), 83–99. https://doi.org/10.17645/si.v4i3.510

Contreras, O. E., Pedraza, A. C., & Herrera, C. (2015). La inclusión social de la fuerza laboral en Colombia . ¿ En contravía de lo sostenible. *Apuntes Del CENES, 34*(60), 131–152.

Crawford-Visbal, J., Olivero, L., Coronado, Y., Lopez, M., Alfaro, A., Orozco, S., & Vasallo, D. (2018). *3C co Comunicación, Capitalismo y Crítica en la Colombia Digital* (U. de la Costa, Ed.) (Universida). Universidad de la Costa.

Cubillos, D. (2018). *¿Políticas de inclusión digital a la latinoamericana?* Universidad Naiconal de la Plata.

Davila, D. (2017). *INCLUSIÓN DIGITAL EN COLOMBIA: UN ANÁLISIS DEL PLAN VIVE DIGITAL I 2010 - 2014.* Pontificia Universidad Javeriana.

Dinero (25, julio, 2019). ¿Rappi-problemas o Rappi-oportunidades? Los desafíos de la gran unicornio colombiana. *Revista Dinero.* Recuperado de https://www.dinero.com/empresas/articulo/que-problemas-enfrenta-rappi/274754

Dinero (3, septiembre, 2020). Transparencia Internacional alerta por concentración del poder en Colombia. *Revista Dinero.* Recuperado de https://www.dinero.com/pais/articulo/alertan-concentracion-del-poder-ejecutivo-en-colombia--noticias-de-hoy/298032#Echobox=1599156127

Domínguez, J., & Rama, C. (2012). *La Responsabilidad Social Universitaria en la Educación a Distancia* (U. C. L. Á. Chimbote, Ed.) (Universida). Chimbote Perú: Universidad Católica Los Ángeles Chimbote.

Goñi, J. (2012). *Mentefactura. El cambio de modelo productivo* (D. de Santos, Ed.) (Diaz de Sa). Diaz de Santos.

Habermas, J., Redondo, M. J., & Garrido, M. (1984). *Ciencia y técnica como" ideología".* Tecnos.

Karatzogianni, A. (2018). Platform ideologies : Ideological production in digital intermediation platforms and structural effectivity in the "sharing economy." https://doi.org/10.1177/1527476418808029

La República. (15, julio, 2019). Rappi suma tres años con pérdidas; van US75 millones. *La República*. Recuperado de https://www.eleconomista.com.mx/empresas/Rappi-suma-tres-anos-con-perdidas-van-US75-millones-20190715-0145.html

Laboratorio de Economía de la Educación—LEE. (2020). Radiografía de la educación virtual para la educación superior. Recuperado de http://economiadelaeducacion.org/radiografia-de-la-educacion-virtual-para-la-educacion-superior/

Latour, B. (2005). *Reassembling the social: An introduction to actor-network-theory*. Oxford University Press.

Lendrys, O., & Crawford-Visbal, J. (2018). Capítulo I Domicilios, Aplicaciones y Economía colaborativa: El caso de Rappi. In U. de la Costa (Ed.), *3C.co Comunicación, Capitalismo y Crítica en la Colombia Digital* (Universida). Universidad de la Costa.

Maestre, M., Páez, A., Mesias, F., & Lombana, J. (2019). Las cooperativas agrarias como modelo generador de negocios con inclusión social: el caso de las cooperativas bananeras del Magdalena (Colombia). *Revsita De Estudios Cooperativos, 132*(132), 195–217. https://doi.org/10.5209/REVE.65488.1

March, J. G. (1991). Exploration and exploitation in organizational learning. *Organization Science, 2*(1), 71–87.

Mendes, B., & Giménez, M. J. (2015). *Generación De Confianza En El "Mundo Real" a Través De Interacciones En El "Mundo Virtual" En El Contexto De La Economía Colaborativa*. FACULTAD DE CIENCIAS ECONÓMICAS Y EMPRESARIALES (ICADE).

Muñoz, W. P. (2018). Inclusión social de actores del conflicto armado colombiano: retos para la educación superior. *Desafíos, 30*(1), 279–308.

Nambisan, S., Siegel, D., & Kenney, M. (2018, July). On Open Innovation, Platforms, and Entrepreneurship. *Strategic Entrepreneurship Journal*. https://doi.org/10.1002/sej.1300

Ojeda, D. (9, septiembre, 2018). ¿Por qué Rappi vale US$1.000 millones si genera pérdidas? *El Espectador*. Recuperado de https://www.elespectador.com/noticias/economia/por-que-rappi-vale-us1000-millones-si-genera-perdidas/

Orozco, L. A., Alarcon, H., Fonseca, F., Herazo, D., Melo, O., Mosquera, A., & Rodríguez, D. (2020). Instrumentos de Planeación Departamental en Materia de Competitividad e Innovación en Colombia. Proyecto Capstone - Universidad Externado de Colombia, Consejería Presidencial para la Competitividad y la Gestión Pública - Privada.

Orozco, L. A., Buitrago, J., & Chavarro, D. A. (2012). Biotecnología y valor social: el emprendimiento científico del CIMPAT para enfrentar la enfermedad de Chagas en Colombia. *Biotecnologías e innovación. El compromiso social de la ciencia. Editorial Javegraf*.

Orozco, L. A., Celli, E., De Francisco, L., Duque, C., Fernandez, W., Monsalvo, A., Pinzón, M., & Rodríguez, E. (2019). Gobernanza multinivel de la agenda digital ELAC a nivel departamental en Colombia. Proyecto Capstone – Universidad Externado de Colombia, Ministerio de Tecnología de la Información y las Comunicaciones – MINTIC. Bogotá.

Ostrom, E. (2000). *El gobierno de los bienes comunes* (F. de C. Económica, Ed.) (Fondo de C). Fondo de Cultura económica.

Pacheco, N. (2016). La Web 2.0 como instrumento esencial en la economía colaborativA: auge de negocios de dudosa legalidad. *Revista CESCO De Derecho De Consumo, 17*, 76–84.

Pérez, E., & Titelman, D. (2018). *La inclusión financiera para la inserción productiva y el papel de la banca de desarrollo.* (CEPAL, Ed.) (CEPAL). CEPAL.

Puyana, A. (2018). Desigualdad horizontal y discriminación étinca en cuatro paises latinoaméricanos. *Revsita Cepal, 125*, 250.

Pyka, A. (2017). Dedicated innovation systems to support the transformation towards sustainability : Creating income opportunities and employment in the knowledge-based digital bioeconomy. *Journal of Open Innovation: Technology, Market, and Complexity, 3*(27), 1–18. https://doi.org/10.1186/s40852-017-0079-7

Ramirez, L., & Sepúlveda, J. (2018). Brecha digital e inclusión digital: Fenómenos socio – tecnológicos. *Revista EIA, 15*(30), 89–97.

Ramis, Á. (2017). Bienes comunes y democracia: crítica del individualismo posesivo.

Rinne, A. (2019). *4 big trends for the sharing economy in 2019.* https://www.weforum.org/agenda/2019/01/sharing-economy/

Rivera, C., & Calva, H. (2015). Análisis comparativo: Colombia, España y México en el uso de las TIC como generadoras de inclusión social. *Revista Internacional De Estudios Sobre Sistemas Educativos, 2*(5), 37–56.

Rohman, S. (2016). The shape of things to come. The on-demand economy and the normative stakes of regulating 21st-century capitalism. *Special Issue on the Risks and Opportunities of the Sharing Economy, 4*, 652–664.

Rueda, R., & Franco-Avellaneda, M. (2018). Políticas educativas de TIC en Colombia : entre la inclusión digital y formas. *Pedagogía y Saberes, 48*(48), 9–25.

Sanabria, J., & Ruiz, M. (2018). *Small farms reach new markets—Comproagro.* Trabajo presentado en Aim2flourish de Weatherhead School of Management—Case Western Reserve University, Tijuana México.

Sanabria, J., & Orozco, L. A. (2021). Del capitalismo liberal a la economía colaborativa, nuevos modelos de negocio y retos para el marco institucional. Colección Así Habla el Externado. Tomo IV "Tecnologías Negocios y Gestión". Universidad Externado de Colombia. Bogotá.

Santos, J. (2017, Junio 7). Lo que no se sabe de Rappi. *Las 2 orillas*. Recuperado de https://www.las2orillas.co/lo-no-se-sabe-rappi/
Selwyn, N. (2002). E-stablishing'an inclusive society? Technology, social exclusion and UK government policy making. *Journal of Social Policy, 31*, 1.
Stępnicka, N., & Wiączek, P. (2018). Sharing economy vs. access economy—wybrane aspekty terminologiczne i metodologiczne. *Prace Naukowe Uniwersytetu Ekonomicznego We Wrocławiu*, (530), 13–25. https://doi.org/10.15611/pn.2018.530.01
Stocker, A., & Stephens, S. (2019). Evaluating the potential of cooperative ridesourcing: A case study of Arcade City in Austin, Texas. Austin Texas.
Sundararajan, A. (2016). *The sharing economy book. The end of employment and the rise of crowd-based capitalism* (M. Publisher, Ed.) (MIT Publis). MIT Press.
Tirole, J. (2017). *Economics for the common good*. https://books.google.es/books?hl=es&lr=&id=MXGYDwAAQBAJ&oi=fnd&pg=PR11&dq=tirole+jean+2017&ots=PfYl-hwwgd&sig=i4zyS0szsEMRiuwsCipRYewGpMk
Turlea, G., Ollé, E., & Ciupagea, C. (2011). Romania and integration into the European model of e-inclusion : From access to the use of advanced communication services The social dimension of internet diffusion in Romania : Examining the connection between internet uses and frequencies. *Romanian Journal of European Affairs, 11*(1), 43–63.
Superintendencia de Sociedades (2019). Superindustria ordena a Rappi S.A.S. cumplir con normatividad de comercio electrónico y formula pliego de cargos. Recuperado de https://www.sic.gov.co/Sic-ordena-a-Rappi-S.A.S.-cumplir-con-normatividad-de-comercio-electr%C3%B3nico-y-formula-pliego-de-cargosWatts, C., & Luz, L. (2017). Las TIC como herramientas de inclusión educativa. *Acta Scienriae Informaticae, 1*(1).
Watts, C., & Luz, L. (2017). Las TIC como herramientas de inclusión educativa. *Acta Scienriae Informaticae, 1*(1).
Wosskow, D. (2014). *Unlocking the sharing economy: An independent review*. (I. and S. Department for Business, Ed.) (Department). Department for Business, Innovation and Skills.
Yu, B., Ndumu, A., Mon, L. M., & Fan, Z. (2018). E-inclusion or digital divide: An integrated model of digital inequality. *Journal of Documentation, 74*(3). https://doi.org/10.1108/JD-10-2017-0148
Yudong, Q., & Ying, L. (2019). New economy in China : Emerging, operation and regulatory reform *. *China Economist, 14*, 2–14.

PART II

Cases on Higher Education as an Agent for STI Governance

CHAPTER 7

Developing Transformative Innovation Through Policy Experimentation in Two Colombian Universities

Diana Velasco, Alejandra Boni, and Salim Chalela

7.1 Introduction: Re-thinking Innovation

Innovation, in a general sense, can be understood as the ability of people and organisations to develop a new or significantly improved product (good or service), process or method to achieve a desired effect (material or social) that responds to an opportunity creatively and that is used and appropriated by a massive group of users (Freeman, 1995; Tidd

D. Velasco (✉)
Universidad de Ibagué, Ibagué, Colombia
e-mail: dcvelmal@ingenio.upv.es

D. Velasco · A. Boni
INGENIO (CSIC-Universitat Politécnica de Valéncia), Valencia, Spain

S. Chalela
Universidad Autónoma Latinoamericana, Medellín, Colombia

L. A. Orozco et al. (eds.), *Science, Technology, and Higher Education*, Palgrave Studies in Democracy, Innovation, and Entrepreneurship for Growth,
https://doi.org/10.1007/978-3-030-80720-7_7

et al., 2005). This innovative activity's consequences (intentional or not) can trigger incremental or radical changes or transformations in social life (Smith, 2017). However, the dominant view and practice of innovation have been based on the private sector activity that governments and universities support. The goal is to make economies more productive by creating knowledge and subsequent business application and societal dissemination (Temple, 2010).

Innovation has predominantly been studied from an economic perspective. Schumpeter (1934) defines it as a new production function that covers new commodities decisive in nations' success. Innovation has also been understood as the result of conducting basic and applied research to produce solutions that can be introduced to large-scale markets (Bush, 1945). This vision of innovation is based on a linear perspective that the innovation systems approach problematises. According to the innovation systems framework, the emphasis must be mainly placed on the optimal interactions of policy, business, academic actors and supporting infrastructures to produce economic effects that are always perceived as positive for thriving countries development (Edquist, 1997; Freeman, 2002). Finally, and in response to the limitations of the two previous approaches, an understanding of innovation from a transformative perspective is introduced. The objective is no longer economic growth but to face the current social and environmental challenges that both Global North and South are facing (Schot & Steinmueller, 2018). Likewise, interactions between policy, business and academic actors are not enough; citizens, communities and civil society organisations must be centrally incorporated. The innovations arise from the response to profound social problems and under a comprehensive sustainability scheme (Pearce et al., 2000), interacting with non-hegemonic groups, which, together with traditional actors, allow changes in prevailing socio-technical systems.[1] Like in the innovation systems approach, the acknowledgement and understanding of norms, values, rules of the game are paramount. However, in the transformative innovation framework, the role of active social groups, as opposed to the view of users as recipients of innovation, that seek for alternatives to solve their needs, is a central element for the innovation policy design, as is highlighted by (Boni et al., 2018;

[1] The socio-technical systems are understood as those links and functions in the relations of production, diffusion and use of technology, which are configured to respond to social needs and challenges, such as energy, water, food production, etc. (Geels, 2004).

Pellicer-Sifres et al., 2017). The Sustainable Development Goals (SDGs), approved by the United Nations in 2015, illustrate the magnitude of challenges such as mitigating climate change, overcoming poverty and inequalities, access to quality education, among others. Failing to reach these goals has a significant affectation on the most vulnerable populations, which now more than ever need innovative solutions pathways (Schot & Kanger, 2018).

This view of innovation is aligned with human development where people, instead of economics, are at the centre. The measure of success is providing means for people to have feasible access to those things they value to have a better life (Alkire & Denehulin, 2009). The human development framework has been developed and expanded through the *Human Development Reports*[2] produced by the United Nations Development Programme (UNDP). Although the conceptual framework of human development has evolved during the years, it has at least five central elements (Boni & Gasper, 2012): (1) a plurality of values such as empowerment and participation, equality and sustainability; (2) capabilities understood as the substantive freedoms or real opportunities to have the kind of life that people value, and functionings understood as the activities people do to expand their capabilities (Sen, 1999); (3) agency, as the ability of people to achieve the objectives they value, it implies power and control not only at the individual but also at the collective level; (4) the multi-dimensionality of well-being beyond economic income, including the sources, means and environmental conditions needed for people to expand their capabilities; and (5) democracy and public debate, to have political freedom and democratic political systems.

Looking at innovation from this point of view also implies re-thinking the role of the University. Suppose policies and practices of innovation are oriented towards objectives where the predominant logic is not increasing economic growth. In that case, we must ask ourselves questions such as: What professionals do we need? What kind of research should we carry out? What types of actors should be included in the University dialogue? What social impact can we produce in the face of local and global challenges?

In this chapter, we respond to these questions, paying particular attention to two regional university initiatives: the definition of a university

[2] The reports can be found in http://www.hdr.undp.org/.

policy at the Universidad de Ibagué, in Tolima Colombia, and the re-significance of the research policy of the Universidad Autónoma Latinoamericana in Medellín, Colombia. The second section details the characteristics of transformative innovation following Schot and Steinmueller (2018) and Schot et al. (2018). In the third and fourth sections, we present the two case studies and analyse them, considering what transformative innovation suggests. The fifth section approaches the discussion, and the sixth section concludes.

7.2 Transformative Innovation

As we pointed out at the beginning of this chapter, the development of STI policy is essential to address social and environmental challenges. For this reason, a relevant question arises: Is the current STI policy fit for purpose? In recent decades, the interest of policymakers and the business sector has focussed mainly on the use of knowledge as an engine for economic growth and innovation to increase competitiveness and job creation. Adverse effects of innovation are not taken into account, as far as there is a positive economic effect.

The Transformative Innovation Policy framework (TIP) implies a direction towards solving social and environmental challenges, expanding the STI policy scope and purpose towards alternatives such as green growth, eco-innovation, social innovation and inclusive innovation (Schot et al., 2018). The causal relationship is altered, giving prevalence to development based on social well-being, participation and empowerment of social groups and equity for social justice (Boni & Gasper, 2012). Therefore, different approaches to measuring "success" other than GDP growth (such as the UN Human Development Index or the OECD Well-being Index) are highly needed. This vision of innovation has unique characteristics that differentiate it from previous frameworks, briefly discussed below.

7.2.1 Socio-technical System Change

The United Nations Agenda to "transform our world" can be interpreted as a call for a new type of innovation. The OECD (2015) also calls for a systemic view of world challenges. Innovation goes beyond the use of technologies and science; it requires changes in the different dimensions of the socio-technical systems that include changes in users' preferences, knowledge creation expressed in science and technology, skills and capacities absorption, infrastructure, policy, industrial structure and cultural significance.

There are many socio-technical systems that fulfil essential social functions in areas such as energy, food, health, mobility and communication. Policy for transformative innovation aims to produce transitions in socio-technical systems towards a more sustainable direction.

7.2.2 *Directionality is the Starting Point*

The transformative change framework proposes the inclusion of different perspectives and broad participation of diverse actors to envisage the consequences of innovation *ex-ante*, opening up pathways towards collective priorities. Such a process implies creating visions on sustainable and desirable scenarios for the different socio-technical systems that connect with concrete trajectories and technical options. Being open and fostering radical new alternatives often not perceived as feasible or even desirable is a critical aspect of the TIP. The change pathways provide contextual technological solutions in tune with social choices and environmental benefits. As a policy principle, directionality opens up the space to assess multiple scenarios aligned with human development values and environment preservation. For this reason, the directionality of transformative innovation is aligned with the SDGs insofar as they represent a global agenda with local commitments.

7.2.3 *Experimentation and Development of Alternative Practices as a Way of Innovation*

Finding new directions requires experimentation. Change implies processes based on experience and second-order learning (also called double-loop learning or deep learning). Socio-technical systems are driven by rule-sets composed of behavioural instructions, cognitive beliefs, norms and values (Geels, 2002; Geels & Schot, 2007; Schot & Steinmueller, 2018). Thus, second-order learning goes beyond understanding and realising ones' assumptions; it implies changes in people's mental and cognitive frameworks, producing changes in behaviour.

Given that the direction towards alternative and sustainable practices implies dealing with uncertainty and complexity, experimentation offers the possibility of exploring various sustainability pathways that ultimately lead to systemic change. Within the framework of transformative innovation, this experimentation is proposed through participatory processes with diverse actors, offering the possibility of agency for non-hegemonic players. As expressed by (Ramírez, 2020: 2): "The experiments in transformative innovation are not intended to confirm an alternative already defined in advance, but rather to try different alternatives, produce prototypes and demonstrative solutions that can inform new paths and, above all, generate deep learning (or second order learning), through a formative evaluation". These alternative practices start at the local and regional level and usually come from the local communities. At the same time, public policy plays an essential role in scaling up and accelerating local initiatives for transformative change. Intermediation between local alternatives, regulatory and institutional frameworks and industrial practices is often required.

7.2.4 *Inclusion as a Prerequisite for Transformative Change*

The inclusion of diverse voices and the agency of non-dominant actors such as organised civil society movements is critical to the emergence of alternative practices. The experimentation process must be inclusive in terms of participation and results and must have a direction that leads to human and sustainable development. Inclusive does not only mean reporting on results, but above all, it implies that those involved have the power to exert influence on alternative solutions. Inclusive processes can lead to the incorporation of conflicting points of view that, instead of being avoided, are discussed and managed. The policy should create appropriate framework conditions for inclusive participation and supporting actors to navigate conflicts and build trust throughout the process.

Table 7.1 summarises the main characteristics of this innovation framework.

The Transformative Innovation Policy Consortium (TIPC) (Schot et al., 2019) has identified five modes of experimentation (or experimental engagements as defined in the text) by which public policy can drive transformative innovation. As its authors state, it is an open proposal that aims to be inspiring. It seeks to open the discussion on possibilities within public policy. Table 7.2 shows the five modes of experimental engagements that we will return to later in the discussion.

Table 7.1 Characteristics of transformative innovation

Change of socio-technical system	Change in consumer practices and needs, skills and capabilities of all the actors involved, infrastructure, government, regulation, industrial structure and cultural significance
Directionality	Creation of visions on sustainable futures connected to development trajectories and technical options. Consideration of multiple directions, embedded in a broader range of options that allow for a second-order learning and formative evaluation process
Experimentation	Change that is based on experience and deep learning. Learning that transforms assumptions and action patterns ingrained in the dominant practices of the different socio-technical systems, such as energy generation, the use and disposal of water, the growth of cities, consumption patterns, among others Experiments can be embedded as alternative practices in niches that compete with an unsustainable dominant practice Governance is critical, to the extent that new intermediations must be designed between local initiatives, new regulatory and institutional frameworks and the alignment of different but complementary policies for the change of socio-technical systems
Inclusion	Incorporate non-dominant actors and actors from diverse sectors, including producers, civil society, users and policymakers. The experimentation process must be inclusive in terms of participation and results. Inclusion and experimentation imply the support of actors to navigate conflicts and to build trust throughout the process

Note Own elaboration based on Schot et al. (2018)

7.3 The Institutional Account for Science, Technology and Innovation of the Universidad Autónoma Latinoamericana

7.3.1 Context and Characteristics of the Universidad Autónoma Latinoamericana

The Universidad Autónoma Latinoamericana (Unaula) was established in 1966 by the university dissidence inspired by the Cordoba Manifesto

Table 7.2 Modes of experimental engagements (Schot et al., 2019: 2)

Modes of experimental Policy Engagement	*Mode 1: Policy design experiments*	*Mode 2: policy instrument and policy process experiments*	*Mode 3: creating experimental spaces*	*Mode 4: supporting, connecting and evaluating societal experiments*	*Mode 5: experimental governance culture*
Role of experimentation in policy	Assists in the formulation, calibration and justification of policy Instruments	Setting up of specific experimental policy interventions in the form of new policy instruments or policy processes tried out temporally or in a small scale	Creates dedicated environments and a constituency for experimentation, where the normal conditions (e.g. regarding permits, taxation) are relaxed	Articulates existing experiments carried out by multiple actors, Facilitates learning from and between experiments, and supports the development of networks	Creates flexible and proactive governance arrangements, including open-ended goals, allowing decentralised and ex perimental interventions by multiple actors
Actors involved	Policymakers, and recipients of the policy treatment	Policymakers and policy analysts, stakeholders involved in the experiments	Lead users, entrepreneurs, technology advocates, designers, civil society actors, policymakers	Networks implicated in experiments, intermediaries and policymakers	As others, but with the aim of broadening participation to actors normally excluded from policy process
Approaches	Randomised Control Trial, Behavioural Experiments	Experimenting with new formats in established policy instruments/ processes (programmes, subsidies, regulation)	Urban Living Labs, policy labs, walk-shops, transition arenas	Intermediary organisations and platforms, workshops, online resources	Strategies and initiatives to promote experimental culture; rewarding reflexivity and learning

of 1918.[3] Unaula has been recognised in the local context for its social commitment in its fifty-three years of existence.

People recognised locally for their direct work within the community, such us Héctor Abad Gómez, Jaime Gil Sánchez, Gilberto Martínez Rave,[4] have given a particular ethos to Unaula. They committed their heritage to an academic cause devoted to popular assistance allowing the entry to higher education of nearly 10,000 students from the lowest socioeconomic strata (working-class and low-income people). This fact made, at the time, the recognition of Unaula as the "University of the Poor" (Durango, 2008).

Unaula maintains its foundational spirit by including institutional policies to support vulnerable local communities, defend human rights, keep an open professorship and decentralise work in different popular neighbourhoods of the city. These actions have allowed the University to be fully immersed in the territory and be recognised as a popular end university (Jaramillo, 2016) with nearly 6,000 students and an academic offering of 27 undergraduate and graduate educational programmes.

Unaula has also invested significant efforts in generating scientific knowledge that aims at the social transformation of communities in the local and regional order. In this sense, its different academic departments have created research groups and social projection units dedicated to the generation and transferring of new knowledge through divulgation strategies for public understanding, aside from the most traditional forms such as scientific publications, patents, consultancy, participation in national and international events, among other activities.

An innovation unit for the Univesity was created in 2015 to consolidate the knowledge transfer processes derived from research results from a linear incremental innovation framework. The assumptions were that the

[3] According to (Arcila, 2011), the Córdoba Manifesto is rooted in the structural changes generated by the collapse of hegemonic eurocentric values (as a result of phenomena such as the First World War, the Russian Revolution and the strengthening of the bourgeoisie on the continent). This antecedent promoted an educational reform that gave rise to university management models that focussed on the training of professionals, in conditions of equality, with a stance and critical thinking regarding the socio-political reality. It sought the vindication of quality in education and allowed to set missionary objectives focussed on the training of the working class and the students representation in the institutional governance.

[4] It is worth mentioning that most of them were persecuted or killed for their fierce defence and opposition to the constant and systematic violation of the human rights of people with limited resources who lived in Medellín, during the 1980s and 1990s.

application of knowledge derived from research or technological development results in introducing a new product or service that creates economic revenue. However, this conceptual approach to innovation is distant from the foundational principles that underpin Unaula's organisational structure. Unaula is committed to contributing to the better coexistence of society, aware that adequate education contributes to greater spiritual, material, cultural and social well-being. In this sense, pluralism, co-government, autonomy and values such as eco-sensitivity, solidarity, equality and respect for difference have characterised the historical evolution of the institution.

7.3.2 *The Construction of an Institutional Narrative*

In 2016, the University reformed its organisational structure creating a Vice-Rectory for Research (Agreement 57 of 2016—Superior Council). This change opened the possibility of reviewing the meaning, orientation, and purpose of research at the University. The Vice-Chancellor started a process to identify organisational capabilities for research, with the support of external advisers on inter-institutional relations and cooperation for development, in coherence with the institutional principles and values (examined in institutional documents such as the foundation act, university statutes, the strategic planning documents, physical master plan, among others) and semi-structured interviews with different institutional and non-institutional actors.

Additionally, 15 semi-structured interviews were conducted with the university leadership (3), deans (3), faculty members (4), employers' associations (2) and social organisations (3) (see Fig. 7.1).

Five organisational capabilities for the development of an institutional research policy were identified and recognised based on the information collected and on the institutional trajectory: (a) critical thinking as the axis of the institutional education project; (b) commitment to good living (Buen Vivir), from a Latin American perspective; (c) the defence of human rights; (d) the existence of a diverse and inclusive academic community; and (e) infrastructure for development in the city centre.

Based on these capabilities, an Institutional Narrative for Science, Technology and Innovation (STI) was built related to the Sustainable Development Goals (SDGs) with five confluences: (a) UniverCity, (b) Human Rights, justice and gender, (c) Economic development, formalisation, creation of wealth and new networks, (d) Social inclusion: culture,

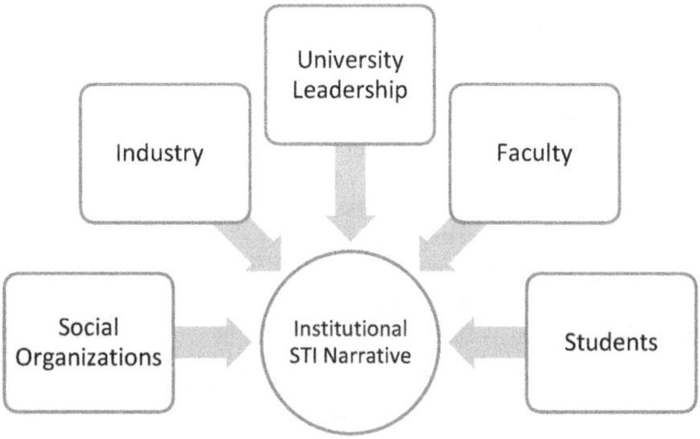

Fig. 7.1 Participative identification of organisational capabilities

disability and education and (e) Eco sensitivity: territory, environment and rurality (see Table 7.3).

Experimentation from these confluences has generated new institutional research processes that involve articulations between academic actors and social organisations, which scope is not limited to academic publications, consultancies or participation in academic events.

An example of alternative practices is the Alliance with Women[5] (at the confluence of Human Rights, justice and gender) that has articulated four universities and two social organisations in order to reveal the humanitarian crisis experienced by women victims of gender violence, in order to mobilise social, political and legal actions that contribute to the eradication of this scourge.

The Alliance with Women defines the objective of this articulation process as follows:

> The union of efforts between civil society and the academy contributes to the construction of spaces for academic, social and political debate that favours the materialisation of women's human rights and the generation of knowledge that explains this social phenomenon [gender violence] and promotes alternatives through research, advocacy processes and strategic litigation, to strengthen access to justice and administrative measures related to their care. For all these reasons, this project seeks to strengthen

[5] Working alliance for strategic litigation in defence of the human rights of women in the city of Medellín, Colombia. Website: https://alianzaconlasmujeres.com/.

Table 7.3 Unaula narrative for STI

Confluences	*Visions of the future*	*SDGs*
UniverCity	The compact city; redefinition of the city centre; public space and heritage; and urban regeneration as conditions for community well-being	Sustainable cities and communities
Human Rights, justice and gender	Contribution to training processes in political culture, the defence of human rights, gender diversity and redistributive justice	Gender equality, Peace, justice and strong institutions
Economic development, formalisation, wealth creation and new networks	Deepen interventions in formalisation, innovation, productivity, decent employment and collaborative networks that address the precariousness and potential of these critical sources of employment and entrepreneurship	Decent work and economic growth Industry, innovation and infrastructure Responsible consumption and production
Social inclusion: culture, disability and education	Commitment to comprehensive education in the city and the region, considering diversity and acting in accordance	Quality education Reduced inequalities
Ecosensitivity: territory, environment and rurality	Human and institutional attitudes aligned with caring for the environment; sincere concern for the current eco planetary problem, our ecosystem and internal and external relations	Climate action Life on land

the Alliance as a space in which, in addition to the production of knowledge, the dialogue of multiple perspectives is launched, generating the reinforcement of the installed capacity of the partners. It does it through the consolidation of work teams compounded by researchers, students, and activists in an interdisciplinary body of knowledge that, from an initial legal emphasis, also addresses violence against women as a social and a public health problem. It seeks local and national projection and impact, thanks, among other things, to the participation of organisations such as the Human Corporation of the city of Bogotá, as well as that of the Collective Corporation for Justice for Women, a focal point of the National

Network of Women, and a social platform with presence in more than 16 cities in Colombia. (Alliance with women, 2018)

The Alliance participated in the elaboration of the gender public policy of Medellín, the creation of the Feminist Legal Clinic to complement the processes of training lawyers from a feminist perspective; likewise, it has generated legal innovations about violence against women in intimate relationships, ex-partners and other relational forms, among other activities.

Another notable example is the Live Experiences programme[6] "School of Systematisation of Local Experiences" (confluence of social inclusion: culture, disability, and education). Live Experiences is conceived as "a space for reflection, appropriation of theories and methodologies that make possible the construction of city and country agendas that are prone to the construction of scenarios of peace and coexistence, as necessary conditions for a good life" (Live Experiences, 2017).

This programme emerged in 2017 as an initiative to systematise local experiences of fourteen social organisations in Medellín. From 2019 it has managed to articulate with more than sixty-two social organisations from other cities such as Bogota, Tunja, Duitama, Ibagué, through activities of knowledge dialogue which implies local knowledge co-production and systematisation projects through methodological tools for the defence of the territory.

7.4 The Participatory Process of Defining the Central Capabilities of the University of Ibagué

7.4.1 Context and Characteristics of the Universidad de Ibagué

The Universidad de Ibagué (UI) is a medium-sized regional private university (by Colombian standards, with around 5,600 students and 330 teachers in 2019) founded in 1980 by a group of businessmen and civic leaders from the Department[7] of Tolima. The UI has contributed to regional development based on human-centred values. Its academic offer, research agendas and programmes are embedded in the territory

[6] Website: https://www.experiencesvivas.com/.

[7] Colombia is politically and geographically divided in departments.

by impacting the regional well-being with tangible results. The UI has a path-dependence towards citizenship training, high standards of academic quality and social projection, making its campus the entire department of Tolima, as can be seen in Fig. 7.2.

Tolima has historically suffered high levels of violence due to the armed conflict between the State, the guerrillas and the illegal armed groups. According to the Departmental Competitiveness Index of Colombia, the conflict has negatively impacted the human development of the territory, placing Tolima in 12th place among 32 departments. In 2016, the peace agreement was signed between the Colombian government and the Revolutionary Armed Forces of Colombia (FARC), which started a disarmament process in 2017. The signing of this peace agreement has led to a crucial moment in the development of the country. In this new post-agreement scenario, words such as truth, justice, reparation, non-repetition, forgiveness, reconciliation, among others, point to the possibility of political and moral routes for conflict resolution. For the regions, particularly for the Tolima region, the peace agreement has opened up an opportunity for centring efforts on much needed social well-being. More now than ever, the UI is a central actor to mobilise knowledge for the region thriving.

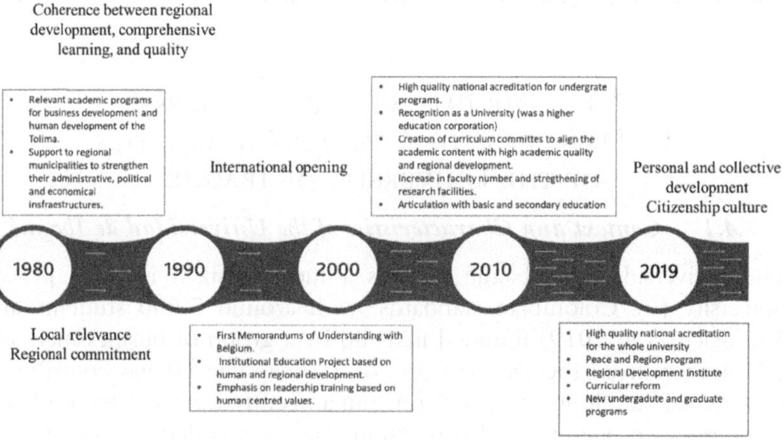

Fig. 7.2 Universidad de Ibagué path-dependancy

Within this context, the UI has played an active role in transformation and building sustainable peace processes by bringing together students, faculty, technical personnel, companies, social organisations, communities and local governments to foster human capabilities.[8]

7.4.2 The Participatory Process to Define Capabilities for Human Development

In 2019, the UI started a journey to define what is valuable for the university community and university partners in terms of capabilities. The process was widely collaborative and participatory by involving faculty, administrative staff, managers, students, alumni, the business sector, municipalities, and social organisations with which the institution collaborates.

A collective vision was expressed in a list of capabilities that characterises the aspirational spirit of the UI. A specific directionality was co-constructed by all participants towards a human-centred transformation inside and outside the University. The process was designed as a mode of experimental governance by creating a flexible and proactive space that allowed multiple actors' decentralised interventions, resulting in the list.

The process started in May 2019, and by December 2019, the final list of capabilities for the UI was finished. During the whole process, it had the drive and support of the rectory team, which gave it legitimacy. The UI Provost led the design of the experiment with an international expert on human development and transformative innovation, and with five researchers of the UI Special Projects Unit.[9] We called this group the designer group. The methodology was designed in three phases, described in Fig. 7.3. In this chapter, we report the results up to the second phase. The horizon phase focussed on gathering different university members (students, faculty, administrative staff, leadership, alumni, entrepreneurs and social organisations) for a co-produced vision of the UI based on

[8] Specific programmes such as Peace and Region (https://pazyregion.unibague.edu.co/), projects developed jointly between local governments, social groups and the UI (https://extension.unibague.edu.co/proyectos) are some of the evidences of this affirmation.

[9] Institute devoted to the study of complexity and systemic thinking. It acts as a think tank for the University and for the region.

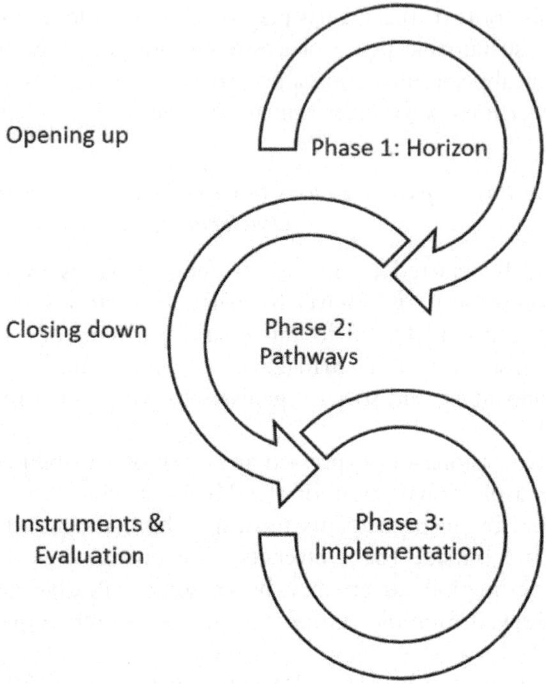

Fig. 7.3 Experiment methodology phases

social and sustainable practices. There were 127 participants in 9 workshops and 13 interviews (64 women and 63 men). The result was a list of eight university capabilities, two related to training, two related to territory, three related to university community and one related to enterprise.

During the pathways phase, a validation process of the eight capabilities list was performed with mixed groups of phase one participants. Besides the validation, the groups drew connections between the capabilities and defined pathways to expand the UI capabilities list. There were 62 participants (35 women and 27 men). The final list collectively built by the UI community is presented in Table 7.4.

The third stage is on hold due to a change in the university leadership. The Special Projects Unit is expected to move forward with instruments

Table 7.4 UI capabilities list

Category	*Capability*	*Definition*
Training	Training of persons and citizens	A university community capable of training people, professionals and citizens with critical thinking, ethical principles and sensitivity regarding social differences and needs
	Integral leadership	A university community capable of training people for reasoned and responsible decisions, in accordance with criteria of justice, fairness, and respect for differences (within the framework of empathic and affective communication) that leads to the realisation of joint actions oriented to the common good
Territory	Social construction of territory	A university community that is capable, in association with the other social actors, of rebuilding and appropriating its territory collectively, through dialogue and mutual understanding, committing itself to nature, culture and diversity of knowledge for connivance and peace
	University that transcends	A university community capable of generating projects and actions aimed at the development of a fair and democratic society that enhances reflection, exchange, and generation and appropriation of knowledge to respond to aspirations, challenges, and problems that affect the various actors in the territory

(continued)

Table 7.4 (continued)

Category	*Capability*	*Definition*
University community	Purposeful Critical reflection	A university community capable of reflecting and building critically on their being and daily work in the light of their identity, history, ethical stakes, bonds of trust, organisational forms, growth opportunities and personal and collective aspirations
	Care	A community that is capable of ensuring conditions that allow the integral growth of the self and the other, through relationships that build trust and recognition among its members as well as of the environment in which they are immersed
	Constructive interaction	A university community capable of stimulating, allowing, and promoting a dialogue that is well informed, clear, transparent and respectful of freedom and differences of opinion. On the one hand, it is oriented to strengthen the social interaction between the members of the community so that they develop the personal power to choose and act in situations of social and political environment. On the other hand, it favours participation, a good working environment, and individual and collective integral human development
Enterprise	Weave nets	A university community capable of fostering interconnections with companies, communities and students to develop innovative projects that respond to territorial needs, build trust and take care of the common good, to make possible a truly local development with a global perspective

and resources to expand the university community capabilities at all levels for every university member and stakeholder.

7.5 Discussion

The Unaula and UI experiences can be understood as a mode five of experimental governance culture. The decision processes and policy documents were based on flexible and proactive governance arrangements. The inclusion of open objectives allowed decentralised and experimental interventions by multiple actors with the active involvement of actors usually excluded from the policy processes. For Unaula, the co-creation of an institutional narrative opened up the possibility of expanding the participation of institutional and non-institutional actors in the construction of policy. In the UI case, designing the list of capabilities gave voice to students, alumni, social organisations, businesses, and administrative officials in a strategic exercise of the university, envisioning a just and sustainable set of real options valued by the university community. Likewise, the methodology based on experiential workshops to create reflexivity spaces provided the means for second-order learning, or learning that enables changes in frames and assumptions and that provides a broader view of the UI beyond the particular role the participants have in university life (Schot et al., 2019). It is noteworthy that in the second pathways phase for the list of capabilities construction, the mixed groups (admin staff, faculty, students, entrepreneurs) allowed the participants to share their views about the University and its role in the regional transformation, increasing the possibilities of learning as suggested by the transformative innovation approach.

It is worth highlighting the directionality that the five confluences and the list of the eight capabilities for human development can give to university policies. The two directions are closely connected to the social and environmental issues that are central to transformative innovation. Unaula's case exemplifies the connection of the narrative with various SDGs. In the UI case, the connection is apparent in the capabilities list, particularly in the training, territory, and enterprise categories. A leadership based on justice, equality, and respect for the differences for the common good; a university community that re-signifies continuously and collectively the territory committed to the preservation of nature, culture, and diversity of knowledge; and a university that is capable of weaving nets to foster innovative projects to respond to territorial needs; give direction to an educational model inspired by comprehensive and humanistic training. Both experiments aim to transform the system (in this case, the University) in a specific direction.

The two university policies can be understood as protected spaces for experimentation, with clear leadership from the Vice Rectories, giving it a strategic policy dimension, and also providing the means to have a collective vision to build and opening up different pathways towards just transitions (Stephens & Graham, 2010). There are two determining factors that made both experiments possible: the first is their *ethos*. Both have a social vocation from their foundation, more political in the case of Unaula and more ethical and oriented towards regional development in the UI case. In both cases, the institutional missions (probably not shared by the entire university community but protected by its founding documents) has protected and legitimised the two innovations. The second issue is the explicit support and direct participation of the two Vice Rectories. These experiments require institutional involvement and political will that needs top-down support. In both cases, the vice-rectors distributed their power to allow a bottom-up policy construction process. In Unaula, the recent creation of a Vice-Rectory for Research as an autonomous dependency on other substantive functions allowed the Vice-Rectory to design the experiment to create the university research policy. For the UI, the Academic Vice-Rectory saw an opportunity to align the capabilities framework with critical foundational documents and the University's policies to expand human capabilities.

Experimenting, empowering different actors, and creating alternative governance arrangements bring tension and sometimes conflict. In Unaula's case, there has been a strong questioning from the Academic Council, which advocates for traditional processes of measurement and evaluation of science. Council members do not believe that it is compatible with scientific production to have a comprehensive university narrative. There were tensions with the Superior Board of the UI, who has final approval on all institutional policies, caused mainly by governance arrangements triggered from the Vice-Rectory.

Finally, it is worth raising questions about the systemic scope of the two initiatives. In terms of transformative innovation, to what extent do both initiatives aim for socio-technical change? This would lead us to a more in-depth discussion (which goes beyond the objective of this chapter) about the characteristics of the knowledge creation socio-technical regime in Colombia. What is certain is that both universities are inserted in a broader quality accreditation system that rewards publication in high-impact journals, generation of economic resources from enrolment, traditional knowledge transfer, the internationalisation of students and teachers, among others, which are necessary but not sufficient conditions. The two policies must fit into this context and coexist with it simultaneously, proposing alternative metrics to evaluate the research performance in the case of Unaula and providing a university vision based on human development, in the UI's case. These different institutional arrangements open new possibilities for experimentation and recognise alternative practices in teaching, research, extension and even university governance.

We present a systemic understanding of the possibilities for transformative innovation from the University. Although our case studies can be considered isolated experiments at this point, they are two examples that can be replicated and adapted to other university realities both in Colombia and abroad. Replication possibilities are also increased thanks to the networks that both institutions have.

7.6 Conclusions

This chapter presents two experiences of defining university policies that can be understood as experimental processes according to the proposed transformative innovation policy framework. Both experiences have a specific directionality aligned with social and environmental challenges. They have been developed following inclusive and participatory processes that have considered voices generally excluded in the formulation of university policy. They have aimed to generate learning and reflexivity among the participants, mobilising and recognising different types of knowledge: experiential, expert, and non-expert, theoretical and practical. The contextual aspect of both experiments is highlighted and linked to both institutions evolution and the participants' aspirations and needs.

The role of experimentation in university governance was taken forward in the Unaula and UI cases. Proactive governance arrangements broadening the spectrum of voices heard and giving agency to the university community and allies to co-create institutional policies is congruent with the principles of transformative innovation policy. Rewarding reflexivity and learning in university policy construction open up the discussion in university management to challenge the current institutional dominant practices.

Considering the above, applying the transformative innovation policy framework to examine the organisational processes in higher education institutions provides possibilities to break with the institutional isomorphism that makes universities behave homogeneously.

Acknowledgements Alejandra Boni acknowledges the support of the BEST-2019 Programme of the Ministry of Education and Culture of the Generalitat Valenciana to write this chapter in the framework of research leave (BEST / 2019/011).

Diana Velasco thanks the Special Projects Unit, particularly the designer group, that thought and implemented the experiential workshops for phases 1 and 2 of the methodology for the capabilities list construction. Also, to Jamith Hernández, a young researcher from the University of Ibagué, and Nidia Chaparro, a lecturer and former Vice-Rector of the UI, for their participation in the capabilities list construction presented in this chapter.

Salim Chalela thanks the Cooperation, Development and Management unit, mainly to Sofía Botero and Hernán Aristizábal, for their dedication to constructing the institutional narrative for the STI. Also to Hernán Jaramillo and Ana María Aldana for their contributions in the framework of the institutional strengthening project of the Alliance for Formal and Inclusive Economy.

References

Acuerdo 308 de 2016. Consejo Académico de la Universidad Autónoma Latinoamericana, Medellín, Colombia, 22 de junio de 2016.

Acuerdo 57 de 2016. Consejo Superior de la Universidad Autónoma Latinoamericana, Medellín, Colombia, 1 de diciembre de 2016.

Alianza con las Mujeres. (2018). Alianza de trabajo para el litigio estratégico en defensa de los derechos humanos de las Mujeres en la ciudad de Medellín. Medellín, Col. Recuperado de. https://alianzaconlasmujeres.com/.

Alkire, S., & Deneulin, S. (2009). *Introducing the human development and capability approach. An introduction to the human development and capability approach*. Earthscan. London. Recuperado de. http://citeseerx.ist.psu.edu/viewdoc/download?doi=10.1.1.383.6231&rep=rep1&type=pdf.

Arcila, R. (2011). *La universidad en América Latina*. Universidad Autónoma Latinoamericana.

Boni, A., Belda-Miquel, S., & Pellicer-Sifres, V. (2018). Innovación transformadora. Propuestas desde la innovación social colectiva para el desarrollo humano. *Recerca. Revista De Pensament y Anàlisi, 23,* 67–94.

Boni, A., & Gasper, D. (2012). Rethinking the quality of universities: How can human development thinking contribute? *Journal of Human Development and Capabilities, 13*(3), 451–470. ADDIN EN.REFLISTX.

Bush, V. (1945). *Science, the endless frontier: A report to the President on a program for postwar scientific research.* US Govt. print. off. Recuperado de. https://apps.dtic.mil/dtic/tr/fulltext/u2/a361303.pdf.

Durango, H. (2008). *Cátedra Universitaria. Evolución de la educación en occidente.* Ediciones Unaula.

Edquist, C. (Ed.). (1997). *Systems of innovation. Technologies, institutions and organisations.* Pinter.

Experiencias Vivas. (s.f.). Experiencias Vivas. Recuperado de. https://www.experienciasvivas.com/.

Freeman, C. (1995). The "national system of innovation" in historical perspective. *Cambridge Journal of Economics, 19*(1), 5–24. https://doi.org/10.1093/oxfordjournals.cje.a035309.

Freeman, C. (2002). Continental, national and sub-national innovation systems-complementarity and economic growth. *Research Policy, 31*(2), 191–211. https://doi.org/10.1016/s0048-7333(01)00136-6.

Geels, F. W. (2002). Technological transitions as evolutionary reconfiguration processes: A multi-level perspective and a case-study. *Research Policy, 31*(8–9), 1257–1274.

Geels, F. W. (2004). From sectoral systems of innovation to socio-technical systems: Insights about dynamics and change from sociology and institutional theory. *Research Policy, 33*(6–7), 897–920. https://doi.org/10.1016/j.respol.2004.01.015.

Geels, F. W., & Schot, J. (2007). Typology of sociotechnical transition pathways. *Research Policy, 36*(3), 399–417.

Jaramillo, R. (2016). *Unaula. Una conquista popular.* Ediciones Unaula.

OECD [OCDE]. (2015). System innovation: Synthesis report. OECD. Recuperado de. http://sro.sussex.ac.uk/id/eprint/61430/1/Rogge.pdf.

Pearce, D., Barbier, E., & Markandya, A. (2000). *Sustainable development economics and environment in the Third World.* https://doi.org/10.4324/9781315070254.

Pellicer-Sifres, V., Belda-Miquel, S., López-Fogués, A., & Boni Aristizabal, A. (2017). Grassroots social innovation for human development: An analysis of alternative food networks in the city of Valencia (Spain). *Journal of Human Development and Capabilities, 18*(2), 258–274.

Ramírez, M. (2020). Una primera introducción al concepto de experimentación. Documento del Consorcio de Política de Innovación Transformadora.

Schot, J., & Kanger, L. (2018). Deep transitions: Emergence, acceleration, stabilisation and directionality. *Research Policy, 47*(6), 1045–1059.

Schot, J., Boni, A., Ramírez, M., & Steward, F. (2018). *Addressing sdgs through transformative innovation policy*, TIPC Research Briefing 2018–01.

Schot, J., Kivimaa, P., & Torrens, J. (2019). *Transformando la experimentación: intervenciones experimentales en materia de políticas y sus alcances transformadores*. Documentos de Políticas TIPC.

Schot, J., & Steinmueller, W. (2018). Three frames for innovation policy: R&D, systems of innovation and transformative change. *Research Policy, 47*, 1554–1567. https://doi.org/10.1016/j.respol.2018.08.011.

Schumpeter, J. (1934). *The theory of economic development*. Transaction Publishers.

Sen, A. (1999). *Development as freedom*. Oxford University Press.

Smith, A. (2017). Innovación social, democracia y makerspaces. *Revista Española Del Tercer Sector, 36*, 49–74.

Stephens, J., & Graham, A. (2010). Toward an empirical research agenda for sustainability in higher education: Exploring the transition management framework. *Journal of Cleaner Production, 18*(7), 611–618. https://doi.org/10.1016/j.jclepro.2009.07.009.

Temple, P. (2010). Education today 2010: The OECD perspective. *UCL Institute of Education Press (UCL IOE Press), 9*(3), 352–354. https://doi.org/10.1080/14748460.2011.616332.

Tidd, J., Bessant, J., & Pavitt, K. (2005). *Managing innovation integrating technological, market and organisational change*. Wiley.

CHAPTER 8

The Contribution in STI of the Higher Education Institutions of Cauca for the Peace Building and Social Inclusion

Alexander Castillo-Garcés, William Chará-Ordóñez, and Paula Andrea Mora-Pedreros

8.1 An Introduction: Territorial Peace Challenges

After the Final Agreement signature for ending the conflict and the building of a stable and durable peace (hereinafter The Peace Agreement) between the government and the Fuerzas Armadas Revolucionarias de

A. Castillo-Garcés (✉) · W. Chará-Ordóñez · P. A. Mora-Pedreros
Universitaria Autónoma del Cauca, Popayán, Colombia
e-mail: alexander.castillo.g@uniautonoma.edu.co; jacastillo@unicauca.edu.co

W. Chará-Ordóñez
e-mail: william.chara.o@uniautonoma.edu.co

P. A. Mora-Pedreros
e-mail: paula.mora.p@uniautonoma.edu.co

L. A. Orozco et al. (eds.), *Science, Technology, and Higher Education*, Palgrave Studies in Democracy, Innovation, and Entrepreneurship for Growth,
https://doi.org/10.1007/978-3-030-80720-7_8

Colombia-Ejército del Pueblo (FARC-EP) guerrilla in La Habana, a huge deployment was carried out in the country in such magnitude that legislators, public servers, governmental and non-governmental institutions and the state in general started to partake in regions and communities to advance with a transformation that transcends economic, politic, social and even cultural fields.

Even though the ending of the conflict spreading, was aligned to the idea of a stable and durable peace, all of these actions are now backed up by the "territorial peace" slogan, a more and popular term, either by the media or by the state investment funds, that have made it a part of a strategy for reaching the vulnerable communities, abandoned and besieged by war actors.

Framed in this state purpose, there are Higher Education Institutions (HEI), which although they tend to train professionals also become fundamental axes for the development of the regions. Rodríguez (2009) points out the challenges of HEI:

> First, university institutions must become a basic element to generate higher levels of competitiveness in the country. (…). Second, university institutions must become an essential source of opportunities for continuing education and social mobility. (…). Third, university institutions must ensure the quality and relevance of their academic offer, a matter of the greatest importance to generate training and research programs that effectively impact the country's competitive capacity and allow the successful insertion of young people from vulnerable families to the work market. Fourth, universities must link with their environment contributing to the development of culture, arts, literature and territorial development. (Rodríguez, 2009, p. 826)

Within the framework of these challenges, the department of Cauca is presented as a favorable scenario for the building of peace, since it has been one of the most affected departments by the armed conflict and after the signing of the Peace Agreement it has experienced the resurgence of other forms of violence. The presence of illegal armed groups, illegal mining, the increase of illicit crops and drug trafficking, shape new expressions of a social, political and economic conflict that requires a priority inter-institutional intervention.

The discussion about interventions to this problem must undoubtedly link the academy. HEI in Popayán have not been oblivious to this reality and have expressed their interest in having the science, technology and innovation systems for designing mechanisms that contribute to the construction of territorial peace in the department of Cauca. Considering the above, it is necessary to inquire about the role and challenges of HEI having as guiding questions for the analysis: What is the role of regional universities in the consolidation of territorial peace? How do their development plans articulate with state purposes? What actions in science, technology and innovation do universities advance to consolidate territorial peace?

Considering these questions, the research performed quantitative and qualitative techniques, which allowed complementing and triangulating the sources. In this regard, it should be mentioned that the collection techniques were applied in five HEI in the department of Cauca: Universidad Del Cauca, Corporación Universitaria Autónoma del Cauca, Fundación Universitaria de Popayán, Institución Universitaria Colegio Mayor Del Cauca y Corporación Universitaria Comfacauca. The selection criteria were determined by the time taken by the educational institution in the Department, at least ten years, and the work of social interaction in the different municipalities. This allowed establishing the design and execution of academic activities, research and relationship with the environment with communities and institutions. These aspects were key, since these criteria referred to the form and type of articulation of HEI with the political, economic, social and cultural dynamics of the territories within the framework of the post-conflict and the building of local peace.

Based on the process of mapping and selection of HEI, analysis units were constructed, according to the proposal of Vargas and Hurtado (2017) sectorial policies (infrastructure, security, justice), institutional capacity (management, participation) and social transformation capabilities and thus guide the process of inquiry based on the notion of building territorial peace. Based on the documentary analysis, the development plans, strategic plans and educational plans in force in HEI were reviewed. In this way, it was possible to identify lines of action linked to the construction of territorial peace, issues and the means to materialize these actions. The work with documentary sources, also included the review and analysis of Web pages, institutional reports and sectorial action plans to contrast the plans with the concrete activities of teaching, social interaction, research and relationship with the environment during the last four years. In addition to the qualitative analysis, it was possible to systematize, classify and process the projection activities of HEI to account for magnitudes around the type of academic, interaction and intervention actions developed by HEI oriented to the construction of territorial peace in Cauca.

8.2 Territorial Peace and Academic Debate for Its Definition

Talking about territorial peace is not of recent date, however, it has become more recurrent after the signing of the Peace Agreement. It is precisely in the search for mechanisms that guarantee the sustainability of the peace that this notion takes relevance, since it is framed in a new interpretation of the political situation. The debate over the reach of a stable peace implies overcoming the old approaches of positive peace or negative peace by that of differential peace, in which the recognition of all peace actions advanced in the territory, even in the framework of structural conflicts, they take relevance for the end of the conflict.

It is precisely the territorial nature of the armed conflict and the notion of territorial peace that have provoked various interpretations by the State, peasant, indigenous, social associations and academy. According to Cairo et al. (2018), the definition of territorial peace that was discussed in the negotiation processes of Havana could "be linked to the notion of democratic peace, not so much in reduce the likelihood of war between democratic states as proposed by Doyle (2000) or Gibler (2007) but to point out the democratic consolidation of the State" (p. 466). Under this idea, territorial peace is the means by which the social, economic and political conditions left by the armed conflict are overcome, much like the notion of positive peace raised by Galtung (1969).

In all eyes, it has been defended from its discursive places, the need to implement a peace bet from the territory as one of the most effective ways to guarantee a peace building. Some of the arguments that support this idea are the following.

For the FARC-EP, the territorial peace, according to one of the leaders called Jesus Santrich: "responds to the idea of sustainable peace in the sense of building peace from within the regions" (Cairo et al., 2018, p. 466). In that sense, the notion of territorial peace can be understood under the premise that the State did not meet the structural needs of the population in rural regions and, precisely, it is there that the voice of those who must make decisions for implementation must be strengthened and guarantee of peace. Sharing the same idea of strengthening the rural territories affected by the armed conflict, but from a vision from security, for the Public Force it can be understood as the return of the institutional armed force and the policies of rural citizen security from a closer relationship with the community of the regions affected by the armed conflict.

Although both notions have discursive differences, in both, the territorial character was essential during the negotiation cycles of the Peace Agreement. It is precisely during their discussion that the notion has its first appearances in the academic debate and institutional planning for the peace process with the FARC-EP. For the commissioner of peace of the moment Sergio Jaramillo, representing the vision of territorial peace from public institutions during a declaration before the United Nations in 2014, he said:

> We have to take advantage of the moment of peace to align the incentives and develop the institutions in the territory that over time will enforce the rights of all equally. To move in that direction, the rights approach must be complemented with a territorial approach. First, because the conflict has affected some territories more than others. And because that change is not going to be achieved if the efforts are not articulated and the population is mobilized in those territories around peace. That is what I call territorial peace. (Jaramillo, 2014, p. 3)

This notion of territorial peace is framed in the thesis that the Colombian armed conflict does not have as an argument the existence of objective conditions for its justification; on the contrary, it is the subjective conditions such as the institutional lag and the weakness of the State in the intervention in the most remote territories that allowed the establishment of agents of the armed conflict. Therefore, with the end of the armed conflict, the institutional task is to rethink the decentralized intervention logics. This vision is evident in the National Development Plan 2014–2018 «Todos por un nuevo país» (National Planning Department, 2015).

According to the governmen in 2014, territorial peace implies two elements. First, the return of the State to the territories devoid of institutional intervention previously co-opted by illegal actors of the armed conflict, recognizing the gradualness of the armed conflict in rural areas, from institutions that guarantee the development and fulfillment of each of the points of the Peace Agreement. In this regard, it is worth mentioning that, in Colombia, especially during the armed conflict there was no absence of the State but a "differentiated presence of the State" (González et al., 2003) that is expressed in the different ways in which the State the territories intervened from particular configurations and the articulation with the local power, the economy and the culture of the regions. Second, from the notion of differentiated presence, recognize the need to privilege the view from the territories and participatory construction through intervention mechanisms in accordance with the State. Hence, participatory planning spaces are proposed, linking all local and community agents.

This institutional vision has allowed the notion of territorial peace to have permeated a certain pragmatism because of the weak explanation about the ways to implement it efficiently. This is how territorial peace has been linked as a public policy approach that translates into a prioritized intervention in rural territories (Ideas para la Paz, 2017), but also as a scenario of territorial autonomy and new administrative decentralization (Zubiría, 2016) that privileges in its implementation the social content and political inclusion of all sectors of the country (García, 2016).

However, it is necessary to clarify that territorial peace is not synonymous with a territorial approach. According to the Peace Agreement, the territorial approach is related to rural development, expressed in the first one that proposes a new intervention approach of the Colombian rural sector. The point of coincidence of the terms, which must be noted, lies in the search for better living conditions of a sector of the population historically affected by the armed conflict. However, territorial peace is not limited only to the rural development of an agrarian reform.

This meeting point of the two interpretations has led the academy to think about how territorial peace should materialize in the search for conditions that improve the quality of life of the population affected by the armed conflict from social inclusion. In this regard, one of the first to express the need to discuss a territorial reform as a prioritized institutional intervention mechanism in the territories was Hernández (2016); For their part, Bautista (2017) and Ríos and Gago (2018), pointed out the need to specify the implementation of territorial peace under formal, normative and public policy mechanisms oriented from the territories, since, without institutional support, the risk of a failure to implement peace would be imminent. The call for the commitment that political elite's must-have in this commitment to peace is set by Cairo and Ríos (2019), for whom the political will in the regions is a factor of articulation of the initiatives postulated by the territories. This argument already allows us to notice the orientation of territorial peace as a planning instrument.

However, the challenges in the territories in the framework of the discussion of territorial peace also occupied the academy, especially from the state's conception of peace for the pacification of the territories. In this regard, Oslender (2018), supported by the argument that before territorial peace, there were efforts to pacify the territories, examines from the notion of superimposed territorialities, the territorial configuration of Afro-Colombian communities in the context of armed conflicts and post-conflict. It points out that pacifying the territories from homogeneity and ignorance of cultural particularities limits the effectiveness of institutional interventions. Along the same lines, for Koopman (2018), new and old social phenomena linked to the armed conflict converge in the territories, hence, territorial peace should be understood as a mechanism to ensure the guarantee of rights of the historically excluded population, including that territories are multi-ethnic settings with multiple needs.

Considering the previous review, the academy has revealed two tensions. The first, a concern for the formalization, monitoring and institutional mechanisms to achieve peace. The second, the need to understand that the territories have their own particularities and needs, which must be intervened with initiatives that are born from the territories and the diagnosis made by their own inhabitants. In both cases, the Academy proposes the review, construction, design and, monitoring of strategies that lead to the closing of social gaps in the territories, since it is from territorial peace, as a planning and intervention mechanism, social inclusion guarantees the compliance and enjoyment of rights.

These academic discussions accompanied the definition of the institutional mechanisms for the implementation of territorial peace. Thus, since 2017, the Colombian Government through the Ministry of Agriculture and Rural Development, based on the territorial approach, has implemented planning and management instruments called Development Plans with a Territorial Approach (PDET) under the premise that "Through a profound change in social, economic and political conditions, it will be possible to lay the foundations for the construction of peace, overcome the conditions that prolonged the armed conflict and guarantee its non-repetition" (Decree 899 of 2017).

To fulfill this goal, the PDET propose the need to strengthen the decentralization and de-concentration processes of the State in each of the territories, based on the reformulation of public institutions and participatory planning, which links the entire community directly or indirectly, to social organizations of all kinds and whose purpose is the intervention of the multiple realities and needs of the territories, and not only as a mechanized and bureaucratic «return of the State». In that sense, the PDET are proposed as the mechanism of public management to intervene in the territories and promote territorial peace. With them you look for:

> Develop in a participatory manner an action plan for regional transformation, which includes all levels of territorial planning, which is arranged with local authorities and communities, and that includes both the territorial approach of the communities, as an objective diagnosis of needs and actions in the territory. (Decree 899 of 2017)

For the implementation of the PDET, 16 subregions were prioritized, grouping 170 municipalities from 11 of the 32 departments of Colombia. Among them, the Department of Cauca is of particular interest due to the long history of conflict it has experienced.

> The dispute between illegal armed actors and the State has intensified since the 1980s, at the end of the 1990s paramilitary groups have entered and since 2005 the armed conflict has worsened, leaving hundreds of victims and deepening the already existing social, economic, and politicians in the region. (Chará et al., 2019, p. 4)

The department of Cauca includes 17 municipalities that make up the Alto Patía, Norte del Cauca, and Pacífico Subregion. These municipalities have been strategic scenarios of control by armed actors that are present in territories under the coexistence of drug trafficking, organized crime, delinquency, and land tenure problems. All these problems are proposed as intervention challenges where HEI will be important to contribute to the transformation of these realities and seek the social inclusion.

In this context, however, and considering the problems of these municipalities, the HEI face another challenge to overcome the barriers in STI. The Colombian State allocates less and less money to finance this sector. For 2018, only 0.5% of GDP was allocated to STI and for 2022 it is proposed to increase by 1.5% of GDP. Little compared to OECD countries that exceed 2% of GDP (Ministerio de Ciencia, Tecnología e Innovación, 2019). In addition to this, there is limited knowledge of the potential of the territories and the little infrastructure in STI for the management, exchange, and promotion of new knowledge that allows the transformation of territorial realities.

In sum, the tracked studies coincide in using the guidelines of the institutional proposal of territorial peace as a starting point and feed the proactive search of the mechanisms for its implementation. In that sense, it is possible to affirm that academic production has been occupied in providing the institutional notion with content, as a focus, overlapping other debates from where the concept can be operationalized and contextualize the old and new problems that evidence the overcoming of the conflict with the FARC-EP and that need to be intervened from a territorial perspective. They also show that the concept and its development are still under construction.

Bearing in mind the above, the challenges of HEI should be, on the one hand, to overcome STI financing barriers, improve departmental agendas for innovation and regional cooperation (Departamento Nacional de Planeación, 2020) and, on the other hand, generate socially useful knowledge and improve the environments for the transformation of multiple conflicts and overcoming the armed conflict in the territories. The intent of the academy is to frame its contributions to the search for mechanisms that guarantee an effective implementation of territorial peace from multiple perspectives and perspectives. In that sense, a review of the HEI development plans will allow us to see the mechanisms designed to contribute to this end.

8.3 The Public Policy of STI and Territorial Peace from the Institutional Development Plans of HEI

The development plans of each HEI are the road map to design, plan and execute program strategies that guarantee both the quality and the role of the academy in the transformation and overcoming of the needs of the territories, especially with contributions in STI. Based on this idea, is important to identify in each development plan those actions in STI and their articulation with territorial peace, peace building and overcoming the armed conflict.

The Corporación Universitaria Comfacauca defined in its 2014–2019 development plan strategies aimed at improving academic programs, becoming an active part of the ITS program, co-creation value for the region, and the productive sector. Regarding STIs, he proposes two scenarios: «positive and negative». On the "negative" side, the emphasis is placed on contextual issues such as the high unemployment rates in the region and extreme poverty in rural areas and the poor results in the Saber Pro test.[1] This last element is key to the evaluation of HEI since, as stated by Orozco et al. (2018) since "the evaluation of teaching could be carried out using the Saber Pro exams as a result of the achievement of the first university mission defined in the formation and formation of capital in the educational activity" (p. 199) with which it would not be fully fulfilled the institutional mission of educational training.

In order to achieve the development plan, it proposes five strategic vectors: (1) academic excellence, (2) institutional visibility and strengthening of social projection, (3) management of institutional well-being, (4) strengthening of research, and (5) research excellence. With these actions, Unicomfacauca is projected at the regional level and in coordination with the companies of the Cauca Family Compensation Fund to think about their own graduate programs and in agreement, design financing models and above all achieve greater local, regional and national visibility (Corporación Universitaria Comfacauca, Agreement 027 of 2014). However, the revision of its plan allows us to affirm that despite making a commitment to articulation with the regional processes led by government agencies and some private sector companies, their actions around territorial peace are not tangible,—without saying that it is not—being one of the reasons, the date of construction of the same, as the conjunctural moment of the post-conflict was not yet latent, nor had the social discourses about peace been transformed.

When inquiring into the Corporación Universitaria Autónoma del Cauca the level of articulation of the «Strategic Development Plan 2016 - 2020 Toward Institutional Accreditation» With the proposal of territorial peace implementation, there is no explicit identification of any component related to the construction of peace, nor does it have strategic axes or objectives in terms of territorial peace. In spite of this, the Institution carries out promotion initiatives and favors the consolidation of peace through academic and social projection activities related to intervention and research projects, chairs, events and congresses that account for the important contribution to the configuration of a territorial peace. These actions are not part of an institutional planning process that allows the

[1] The higher education quality exam -Saber Pro (formerly ECAES) in Colombia is designed to evaluate students in the last semesters of higher education to inquire about the professional skills acquired within the training process.

articulation of governmental and non-governmental efforts to achieve a greater impact on society. In that perspective, their actions are isolated and to some extent discontinuous.

This aspect, although it represents a weakness, can also be seen in terms of opportunity in the phase of implementation of the Peace Agreement provided that they are strategic axes or actions articulated with other national and regional initiatives. In this regard, it is worth mentioning that the Strategic Development Plan proposes among its objectives: (1) strengthen the presence of the Corporation in the region and improve integration with the environment, (2) strengthen the Research System that aims to improve research processes in social intervention in the perspective of the needs of the environment and (3) social transformation and regional entrepreneurship to generate conditions for social and economic development from initiatives designed in an articulated manner between the academy and the productive sector in relation to the needs of the territories (Corporación Universitaria Autónoma del Cauca, Agreement 023 of 2015).

Similar situation is presented with the "Institución Universitaria Colegio Mayor del Cauca", since its development plan «Transformative management with human quality 2016 - 2020» does not identify specific axes, components, strategies, plans or programs linked to territorial peace. However, there are elements that should be considered in a possible articulation with the implementation of Peace Agreement at the regional level. The description of the mission and institutional vision highlights the inclusive nature of the training of professionals from the municipalities of the department of Cauca and other southwestern regions, based on a model of social commitment based on good educational practices. The strategy of social projection of the Institution is striking, since under the principle of approach to society, it proposes the construction of initiatives for development, entrepreneurship and resolution of conflicts caused by poverty, displacement, unemployment, illiteracy or dissatisfaction of needs (Institución Universitaria Colegio Mayor del Cauca, Agreement 014 of 2016).

The "Fundación Universitaria de Popayán" and its development plan 2013–2018 is based on the National Development Plan 2010–2014 "Prosperity for all", and in particular on "Peace building". Likewise, in the Ten-Year Education Plan 2006–2016, one of the challenges of education in Colombia stands out "An education in peace and for peace, coexistence and citizenship" (Fundación Universitaria de Popayán, Agreement 005 of 2004). These two dimensions are configured as articulating axes in the implementation of territorial peace in the department of Cauca. In terms of action for the construction of territorial peace, the institutional orientation toward the development of the region can be rescued in the tourism, mining, agricultural chains, the preservation of the Colombian Massif, and the strengthening of human rights and coexistence citizen, who become the only elements that are potentially linked to the axes of the construction of territorial peace.

Finally, the development plan of the "Universidad del Cauca" «Toward a University committed to territorial peace 2018–2020» reports a different case within the studied HEI, since it is possible to establish mentions, strategies and training actions, research and social projection oriented to the construction of peace. In components such as mission and vision, the permanent commitment to social development, the formation of democratic professionals and the construction of a fair and equitable society are highlighted (Universidad del Cauca, 2018). Likewise, it is pertinent to mention that among the values and principles provided in the development plan there are important references to the design of plans, programs and professional training projects that allow the cultural, scientific, productive and technological development of the region and the country; the construction of spaces of tolerance and coexistence, the achievement of national peace; promotion of democracy and participation in the framework of the Social State of Law (Universidad del Cauca, 2018).

The foregoing accounts for an institutional planning instrument in which the construction of territorial peaceis proposed as a transversal axis to the strategies, programs and actions designed. In addition, it highlights the research, innovation and social interaction component (part of Strategic Axis 3) in terms of strengthening research and social interaction at all levels of training for institutional and social development, based on management, transfer and appropriation of knowledge from a territorial peace approach (Universidad del Cauca, 2018). The document also provides an action called «Unicauca for you. Recognition and social interaction for territorial peace» (Universidad del Cauca, 2018) that gives an account of how the strategy will be materialized in the coming years. Finally, it proposes the construction of territorial peacefrom the formation processes linked to the characteristics of the environment and social interaction, promotion of research and intervention as a means for the transfer and social appropriation of knowledge, and projection actions social who seek greater presence of the University in the region and the inclusion of communities in their institutional action.

In summary, in matters of STI, HEI establish in their development plans strategies aimed at promoting two scenarios, the strengthening of research and the relationship with the environment. From the first they have proposed: the transfer of knowledge, the production of new knowledge in terms of contributions to peace and the articulation of projects with communities in order to improve the conditions of rural populations in the department of Cauca. Since the second they have been proposed: social interaction and social intervention with communities and government programs in relation to overcoming the conflict. Under this argument, it is pertinent to expose the vocation of HEI from those actions aimed at the construction of territorial peace.

8.4 HEI Activities in STI and Peace

The link between education and peace building is promoted by Law 1732 of 2014 and is regulated by Decree 1038 of 2015. It is indicated that all educational institutions must implement the peace chair with the primary objective of creating and consolidating spaces for learning, reflection and dialog on the culture of peace and sustainable development, thus contributing to the general well-being and improvement of the population's quality of life.

Although the regulations bind the institutions of basic and secondary education in a compulsory way, with the institutions of higher education, the obligation is subject to their constitutionally consecrated autonomy, which allows them to establish, in addition to the chair of peace, other curricular actions, of research and social projection as strategies to contribute to the construction of territorial peace scenarios. Under this idea, when reviewing the institutional actions developed by the regional HEI in the Department, it is noted that the academic scenario does not depart from the normative and contextual provisions around the most sensitive and purposeful discussions of the national, regional and local political context. Hence, that the activities carried out by the HEI consulted in terms of territorial peace are relevant as they are part of new constructive and propositional debates from the region. From 2012 to 2019, about 215 experiences support this argument.

Although Colombian legislation indicates that these activities should be carried out since 2015, the HEI institutions consulted have developed curricular, research and projection actions since before the enactment of the aforementioned legislation. Thus, from 2012 to 2014, 18.7% of the total activities reported (Advice and training to local governments, (2) Postgraduate education, (3) Technological innovation projects, (4) Promotion of entrepreneurship, (5) Training of human talent, and (6) Social research projects) in STI were carried out.

A not less percentage since it shows that, if we consider that during this period the negotiations in Havana with the FARC-EP guerrillas are barely in an exploratory and dialog phase, the HEI continued to debate, expose and denounce the strong incidence of the conflict armed in the social, political and economic context of the department of Cauca. On the other hand, since 2015 there is a greater correspondence with the regulations. According to Fig. 8.1, institutional actions increase, from 9.8% to 18.6% in 2016 and 23.7% in 2019.

When inquiring, what are the HEI that carried out the most academic events in the key to peace education developed in the period studied: The Universidad del Cauca records 57.3%, the Corporación Universitaria Comfacauca 12.7%, the Corporación Universitaria Autonoma del Cauca 12% stand out as the three HEI with the highest number of academic events (See Fig. 8.2).

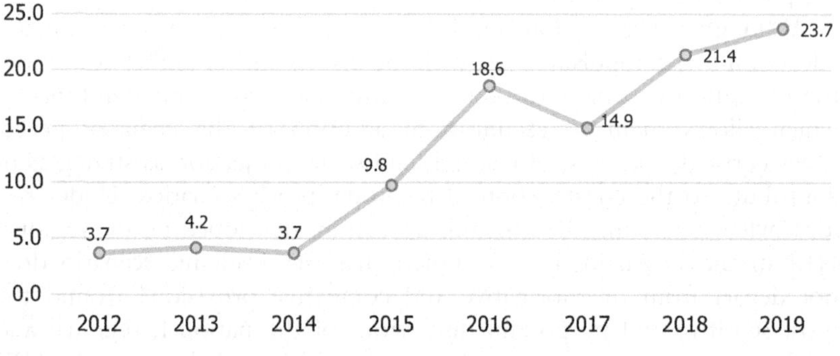

Fig. 8.1 Percentage of institutional activities carried out in terms of territorial peace during 2012–2019 (*Source* based on www.unicauca.edu.co, www.uniautonoma.edu.co, www.fup.edu.co, www.unicomfacauca.edu.co, www.unimayor.edu.co)

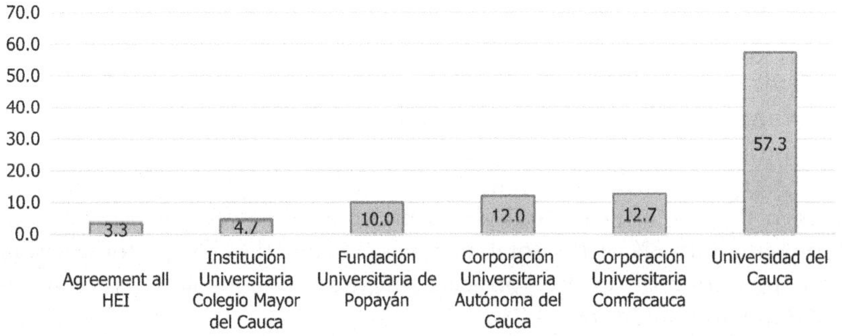

Fig. 8.2 Percentage of institutional activities carried out in terms of territorial peace by the HEI of the department of Cauca. 2012–2019 (*Source* based on www.unicauca.edu.co, www.uniautonoma.edu.co, www.fup.edu.co, www.unicomfacauca.edu.co, www.unimayor.edu.co)

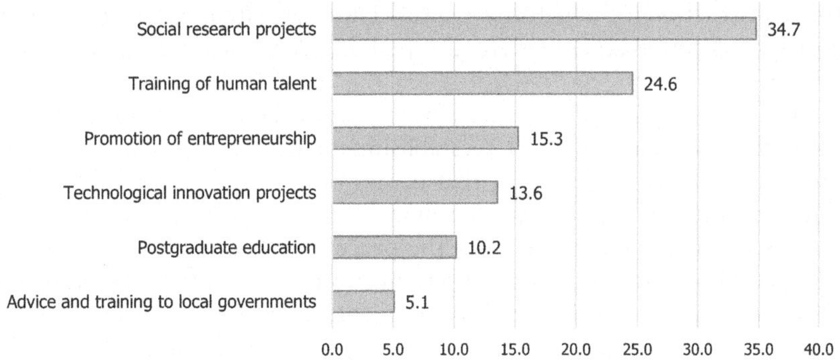

Fig. 8.3 Percentage of classification of institutional activities carried out in terms of territorial peace by the HEI of the department of Cauca. 2012–2019 (*Source* based on www.unicauca.edu.co, www.uniautonoma.edu.co, www.fup.edu.co, www.unicomfacauca.edu.co, www.unimayor.edu.co)

On the other hand, the review of the type of academic activities carried out by the HEI of Popayan in terms of territorial peace and peace education allowed to establish six types of activities (See Fig. 8.3). To a lesser extent (5.1%), decisive advisory and training activities were carried out for the city on issues of conflict and peace. Postgraduate academic activities are also carried out (10.2%). Those academic activities dedicated to the training of human talent, especially public, private and civil society officials, oriented to the socialization of progress in the negotiation process with the armed actors of the conflict, routes of attention and pedagogy for peace meant 24.6% of HEI events. In terms of STI, technological innovation projects were carried out, especially in communication technologies, they were 13.6%. In addition, projects based on productive undertakings in the key of peace and performative actions were carried out and represented 15.3% of the total activities. Finally, the design, formulation and application of research projects aimed at finding solutions for social inclusion accounted for 34.7%

In the same way, it was possible to identify STI actions aimed at the social inclusion of communities, the transfer of knowledge, and social intervention in territories historically affected by the armed conflict. Although some are not articulated in a specific way to the development plans of the HEI, they constitute STI initiatives that have intervened in specific realities of Cauca to rebuild the social fabric and promote the construction of territorial peace. These research, interaction, and social intervention strategies are grouped into the following six categories (Fig. 8.4).

In the first one, there are initiatives of articulation with the environment for the guarantee and reestablishment of the rights of the rural population of the department, that is, the work of the universities in the different municipalities from consultancies and legal brigades for advice victims of the armed conflict and the peaceful resolution of conflicts. In the second one, social projection strategies are grouped for entrepreneurship and regional productivity improvement, which seek the construction of networks and spaces for interaction and innovation for small agricultural production and marketing processes developed by communities in the different territories of the department of Cauca.

In a third group, it is possible to identify intervention projects aimed at innovation and the construction of social fabric in communities, social organizations and territories that were affected by the armed conflict. In this sense, the work to guarantee the rights of early childhood and adolescence, psychosocial care for vulnerable populations, education for peace based on virtual platforms and the construction of spaces for coexistence, community leadership, training and promotion of innovative production processes for ex-combatants and the training of the population in digital technologies, web pages and email.

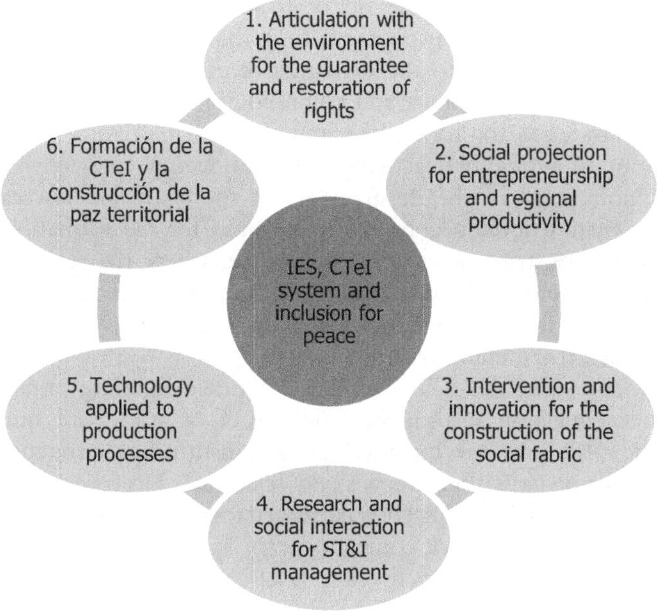

Fig. 8.4 STI strategies in research, interaction and social intervention carried out by IES of the department of Cauca (*Source* based on www.unicauca.edu.co, www.uniautonoma.edu.co, www.fup.edu.co, www.unicomfacauca.edu.co, www.unimayor.edu.co)

Likewise, it was possible to trace research and social interaction strategies for STI management in municipalities and rural areas of the department of Cauca that have a low technical and administrative capacity for the development of technological processes and social innovation applied to specific problems in the post-conflict. In this regard, the offer of higher education institutions has been related to the constitution of observatories, offices for social interaction and articulation with the environment as instances for the application of socially useful technical studies and support in decision-making; the design and construction of toolboxes for the social appropriation of science, technology and innovation; the transference of knowledge to the municipalities and communities from applied social research and; the constitution of project banks and information systems of STI.

The fifth category is made up of technology initiatives applied to production and connectivity processes for remote areas of the department, where proposals related to the exchange of experiences and knowledge to promote social, economic, and technological development stand out. Likewise, strategies for technology transfer and improving productivity in community agricultural activities and optimizing connectivity in the most remote areas of the department. In the sixth and last category, are the activities developed by the universities for the formation of the STI and the construction of territorial peace, where the regionalization of academic programs toward the north and south of the department stands out, and the offer of courses of extension, face-to-face and virtual, to strengthen the training of human talent.

As can be seen, the STI initiatives for peace building implemented by higher education institutions, the object of study, are numerous, although some are not included in the institutional strategic plans, which does not limit their impact and relevance. However, to improve coverage and enhance results, it is necessary to advance in the articulation between the strategies, seek complementarity and, from that perspective, improve efficiency and effectiveness levels. In fact, within the framework of the implementation of the peace accords, the construction of a common agenda among higher education institutions is required to direct and strengthen the investigation, intervention, and interaction processes carried out in the different territories of the department. In the same way, a greater synergy between the actors of the STI system with the Cauca Government, the different municipalities, and the HEI, to achieve greater effectiveness of public actions and evaluate the impact of the strategies related to the STI for including social and peace building.

8.5 Final Considerations: STI and Peace Building from HEI

It is not possible to think of the existence of a single way of intervening in the territories. It is necessary to continue the debate on the scope of peace and learn from the lessons already applied. Other points of view that link new ways of understanding the territory, as well as the participation and legitimacy of the processes will be of vital importance in the construction of territorial peace. Here, HEI have the responsibility of institutionalizing science, technology, and innovation systems for the fulfillment of this objective.

The review of the development plans of the HEI of the department of Cauca and their institutional actions in the key to peace makes it possible, first of all, to determine that the HEI of the region have not included in their development plans visible aspects around the consolidation of a territorial peace, at least in those that are private. However, it is important to bear in mind that these documents were drawn up during the negotiation phase between the national government and the FARC-EP, that is, before the signing of the Peace Agreement. Of course, this did not limit the performance of HEI at least during these early post-conflict years. On the contrary, there was a sample of actions linked to research, intervention and social interaction as a motor for social inclusion based on STI strategies which allowed, among other things, to contribute directly to the social appropriation of new discourses such as the peace, the reconstruction of the social fabric and the transfer of knowledge to mitigate serious problems in the territories of the department of Cauca.

Despite the challenges such as the low budget for research and the limited technical and technological capacities of local governments, the valuable contribution of HEI in the construction of territorial peace through STI initiatives that have sought social inclusion cannot be ignored. Starting from work with communities, the transmission of knowledge to strengthen productive and community processes, the development of technologies to reduce the digital divide and the training of human talent to promote competitiveness and innovation. In the same way, the research and social interaction activities developed from the HEI generate a significant contribution to the processes of design, execution and evaluation of policies, plans and programs oriented toward peace and social inclusion.

References

Bautista, S. (2017). Contribuciones a la fundamentación conceptual de paz territorial. *Revista Ciudad Paz-ando, 1*(10), 100–110. DOI: https://doi.org/10.14483/2422278X.11639.

Cairo, H., & Ríos, J. (2019). Las élites políticas y la paz territorial en Colombia: un análisis de discurso en torno al Acuerdo de Paz. *Revista Española de Ciencia Política, 50,* 91–113. https://doi.org/10.21308/recp.50.04.

Cairo, H., Ulrich, O., Piazzini, C., Ríos, J., Koopman, S., Montoya, V., Rodríguez, F., & Zambrano, L. (2018). "Territorial peace": The emergence

of a concept in Colombia's peace negotiations. *Geopolitics, 23*(2), 464–488. https://doi.org/10.1080/14650045.2018.1425110.
Chará, W., Méndez, D., & Betancourt, A. (2019). La justicia y la paz territorial: Experiencias, retos y desafíos del sistema local de justicia en el departamento del Cauca 2017–2018. *Via Iuris, 27*, 247–277.
Corporación Universitaria Comfacauca. Acuerdo 027 del 2014 (2014, de diciembre de 11). Por medio del cual se aprueba el Proyecto Educativo Institucional. Recuperado de http://www.unicomfacauca.edu.co/phocadownload/Acuerdos/PEI%20Unicomfacauca.pdf.
Corporación Universitaria Autónoma del Cauca. Acuerdo No. 019 de 2015 (2015, de enero de 13). Por el cual se aprueba la Reforma al Proyecto Educativo Universitario de la Corporación Universitaria Autónoma del Cauca. Recuperado de ttps://www.uniautonoma.edu.co/universidad/documentos/acuerdo-no-019-2015-peu.
Corporación Universitaria Autónoma del Cauca. Acuerdo No. 023 de 2015 (2015, de diciembre de 7). Por el cual se aprueba el Plan de Desarrollo Estratégico de la Corporación Universitaria Autónoma del Cauca. Recuperado de. https://www.uniautonoma.edu.co/institucion/estatutos.
Corporación Universitaria Autónoma del Cauca. Acuerdo No. 022 de 2017 (2017, de agosto de 1). Por el cual se aprueba la Misión de la Corporación Universitaria Autónoma del Cauca. Recuperado de https://www.uniautonoma.edu.co/universidad/documentos/acuerdo-no-022-1-agosto-2017-mision-corporacion-universitaria-autonoma-cauca.
Departamento Nacional de Planeación. (2020). Documento CONPES Política Nacional de Ciencia, Tecnología e Innovación 2021–2030. Recuperado de. https://minciencias.gov.co/sites/default/files/documento_conpes_ciencia_tecnologia_e_innovacion.pdf.
Doyle, W. (2000). A more perfect union: The liberal peace and the challenge of globalization. *Review of International Studies, 26*(5), 81–94. https://doi.org/10.1017/S0260210500000814.
Fundación Universitaria de Popayán. Acuerdo 005 de 2004 (20 de abril del 2014). Fundación Universitaria de Popayán.
Galtung, J. (1969). Violence, peace and peace research. *Journal of Peace Research, 6*(3), 167–191. https://doi.org/10.1177/002234336900600301.
García, S. (2016). "Paz territorial: ni territorios, ni paz". *Revista Nova et Vera, 2*(18). Recuperado de http://www.urosario.edu.co/revista-nova-et-vetera/Vol-2-Ed-18/Omnia/Paz-territorial-ni-territorios,-ni-paz/.
Gibler, D. (2007). Bordering on peace: Democracy, territorial issues, and conflict. *International Studies Quarterly, 51*(3), 509–532. https://doi.org/10.1111/j.1468-2478.2007.00462.x.
González, F., Bolívar, I., & Vásquez, T. (2003). Violencia política en Colombia. De la nación fragmentada a la construcción del Estado. CINEP.

Hernández, A. (2016). *Paz Rural y Reforma Territorial: Impacto del Proceso de Paz en la descentralización territorial* (Serie Documentos de Trabajo No. 51). Universidad Externado.

Ideas para la Paz. (2017). Dilemas de la paz territorial y la participación ciudadana. Recuperado de. http://www.ideaspaz.org/publications/posts/1275.

Institución Universitaria Colegio Mayor del Cauca. Acuerdo 014 de 2016. Por medio del cual se aprueba el Plan de Desarrollo Institucional 2016–2020. Recuperado de. https://unimayor.edu.co/web/21-unimayor/planeacion/planes-de-desarrollo/1372-plan-de-desarrollo-institucional-2016-2020.

Jaramillo, S. (2014). La paz territorial. Recuperado de. http://equipopazgobierno.presidencia.gov.co/prensa/declaraciones/Paginas/paz-territorial-sergio-jaramillo-alto-comisionado-paz--proceso-paz.aspx.

Koopman, S. (2018). "Territorial peace": The emergence of a concept in colombia's peace negotiations. *Geopolitics, 23*(2), 464–488. https://doi.org/10.1080/14650045.2018.1425110.

Ministerio de Ciencia, Tecnología e Innovación. (2019). MinCiencias. (07 de 05 de 2019). La Ciencia, la Tecnología y la Innovación en el Plan Nacional de Desarrollo 2018 - 2022. Recuperado de. https://minciencias.gov.co/sala_de_prensa/laciencia-la-tecnologia-y-la-innovacion-en-el-plan-nacional-desarrollo-2018-2022.

National Planning Department. (2015). Bases del Plan Nacional de Desarrollo 2014–2018. "Todos por un nuevo país: Paz, Equidad y Educación". Recuperado el 15 de mayo de 2018, de. https://colaboracion.dnp.gov.co/CDT/Prensa/Bases%20PND%202014-2018F.pdf.

Orozco, L., Aristizabal, J., & Villaveces, J (2018). Management challenge in the Entrepreneurial University and academic performance. In F. Altinay (Ed.), *Open and equal access for learning in school management*. Recuperado de. https://www.intechopen.com/books/open-and-equal-access-for-learning-in-school-management/management-challenge-in-the-entrepreneurial-university-and-academic-performance.

Oslender, U. (2018). Another history of violence: The production of geographies of terror in Colombia's Pacific coast region. *Latin American Perspectives, 35*(5), 77–102. https://doi.org/10.1177/0094582X08321961.

Presidencia de la República de Colombia. (2018). Decreto 899 de 2017. Por el cual se establecen medidas e instrumentos para la reincorporación económica y social colectiva e individual de los integrantes de las FARC-EP conforme al Acuerdo Final, suscrito entre el Gobierno Nacional y las FARC-EP el 24 de noviembre de 2016. Presidencia de la República de Colombia.

Ríos, J., & Gago, E. (2018). Realidades y desafíos de la paz territorial en Colombia, *Papers. Revista de Sociología, 103*(2), 281–302. Disponible en: https://doi.org/10.5565/rev/papers.2361.

Rodríguez, E. (2009). El rol de las universidades en la sociedad del conocimiento y en la era de la globalización: evidencia desde Chile. En: Interciencia, 34. Disponible en. http://www.redalyc.org/articulo.oa?id=33913148011.

Universidad del Cauca. (2018). Plan de Desarrollo Institucional 2018–2022. Hacia una Universidad comprometida con la Paz Territorial. Disponible en: https://www.unicauca.edu.co/versionP/sites/default/files/files/Plan_Desarrollo_Institucional_2018-2022.pdf.

Vargas, G., & Hurtado, R. (2017). *Los retos de la paz territorial*. Centro Interdisciplinario de Estudios sobre Desarrollo Cider. Universidad de Los Andes.

Zubiría, F. (2016). La Paz territorial. Recuperado de. https://www.youtube.com/watch?v=l1xQ_pi8bkE.

CHAPTER 9

A Classification Model to Analyze Inclusion in Higher Education Systems: An Approximation from Contingency Theory

Cristhian Fabián Ruiz Ramos, Ricardo Bonilla Jiménez, Javier García-Estévez, and Luis Antonio Orozco

9.1 Introduction

Inclusion in higher education systems (HES) is an issue of great importance because it allows nations to generate development opportunities. It also represents a way to provide opportunities to different population groups, especially those with vulnerable conditions or who are excluded. UNESCO initiated the promotion of inclusion in education at the 1994

C. F. R. Ramos (✉)
Senior Consultant in Innovation Management, Bogotá, Colombia

Director of the Research Group "Gestión Ambiental y Competitividad", Bogotá, Colombia

R. B. Jiménez
Corporación Universitaria Minuto de Dios UNIMINUTO, Bogotá, Colombia
e-mail: ricardo.bonilla.j@uniminuto.edu.co

L. A. Orozco et al. (eds.), *Science, Technology, and Higher Education*, Palgrave Studies in Democracy, Innovation, and Entrepreneurship for Growth,
https://doi.org/10.1007/978-3-030-80720-7_9

World Conference on Special Educational Needs: Access and Quality held in Spain (UNESCO, 1994). Since then, this UN organization has encouraged the development of national and organizational policies that promote attention not only to people with disabilities but also for different groups that could be marginalized by their social conditions.

Latin American countries have introduced legislative reforms and public policies to improve access, permanence, and the achievement of graduation diplomas from higher education institutions (HEI) with a focus on disabled students. However, the discourse on diversity and social inclusion based on moral imperatives (also sponsored by public policies) differs significantly from current university practices. Elite universities maintain a low inclusion of students from low socio-economic status (LSES) and generally incorporate talented students (Hughes, 2015).

One of the most important indicators from university rankings takes into account the capacity of HEI to carry out the three missions of higher education: teaching, research, and technology transfer through innovation and entrepreneurship. According to Hughes (2015), the lowest ranked universities are teaching-oriented organizations. They concentrate their efforts on achieving excellent teaching processes on populations that have complex needs such as LSES. For these types of universities, neither enhanced research through hiring PhDs nor assuming challenges of the third mission are a priority.

Inclusion in HES has been mainly understood as a diversity issue in which any person has the right to access an HEI regardless of abilities, race, gender, nationality, or any other characteristic (Wood, 2015). Therefore, there is a concern about including students from different social and cultural backgrounds (Dassin, Enders & Kottmann, 2014).

Inclusion involves "organizational strategies and practices that promote meaningful social and academic interactions among persons and groups

J. García-Estévez
Universidad de Los Andes, Bogotá, Colombia
e-mail: jh.garcia@uniandes.edu.co

L. A. Orozco
School of Management, Universidad Externado de Colombia, Bogotá, Colombia
e-mail: luis.orozco@uexternado.edu.co

who differ in their experiences, their views, and their traits" (Tienda, 2013, p. 467).

Inclusion is a multidimensional concept that addresses issues for students, teachers, and administrative staff related to diversity, equity, coverage, and student dropout, as well as access, success, and participation of different interest groups. However, empirical studies on inclusion focus on the student population, mainly in particular social groups (Contini & Salza, 2020; Cupito & Langesten, 2011; Sahni & Shankar, 2012). There are conflicts among access—as a measure of social inclusion—and quality—seen through success that reflects performance and outcome indicators—(Contini & Salza, 2020; Gidley et al., 2010) and the results of university rankings. It can be expected that universities will seek to allocate resources to increase indicators related to quality in terms of the number of PhDs and indexed publications rather than expanding coverage to populations that may not be able to get good results from tests such as the SAT. This phenomenon is known as the tension between elite institutions and extensive higher education (Gidley et al., 2010) and the dichotomy between inclusion and effectiveness in terms of graduation rate (Contini & Salza, 2020).

Access, not only for students but also for teachers and administrative staff, is the first step of inclusion, and this may vary according to contingent factors such as the geographic location of the universities and their immediate surroundings. Success of inclusion should not only take into account fulfilling a university's educational objectives and the level of incorporation and professional development of a university community (Gidley et al., 2010); it should also be reflected as a mechanism to promote regional development.

In Colombia, inclusion has been understood from a management perspective, in which IES are transformed and adapted to overcome the limitations and barriers that students have for learning, especially certain vulnerable social groups (Ministerio de Educación Nacional [MEN], 2013, cited by Arizabaleta Domínguez & Ochoa Cubillos, 2016). This approach to inclusion focuses mainly on populations "from ethnic groups, victims of the armed conflict, people with disabilities, gypsy populations, LGBTI, border residents, and peasants, among others, to create inclusive-learning environments with social impact" (Arizabaleta Domínguez & Ochoa Cubillos, 2016).

The launch of the *Guidelines Policy for Inclusive Higher Education* in 2014 is one of the processes that the MEN carried out to improve inclusion in higher education. This document provides policies to care for the particular populations that, due to their conditions, require specific treatment according to current law (see Decree 780 of 2016). In this framework, inclusion is measured considering students, teachers, and administrative populations in terms of the perception they have about the policies, programs, plans, and actions of IES to serve target groups comprehensively. However, we do not have studies that analyze inclusion taking into account how IES incorporate students and PhDs according to their regional features where IES have influence.

According to the statistics reported by the National Information System of Higher Education (SNIES - MEN, 2016), in 2018, 637 municipalities in Colombia had enrollment of at least one person in higher education programs, representing about 57% of the total number of municipalities in the country. However, most of the higher education programs are highly concentrated in a few departments or cities of the country, representing a significant coverage gap. For example, 33% of higher education students are enrolled in Bogotá, 13.9% in Antioquia, 7.5% in Valle del Cauca, 5.5% in Atlántico, and 5.3% in Santander. Therefore, Bogotá and these four departments represent 65.2% of the higher education enrollment while the other 28 departments represent just 34.8%. In Arauca, Amazonas, Guainía, Vaupés, and Vichada, the coverage rate is below 10%. This shows a high disparity in terms of access to higher education.

Figure 9.1 shows the Gini Index of Undergraduate Enrollment in Colombia from 2006 to 2015. The index had a 0.8 percentage point reduction during this period (going from 66 in 2006 to 65.2% in 2015). This variation suggests a marginal reduction in territorial inequality related to access to higher education. Colombia has made progress in reducing dropout rates, achieving a national university dropout rate of 9% in 2016. In comparison, the university dropout rate in technical, professional, and technological subjects (T&T) was 17.1% (SPADIES).

This chapter analyzes the inclusion of PhDs and students in the Colombian university system from a regional perspective. We propose a model to classify and forecast the inclusion of students and PhDs within a contingency theory framework to contribute to resource planning according to environmental conditions and to allow for better adjustment of governance efforts in the STI system.

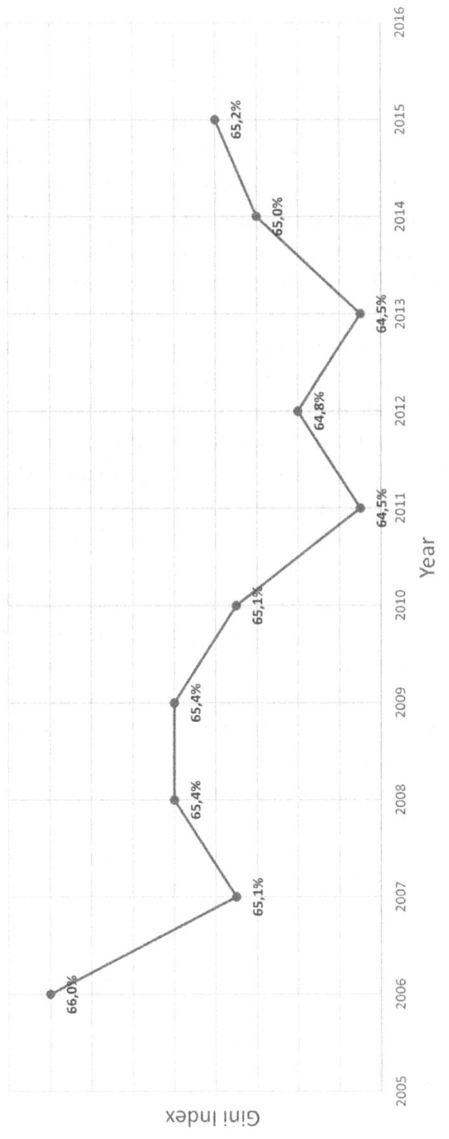

Fig. 9.1 Gini Index of Undergraduate Enrollment in Colombia from 2006 to 2015 (*Source* SNIES - MEN 2016, p. 3)

Over the last two decades, the contribution of higher education in inclusive and sustainable socio-economic development has significantly increased through several channels such as fostering innovation, increasing higher skills, and widening access. HES can contribute to inclusive development by preparing citizens and creating new knowledge to face technological change and socio-economic challenges.

There has been a growing demand to widen the access to higher education and change the elitist nature of universities. The massive expansion of higher education across all continents has been one of the defining features of the late twentieth and early twenty-first centuries (Guri-Rosenblit et al., 2007). Including more students as a means to contribute to social development has increased due to national policies and the natural growth of higher education institutions (Ferreyra et al., 2017).

In the early 1980s, several countries started to develop quality assessment systems for higher education (Van Vught & Westerheijden, 1994). Accreditations and rankings have increased in national and international realms as institutional instances that define legitimacy (Marope et al., 2013), exerting pressures to increase the number of PhDs and the teaching-student related indicators (Wächter et al., 2015) seen as part of what is considered quality in higher education (Reyes, 2016). Universities tried to hire more PhDs to accomplish teaching and research missions and move to the third mission that is oriented toward innovation, technology transfer, and entrepreneurship (Villaveces & Orozco, 2015). Larger numbers of PhDs means a university's human capital can encompass training as well as creating new knowledge in a virtuous cycle, implying signals of quality that could subsequently more students.

Two of the main concerns and central indicators in HES are the inclusion of undergraduate students and Ph.Ds. In addition to the oversupply of PhDs in universities, the number of freshmen has also decreased in recent years in several Colombian HES. This imbalance leads to a governance problem in terms of adjusting the inclusion of human capital in HEIs.

During the twentieth century's last two decades, STI policies provided several incentives to train PhDs worldwide, despite the absorptive capacity of STI systems (Mangematin, 2000). At the beginning of the second decade of the twenty-first century, Cyranoski, Ledford, Nayar, and Yahia (2011) analyzed the overproduction of PhDs in the world and the problems incorporating doctors into stable jobs in developed economies. The authors found that the number of scientists with PhDs grew 40% from

1998 to 2008. However, the labor market began to constrain. Mangematin (2000, p. 741) indicated that "It is becoming more and more difficult for PhD graduates to find a job corresponding to their qualifications". Also, Cyranoski et al. (2011, p. 276) observed that "science Ph.D. graduates may never get a chance to take full advantage of their qualifications. In some countries, including the United States and Japan, people who have trained at great length and expense to be researchers confront a dwindling number of academic jobs".

Over the last decade, the number of PhDs in Colombia has increased. There were 6,665 PhDs in 2007 and 17,224 in 2016. The number of PhDs linked to research activities was 520 in 2007 and 3,029 in 2016 (OCyT, 2018). The number of professors increased from 5,649 in 2010 to 13,797 in 2018. In addition, the number of PhD programs grew from 78 in 2007 to 266 in 2016. As a consequence, the number of students that received a PhD degree rose from 97 in 2007 to 803 in 2018 (SNIES, 2019).

Inclusion in terms of an increase in number of students has been significant over the last several decades in the Colombian HEIs. Student numbers have steadily grown from 1990 to 2016, from around 487,448 to 2,320,148 (Observatorio de la Universidad Colombiana, sf). Despite this increase, Colombia still has one of the lowest shares of tertiary-educated adults among OECD countries. In 2018, 15.4% of Colombia's population of 25–64 year-olds had a tertiary education, where 27% have a tertiary education in the OECD countries, almost double. Although the share of Colombia's tertiary-educated younger adults (25–34 year-olds) is slightly higher at 29%, it is still among the lowest of the OECD countries (44.5% for younger adults) (OECD, 2019).

The private sector plays an important role in Colombian tertiary education, particularly at the bachelor's and master's levels where 60–70% of students are enrolled compared to 30% on average across OECD countries. In contrast, only 20% of short-cycle tertiary students are enrolled in private institutions in Colombia compared to 40% on average across OECD countries (OECD, 2019).

The Ministry of Education—MEN reported Colombia had 2,280,327 undergraduate students in 2017. This number dropped to 2,267,140 in 2018, a reduction of 0.6%. New students in Colombian HES decreased between 2017 and 2018 by 13.6%, as the number of students went from 798,431 to 690,168 (SNIES, 2019).

The phenomena described above reveals a tension in the trend of universities. They want to engage PhDs but simultaneously have problems recruiting more students. There is no evidence that the number of students is growing in Colombia, but more students are needed to engage PhDs.

One of the STI system governing goals is including more people in HES, promoting developing and creating capacities to produce more citizens and knowledge. In developing economies in Latin America, the labor market for PhDs in HES has not been evaluated. Developing models to explain and classify social inclusion in universities according to their capacity to hire PhDs and grow in terms of students has been neglected.

Studies of higher education are emerging in the literature that use the contingency theory framework to explain the relationship between changes in the environment and the universities' response (Kováts, 2018). This research proposes a model to explain the relationship between university size in terms of students and the absorptive capacity to incorporate doctors in their faculties, using the contingency theory framework developed in organizational studies. The model helps plan resources to improve social inclusion in HEIs. The model was applied to universities with different environmental conditions in the labor market (country capital vs. regions) and helps identify groups of universities according to their organizational mission—from teaching to research and entrepreneurship—and forecast their capacity to grow with new students and PhD professors. Also, the model helps organize the number of PhDs according to the demand of HES in terms of students in undergraduate programs.

The chapter is structured as follows. The next section presents a review of the literature used to develop the model. The second part presents the methodology defined to construct the model using the case of Colombian HEIs. The third part shows the results, and the fourth part present the conclusions.

9.2 Theoretical Background

9.2.1 *Inclusiveness in HES as a Means of Development and Regional Inequality*

Inclusive development emerged on the global development discourse in the early 2000s. According to UNDP, development can be inclusive and reduce poverty only if every social group contributes to creating opportunities, shares benefits from development, and participates in the decision-making process (UNDP, 2013). This inclusiveness allows more governance of the HEIs. The word inclusiveness has gained a wide content in the debate both at the academic and policy levels.

Inclusiveness can be defined in terms of the capability of providing wide opportunities along with race, ethnicity, gender, income, and social class lines to attain higher education degrees. It also aims at promoting equity and social cohesion (European Commission, 2018). Inclusiveness can also be defined in terms of access—if the enrollment probability is high for all social groups, or completion—if the (timely) completion probability given enrollment is high for all social groups. Inclusiveness can mean emphasizing the needs of disadvantaged and marginalized people; peri-urban areas, sectors, and regions; participation in policy and politics (Lawson, 2010); a broad education processes; social infrastructure for all; capacity building to enable the marginalized to use opportunities; recognition of a plural system of rights, that is, also customary rights; enabling people to help themselves; and the redistribution of power to allow for redistribution of resources (Pouw & Gupta, 2017).

The global development discourse has broadened its focus beyond a narrow definition of development as a primarily economic process to one with an integral focus on the achievement of equity and the rights of citizenship (Hickey et al., 2015). From a higher education perspective, inclusive development implies widening access since a broad education is one of the most important ways to reduce inequalities across social groups, gender, and regions (Conceição et al., 2001). Higher education may help reduce inequality, foster social inclusion, and deal with social challenges. In fact, there is evidence of the role of HEIs as technological promoters, which help solve social problems and connect directly with people's daily needs, supporting the dynamics of inclusion, justice, and well-being (Kruss et al., 2015).

The importance of higher education is rising in modern societies in which economies are based on knowledge and innovation. For instance, the EU2020 strategy defined in 2010 set the goal that 40% of the individuals aged 25–34 have a tertiary education by 2020. HES are no longer purely elite systems so there are greater societal expectations for fair access to them (Brewis, 2019). Nonetheless, inequality in access to HES remains pervasive around the world (Atherton et al., 2016).

Social inclusion in higher education refers to the increasing access to higher education and degree completion for underrepresented groups, improving countries' human capital, and innovation capacity while fostering social inclusion of citizens and increasing their labor market opportunities (Kottmann et al., 2019). A recent progress report on the Bologna process implementation confirms that students from low socio-economic backgrounds, migrant backgrounds, and students with chronic illnesses or disabilities are still underrepresented in higher education (Kottmann et al., 2019). The Italian higher education system demonstrates that inclusiveness is not just a matter of access because, despite the absence of formal entry barriers, Italy is lagging behind the majority of the developed countries in the share of young individuals with tertiary education (Contini & Salza, 2020).

From a regional development perspective, inclusion in HEIs provides several mechanisms to improve standards of living. HEIs can support the specific needs and circumstances of regional economic, social, and cultural development. They can link with public and private regional partners to develop local industries. They contribute to a region's comparative advantage in knowledge-based industries and to its human capital base, as they train professionals who may be more likely to remain in the regions after graduation (OECD, 2017).

The capacity of HEIs to contribute to the development of STI systems mainly depends on the inclusion of PhDs and students. First, PhDs contribute to the creation of knowledge, consultancy services, improvements in teaching, and the incorporation of new technologies, among others. Second, it is recognized that the inclusion of students is important for improving the lives of people, job creation, economic growth, and social fairness. Therefore, there is a growing need to widen opportunities for access and completion for students from disadvantaged backgrounds.

9.2.2 The Shortcomings of the Inclusion of Students and PhD in HES

The increase of PhDs has risen in recent years, creating pressures in the labor market in developed economies (Cyranoski et al., 2011) to the point that a doctoral education is in crisis (Halse, 2007). In European countries like Italy, the number of PhDs increased between 2000 and 2012 by more than 300%, "while a decrease has been reported by the Universities' personnel" (Gaeta et al., 2017, p. 245). Moreover, according to Santos, Horta and Heitor (2016, p. 354), citing Miller and Feldman

(2014), the complexity of academic work includes "unpredictable and unsatisfactory career prospects... where contingent faculty, postdoctoral positions followed by more postdoctoral positions, and limited research and academic freedom is the expected career path". In terms of the capacity of universities to engage PhDs, Soucek et al. (2017) found that obtaining a PhD does not imply an improvement in salary. Rather, self-employment allows better income. Finally, studies in countries like Norway (Wiers-Jenssen & Try, 2005) and Colombia (Orozco, 2016) reveal the rising competition between national and immigrant academics. The labor market in fields like management, pressured by the need for internationalization, tends to hire and value immigrants with PhDs more than national professors (Orozco, 2016).

In Portugal, a critical analysis of the claim "too many Ph.D.s" was addressed by Santos et al (2016), showing that PhDs tend to move beyond stable jobs at universities. Cuthbert and Molla (2015) show how developed economies tend to enhance doctoral programs to include training that allow graduates to get a job outside HES. In Australia, nearly 50% of PhDs find a job outside of academia due to the reframing of doctoral education to train people in a wide skillset to overcome unemployment. The current frame in the fourth industrial revolution brings new opportunities to high-level training, especially in research (Schwab, 2017). In fact, previous research reveals that firms in the Colombian manufacturing industry that engage PhDs tend to innovate more (Orozco et al., 2010), aiming for the incorporation of PhDs in the industry. Also, PhDs may contribute to high technological entrepreneurship (Villaveces & Orozco, 2015) and lead public administration and non-profit organizations (Cuthbert & Molla, 2015). In conclusion, universities may present disadvantages to compete for hiring PhDs.

The contingency theory stated that changes in the environment that lead to uncertainty influence organizations to define strategies and structures that can respond and fit the external conditions to perform better (Donaldson, 2001). Subsequently, differing environmental conditions lead to a variety of types of organizational strategies and structures. Universities have adjusted their organizational mission according to the changes presented in the environment (Scott, 2006). Since the first industrial revolution, three university models can be identified: the Napoleonic devoted to teaching, the Humboldtian oriented toward research, and the Anglo-Saxon and Anglo-American model that promotes the so-called "third mission" based on innovation, entrepreneurship and knowledge commercialization (Sam & Van der Sijde, 2014).

Kováts (2018) introduced the contingency theory to explain faculty growth and the increase of decentralization to accomplish teaching and research activities due to the rise of university size in terms of new students and the changes in legal conditions. Universities that want to reach the third mission and adjust their organizational capacity to survive and grow in the changing environment need to increase the number of PhDs at faculties to comply with the institutional request of what is defined as a quality in HES (Orozco et al., 2018).

In Latin America, researchers in the region almost doubled between 2000 and 2010, especially in countries like Argentina, Colombia, and Mexico (Barro & Fernández, 2015). However, as Barro and Fernández (2015, p. 532) concluded, "The number of PhDs is still insufficient to establish an intensive R&D program in most of the countries in the region". If the PhD supply is low, universities postpone hiring and increase teaching loads and class sizes from staff and faculty members (Basil & Basil, 2006).

HES in Latin America present shortcomings in moving toward accomplishing the third mission and adjusting their structures to changing environments framed by the fourth technological revolution. As Orozco et al. (2018) found, an elite group of universities that show good performance in teaching also present better results in activities related to the third mission in Colombia despite variables like student size and geographical location. However, universities rely on tuition and the number of students. So, good universities may search for an increase of students by an increase of PhDs.

The contingency model developed below differentiates universities by environments (given by location) and its organizational strategy, whose mission can be identified and inferred by its growth trend.

From a complex science approximation, it is not enough to describe and characterize a phenomenon; it is necessary to propose an explanation for its behavior. As Levy (2000) stated, "Dynamic nonlinear systems with feedback mechanisms can exhibit complex, unpredictable behavior within which underlying patterns and structure can be discerned" (p. 83). We expect the same from this complex system composed by different types of universities inside the HES.

9.3 Methodology

The proposed model is based on the principle of contingency theory that the evolution of an element of a system depends on its current state and its ability to respond to environmental conditions. Although all Colombian universities have the same regulatory framework, their conditions, like the regional munificence or financial generosity, in terms of PhDs as a labor market and the number of students differ significantly.

To be coherent with the contingency theory, we propose a model based on probability distribution functions over linear or deterministic models. It is possible to locate regions of statistical order and disorder of elements within a distribution function. This model will consider the current state of each of its elements, Colombian HEIs. Their positions in the distribution can reveal possible underlying dynamics.

According to theories of Complex Science, analyzing distribution functions can point out regions of statistical disorder among subgroups of its agents. These regions of disorder highlight HEIs that could be exploring the system and are usually identifying opportunities. The distribution functions can also point out regions of statistical order among a subgroup of its agents. These HEIs could be interpreted to have overcome the exploration of opportunities and instead have moved to exploiting them.

Statistical disorders are usually displayed by normal or exponential distributions, and statistical order are represented by Power Law or Pareto distributions (Andriani & McKelvey, 2007, 2009). Working with a distribution function implies that a response given the same stimulus depends on its agents and context. This model calculates distribution functions for PhD distribution on HEI and distribution function of freshmen on HEI and the possible relations.

The model does not intend to predict the increase of PhDs given an increase in the number of students. It intends to show that a growth stimulus in students does not generate the same stimulus in the growth of PhDs. It will be shown that a complex system composed of heterogeneous actors translates the same stimulus into different responses. From the contingency theory point of view, the strategies of each system element are conditioned both to the environment and to its capacity to act on it.

To calculate changes in the distribution function to identify order or disorder regions it is needed to create a fit of the observed distribution function. The difficulty of this construction is that the distribution fit must be smooth and for the entire distribution. For this, the parametric fit for long-tail distribution proposed by Bonilla and Zarama (2012) is used.

Bonilla and Zarama (2012) propose a fit using a piecewise function with continuous derivatives. The piecewise function will be possible changes in the underlying dynamic.

The piecewise functions used to fit long-tail distributions is:

$$f_1(x) = x^\lambda(x^{k_1}A_1 + x^{-k_1}B_1) for 1 \leq x \leq x_1$$

$$f_2(x) = x^\lambda(x^{k_2}A_2 + x^{-k_2}B_2) for x_1 < x$$

where k_i, A_i, B_i, λ, and x_i are fit parameters.

An advantage of using a piecewise function model to fit the distributions is the ability to identify thresholds where the distribution changes. As presented by Bonilla and Zarama (2011), the piecewise adjustment function is theoretical. Therefore, predictions based on changes in the distribution relate to actual changes in the behavior of the system. Fitting the distribution functions in this way allows us to identify points at which the dynamics of the system change. Figures 9.2 and 9.3 show

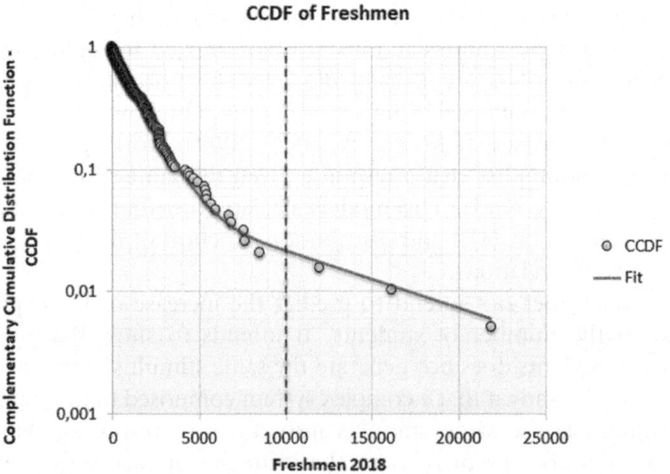

Fig. 9.2 Complementary cumulative distribution function of the number of students enrolled by HEI (*Source* Education Information System [SNIES], January 2018. Dashed vertical lines show the change in the stepwise function at 10,000 freshmen. The KS-test gives a pValue = 0.36 greater than 0.05, then the null hypothesis the data follow a specified distribution is accepted)

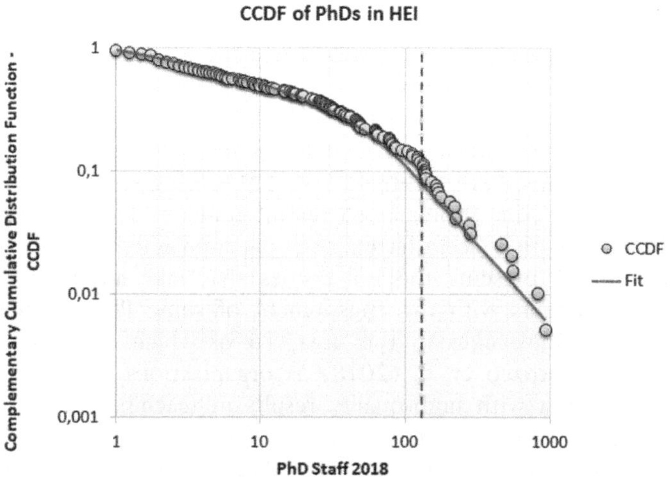

Fig. 9.3 Complementary cumulative distribution function of PhDs hired by HEI (*Source* Education Information System [SNIES], January 2018. Dashed vertical lines show the change in the stepwise function so in the underlying dynamic at 130 PhDs. The KS-test gives a pValue = 0.18 greater than 0.05, then the null hypothesis the data follow a specified distribution is accepted)

the fit for PhDs in HEI and for freshmen. Mathematically the fit is over the Cumulative Distribution Function to calculate Kolmogorov–Smirnov Goodness-of-Fit Test (KS-Test).

9.4 Results

Combining results from freshmen and PhDs fits, a model can be defined with four areas. In three quadrants, universities are grouped by their order–disorder dynamic (see Fig. 9.4). These areas and their quadrants are defined from the changes in the curve of the distribution function of the variables shown in Figs. 9.2 and 9.3.

In quadrant A1 there are 168 HEIs in a disordered state for both the freshmen distribution and PhD distribution that can be interpreted as HEI that are looking for opportunities or strategies on recruiting new students and understanding opportunities around hiring PhDs. In quadrant A2 there are 3 HEIs that are in an ordered state given the freshmen distribution but in a disordered state given the PhD distribution. The

HEI in this quadrant have a deep understanding of the academic market and clear strategies to take advantage attracting undergraduate students, but in terms of PhDs they do not seem to be interested or do not have a clear understanding what to do. Finally, in quadrant A3, there are 22 HEI that display a statistical order relating to PhDs but show disorder for freshmen. These have identified how PhDs bring value to their institutions but lack clear strategies to recruit undergraduate students, for example, because they don't have a large program offering.

Quadrant Al presents the universities that take advantage of the increase of students with the engagement of some PhDs. The model classified 168 universities in this area, 16 of which were defined by the model of Orozco et al. (2018) as organizations able to perform the third mission with high-quality results in teaching. Orozco et al. (2018, p. 206) found that universities in this group "are capable of being involved in academic entrepreneurship while generating synergies with the professional education that constitutes the basis of their mission".

The methodology proposed brings insight to create categories to analyze the HES and clearly invites us to perform deeper studies to explore how regions overcome the imbalance between a decrease in freshmen and increase in PhDs. Figure 9.5 shows the change in freshmen between 2017 and 2018 on average by region on the x-axis, and the

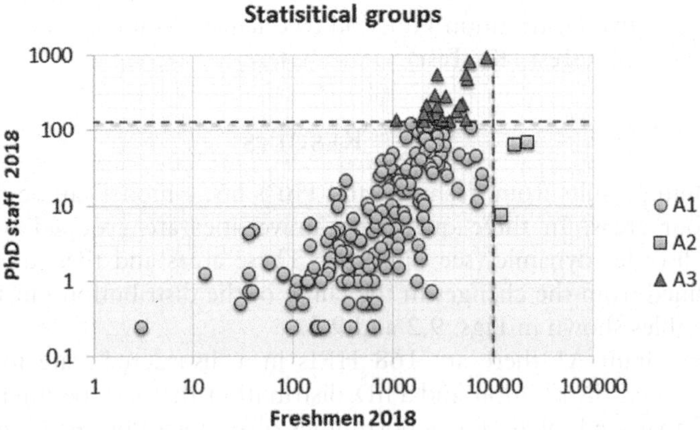

Fig. 9.4 Clusters that determine HEI on statistical order or disorder state

change in PhDs in the same period on the y-axis. On this figure, development Level 1 indicates a region with low development conditions and Level 4 with high development conditions on a logarithmic scale.

Figure 9.5 shows HEIs in all four quadrants, meaning there are HEIs displaying growths in both freshmen and PhDs and all possible other combinations. Although there is at least one regional development level in each quadrant, there are no obvious relations between average change in Freshman or PhD population with the regional development Index (Consejo Privado de Competitividad and Universidad del Rosario, 2019). The figure shows that the HEI in Atlantico is the only one that tried to engage more students despite creating research capacities, including more Ph.D. However, this type of tendency does not seems adequate to improve the quality, and the trend of the most developed regions is to grow more in doctors than in first-year students. As Ochoa (2019) stated, the increase of students does not mean more quality in a HES that 50% of students withdraw from their careers.

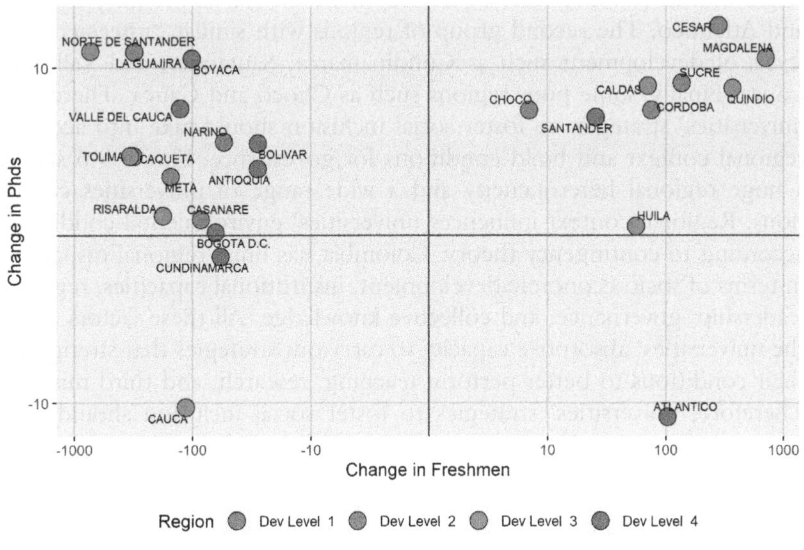

Fig. 9.5 Average Change in freshman vs. Change in PhDs by Region and Development Between 2017–2018 at Colombian HEIs

To explore the relation by region more deeply, Fig. 9.6 presents the change in freshmen between 2017 and 2018 on the x-axis, and the change in PhDs in the same period on the y-axis for each HEI in a region at each development level. In this figure, it is possible to see that HEIs in the same region experience different conditions or opportunities given their knowledge or strategies.

Figure 9.6 shows that an analysis of individual conditions by HEI is needed. Regions with more than three HEIs have institutions in more than one quadrant, showing there are HEIs with strategies adapted to conditions but also institutions that fail to grow in Freshmen and PhD simultaneously. In addition, Figure 9.6 shows a huge regional heterogeneity and a wide range of universities' conditions. Regional context influences universities' environmental conditions according to contingency theory. Colombia has huge regional disparities in terms of socio-economic development, institutional capacities, regional leadership, governance, and collective knowledge. All these factors affect the universities' absorptive capacity to carry out strategies that strengthen their conditions to better perform teaching, research, and third mission. In Figure 9.6, we can classify the regional patterns into three groups. Regions with a better level of development such as Antioquia, Bogotá, and Atlantico. The second group of regions with similar "intermediate" levels of development such as Cundinamarca, Santander, and Valle del Cauca. Finally, some poor regions such as Chocó and Cauca. Therefore, universities' strategies to foster social inclusion should take into account regional context and build conditions for governance. Figure 9.6 shows a huge regional heterogeneity and a wide range of universities conditions. Regional context influences universities' environmental conditions according to contingency theory. Colombia has huge regional disparities in terms of socio-economic development, institutional capacities, regional leadership, governance, and collective knowledge. All these factors affect the universities' absorptive capacity to carry out strategies that strengthen their conditions to better perform teaching, research, and third mission. Therefore, universities' strategies to foster social inclusion should take into account regional context and build conditions for governance.

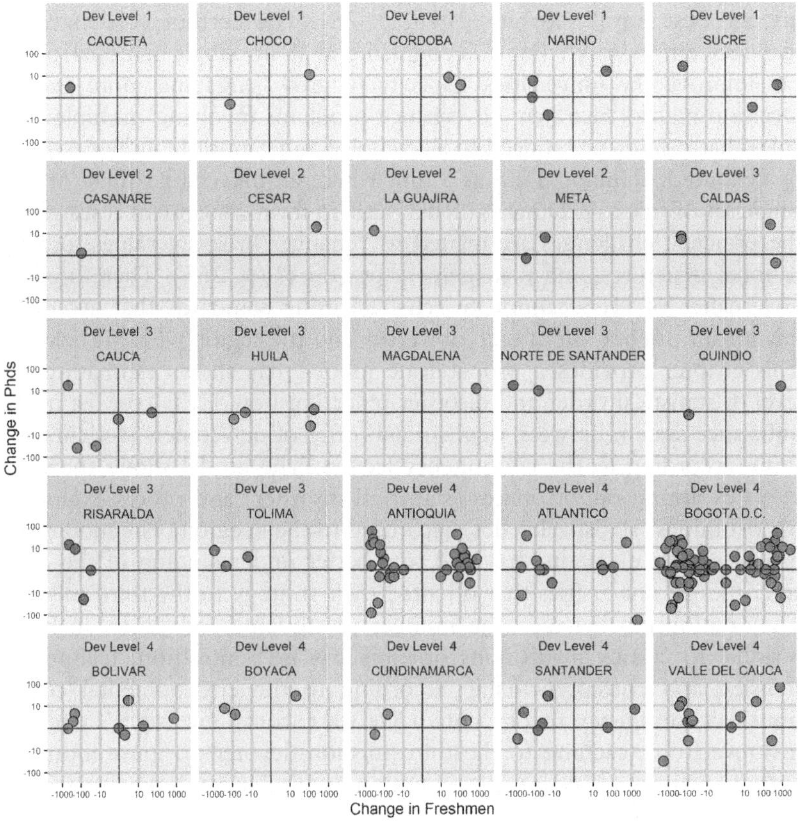

Fig. 9.6 Change in Freshman vs. Change in PhDs Between 2017–2018 for each Colombian HEI by Region and Development level

9.5 Conclusion

In recent years, the institutional pressures to increase social inclusion in the HES have been increasing in an imbalance between the incorporation of students and Ph.D. to achieve the university mission in education and research. Therefore, the governance of social inclusion in the HES needs tools to evaluate the absorptive capacity according to the environmental demands. The contingency theory of organizations asserts that "there is no structure which is effective in every environment (there is no one best way)" (Kováts, 2018, p. 75). The current challenges for management research imply recognizing that no single national policy can improve the universities' capacity to grow, engaging more people. Decision-makers face new governance problems involving multiple variables that cannot be reduced to one choice and cannot be fully described or delimited, thinking HES as a unit where all universities must fit in a single set of rules. As Duncan (1993) argued for management researchers, the principal challenges are related to "changes in social values, organizational structures, and management practices" (p. 255). Therefore, the governance of HES cannot be achieved using standards that avoid the missionary orientation of each university and the region where it belongs. This chapter provides a probabilistic model that allows estimating the level of statistical order and disorder reflecting how HEIs co-exist in the imbalance system between demand and offer of newcomers students and PhDs according to the contingency factors. The model shows there are HEIs exploring opportunities (statistical disorder) and others exploiting opportunities (statistical order) according to their region. The model also provides basic elements that lead to a better understanding of the characteristics of universities that oriented their strategy to the third mission. The relationship between the number of students and Ph.D. makes it possible to classify institutions oriented toward innovation, technology transfer, and entrepreneurship according to the environmental conditions as contingency theory stated. We start from universities' tendency to move from teaching to the third mission devoted to innovation and entrepreneurship. Under this assumption, we find institutions that require more significant growth in their Ph.D. staff. However, in an emerging economy like Colombia, the trend of the universities shows greater growth in students than in doctors. Universities in Colombia have been raising their infrastructure by 37% per year (Dinero, 2019), and the Covid-19 effect will enhance the tendency to grow using digital technologies for virtual and remote education. The question remains if social inclusion is oriented toward student engagement while universities tried to achieve financial efficiencies with fewer Ph.Ds, promotes the quality of the HES (Aristizabal and Orozco, 2020; Orozco et al., 2018). We hope to contribute to new forms of researching the trends of HES according to the variables that define mission statements oriented toward the particular conditions of each university and promote the idea that good governance needs to go beyond policies that seek that one size fits all.

References

Allen, P., Maguire, S., & McKelvey, B. (2011). *The Sage handbook of complexity and management*. Sage.

Andriani, P., & McKelvey, B. (2007). Beyond Gaussian averages: redirecting. *Journal of International Business Studies, 38*(7), 1212–1230.

Andriani, P., & McKelvey, B. (2009). Perspective—from Gaussian to Paretian thinking: Causes and implications of power laws in organizations. *Organization science, 20*(6), 1053–1071.

Aristizabal, J., & Orozco, L. A (2020). Más allá de los rankings: propuesta para medir la calidad y la eficiencia de la educación superior. *Experto, 11*(2), 19–23.

Arizabaleta Domínguez, S. L., & Ochoa Cubillos, A. F. (2016). Hacia una educación superior inclusiva en Colombia. *Pedagogía y Saberes, 45*, 41–52.

Atherton, G., Dumangane, C., & Whitty, G. (2016). *Charting equity in higher education: Drawing the global access map—Research database*. University of York.

Barro, S., & Fernández, S. (2015). *La transferencia de I + D, la innovación y el emprendimiento en las universidades*. Centro Interuniversitario de Desarrollo (CINDA).

Basil, M. D., & Basil, D. Z. (2006). The marketing market: A study of Ph.D. supply, demand, hiring institutions, and job candidates. *Journal of Business Research, 59*(4), 516–523.

Bonilla, R., & Zarama, R. (2012). An information approach to deriving domestic water demand: An application to Bogotá, Colombia. In *Production systems and supply chain management in emerging countries: Best practices* (pp. 25–44). Springer.

Borgman, C. L. (Ed.). (1990). *Scholarly communication and bibliometrics*. Sage.

Brewis, E. (2019). Fair access to higher education and discourses of development: A policy analysis from Indonesia. *Compare: A Journal of Comparative and International Education, 49*(3), 453–470. https://doi.org/10.1080/03057925.2018.1425132.

Conceição, P., Gibson, D. V., Heitor, M. V., & Sirilli, G. (2001). Knowledge for inclusive development: The challenge of globally integrated learning and implications for science and technology policy. *Technological Forecasting and Social Change, 66*(1), 1–29. https://doi.org/10.1016/S0040-1625(00)00075-5.

Consejo Privado de Competitividad & Universidad del Rosario. (2019). Indice Departamental de Competitividad. Bogotá: Universidad del Rosario. Available at: https://compite.com.co/wp-content/uploads/2019/11/CPC_IDC_2019_WEB.pdf.

Contini, D., & Salza, G. (2020). Too few university graduates. Inclusiveness and effectiveness of the Italian higher education system. *Socio-Economic Planning Sciences*, 100803. https://doi.org/10.1016/j.seps.2020.100803.

Cupito, E., & Langsten, R. (2011). "Inclusiveness in Higher Education in Egypt." *Higher Education, 62*(2), 1–15.

Cuthbert, D., & Molla, T. (2015). Ph.D. crisis discourse: A critical approach to the framing of the problem and some Australian 'solutions'. *Higher Education, 69*(1), 33–53.

Cyranoski, D., Gilbert, N., Ledford, H., Nayar, A., & Yahia, M. (2011). Education: The Ph.D. factory. *Nature, 472*(7343), 276–279.

Dassin, J., Enders, J., & Kottmann, A. (2014). Social inclusion in international higher education: approach and achievements of IFP. In *Leadership for social justice in higher education* (pp. 15–33). Palgrave Macmillan.

Dinero, R. (2019). La expansión de las obras en las universidades. Disponible en https://www.semana.com/edicion-impresa/negocios/articulo/en-que-van-las-obras-de-infraestructura-en-las-universidades/266401/.

Donaldson, L. (2001). *The contingency theory of organizations.* Sage.

Donaldson, L. (2006). The contingency theory of organizational design: Challenges and opportunities. *Organization Design*, 19–40.

Duncan, G. T. (1993). Management research methodology: Prospects and links to practice. *The International Journal of Organizational Analysis, 1*(3), 255–272.

European Commission. (2018). *The European higher education area in 2018: Bologna process implementation report Publications Office of the European Union/EACEA/Eurydice.*

Ferreyra, M., Avitabile, C., & Paz, F. H. (2017). *At a crossroads: Higher education in Latin America and the Caribbean.* World Bank Publications.

Gaeta, G. L., Lavadera, G. L., & Pastore, F. (2017). Much ado about nothing? The Wage Penalty of holding a Ph.D. Degree but not a Ph.D. job position☆. *In Skill Mismatch in Labor Markets* (pp. 243–277). Emerald Publishing.

Gidley, J. M., Hampson, G. P., Wheeler, L., & Bereded-Samuel, E. (2010). From access to success: An integrated approach to quality higher education informed by social inclusion theory and practice. *Higher Education Policy, 23*(1), 123–147.

Guri-Rosenblit, S., Sebkova, H., & Teichler, U. (2007). *Massification and diversity of higher education systems: Interplay of complex dimensions.* UNESCO Forum.

Halse, C. (2007). Is the doctorate in crisis? *Nagoya Journal of Studies in Higher Education, 7*(1), 321–337.

Hickey, S., Sen|, K., & Bukenya, B. (2015). *The politics of inclusive development: Interrogating the evidence.* Oxford University Press.

Hughes, K. (2015). The social inclusion meme in higher education: Are universities doing enough? *International Journal of Inclusive Education, 19*(3), 303–313.

Hussar, B., Zhang, J., Hein, S., Wang, K., Roberts, A., Cui, J., Smith, M., AIR; Bullock Mann, F., Barmer, A., & Dilig, R. (2020). *The condition of education 2020*. National Center for Education Statistics. IES. NCES 2020144. Available at https://nces.ed.gov/pubsearch/pubsinfo.asp?pubid=2020144.

Kemper, A. (2010). *Complex networks theory*. Physica-Verlag HD.

Kottmann, A., Vossensteyn, J. J., Kolster, R., Veidemane, A., Blasko, Z., Biagi, F., Sánchez-Barrioluengo, M., European Commission, & Joint Research Centre. (2019). *Social inclusion policies in higher education: Evidence from the EU—Overview of major widening participation policies applied in the EU 28*.

Kováts, G. (2018). The change of organizational structure of higher education institutions in Hungary: A contingency theory analysis. *International Review of Social Research, 8*(1), 74–86.

Kruss, G., McGrath, S., Petersen, I., & Gastrow, M. (2015). Higher education and economic development: The importance of building technological capabilities. *International Journal of Educational Development, 43*, 22–31. https://doi.org/10.1016/j.ijedudev.2015.04.011.

Lawson, V. (2010). Reshaping economic geography? Producing spaces of inclusive development. *Economic Geography, 86*(4), 351–360. https://doi.org/10.1111/j.1944-8287.2010.001092.x.

Levy, D. L. (2000). Applications and limitations of complexity theory in organization theory and strategy. *Public Administration and Public Policy, 79*(1), 67–88.

Mangematin, V. (2000). Ph.D. job market: professional trajectories and incentives during the Ph.D. *Research Policy, 29*(6), 741–756.

Marope, P. T. M., Wells, P. J., & Hazelkorn, E. (Eds.). (2013). *Rankings and accountability in higher education: Uses and misuses*. UNESCO.

Observatorio de la Universidad Colombiana. (s.f.). *Matrícula en las IES colombianas*. Available at https://www.universidad.edu.co/matricula-en-las-ies-colombianas/.

Ochoa, M. (2019). Las bondades del nuevo decreto: 1331 de julio de 2019. *Semana Educación, 44*, 49.

OCYT. (2018). *Informe anual de indicadores de ciencia, tecnología e innovación*.

OECD. (2000). *Science, technology, and innovation in the new economy*.

OECD. (2017). *Enhancing higher education system performance benchmarking higher education system performance: Conceptual framework and data*.

OECD. (2019). *Education at a glance: OECD indicators*.

Orozco, L. A., Chavarro, D. A., & y Ruiz CF, . (2010). R&D departments and innovation in the manufacturing industry of Colombia: A comparative analysis from the perspective of organizational behavior. *Innovar Journal, 20*(37), 101–116.

Orozco, L. A. (2016). La formación doctoral en administración en Colombia: Reflexión fenomenológica de un investigador. *Cuadernos De Administración, 29*(52), 115–139.

Orozco, L. A., Aristizabal, J., & Villaveces, J. L. (2018). The entrepreneurial university and academic performance in the Latin American context: The Colombian case. In F. Altinay (Ed.), *Open and equal access for learning in school management*. Intech Open.

Pouw, N., & Gupta, J. (2017). Inclusive development: A multi-disciplinary approach. *Current Opinion in Environmental Sustainability, 24*, 104–108. https://doi.org/10.1016/j.cosust.2016.11.013.

Reden, E (2019). Number of enrolled international students drops. https://www.insidehighered.com/admissions/article/2019/11/18/international-enrollments-declined-undergraduate-graduate-and.

Reyes, C. (2016). Medición de la calidad universitaria en Chile: La influencia de los rankings. *Calidad En La Educación, 44*, 158–196.

Sahni, R., & Shankar, V. K. (2012). Girls' higher education in India on the road to inclusiveness: on track but heading where? *Higher Education, 63*, 237–256. https://doi.org/10.1007/s10734-011-9436-9.

Sam, C., & Van der Sijde, P. (2014). Understanding the concept of the entrepreneurial university from the perspective of higher education models. *Higher Education, 68*(6), 891–908.

Santos, J. M., Horta, H., & Heitor, M. (2016). Too many Ph.D.s? An invalid argument for countries developing their scientific and academic systems: The case of Portugal. *Technological Forecasting and Social Change, 113*(1), 352–362.

Schwab, K. (2017). *The fourth industrial revolution*. Crown Business.

Scott, J. C. (2006). The mission of the university: Medieval to postmodern transformations. *THe Journal of Higher Education, 77*(1), 1–39.

SNIES - MEN (2016) Boletín Educacion Superior en cifras. Subdirección de Desarrollo Sectorial. Available at: https://www.mineducacion.gov.co/1759/articles-359643_recurso_1.pdf.

SNIES. (2019). *Statistics*. Sistema Nacional de Información de la educación superior. Available at: https://snies.mineducacion.gov.co/portal/ESTADISTICAS/

Soucek, R., Göritz, A. S., & Moser, K. (2017). *Does it pay off to complete a doctorate?*. Zeitschrift für Arbeits-und Organisationspsychologie A&O.

Tienda, M. (2013). Diversity ≠ Inclusion: Promoting integration in higher education. *Educational Researcher, 42*(9), 467–475.

UNDP. (2013). Human Development Report 2013. *The Rise of the South: Human Progress in a Diverse World*. New York.

Unesco. (1994). *The Salamanca Statement and Framework for action on special needs education: Adopted by the World Conference on Special Needs Education; Access and Quality. Salamanca, Spain, 7–10 June 1994*. Unesco.

Van Vught, F. A., & Westerheijden, D. F. (1994). Towards a general model of quality assessment in higher education. *Higher Education, 28*(3), 355–371.

Villaveces, J., L., & Orozco, L. A. (2015). Colombia. In S. Barro (Coord), *La transferencia de I+D, la innovación y el emprendimiento en las universidades*. Educación superior en Iberoamérica - Informe. CINDA – RedEmprendia-Universia. Santiago de Chile.

Wächter, B., Kelo, M., Lam, Q., Effertz, P., Jost, C., & Kottowski, S. (2015). University quality indicators: A critical assessment. *Study: European Parliament, 4*.

Wiers-Jenssen, J., & Try, S. (2005). Labour market outcomes of higher education undertaken abroad. *Studies in Higher Education, 30*(6), 681–705.

Wood, D. (2015). Problematizing the inclusion agenda in higher education: Towards a more inclusive technology enhanced learning model. *First Monday, 20*(9).

CHAPTER 10

Methodology for the Governance and Management of the University as a Complex Adaptive System Based on the Three Missions: Research, Education, and Connecting with Its Surroundings

Ronald Cancino, Luis Antonio Orozco, Javier Medina, Mauricio García, José Coloma, Felipe Bustos, and Cristian Alister

10.1 Introduction

The transformations in university environments seem to be becoming more compelling. On the one hand, a trend that has been ongoing for some time now places the Sustainable Development Goals (SDGs) as a

R. Cancino (✉) · M. García · F. Bustos
Social Sciences Department and Researcher at Centro de Investigaciones Sociológicas (CIS), Universidad de la Frontera, Temuco, Chile
e-mail: ronald.cancino@ufrontera.cl

L. A. Orozco et al. (eds.), *Science, Technology, and Higher Education*, Palgrave Studies in Democracy, Innovation, and Entrepreneurship for Growth,
https://doi.org/10.1007/978-3-030-80720-7_10

frame of reference for all strategic actions of the systems of higher education. On the other hand, the present and future pandemic and syndemic scenarios do not only seem to transform society, but also, they place at the forefront a relation problem between science and society where the principal actor is the university. In Latin America, there appear to be two principal tensions regarding university development, and they place the current capabilities and the models of governance and management of STI capabilities to the test. In the first place, the particularities of the social, cultural, territorial, and productive environments faced with cultural dilemmas, problems of poverty, productive stagnation, and the lagging of STI, are added to the global megatrends with strong local impacts in pandemic scenarios, and the continuous activations of disasters and catastrophes all of which the university must confront. Secondly, universities are oriented—by science and innovation systems—to reorganize and prioritize those capacities that perform best in the service of the interests of those who finance or exercise ideologies with political power, generating problems of increasing internal gaps as well as causing fractures in academic communities around the three university missions: training of human capital, generation of knowledge, and connecting to the surroundings through innovation and technology transfer.

In the last three decades in Latin America, the notion of the National Innovation System has been strongly disseminated as a policy model that was originally conceived as an explanatory model for the socio-institutional and technical changes and the relationship between agents with STI capabilities, has become a normative model in the region, which has transformed institutional architectures, incentive systems, and relationship models between agents that produce, intermediate and demand

L. A. Orozco
School of Management, Universidad Externado de Colombia, Bogotá, Colombia
e-mail: luis.orozco@uexternado.edu.co

J. Medina
Universidad del Valle, Cali, Colombia

J. Coloma
Alberto Hurtado University, Santiago, Chile

C. Alister
Catholic University, Temuco, Chile

knowledge and technologies, without generating the expected impacts obtained in developed countries (Arocena & Sutz, 2000). We argue that this systemic model has expressed a development model that has failed to transform the low knowledge and technology-intensive forms of industry (its foundational mission as a normative model), and furthermore, has activated a set of social, cultural, territorial, and environmental dilemmas, consequences of what today is called "neo-extractivism" (Svampa, 2019), and which continuously present strong socio-technical problems, conflicts, and controversies between science for development and freedom, as Sen would say, or science at the service of the ideology of competitiveness and the struggle for the supremacy of economic and commercial domination.

This has caused universities to have to face a heterogeneous environment: changes in the normative priorities in the societies in which they operate, changing scientific productivity dynamics, high competition, gaps in the needs of immediate environments, change in the behavior of their researchers, emphasis on diverse management models (Barra, 2019; Jurado-Paz & Morán-Vallejo, 2019; Rivero et al., 2018). Hence, university institutional management is constituted as a space of mediation between the environment, its dynamics, and the university's own operations (Krog, 2018). However, it should be noted that the installation of units oriented to the analysis and generation of inputs for evidence-based decision-making is not devoid of internal tensions between the academic dynamics themselves, within the framework of the three university missions—training, research, and extension—(Orozco et al., 2018), and the demands attributable to the environment in the framework of the SDGs in which there is a lack of translating agents between the university with the demands of knowledge, and the integration to the global circuits of knowledge circulation in unfavorable and significantly asymmetrical conditions between organizations (Correa, 2014; Feld & Kreimer, 2020; Kreimer & Ugartemendía, 2007).

Given the definitions of a university in the twenty-first century (Araneda & Pedraja, 2017), systematically challenged to provide human capital, knowledge, and technologies to the environment for the resolution of problems of different orders, and the growing pressure to assume in a third mission the role of agent of innovation and entrepreneurship (Orozco & Chavarro, 2008), studies on this institution have assumed a similarly parceled form. Thus, each function operates as its own field of knowledge and research, highlighting specific challenges for each of the university missions (Altbach, 2006; Correa, 2014; Orozco et al., 2018). The university-environment gaps (Casas et al., 2014; Etzkowitz & Leydesdorff, 1995; Wright et al., 2004), the tensions provoked by regulatory schemes on scientific productivity and their impact on research practices (Abbott, 2020; Bloch & Schneider, 2016; Feld & Kreimer, 2020; Kanchan & Krishan, 2019; Liu et al., 2009) and the impact of globalization and the new demands of labor markets on university training processes (Escudero et al., 2010; Moreno, 2009; Wit, 2020), evidence the tensions inherent to the university in our time, and require opening new transdisciplinary approaches, which at different hierarchical levels promote rethinking the university from the paradigm of complexity.

Regarding university governance and the role it plays to manage the scientific capabilities of the organization—at the normative, technological, financial, and relational levels—, the literature tends to identify the growing challenge of understanding the university as a CAS (Oliva, 2008), which is involved in a heterogeneous network of agents and socio-technical contexts (Casas, 2001, 2004, 2015). Information systems and the use of information technologies are central tools for the effective implementation of institutional changes and provide capabilities that allow managing the operations and functions of a complex university (Acosta et al., 2017; Dastan et al., 2011).

In the university dynamic itself, these trends have effects on academic policy, on governance models and management practices, and on the unique forms of scientific activity. The competitive relationship between institutions, networks, and groups of researchers is becoming more acute in the search for resources for research funding and the legitimization of research work, as understood by Merton in the Matthew Effect in science and Bourdieu's scientific field, but with new instances such as university rankings and institutional accreditations (Orozco, 2015).

The central aspect here, since at least the 1990s, is that competitiveness has become a part of the university system, tending to promote a dynamic ethos of competition, which assumes a management of complexity in functional and parceled terms. Functional, in that there is competition for the acquisition of resources through the fulfillment of indicators, operates from the environment toward the system—national regulatory frameworks that provide resources for which universities compete—and that marks the dynamics of university management, reproducing competitiveness at the system level—search for prestige, funds, symbolic capital, etc.—to the detriment of the rationalities of cooperation and sustainability. Parceled, given that the traditional condition of university systems operates in the logic of differentiation of tasks on the three missions (training, research, and connecting with the surroundings), where institutional designs and normative strategies attempt to respond to the requirements of the university functions themselves in a culture that is Taylorized in the division of labor for the lines of production. To this, we must add that the institutional division of the missionary functions is not symmetrical with respect to the allocation of resources, incentives, and execution of the same tasks. Academics and researchers are the main agents who are evaluated through training, research, and connection with the surroundings. This suggests a key idea: the institutional design must be understood from complexity, for the development of the capacities of the main agents with the aim of understanding their interactions among the activities of the three university missions.

In addition, there is an ongoing tendency to design and use scientometrics focused on the quantity and recognition of scientific production. This metric is not only used for discerning the quality of academic work (its original mission), but also has political effects given its strong institutionalization in the science and innovation systems in the region: it establishes a hierarchy among researchers, academic management units, research results transfer offices (OTRIs) and universities as a whole, which has a strong impact on public funding for research and on the prosperity of university systems. Thus, scientometric measurements are no longer just a certification of quality and a tool for mapping what the agents do, but also a space for mediation between institutional architectures, incentive systems, and efforts to steer toward one goal or another. This, in the relations between the agents of the national innovation systems has been operating as a cornerstone with the forms of governance and as a form for legitimizing determinants of the results of management. A university president presents indicators, many of them scientometric in nature, as a means of showing the results of his management and uses them as a means to appear in the standardized legitimacy benchmarks such as rankings and accreditations.

In this context, this chapter proposes that in the face of these megatrends, it is necessary to understand and manage the complexity of the activities and products of university work. This implies not focusing the evaluation of capacities only on scientific products, but on a vision regarding the heterogeneity of processes and products: forms of management and institutional design, publications, human capital formation, relational capital with environmental entities, and creation of scientific capital (Orozco, 2015). Therefore, we propose that this requires a theoretical conception that takes into account complexity in order to outline methodologies conducive to designing governance systems that improve university management. The chapter is structured as follows: first, it presents a state of the art based on a theoretical convergence between approaches from Complex Adaptative Systems (CAS) theory and social and computational studies of science. From there, it proposes the theoretical model that explores two types of mechanisms: one socio-organizational and the other socio-cognitive. The second section presents the methodology for modeling capabilities. The method consists of the development of a distinction of levels that articulates data management and university scientific information, systemic modeling of university management capabilities with bibliometric indicators, lexicometric analysis, and analysis of social and cognitive networks. It ends with conclusions and an agenda for future research.

10.2 A Theoretical Model of the University as a CAS

We begin by pointing out that conceiving of universities as Complex Adaptative Systems CAS implies understanding them, in the first place, as organizations. In the classic sense proposed by the social sciences, they are institutionalized environments that operate as a form of social coordination, where, like other forms of social coordination such as communities and markets, the actors coordinate expectations and actions, seeking to adapt them to certain established and expected processes and results (Beckert, 2009; Ostrom, 2005). To achieve social coordination, organizations, studied as companies or corporations and as bureaucratic organizations or state agencies, function on the basis of decision-making procedures made viable through (a) hierarchical levels of power; (b) specialized and functionally differentiated management units; (c) operations of exchange of services and rewards, and; (d) operations of administration, control, and evaluation of management.

In order to understand universities as agent-based complex adaptive systems, it is necessary to make explicit that complexity is basically referred to, from the paradigm developed by researchers nested around the Santa

Fe Institute in New Mexico, as the coupled, interwoven, or intertwined property (plexus) of natural and social phenomena (Gell-Mann, 1995). Focusing attention on social phenomena, a complex system is constituted by two interdependent levels of organizations. One level is that of the adaptive agents, who interact in a context or environment with specific conditions (natural, institutional, technological) and as a consequence of these local interactions, a second level is produced, which is the emergent level, which emerges as a global property of the system, and which, in turn, influences the specific conditions in which the agents interact. Complexity as interweaving or coupling translates, on the one hand, into the connection and feedbacks between the two levels indicated and, on the other, into the connection between the diversity of elements that concur in the processes at each of these levels (Carmichael & Hadžikadić, 2019; Cumming & Norberg, 2008; McMillan, 2004).

This demands we take the understanding of the complexity of university management seriously. In organizations as complex adaptive systems, the agents are the individuals that integrate them, among others, politicians, bureaucrats, managers, shareholders, entrepreneurs, and scientists. These agents, in accordance with institutional economics (Aoki, 2010; Mantzavinos et al., 2004), evolutionary game theory (Gintis, 2007) and analytical sociology (Hedström & Bearman, 2009; Macy & Flache, 2009), have different attributes from those pointed out in the theoretical assumptions of neoclassical economics, which are complete information processing capacity and orientation toward utility maximization around self-interest. The theories developed within this paradigm, based on simple agents, simple environments, and linear results related to efficiency in exchanges and, at the aggregate level, in markets, have had low predictive capacity due to their poor fit with empirical evidence (Bowles, 2006).

Aware of these limitations, the agent-based complex adaptive system paradigm develops a different perspective. In this framework, the first attribute of agents is that they are endowed with intentionality, i.e., they have intentional elements, specifically, willful desire for something to happen, and beliefs about the actions and motivations of others and about the consequences of their own and others' actions (Searle, 2010). Secondly, and in relation to the above, agents are endowed with rationality, which means that their desires and beliefs guide their social action in specific and dynamic ways.

Here it should be noted that agents' beliefs include, in addition to the aforementioned, those they use to evaluate their opportunity structure, i.e., the action alternatives available to achieve a purpose or objective adjusted to their desires (Hedström, 2005; Petersen, 2009). It is in this sense that agents are constituted as such, since they have the capacity for agency, i.e., to use certain means, interpreting their environment, to achieve an end and social action is therefore deployed as a means of becoming agents in that environment. However, based on the seminal contributions of Herbert Simon, it is evident that agents have limited rationality, expressed within a restricted capacity to process information from a complex and dynamic environment, which generates a scenario of uncertainity, since it is not absolutely predictable and controllable (Cowan & Arrow, 2019).

Despite this, the third attribute of agents is their adaptive capacity. They are adaptive agents because, based on their cognitive resources, they constantly seek to adapt to their environment, using internal models to represent it. From the use of heuristics as fast and precise cognitive devices for information processing, agents generate evolutionary learning processes, endogenously adjusting their internal models, thanks to the information extracted from experience. Thus, they establish regularities (patterns) that allow the formation of internal rules or behavioral orientation schemes, improving their adaptive capacity, mainly through the deployment of adaptive strategies as forms of anticipation (Beinhocker, 2006; Gell-Mann, 1994; Holland, 1995; Miller & Spage, 2007).

The emergent level of the complex system is produced by the interactions between the adaptive agents that compose it, who act in accordance with their internal rules and the environment in which they are situated, composed of other adaptive agents (articulated in social networks as spaces of mutual influence—exchange, social contagion)—and by external rules that constrain their decisions and actions. The emergent state, as a macro level, has properties different from those of the micro level elements that cause it, and the generative process is not linear, as it is highly sensitive to specific conditions. Therefore, the process of aggregation, combination, or composition and its emergent results are not entirely predictable. Rather, there are degrees of uncertainty, randomness and change is permanent, due, among other factors, to the effect of focal points, to modifications in the co-evolution of strategies among agents and to critical mass effects.

In the case of organizations as agent-based complex adaptive systems, the emergent properties include expected results or collective goals of public interest, such as the generation of innovations, efficiency, transparency in management, and increased competitiveness (Arthur, 2015; Colander & Kupers, 2016; Geyer & Rihani, 2010; Lane, 2017).

Having made reference to complex adaptive systems, we now have elements to return to the question about the management of research, training, connection, and innovation capabilities in universities and also to return to the proposals put forward in reference to conceiving universities as organizations, as agent-based complex adaptive systems, in which the capabilities of the agents and the processes and results they generate need to be managed through the use of governance devices. If, in line with Lemos and Agrawal (2006), we understand governance as the set of regulatory processes through which the actions of the different agents and their results are influenced, we propose, more specifically, that it is necessary to activate governance devices at the two levels of the complex adaptive systems mentioned above, i.e., at the adaptive agent local level and at the global or emergent level.

At the level of adaptive agents, we assume the approach of governance in organizations which refers to the regulation or conduction by means of administrative structures and processes, managerial criteria, and systems of incentives and rules that favor cooperation and social coordination (Christensen and Tschirhart, 2011). Furthermore, assuming an institutional path of rule-based governance (Peters, 2011), we situate ourselves in the perspective of institutional design theory, which states that institutions are formal and informal rules that have the power of enforceability and that institutional design is the intentional creation of rules, in order to promote valuable results in a given context that coordinates expectations, shared visions of meanings and constitutes a basis for action (Brousseau et al., 2011; Goodin, 1996). The fundamental ideas surrounding institutional design are: (a) agents are oriented toward action based on different motivations and purposes; (b) agents are sensitive to incentives that constitute opportunities to achieve their purposes; (c) the incentives that shape opportunities can be intentionally designed in order to lead agents, considering their motivations, toward certain actions; (d) the actions of individuals are intended to generate, at an aggregate level, socially valued expected results (Pettit, 1996; Ostrom, 2006).

The fundamental consequence for governance in CAS is that there are multiple possible outcomes at the agent and emergent level (Edelenbos et al., 2009; Klijn & Snellen, 2009), and therefore not necessarily what is expected and normatively valued as positive. On the contrary, among the plurality of outcomes, there are also those that sociology has called unintended and undesired consequences or perverse aggregate effects of social action (Boudon, 1982; Merton, 1976). In this framework, the presence or absence of organizational elements such as information (Arrow, 1999), organizational culture (DiMaggio, 2015), social networks (Granovetter, 2017), hierarchical monitoring processes (Miller, 2004), incentives (Bowles, 2016), and social norms (Gambetta & Origgi, 2013), under certain conditions, can result in negative effects such as lack of coordination, passivity, opportunism, corruption, organizational capture, resistance, conflict, increased transaction costs, distrust, and erosion of prosocial motivations.

From this perspective then, we propose understanding a university as a CAS as shown in Fig. 10.1. Specifically, a network of agents (in the form of groups, centers, institutes) that interact in the production (in the form of research, development, and innovation projects) and dissemination of knowledge (in the form of teaching, interactions with its surroundings, research, technology transfer, and innovation). This interaction occurs within the framework of rules and incentives of the university itself, or of the territorial and national science and technology system environment, or

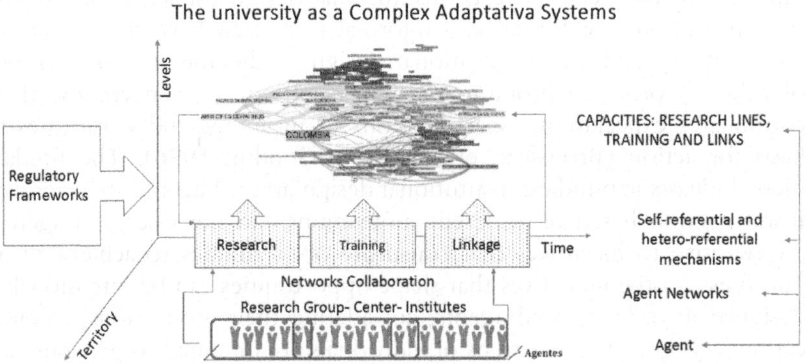

Fig. 10.1 The university as a CAS (*Source* Based on Cancino and Univalle [2017])

of other forms of institutional pressure such as rankings and the media. From this relationship, scientific and technological knowledge emerges, capacities for interacting with priorities of the environment and knowledge networks that constitute the dynamic heritage of the STI (Cancino, 2017), in which diversity and heterogeneity are sought as desirable but complex goals to govern in universities and their schools (Orozco, 2015).

Based on this we understand that in a university, scientific agents interact within a framework of specific rules and incentives that are oriented to at least three mission areas that may enter into conflict for the management of resources and rewards (Orozco et al., 2018). Additionally, these do not unidirectionally determine the actions of the agents, but rather the agents, through interactions with others (whether or not materialized in specific scientific collaborations) generate research projects, scientific publications, processes of human capital formation, and various forms of interaction with the surrounding environment. The forms of scientific collaboration and the topics selected by the agents at the micro level give rise to macro forms. Recognizable lines of research, training, and linkage are generated as well as emerging phenomena. And these lines are what we come to understand as university capacities: a set of scientific activities and knowledge expressed in scientific products (publications), in processes of human capital formation (teaching, theses), activities of connection with the surrounding environment, and the very forms of collaboration that support these capacities.

In these interaction processes that give rise to the emergence of focused capabilities such as lines of research, training, and liaisons with their surroundings, there are mechanisms that must be considered to explain both the structure and the evolutionary and adaptive dynamics of the capacities. We consider at least two mechanisms to be relevant: self-referential mechanisms and heteroreferential mechanisms (Cancino, 2017). The first refers to the criteria that the agents put into play (their internal models) to select with whom to link and what topics they work on in the search for creating a scientific knowledge footprint, while the second refers to the strategy they deploy to link with agents and topics in relation to those defined by the regulatory framework and incentive system, whether in the form of academic careers and promotion instruments done both internally and externally to the university. Both mechanisms act together, and an analytical task is to unveil the way they interact and the effects they generate in the structuring of capabilities.

Regarding this perspective, we explore a methodology for modeling scientific capabilities, which aims at identifying them, placing them in a relational perspective (among themselves and as a result of the action of agent networks), and identifying the governance structure and management processes that make the existence of these distributed capabilities understandable, as well as identifying the self- and heteroreferential mechanisms that influence this structuring.

10.3 Methodology for Modeling of Scientific Capabilities

Information on scientific activity is obtained from authors and personnel with time allocation to the STI who are organized in projects and research groups to generate results in terms of research products, training, and connections with the surrounding environment. For an example of information sources in a Colombian-Chilean comparative case, see Cancino et al. (2014). Figure 10.2 shows the information capture method for the case of Colombia.

Based on these variables, different types of bibliometric and modeling analyzes were carried out. From the point of view of a CAS, we conceived interaction levels and mechanisms that explain them: a micro level,

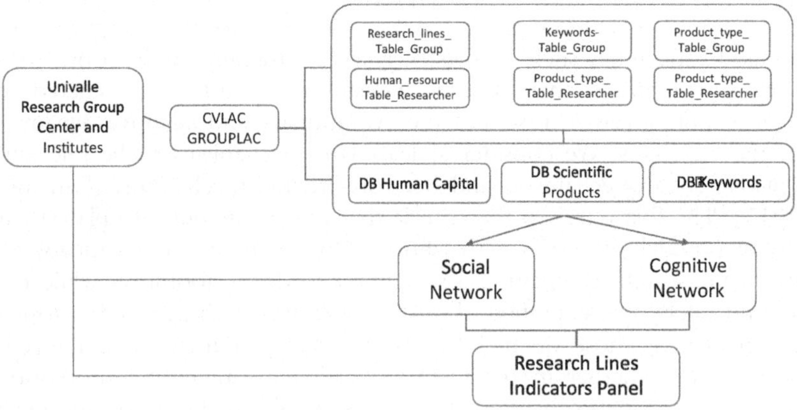

Fig. 10.2 Method for information processing (*Source* based on Cancino et al./Univalle [2017])

consisting of the identification of forms of collaboration of the agents in the different types of products for the three university missions in the framework of strategic areas defined by the analyzed university. A macro level referring to the research lines, their cognitive structure, and the comparative positioning of the research lines with respect to their volume (size) and intensity (cognitive integration). Now, in the search for the mechanisms that affect the structure and dynamics of the lines of research, we explore the analysis of STI management processes and the identification of factors that affect the structuring of the lines (Cancino, 2017).

1. Micro level. Agents, networks, and forms of collaboration.

At this level, we place the agents and their interactions, that is, the conformation of scientific collaboration networks and their structural indicators. Researchers select with whom to collaborate, generating aggregate effects in the structure of the networks, and shaping qualities of collaboration in the major areas of development defined by the university, and in particular, with respect to the types of products that are generated for the three missions as shown in Table 10.1.

Table 10.1 Micro level

Area/Line /Product type	*Social Network (Human Resources)*
Size of network	Number of human resources in the Strategic Area, Research line, or Product type
Number of groups	Number of human resource groups in the Strategic Area, Research line, or Product type
Modularity	Strength of the division of a network in human resource modules (also called groups, clusters, or communities). Networks with high modularity have strong connections between nodes within modules, but few connections between nodes in different modules (Newman, 2006)
Network density	Total of the relationships established between human resources in relation to the total possible, within the framework of a Strategic Area, Research line, or Product type
Network centrality	Average number of links possessed by human resources of a Strategic Area, Research line, or Product type

Source Based on Cancino (2017)

Structural Indicators of Scientific Network According to Development Areas and Product Types, Univalle 2017

ARTS

Product types	Productos	Network size	Number of groups	Modularity	Network density	Network centrality
Training	Directed training activities/Tutorials	47	3	0,521	0,200	1,000
Research	Bibliographic production	75	7	0,645	0,076	1,524
Linkage	Technical production	36	3	0,203	0,194	1,556
	Artistical/cultural production	19	1	0,000	1,000	1,000
	Other activities	25	2	0,111	0,238	1,429
	Supplementary data	32	2	0,500	0,333	0,500

LIFE SCIENCES

Product types	Productos	Network size	Number of groups	Modularity	Network density	Network centrality
Training	Directed training activities/Tutorials	119	9	0,83	0,058	1,1
Research	Bibliographic production	231	20	0,889	0,023	2,260
Linkage	Technical production	120	11	0,625	0,067	2,062
	Artistical/cultural production	7	0	0,000	0,000	0,000
	Other activities	54	1,000	0,000	1,000	3,000
	Supplementary data	92	2,000	0,320	0,333	1,000

TERRITORIAL DEVELOPMENT

Product types	Human Resources	Network size	Number of groups	Modularity	Network density	Network centrality
Training	Directed training activities/Tutorials	24	3	0,560	0,238	1,429
Research	Bibliographic production	36	5	0,283	0,109	1,091
Linkage	Technical production	28	1	0,000	1,000	1,000
	Artistical/cultural production	3	0	0,000	0,000	0,000
	Other activities	13	0	0,000	0,000	0,000
	Supplementary data	18	1	0,000	0,500	1,500

TECHNOLOGICAL DEVELOPMENT

Product types	Human Resources	Network size	Number of groups	Modularity	Network density	Network centrality
Training	Directed training activities/Tutorials	151	15	0,730	0,032	2,324
Research	Bibliographic production	224	22	0,875	0,019	2,391
Linkage	Technical production	132	12	0,787	0,053	1,892
	Artistical/cultural production	10	0	0,000	0,000	0,000
	Other activities	48	2	0,500	0,300	1,200
	Supplementary data	133	11	0,712	0,045	2,407

PEACE

Product types	Human Resources	Network size	Number of groups	Modularity	Network density	Network centrality
Training	Directed training activities/Tutorials	65	3	0,642	0,179	1,250
Research	Bibliographic production	133	10	0,728	0,059	2,256
Linkage	Technical production	69	4	0,281	0,182	1,818
	Artistical/cultural production	8	1	0,000	1,000	2,000
	Other activities	29	1	0,000	0,667	1,333

ENERGY

Product types	Human Resources	Network size	Number of groups	Modularity	Network density	Network centrality
Training	Directed training activities/Tutorials	53	2	0,256	0,288	3,167
Research	Bibliographic production	86	5	0,178	0,071	2,829
Linkage	Technical production	47	2	0,018	0,311	2,800
	Artistical/cultural production	2	0	0,000	0,000	0,000
	Other activities	25	3	0,215	0,178	1,600

The identification of the structure of research collaboration, training, and bonding, allows identifying the specialization in one or more activities associated with the missions of the university, dimensioning the human capital dedicated to each of these activities, as well as understanding whether the relationships Bbetween the agents they have levels of internal cohesion that allow identifying a specialization in the activity based on collaboration.

The attached table indicates the structure of indicators of networks of human capital dedicated to Research (Bibliographic Production), Training (Directed Works / Tutorials), and Linkage with the Environment (Technical Production, Artistic/cCultural Production), Other works and Data complementary) of the Universidad del Valle with data accumulated as of 2017.

The high heterogeneity between the six strategic areas can be observed and the differences in the specialization of human capital and their forms of collaboration in the university's three missionary activities. This is the first way, at the micro -level, to understand the decisions and strategies that agents make, selecting with whom to collaborate and around what type of activities to collaborate.

2. Macro level. Research lines as emerging phenomena.

The aim here is to identify and characterize the lines of research understood as emerging phenomena of the interaction of the agents and their forms of scientific collaboration in strategic areas and in the construction of products derived from the work of the three missions. In turn, the aim is to comparatively understand the lines themselves, for which reason indexes are designed to understand their relative positioning according to the size of the lines and the intensity of the internal relationships within them (Cancino, 2017).

2.1. Identification of research lines. The main purpose was to identify lines of research based on the keywords of the products as a means of visualizing the cognitive capabilities deployed by the university to identify these lines. An analysis of associated words was performed using Gephi network analysis software. Specifically, we sought to detect modules or clusters of keywords sufficiently independent of each other by applying the modularity algorithm (Blondel et al., 2008). Each of these groups of keywords were interpreted as lines of research, supported by expert analysis with researchers and university administrators.

The indicators used are defined in Table 10.2. As can be seen, the measures that can be obtained from these indicators are generally applied to all types of database groupings, whether research lines or product types. Also, these indicators are applied to both types of agents: human capital, which correspond to the social networks; and keywords, which constitute the cognitive network, in the form proposed for the analysis of scientific communities (Orozco & Chavarro, 2006). In short, the indicators, shown in Table 10.2, make it possible to observe the structure of each of these dimensions and levels of analysis in a comparative manner.

Table 10.2 Macro level

AREA/LINE/PRODUCT TYPE	*COGNITIVE NETWORK (Key words)*
Size of Network	Number of key words contained in the Strategic Area, Research Line, or Product Type
Number of groups	Number of groups of key words contained in the Strategic Area, Research Line, and Product Type
Modularity	Strength of the division of a network into keyword modules (also called groups, clusters, or communities). Networks with high modularity have strong connections between nodes within modules, but few connections between nodes in different modules (Newman, 2006)
Network density	Total of the relationships established between the keywords in relation to the total possible, within the framework of a Strategic Area, Research Line, or Product Type
Network centrality	Average number of links to the keywords of a Strategic Area, Research Line, or Product Type

Source based on Cancino (2017)

Once the lines of research were identified, the next step was to build sub-databases of products for each of these lines of research, with the purpose of identifying the capacities for the three missions: research (bibliographic production), human capital formation (directed work/tutoring), and connection to the surrounding environment (technical production, cultural-artistic production, other complementary work, and data), in order to identify the performance of each of these capacities with respect to the line of research. The presence/absence of these types of products in the line was identified, as well as the cognitive contents, structure, and network indicators of each.

Structural Indicators of Keywords Networks According to Development Areas and Product Types, Univalle 2017

ARTS AND HUMANITIES

Products type	Products	Network size	Number of groups	Modularity	Network density	Network centrality
Directed training activities/Tutorials	Directed training activities/Tutorials	323	42	0,703	0,014	4,5
Bibliographic production	Bibliographic production	675	78	0,705	0,008	5,133
Lynkage	Technical production	187	29	0,583	0,027	4,968
	Artistical/cultural production	20	4	0,519	0,255	4,333
	Other activities	123	16	0,455	0,056	6,605
	Supplementary data	164	32	0,938	0,025	3,753

LIFE SCIENCES

Products type	Products	Network size	Number of groups	Modularity	Network density	Network centrality
Directed training activities/Tutorials	Directed training activities/Tutorials	1106	145	0,904	0,004	4,157
Bibliographic production	Bibliographic production	2338	246	0,918	0,002	4,735
Lynkage	Technical production	482	80	0,892	0,008	3,726
	Artistical/cultural production	3	1	0	1	1
	Other activities	78	18	0,863	0,043	2,836
	Supplementary data	245	52	0,898	0,014	3,059

TERRITORIAL DEVELOPMENT

Products type	Words	Network size	Number of groups	Modularity	Network density	Network centrality
Training	Directed training activities/Tutorials	1872	173	0,911	0,003	4,571
Research	Bibliographic production	2614	255	0,909	0,002	4,699
Linkage	Technical production	568	91	0,932	0,007	3,945
	Artistical/cultural production	11	4	0,302	0,2	2
	Other activities	109	27	0,873	0,031	3,184
	Supplementary data	499	86	0,899	0,007	3,23

The identification of structural indicators of word networks (cognitive networks) in the activities of research, training, and connection with the environment allows identifying the cognitive specialization in all, some, or each of them, as an effect of the agents'' strategies. At this emerging level, cognitive specialization in the strategic areas of the University allows identifying the size of cognitive activity in each type of activity, the number of groups that comprise it (a proxy for internal diversification), and levels of relationship between the themes and the internal cohesion existing in them. Thus, an image of how specialized activity is within a strategic area can be obtained and, thus, structurally understand the university''s cognitive complexity.

2.2 Comparison of research lines. Volume and intensity: in the University as a CAS, there is a plurality of research lines with heterogeneous relative developments, both in relation to the network structure they have formed, as well as to the levels of complexity and cognitive size of these lines. This forces us to think in adaptive terms: the lines have heterogeneous developments and, therefore, their growth possibilities depend on both their internal and external conditions. To achieve this understanding, once the indicators in the social and cognitive network for all the lines of research and types of products have been obtained, the "Volume" and "Intensity" indexes are constructed. The purpose of this is to visualize the cognitive structure acquired by the social and cognitive networks according to the volume of their actors and the intensity of their interactions, as well as the cognitive volume of the lines and the interactions between keywords, as shown in Table 10.3.

This identification of the macro characteristics of the Research Lines permits a global analysis of the University's Research Lines. Since it is represented in a Euclidean plane, it is then possible to compare the size of the lines with the levels of internal integration. That is: it is possible to identify large or small lines according to their volume (the number of words and the number of groups that comprise these), and lines that are intensive or not very intensive in average internal relations according to their modularity and network density as shown in Table 10.3.

Table 10.3 Indicators of volume and intensity

Indicator	*Index*	*Definition*	*Expression on Graph*
Size of Network Number of Groups	Volume	This is a measure of the relative size of a line of research in relation to the other line (comprised of network size and number of groups)	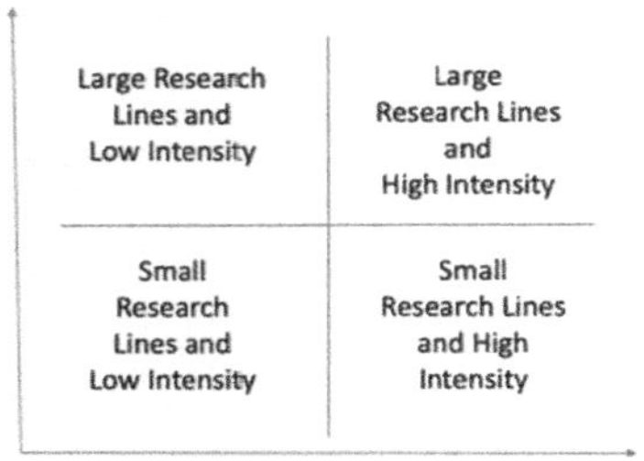
Modularity Density of Network	Intensity	This is a measure of the internal relations between the contents of a line of research. A higher indicator shall indicate greater relations between the cognitive contents (greater thematic integration)	

Source Based on Cancino (2017)

Comparative Analysis of Research Lines in Strategic areas According to Volume and Intensity Index and Diversification of research, Training, and Linkage Activities, Univalle 2017

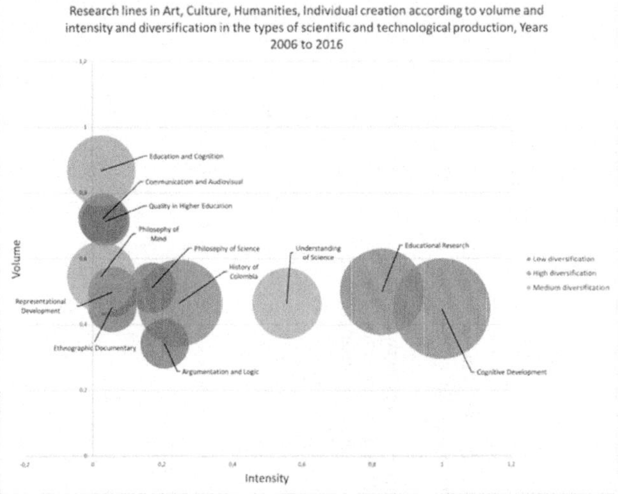

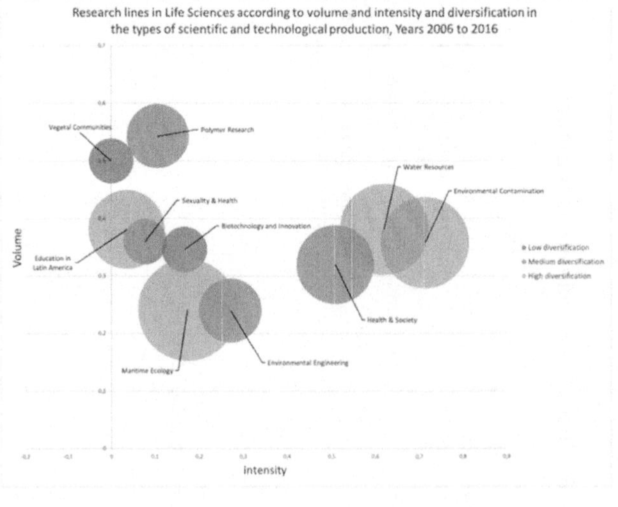

A strategic area can contain several lines of investigation. These can achieve differential positions between them if the volume (the number of cognitive contents and the number of researchers who participate in it) and the intensity of their internal relationships (the researchers' internal cohesion) are analyzed. In this way, it is possible to identify large and highly cohesive lines (a large volume of cognitive contents and groups of researchers with sustained relationships); loosely cohesive large lines (large lines in cognitive volume, but with loosely cohesive researchers); small and very cohesive lines (small lines in cognitive terms, but with very cohesive researchers), and small lines that are not very cohesive (small lines in cognitive terms, and with little cohesion of their researchers).

This comparative visualization is a powerful tool for the management of research lines since it makes it possible to identify the relative positions among them. This implies assuming the complexity of the university: the existence of heterogeneous capacities, whose dynamics cannot be univocally prescribed by the instruments of promotion. This, due to the fact that their impact depends on the internal conditions of the lines, and on the way in which the agents react by forming networks, selecting topics and focused research, training and liaison. This is a central aspect for the governance of university capacities in the three missions.

3. In search of mechanisms. Forms of management and factors that indicate the structuring of lines of research.

Here, two types of analysis are developed that allow us to understand the structure of the university's lines of research. These are two types of mechanisms: one normative and the other cognitive.

Systemic modeling of management processes. One of the qualities of CAS is non-linearity and learning capacity. We propose that these qualities are observable in the way management agents drive and implement regulatory frameworks and incentive systems. In this process, agents mediate the norm with scientific agents, and they experiment and learn from processes that generate positive or negative management outcomes. In turn, scientific agents learn to improve their interaction with management agents. Through qualitative and ethnographic work, consisting of meetings, field observations and interviews, systemic models are constructed regarding the main management operations of the university research system. Variables are identified and linked to each other, evidencing the key feedbacks that act as sets of variables that especially affect the emergence of lines of research. These feedbacks are relevant in theoretical terms since they are indicative of the quality of flow in the university CAS, inasmuch as, despite the rules defining procedures, in practice they generate processes beyond what is expected regarding their operation, activating transformations that can go in the desired direction or in other directions.

Systemic Modelling of STI Management Process, Univalle 2017

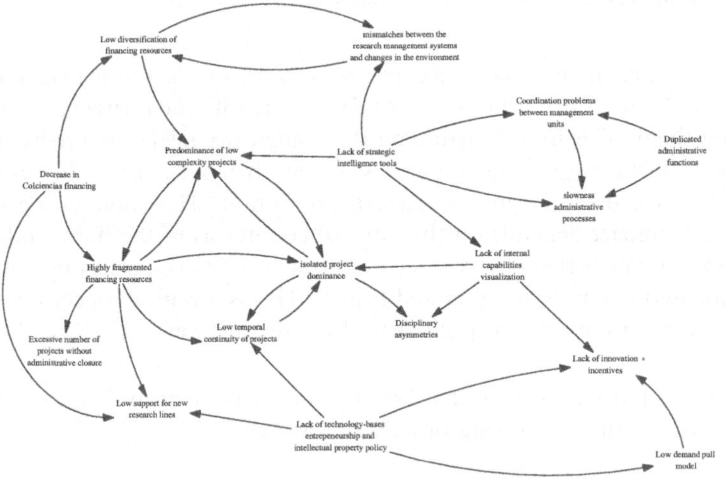

Systemic modeling allows us to understand how management processes operate in practice. These, in the SAC model, constitute updates of the regulatory frameworks and incentive systems and are under constant pressure as a result of the development of capacities, requiring new adjustments and/or institutional changes. To achieve this, through ethnographic and qualitative work, systemic models are built that link identified key variables, in such a way that a complex network of variables is understandable and the transversal axes (feedback or loops) that constitute the bottlenecks of management dynamics are identified.

Factor analysis. Regarding the cognitive mechanisms, a factor analysis is performed to identify new cognitive categories that emerge from the convergence of the available variables and indicators. A set of indicators is extracted based on the research lines data, which are subsequently used as input variables in the factor analysis. Part of these indicators reveal the structural characteristics of the keyword network of each research line and the relationship that these cognitive elements have with priorities of the political environment of the university. The indicators of the factor analysis are shown in Table 10.4.

From these indicators, it is possible to perform an exploratory factor analysis. The Principal Axis Factorization extraction method and the Varimax rotation method with Kaiser Normalization were used. Additionally, the Factor graph was used to visualize the variables and cases (lines of research) according to this identified underlying structure. With the identified factors, a Spearman correlation analysis was performed, considering discrete variables. Three variables obtained by disaggregating the indicator "types of products" were added. We used "bibliographic production," "technical production," and "directed work/tutoring," counting the number of words that each line had in each of these types of products. This sought to identify whether or not the place of the research lines in terms of the underlying factors is related to the number of words they have in the products that are developed. In other words, this could mean that the structure of the lines of research at Universidad del Valle, observed in the light of the study variables, is associated with the number of keywords that these lines have in each type of product.

Considering the distribution according to these dimensions in quadrants (Fig. 10.2), the most representative lines of research are as follows:

1. complex/convergent: these are positioned in quadrant I. They have high cognitive complexity and simultaneously high convergence with policy.
2. Complex/divergent: positioned in quadrant II. These are highly complex in their cognitive composition but do not converge with policy instruments.
3. Simple/divergent: located in quadrant III, these are the most incipient in terms of what is measured by these dimensions. They have low cognitive complexity and diverge from policy instruments.

Table 10.4 Factoria study indicators

Indicator	*Operationalization*
1. Number of key words (N_PC)	Count of the number of keywords that make up each line of research of the university. Values are ≥ 1
2. Medium grade (Grade_M)	Average of the number of links that each keyword has with the others. Values are ≥ 1
3. Number of groups of key words (N_Grup)	Count of the number of groups that compose the keyword network of each research line, as a function of the modularity index. The values are ≥ 1
4. Modularity Index	Strength of the division of a network into modules (also called groups, clusters, or communities). Networks with high modularity have strong connections between nodes within modules, but few connections between nodes in different modules (Blondel et al., 2008). The values range from −1 to 1
5. Number of types of products (Divers)	Count of the types of products that each research line has. There are six types of products: (1) complementary data, (2) other work, (3) artistic/cultural production, (4) bibliographic production, (5) technical production, (6) directed work/tutorials. Values are ≥ 1
6. Regional development convergence plan (Con_PRD)	Degree of cosine similarity between Univalle research lines and the Regional Development Plan
7. Convergence vision 2032 (Conv_V)	Degree of cosine similarity between Univalle's lines of research and Colombia's Vision 2032 Plan
8. National convergence plan(Conv_PEN)	Degree of cosine similarity between Univalle research lines and the National Development Plan

Source Prepares by the authors, 2020

4. Simple/convergent: Are Those Lines in Quadrant IV, Which Have a Simpler Cognitive Composition, but Converge with Policy Priorities.

Factor Analysis. Cognitive Complexity and Linkage with the Media Development Policy, Univalle 2017

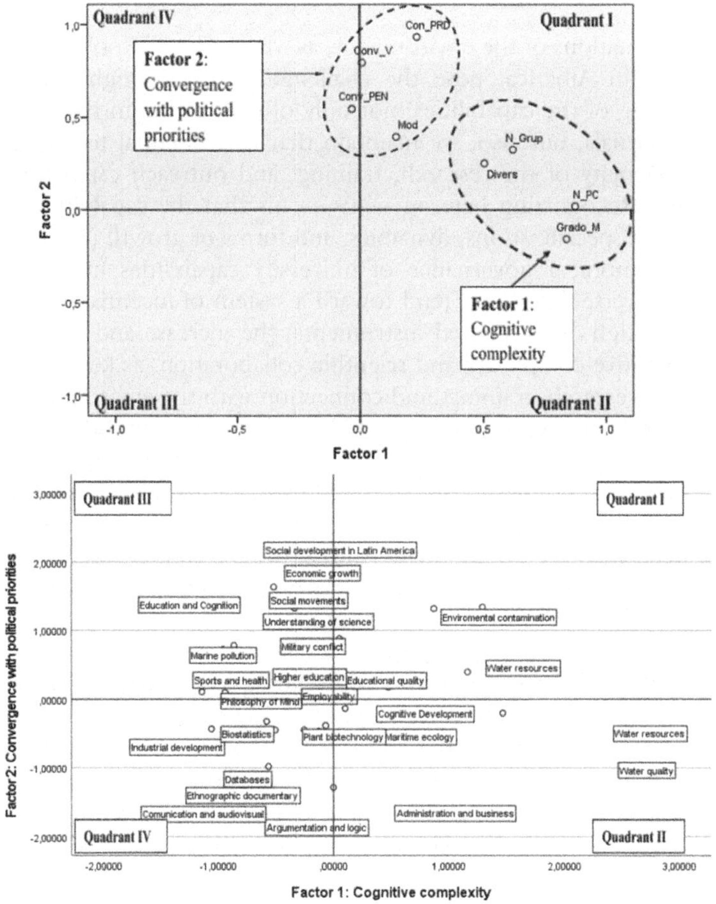

The factor analysis, based on the set of available structural indicators, makes it possible to identify their incidence in the research lines' general configuration. This typology of factors can be used to distribute the Lines according to those factors. In the case analyzed, the central factors are the internal of a line and the link it establishes with the environment''s policies.

10.4 Conclusions and Research and Management Agenda: For the Governance of the University as a Complex Adaptive System

The transformations of the environment, as well as the STI policies themselves in Latin America, pose the challenge of a thorough and deep understanding of the capabilities, not only of publication in high-impact scientific journals, but also, we maintain that it is essential to recognize the heterogeneity of the research, training, and outreach capabilities of universities. Recognizing heterogeneity means that the capabilities have differentiated specializations, dynamics, and forms of growth (Ruiz et al., 2010). Therefore, a governance of university capabilities must recognize these diverse forms and tend toward a system of incentives that can manage through differentiated instruments, the increase and diversification of cognitive complexity and scientific collaboration, as key processes to articulate research, training, and connection with the environment. To advance in this, we propose that the University be understood as a CAS, in which networks of agents are articulated to generate activities leading to the emergence of lines of research, training, and liaison whose expressions can be differentiated, with greater or lesser degrees of specialization and/or heterogeneity among them. And, in order to understand the form and dynamics of capabilities, there are explanatory mechanisms that help to understand and improve management.

A central aspect of the governance of complex adaptive systems indicates that the rules and incentives must be aimed at the agents, their motivational structures, and configuration of opportunities, in such a way that the emerging results are multiple and must therefore be recognized in multilevel terms. In this sense, the methodology proposed here conceives that at the micro level, scientific agents collaborate/do not collaborate in the development of research, training, and liaison activities, and that this generates conditioning factors in the system that are expressed at the macro level. This can be understood as an emerging level in which it is possible to identify lines of research that go further than the statements of the scientific agents taken individually and that therefore their cognitive and social structures can be analyzed. We have proposed that from traditional network indicators, it is possible to build Indices (Volume and Intensity) that allow comparing lines of research in universities, allowing thusly for a global and systemic vision of the capacities that are developed (Cancino, 2017). In addition, this methodology makes it possible to identify the levels of strategic alignment of the research lines in relation to the priorities of the environment, both in quantitative terms and in terms of scientific and technological content.

A fundamental consequence of understanding a university as a CAS is that the development of the lines of research is heterogeneous and can move toward variable growth, whether in research, training, and/or correlation. These possible forms of specialization could generate unex pected effects, such as a strong internal differentiation between highly developed capacities and capacities with low or very low development. This is the effect of incentives placed exclusively on the high productivity of scientific articles in international journals. We believe that the future of university management will move toward the challenge of promoting harmonious development of the capabilities of its three missions. To this end, we propose that the participatory and empirically based construction of research, education, and outreach agendas can contribute to a governance that recognizes the systemic, adaptive, and complex nature of the generation and evolution of capabilities in Latin American universities.

Bibliography

Abbott, A. (2020). Stress, anxiety, harassment: Huge survey reveals pressures of scientists' working lives. *Nature, 577*(7791), 460–461. https://doi.org/10.1038/d41586-020-00101-9.

Acosta, L. A., Becerra, F. A., & Jaramillo, Y. D. (2017). Sistema de información estratégica para la gestión universitaria en la universidad de Otavalo (ecuador). *Formación Universitaria, 10*(2), 103–112.

Adelt, F., Weyer, J., Hoffmann, F., Ihrig, A. (2018). "Simulation of the Governance of Complex Systems (SimCo): Basis Concepts and Experiments on Urban Transportation", *Journal of Artificial Societies and Social Simulation*, 21 (2).

Altbach, Philip (2006). «Globalization and the University: Realities in an Unequal World». En Phillip Altbach, James Forest, *International Handbook of Higher Education. Dordrecht* (pp. 23–48): Springer.

Aoki, M. (2010). *Corporations in Evolving Diversity*. Cognition, Governance, and Institutions. New York: Oxford University Press.

Araneda-Guirriman, C., & Pedraja-Rejas, L. (2017). Las universidades y el nuevo perfil de estudiantes: nuevas realidades y retos para América Latina. *Interciencia, 42*(12), 786–788.

Araneda, C., Pedraja, L., & Rodriguez, E. (2017). Sistema nacional de innovación: Reflexiones y análisis del caso chileno. *Idesia, 35*(4), 111–117.

Arocena, R., & Sutz, J. (2000). Looking at national systems of innovation from the South. *Industry and Innovation, 7*(1), 55–75.

Arrow, K. (1999). "Information and the organization of industry", en G. Chichilnisky *Markets, information, and uncertainty Essays in economic theory in honor of Kenneth J. Arrow*. New York: Cambridge University Press.

Arthur, B. (2015). *Complexity and the Economy*. Oxford University Press.

Axelrod, R. (1997). *The complexity of cooperation*. Princeton University Press.

Barra, A. M. (2019). La Importancia de la Productividad Científica en la Acreditación Institucional de Universidades Chilenas. *Formación Universitaria, 12*(3), 101–110.

Beckert, J. (2009). The social order of markets. *Theory and Society, 38*(3), 245–269.

Beinhocker, E. (2006). *The Origin of Wealth: Evolution, Complexity, and the Radical Remaking of Economics*. Harvard Business School Press.

Bennet, A., & Bennet, D. (2011). *Organizational survival in the new world. The intelligent complex adaptative systems*. Routledge.

Bloch, C., & Schneider, J. W. (2016). Performance-based funding models and researcher behavior: An analysis of the influence of the Norwegian publication indicator at the individual level. *Research Evaluation, 25*(4), 371–382. https://doi.org/10.1093/reseval/rvv047.

Blondel, V; Guillaume, J-L; Lambiotte R; Lefebvre, E (2008). Fast unfolding of communities

Boudon, R. (1982). *The Unintended Consequences of Social Action*. Basingstoke: Palgrave Macmillan UK.

Bowles, S. (2016). *The Moral Economy: Why Good Incentives Are No Substitute for Good Citizens*. Yale University Press.

Bowles, S. (2006). *Microeconomics: Behavior, Institutions, and Evolution*. Princeton University Press.

Brousseau, E., Garrouste, P., & Raynaud, E. (2011). Institutional changes: Alternative theories and consequences for institutional dessign. *Journal of Economic Behavior & Organization, 79*, 3–19.

Cancino, R. (2017). *Sistemas Adaptativos Complejos de Ciencia y Tecnología. Aproximación a la complejidad sociocientífica contemporánea. El caso de la Antropología Social chilena entre los años 1989 y 2011*. Tesis Doctoral, Universidad de Chile.

Cancino, R., Orozco, L. A., Ruiz, C. F., Coloma, J., García, M., & Bonilla, R. (2014). Formas de organización de la colaboración científica en América Latina: un análisis comparativo del sistema chileno de proyectos y el sistema colombiano de grupos de investigación. In P. Kreimer, H. Vessuri, L. Velho, & A. Arellano (Eds.), *Perspectivas latinoamericanas en el estudio social de la ciencia, la tecnología y la sociedad* (1st ed., p. 603). México DF: Siglo XXI Editores.

Cárdenas, J. C. (2009). Experiments in Environment and Development. *Annual Review of Resource Economics, 1*, 157–182.

Carmichael, T., Hadžikadić, M. (2019). "The Fundamentals of Complex Adaptative Systems", en T. Carmichael, A. Collins y M. Hadžikadić (Eds.), *Complex Adaptative Systems.* Views from the Physical, Natural, and Social Sciences. Cham: Springer

Casas, R. (2001). El enfoque de redes y flujos de conocimiento en el análisis de las relaciones entre ciencia, tecnología y sociedad. *Revista Kairos, 5*(8).

Casas, R. (2004). Conocimiento, tecnología y desarrollo en América Latina. *Revista Mexicana De Sociología, 66*, 255–277.

Casas, R. (2015). Hacia un enfoque analítico y de políticas para las interacciones entre ciencia, universidad y sociedad en la región latinoamericana. *Cuestiones de Sociologia, 12.* http://www.cuestionessociologia.fahce.unlp.edu.ar/article/view/CSn12a04.

Casas, R., Corona, J., & Rivera, R. (2014). Politicas de ciencia, tecnologia e innovacion en America Latina: Entre la competitividad y la inclusion social. In P. Kreimer, H. Vessuri, L. Velho, & A. Arellano (Eds.), *Perspectivas latinoamericanas en el estudio social de la ciencia, la tecnología y la sociedad* (pp. 352–364). Siglo XXI Editores.

Cohen, M., & Axelrod, R. (2000). *Harnessing Complexity: Organizational Implications of a Scientific Frontier.* The Free Press.

Colander, D., & y Kupers, R. . (2016). *Complexity and the Art of Public Policy: Solving Society's Problems from the Bottom Up.* Princeton University Press.

Correa, H. (2014). Estudios sobre ciencia, tecnología y sociedad: En favor del compromiso político. *Scientiae Studia, 12*(3), 511–534.

Cowan, G., Arrow, K. (2019). "Bounded rationality and other departures", en D. Krakauer *Worlds Hidden in Plain Sight: The Evolving Idea of Complexity at the Santa Fe Institute.* Santa Fé, NM: The Santa Fe Institute Press.

Christensen y Tschirhart, (2011). "Organization Theory", en M. Bevir (Ed.). *The SAGE Handbook of Governance.* London: SAGE Publications.

Cumming, G., Norberg, J. (2008). "Scale and complex system", en J. Norberg y G. Cumming (Eds.), *Complexity theory for a sustainable future.* New York: Columbia University Press.

Dastan, Đ, Çiçek, M., & Naralan, A. (2011). The Effects Of Information Technology Supported Education On Strategic Decision Making: An Empirical Study. *Procedia - Social and Behavioral Sciences, 24*, 1134–1142.

DiMaggio, P. (2015). New Institutionalism in the Analysis of Complex Organizations. *International Encyclopedia of the Social & Behavioral Sciences, 16*, 764–769.

Durlauf, S., & Ioannides, Y. (2010). Social Interactions. *Annual Review of Economics, 2*, 451–478.

Edelenbos J., Klijn, E., Kort, M. (2009). "Managing Complex Process Systems: Surviving at the Edge of Chaos", en G. Teisman, A. van Buuren y L. Gerrits (Eds.), *Managing Complex Governance Systems.* New York: Routledge.

Escudero, T., Pino, J., & y Rodriguez, C. . (2010). Evaluacion del profesorado universitario para incentivos individuales: Revisión metaevaluativa. *Revista De Educación, 351*, 513–537. https://idus.us.es/handle/11441/44864.

Etzkowitz, H., & Leydesdorff, L. (1995). The triple helix—university-industry-government relations: A laboratory for knowledge based economic development. *EASST Review, 14*(1), 14–19.

Feld, A., & Kreimer, P. (2020). Latinoamericanos en proyectos europeos: Asimetrías en la cooperación científica internacional. *Ciencia, Tecnología y Política, 3*(4), 1–12.

Gambetta, D., & Origgi, G. (2013). The ll game the curious preference for low quality and its norms. *Politics Philosophy & Economics, 12*(1), 3–23.

Gell-Mann, M. (1994). "Complex Adaptative Systems", en G. Cowan, D. Pines y D. Meltzer (Eds.), *Complexity. Methaphors, Models and Reality. Reading,* MA: Addison-Wesley Publishing Company.

Gell-Mann, M. (1995). Plectics. In J. Brockman (Ed.). *The Third Culture: Beyond the Scientific Revolution* (pp. 316–332). New York: Simon & Schuster

Geyer, R., & Rihani, S. (2010). *Complexity and Public Policy: A new approach to twenty-first century politics, policy and society.* Routledge.

Gintis, H. (2007). A framework for the unification of the behavioral sciences. *Behavioral and Brain Sciences, 30*, 1–61.

Goodin, R. (1996). "Institutions and theur design", en R. Goodin (Ed.), The theory of institutional design. Cambridge, MA: Cambridge University Press.

Granovetter, M. (2017). *Society and Economy. Framework and Principles.* Harvard University Press.

Hedström, P., Bearman, P. (2009). "What is Analytical Sociology All About? An Introductory Essay", en P. Hedström y P. Bearman (Eds.), *The Oxford Handbook of Analytical Sociology.* Oxford: Oxford University Press.

Hedström, P. (2005). *Dissecting the Social. On the Principles of Analytical Sociology.* Cambridge University Press.

Holland, J. (2014). *Complexity: A Very Short Introduction.* Oxford University Press.

Holland, J. (1995). *Hidden Order. How Adaptation Builds Complexity.* Addison-Wesley Publishing Company.

Jurado-Paz, I. M., & Morán-Vallejo, M. A. (2019). Gestión universitaria de la innovación social promovida desde espacios académicos relacionados con el emprendimiento, la investigación y la proyección social. *Revista De Investigación, Desarrollo E Innovación, 9*(2), 261–272.

Kanchan, T., & Krishan, K. (2019). The Leiden manifesto and research assessment. *Science and Engineering Ethics, 25*(2), 643–644.

Klijn, E., Snellen, I. (2009). "Complexity Theory and Public Administration: A Critical Appraisal", en G. Teisman, A. van Buuren y L. Gerrits (Eds.), *Managing Complex Governance Systems.* New York: Routledge.

Knight, J., & Johnson, J. (2011). *The Priority of Democracy. Political Consequences of Pragmatism.* Princeton University Press.

Kreimer, P., & Ugartemendía, V. (2007). Ciencia en la Universidad: dimensiones locales e internacionales. Mecanismos de reproducción de la investigación en grupos universitarios de la Argentina. *Atos de pesquisa em educacao, 2*(3), 461–485.

Krog, J. (2018). The missing link : How university managers mediate the impact of a performance-based research funding system. *Research Evaluation, 28*(1), 1–10.

Lane, R. (2017). *The Complexity of Self Government. Politics from Bottom Up.* Oxford University Press.

Lemos, M., & Agrawal, A. (2006). Environmental Governance. *Annual Review on Environmental and Recources, 1*(31), 297–325.

Liu, X., Yu, S., Moreau, Y., De Moor, B., Glänzel, W., & Janssens, F. (2009). Hybrid Clustering of Text Mining and Bibliometrics Applied to Journal Sets. In *Proceedings of the 2009 SIAM International Conference on Data Mining* (Vol. 1–0, pp. 49–60). Society for Industrial and Applied Mathematics. https://epubs.siam.org/doi/abs/10.1137/1.9781611972795.5.

Macy, M., Flache, A. (2009). "Social Dynamics from Bottom Up: Agent-based Models of Social Interactions", en P. Hedström y P. Bearman (Eds.), *The Oxford Handbook of Analytical Sociology.* Oxford: Oxford University Press.

Mantzavinos, K., North, D., & Shariq, S. (2004). Learning, Institutions, and Economic Performance. *Perspectives on Politics, 2*(1), 75–84.

Maskin, E. (2008). Mechanism design: How to implement social goals. *American Economic Review, 98*(3), 567–576.

McGee, S., & Edson, R. (2014). Challenges of Governance in Complex Adaptative Systems: A Case Study of U.S. Public Education. *Procedia Computer Science, 36*, 131–139.

McMillan, E. (2004). *Complexity, Organization and Change.* Routledge.

Merton, R. (1976). *Sociological Ambivalence and Other Essays.* The Free Press.

Miller, J., & Spage, S. (2007). *Complex Adaptive Systems an introduction to computational models of social life.* Princeton University Press.

Miller, G. (2004). "Monitoring, Rules, and the Control Paradox: Can the Good Soldier Svejk Be Trusted?, en R. M. Kramer y K. S. Cook (Eds.), *Trust and Distrust in Organizations.* New York: Russell age Foundation.

Moreno, T. (2009). La enseñanza universitaria: Una tarea compleja. *Revista de la educación superior, 38*(151), 115–138. http://www.scielo.org.mx/scielo.php?script=sci_abstract&pid=S0185-27602009000300007&lng=es&nrm=iso&tlng=es.

Nee, V. (2005). "The New Institutionalism in Economics and Sociology", en N. Smelser y R. Swedberg (Eds.*), The Handbook of Economic Sociology*. Princeton, NJ: Princeton University Press.

Oliva, I. (2008). Conocimiento, universidad y complejidad: Bosquejos epistemicos y metodologicos para unavinculacion transdisciplinaria. *Estudios Pedagogicos, 34*(2), 227–243.

ONU. (2015). *Transformar nuestro mundo: La Agenda 2030 para el Desarrollo Sostenible*. [Resolucion aprobada por la Asamblea General]. Organizacion de Naciones Unidas.

Orozco, L. A. (2015). *Diversidad y heterogeneidad en redes de colaboración científica: Un estudio de las escuelas de administración de América Latina*. Universidad Externado de Colombia.

Orozco, L. A., Aristizabal, J. P., & Villaveces, J. L. (2018). Management challenge in the entrepreneurial university and academic performance. *Open and Equal Access for Learning in School Management*, 196–213.

Orozco, L. A., & y Chavarro, D.A, . (2008). Universidad y emprendimiento. *Hallazgos Revista De Investigaciones, 10*, 65–97.

Orozco, L.A y Chavarro, D.A. (2006). *De la historia y sociología de la ciencia a indicadores y redes sociales. Análisis de la biotecnología para el estudio de comunidades científicas en el marco de los programas nacionales de Ciencia y Tecnología*. OCyT. Bogotá.

Ostrom, E. (2006). "The complexity of rules and how may evolve over time", en C. Schubert y von Wangenheim (Eds.), *Evolution and Design of Institutions*. New York: Routledge.

Ostrom, E. (2005). *Understanding institutional diversity*. Princeton University Press.

Otte, V., & Rousseau, R. (2002). Social network analysis: A powerful strategy, also for the information sciences. *Journal of Science Information, 28*(6), 441–453.

Peters, G. (2011). "Institutional theory", en M. Bevir (Ed.). *The SAGE Handbook of Governance*. London: SAGE Publications.

Petersen, T. (2009). "Opportunities", en P. Hedström y P. Bearman (Ed.), *The Oxford Handbook of Analytical Sociology*. Oxford: Oxford University Press.

Pettit, P. (1996). "Institutional Design and Rational Choice", en R. Goodin (Ed.), *The theory of institutional design*. Cambridge, MA: Cambridge University Press.

Rivero, P., Echeverry-Mejia, J., & Vessuri, H. (2018). Más allá de las ciencias, los científicos y la gestión de la ciencia y la tecnología. Conversación con Hebe Vessuri. *Cuadernos de Antropología Social, 48*, 129–144.

Roth, A. (2018). Marketplaces, Markets, and Market Design. *American Economic Review, 108*(7), 1609–1658.

Ruiz, C., Bonilla, R., Chavarro, D., Orozco, L. A., Zarama, R., & Polanco, X. (2010). Efficiency measurement of research groups using Data Envelopment Analysis and Bayesian networks. *Scientometrics, 83*(3), 711–721.

Schneider, V. (2012). "Governance and complexity", en D. Levi-Faur (Ed.), *The Oxford Handbook of Governance*. Oxford: Oxford University Press.

Searle, J. (2010). *Making the Social World: The Structure of Human Civilization*. Oxford University Press.

Simon, H. (1997). *Models of Bounded Rationality. Empirically Grounded Economic Reason. Volumen 3*. Cambridge, MA: The MIT Press.

Simon, H. (1996). *The Sciences of the Artificial. Cambridge*. The MIT Press.

Stiglitz, J. (2000). The contribution of economics of information to the twentieth century economics. *The Quarterly Journal of Economics, 115*(4), 1441–1478.

Svampa, M. (2019). *La fronteras del neoextractivismo en América Latina. Conflictos socioambientales, giro ecoterritorial y nuevas dependencias*. Mexico: Universidad de Guadalajara - CALAS.

Teisman, G., Gerrits, L., van Buuren, A. (2009). "An introduction to Understanding and Managing Complex Process Systems", en G. Teisman, A. van Buuren y L. Gerrits (Eds.), *Managing Complex Governance Systems*. New York: Routledge.

Tirole, J. (2001). Corporate governance. *Econometrica, 69*(1), 1–35.

Vázquez-Cano, E., Mengual-Andrés, S., & Roig-Vila, R. (2015). Análisis lexicométrico de la especificidad de la escritura digital del adolescente en whatsapp. *RLA. Revista de Lingüística Teórica y Aplicada, 53*(1), 83–105.

Williamson, O. (2017). *Contract, Governance and Transaction Cost Economics*. World Scientific Publishing.

Wit, H. de. (2020). Internationalization of higher education. *Journal of International Students, 10*(1), i–iv. https://doi.org/10.32674/jis.v10i1.1893.

Wright, M., Birley, S., & Mosey, S. (2004). Entrepreneurship and university technology transfer. *The Journal of Technology Transfer, 29*(3/4), 235–246. https://doi.org/10.1023/B:JOTT.0000034121.02507.f3.

CHAPTER 11

Science, Technology, Innovation, and Inclusive Development: A Country Comparison Between Colombia and Mexico

Jaime Humberto Sierra-González and Carlos Eugenio Ramos-Pérez

11.1 Introduction

The XVI edition of the Hay Festival (celebrated in Cartagena de Índias, Colombia, in January 2020) saw the participation of Cambridge Professor of Political Economy of Development Ha-Joon Chang. Chang remarked that at the heart of the social protests that occurred in late 2019 and early 2020 in Latin America (e.g., Chile and Colombia) was generalised discontent and frustration with current socio-economic policies. This happens because natural resources-based economies that generate basic

J. H. Sierra-González (✉) · C. E. Ramos-Pérez
Business Department, School of Business and Economics, Pontificia Universidad Javeriana, Bogotá, Colombia
e-mail: jhsierra@javeriana.edu.co

L. A. Orozco et al. (eds.), *Science, Technology, and Higher Education*, Palgrave Studies in Democracy, Innovation, and Entrepreneurship for Growth,
https://doi.org/10.1007/978-3-030-80720-7_11

export commodities[1] favour wealth concentration in old elites and barely generate highly qualified better-paid jobs for younger, more educated citizens (Chang, 2020). That is, Latin American elites have failed to invest in innovation and in building more egalitarian economies.

Furthermore, IADB economist G. Rivas (2020) has stated along the same line that:

> It is clear from those policies that better procure social inclusion must be a priority. However, it is also imperative to remark that without an important increase of productivity, it will be very difficult to sustain a greater level of social expenditure and, even less, to create better jobs, which are a key factor in diminishing inequality.
>
> And so it happens that over the recent decades, economic expansion in the region has been fundamentally sustained by demographic growth and the extensive exploitation of natural resources. Nevertheless, several countries are already experiencing a demographic transition that implies that a greater proportion of elder adults need to be supported by a few proportion of younger employed adults.
>
> That can only be done with a bigger increase in productivity and the evidence accumulated through years of research tells us that innovation is the factor that will help us achieve these changes. (Our own translation)

Chang and Rivas' assertions can be illustrated through the experiences of Colombia and Mexico, two Latin American countries in which there have been National Systems of Science, Technology, and Innovation (NSSTI) in place since the decade of 1990s. Despite the existence of these systems, there is evidence that shows that both Colombia and Mexico underperform in terms of investment in Science, Technology, and Innovation (STI) activities, scientific production, and training of highly specialised human resources for STI when compared to other members of the Organization for Economic Cooperation and Development (OECD) group.

Actually, a quick look at the Global Innovation Ranking shows that Latin American economies are literally stock in the mid-to-lower percentiles of innovative nations. Moreover, even if three of the top four Latin American economies now belong to OECD (Brazil is a partner and non-member contributor), their relative standing among the other more advanced members of such club once again unveils serious deficiencies

[1] Which often are not even well-known enough so that their exploitation and international trade at low value-added levels is all the more so sub-optimal (Mejía, 2020).

concerning the social, economic, and political welfare conditions they can offer their citizens (Tables 11.1 and 11.2).

As a matter of fact, recent work explores a comparative approach to innovation efforts and performance of Bogota (Colombia) and the other capital cities of OECD members (Chile and Mexico included), and the European Union (Malaver & Vargas, 2020). The conclusion reached indicates that the Colombian and Mexican capital cities (25% of Colombia's GDP and 17% of Mexico's GDP, respectively) lags well behind all the OECD capitals (in per capita terms) and, furthermore, the gap will likely grow in the near future if STI initiatives do not live up to the expectations generated by the OECD membership. even

This is all in line with the profile of the situation that has recently surfaced in most Latin American nations, summed up in Table 11.1. Facts seem to stand behind Chang's assumptions. Although relatively stable, the socio-economic and political systems in operation in Latin America do lack steam on the structural drive to reinvigorate societies and lead them towards a wider and deeper state of welfare.

This is what motivates this paper. Essentially, we wonder why have Colombia and Mexico not moved through knowledge production and innovation faster and closer to knowledge-based economies where opportunities and superior performance may contribute to change inequality and wealth concentration into greater and better spread resources, opportunities, and social welfare. And we ponder about the consequences and challenges of such situations.

This paper is structured as follows; in Section two, we offer a brief characterisation of both countries so the traits that link STI and inclusive development are broadly described. Section three explores the main theoretical underpinnings of inclusive development. Section four discusses what are considered the key reasons for the current state of affairs and the evolution of the links between STI and inclusive development in Colombia and Mexico. Finally, Section five states final remarks, implications, and feasible recommendations that might help lead a transformation in the two countries.

11.2 STI Systems and Inclusive Development in Colombia and Mexico

Studies on Innovation Systems and the so-called Triple Helix approach (e.g., Etzkowitz & Leydesdorff, 2000; Lundvall, 1992; Nelson, 1993)

Table 11.1 A snapshot of the top four Latin American countries

Country	*Trends in government transition*	*Human Development Index*[a]	*Social situation*	*Regional ranking in terms of GDP and value*[b]	*Growth mean % (2013–2018) in terms of GDP*[c]	*Ranking OECD*[d]	*Global Innovation Index*[e]
Brazil	Left>>>Right	79 (0.761)	Discontent, no protests	1 (3,255,145)	−0.19	4	62 (31.94)
Chile	Left>>>Right	42 (0.847)	Discontent and sustained protests	4 (463,790)	2.51	21	54 (33.86)
Colombia	Right>>Further right	79 (0.761)	Discontent, less sustained protests	3 (709,421)	3.04	16	68 (30.84)
Mexico	Right>>>Left	76 (0.767)	Discontent, no protests	2 (2,573,848)	2.43	8	55 (33.60)

[a]Human Development Index, 2019 (UNDP, 2020). Value and score (max = 1)
[b]OECD (2020a). GDP in current prices, total million USD (2019 or latest available)
[c]World Bank (2020a). Growth average 2013–2018
[d]OECD (2020a). GDP ranking
[e]Cornell University, INSEAD, WIPO (2020). Global ranking (out of 131 economies) and score (max = 100)
Source Own elaboration based on different sources

Table 11.2 Colombia and Mexico compared—selected indicators 2015–2019

Indicator	*Country*	*2015*	*2016*	*2017*	*2018*	*2019*
Population (millions)	Colombia	48.2	48.7	49.3	49.8	50.4
	Mexico	121	122	124	125	126
GDP per capita (USD)	Colombia	6075	5808	6322	6689	6421
	Mexico	9665	8809	9389	9805	9999
GDP (USD billion)	Colombia	293	283	312	333	324
	Mexico	1169	1077	1160	1223	1259
Economic growth (GDP, annual variation in %)	Colombia	3.0	2.1	1.4	2.5	3.3
	Mexico	3.3	2.6	2.1	2.2	−0.3
Unemployment rate	Colombia	8.9	9.2	9.4	9.7	10.5
	Mexico	4.0	3.4	3.1	3.4	2.9
Trade balance (USD billion)	Colombia	−13.5	−9.2	−4.5	−5.1	−8.5
	Mexico	14.7	−13.1	−11.0	−13/6	5.4
Exports (USD billion)	Colombia	38.6	34.1	39.8	44.4	42.4
	Mexico	381	374	409	451	461
Imports (USD billion)	Colombia	52.1	43.2	44.2	49.6	50.8
	Mexico	395	387	420	464	455
Public debt (% GDP)	Colombia	42.9	43.8	44.9	48.2	47.2
	Mexico	45.4	49.4	46.9	46.8	47.1
Inflation rate (CPI, annual variation in %)	Colombia	5.0	7.5	4.3	3.2	3.5
	Mexico	2.7	2.8	6.0	4.9	3.6
External debt (% of GDP)	Colombia	38.2	42.5	40.0	39.6	42.7
	Mexico	35.6	38.3	37.6	36.5	36.8
International reserves (USD)	Colombia	46.7	46.7	47.6	48.4	53.2
	Mexico	177	177	173	175	181
Investment (annual variation in %)	Colombia	2.4	−2.9	1.9	1.5	4.3
	Mexico	5.0	1.0	−1.6	0.9	−4.9
Consumption (annual variation)	Colombia	3.4	1.6	2.3	3.7	4.4
	Mexico	2.7	3.8	3.2	2.3	0.6
Domestic demand (annual variation as %)	Colombia	2.4	1.2	1.1	3.4	4.3
	Mexico	3.0	3.1	1.8	2.0	−0.9
Industrial Production (annual variation in %)	Colombia	2.0	4.1	−0.5	3.8	1.5
	Mexico	1.1	0.3	−0.3	0.5	−1.7

Note All USD values are current prices
Source Own elaboration with information from Focus Economics (2020a, 2020b)

have been introduced but insufficiently interpreted/adapted in most developing countries and, particularly, in Latin America. Such frameworks, which were originally developed before the creation of the Systems of Innovation in Latin America and were meant to understand other contexts, have been adopted as prescriptive models that are explicitly used to guide the process of creation of "ideal" Systems of Innovation in these countries.

As a result, we posit, the Systems of Science, Technology and Innovation designed in Colombia and Mexico are essentially top-down, State-driven, centralised, and linearly conceived regarding different dimensions (national, regional, sectoral). This, in turn, affects the governance and performance of such systems and, unsurprisingly, the outcomes and challenges that can be identified in each case widely differ from those of developed countries. In fact, a few exploring studies already show that Latin America, and particularly the Colombian and Mexican STI systems, have a long way to go to close the gap with developed economies and to further advance in the locally desired direction, particularly if it regards boosting inclusive development (Kuhlmann & Ordoñez, 2017; Malaver & Vargas, 2020).

Both, Colombia and Mexico have promoted some inclusive policies which, to a certain extent, relate to a few STI topics as it is recognised that such inclusive measures[2] are central to economic growth (Bortagaray, 2016; Casas et al., 2013; Planes-Satorra & Paunov, 2017). Nevertheless, far less importance has been given to generate strategies that jointly promote social, territorial, and business inclusion.

11.2.1 Colombia at a Glance

Colombia is the third biggest economy (measured by GDP) of Latin America and the Caribbean, behind Brazil and Mexico. It is a country of great biodiversity with a growing, though ageing, population that reaches almost 50 million inhabitants (FocusEconomics, 2020a). Colombia

[2] Such policies refer to instruments which "*aim to remove barriers to the participation of individuals, social groups, firms, sectors and regions that are underrepresented in innovation activities in order to ensure that all segments of society have the capacities and opportunities to successfully participate in and benefit from innovation*" (Planes-Satorra & Paunov, 2017, p. 4). Understood as a process, inclusive innovation involves the coordination of several actors from specific contexts for sharing information and, ideally, generating knowledge (Sampedro, 2013).

became the most recent member of the Economic Cooperation and Development Organisation (OECD) in 2018 as the 37th member State.

Since the liberation from Spanish rule, Colombia went through unceasing turmoil and experienced continued changes that meant the publication of nine constitutions between 1811 and 1886. After the separation of Venezuela, Ecuador, and Peru/Bolivia, the Republic of Colombia was finally consolidated, but political instability was its trademark. The start of the twentieth century saw the separation of Panama, fabricated by the local elites and the USA, amid the "one-thousand-day" war.

In 1948, another major period of politically born violence started with the assassination of Jorge Eliecer Gaitán, and the last *coup d'Etat* took place in 1953. In 1958, the two major traditional parties (conservatives and liberals) signed a deal to alternate in power for sixteen years (four presidential terms) (the so-called *Frente Nacional*). It came to its end in 1974. The ensuing period, however, still saw political violence enacted by the confrontation between State forces, several guerrillas and, later, paramilitary forces created by drug lords and big landholders. Amid such harsh circumstances, the tenth Constitution was proclaimed in 1991.

Politically, according to such Constitution, the Colombian State is organised in two main parts: the branches of public power and the State organisms. Regarding the former, the public power has three branches: (1) The Executive branch, subdivided into three levels: national, departments, and municipalities. The Executive is represented by a democratically elected President of the Republic, serving a four-year term, and who is the head of State and the government; (2) the Legislative branch, integrated by the Congress of the Republic (Senate and Chamber of Representatives); (3) the Judiciary powers (Supreme Court and Courts of Justice). The nation also includes autonomous and independent organs such as Banco de la República (Central Bank), Regional Autonomous Corporations (in charge of regulating environment-related issues, among other things), autonomous State-owned universities, and regulators such as the Autoridad Nacional de Televisión (the broadcasting regulator) (Función Publica, 2020).

Colombia has started implementing a series of macroeconomic policies that have enabled it to sustain a certain trail of development for the past decade (OECD, 2019a). Among these, the Colombian government has produced policies for fostering education, incentivising greater commercial openness, and has nearly ended a 50-year internal armed conflict with politically dissident groups.

Despite these advances, and although Colombia initiated its internationalisation process with the *Apertura Económica* (economic opening)—and an extensive privatisation process of State-owned companies—boosted by President Gaviria during the 1990s, the country's insertion into global markets has remained stagnant even after signing fifteen Free Trade Agreements so far. This is so as the country's exports have been, for the past two decades, concentrated in only five products (mineral fuels and oil, coffee, precious stones, plastics, and live trees) (CPC, 2020). Similarly, these products are traded to mainly four partners: USA, Panama, China, and Ecuador. Colombia's net exports reached 42.4 USD billion in 2019 (FocusEconomics, 2020a; OEC, 2020), making it the 55th largest exporter in the world (OECD, 2019a).

In economic terms, although growth potential has fallen substantially during the last decade, economic growth in Colombia has been resilient to external macroeconomic crises thanks, in part, to sound and credible macroeconomic policy framework, prudent fiscal management, and a smooth adjustment to the oil prices shock of 2014–2016 (OECD, 2019a; World Bank, 2020a). Inflation was meant to remain near the 3% target before the COVID-19 crisis, supporting real income and consumption (Table 11.2). Additionally, the country has increased its exposure to global financial conditions. Similarly, poverty and informality levels had also fallen (OECD, 2019a).

After nearly 70 years of internal conflict, Colombia signed a peace treaty with the biggest guerrilla (FARC) that has enabled the country to slightly concentrate more on some social progress (OECD, 2019a). However, internal regional inequalities remain large, informal employment substantial, poverty high and spread, with most social policies not well-targeted.

Although access to finance has improved, thanks in part to changes in tax schemes introduced by the Financing Law of 2018 (*Ley de Financiamiento*), financial markets remain less developed than their counterparts from countries in the region (OECD, 2019a), even if it has it has integrated into MILA (Integrated Latin American Markets made up by Chile, Colombia, Mexico, and Peru). Colombians' in general have an asymmetrical access to the finance system. For example, in 2017 34.4% of the country's SMEs had access to a bank credit, a number below the 41.4% with access in 2015 (CPC, 2020). Moreover, there are few investment angels supporting the entrepreneurial base in the country, leaving entrepreneurs with the necessity to access alternative (e.g., family or friends) sources of finance as main investors to support innovation (CPC, 2020). The former is coupled with a banking system with low levels of integration with the innovation system (García & Prado, 2019).

The main Colombian development policy document is the National Development Plan created by the National Planning Department (DNP for its acronym in Spanish). For its current edition (2018–2022), it proposes and follows the formula: Legality + Entrepreneurship = Equity. The plan's operative lines include security, legality, anti-corruption advance, Colombia and globalisation, and citizen participation. Science, Technology, and Innovation is said to be a transversal element of the plan.

The long-term focus (2030) of the plan targets Colombia's investment in STI activities at 1.5% of its GDP by 2022 (2019 value was 0.67%) (DNP, 2020). Such an increase would be significant as Colombia is outperformed by other big Latin American economies (Chile, Mexico and Brazil) in terms of innovation capabilities (OECD 2019a; WIPO, 2020) (Table 11.1). In fact, the Global Innovation Index ranks Colombia as the 68th economy in the world in terms of its innovation capabilities and 5th among 18 economies in Latin America and the Caribbean (Cornell University, INSEAD, WIPO, 2020). Although some progress has occurred, an important effort still needs to be done to take Colombia into a more competitive position. Yet, we agree with Centeno et al. (2020), who argue that such effort needs to go beyond the typical discussions regarding R&D and innovation budget increases and uses, and the traditional corrective measures adopted (e.g., enactment of law or additional reforms).

Thus, the main discussion needs to be oriented towards generating a more substantial change in terms of what is relevant for Colombia; for example, how STI resources would be more efficiently used, how, and by whom. Also, the scientific development of the country and the related advancements of its innovation system should be substantially transformed from a resource-based economy into a knowledge-based one to better exploiting the natural endowment of the country and its bio and cultural diversity (Mondragón, 2020). Moreover, the current STI system has other impending needs to tackle at the governmental level: its high level of bureaucracy and the partial (mis)understanding of the Colombian elites who have designed the STI system exclusively from a technology standpoint and which paradoxically observes technology as exogenous to the system (Centeno et al., 2020; Mondragón, 2020).

11.2.2 Mexico at a Glance

Mexico, with a population of almost 130 million, has the eleventh largest economy in the world and the second in Latin America and the Caribbean. The country became a member of OECD in 1994, the same year it signed the North American Free Trade Agreement (NAFTA), later renegotiated into what is now known as USMCA (USA, Mexico, and Canada). Currently, Mexico has strong macroeconomic institutions and ranks as the world's 15th largest exporter due to the strengthening of its productive capacities, diversifying away from raw materials such as oil, and deepening its production complexity on manufactured products that are integrated into regional and global value chains (OECD, 2013a; World Bank, 2019, 2020b).

Mexico, following its independence from Spanish rule in 1821, became a representative, democratic, and Federal Republic according to the Constitution of 1824. What followed was a period of political and economic turmoil, which culminated in the Mexican Revolution of 1910 and the publication of the Political Constitution of 1917 (still in force). Though organised as a democracy, the country was ruled between 1930 and 2000 by the *Partido Revolucionario Institucional* (PRI)—a centre-right political party—and by far-right PAN between 2000 and 2012, with PRI returning to Government from 2012 to 2018. Currently, the government is headed by leftist Andres Manuel Lopez Obrador, who became elected president in December 2018.

The Mexican State is organised around three branches of public power: (1) The Executive power, represented by a democratically elected President of the country who serves a six-year period. (2) the Legislative power deposited in the Congress and divided in the Senate and the Deputies, and (3) The Judiciary power which is represented by the Supreme Court of Justice.

In economic terms, although some moderate economic improvement has occurred, this has not enhanced relative living standards. Over the last three decades, Mexico has underperformed in terms of economic growth. Growth rates averaged only 2.4% between 1980 and 2017, with declining oil production impacting both the economy and its fiscal revenues (OECD, 2013a, 2019b; World Bank, 2019). Over the last decade, the country has experienced a robust export growth that is driven by integration into lower value-added activities connected to global value chains aided by NAFTA; the exports' share of GDP has climbed from 19% of GDP in 1990 to 38% of GDP in 2017. Manufactured goods account for 80% of exports and go mostly to the United States (OECD, 2019b) (Table 11.2).

During the 1980s, some relevant macroeconomic changes occurred in the country following two crises, the energy crisis of the late 1970s and the national crisis of 1982 (Villavicencio, 2012). As a consequence, the country redefined its development model by introducing market-oriented structural reforms (first generation reforms) such as greater commercial openness, trade liberalisation, and the privatisation of several State-owned enterprises (e.g., Telmex) (Casas et al., 2013) following policy recommendations from the Washington Consensus.

The country still faces problems with a weak rule of law and deteriorated institutions, impunity levels are high, violent crime continues to grow, and control of corruption is weak when compared to OECD countries, but also against Asian economies (OECD, 2019b). There are obstacles to competition and widespread informality which encompasses nearly 60% of jobs; similarly, perceived corruption is the highest in the OECD (OECD, 2019b). There are also problems with social inclusion and poverty reduction. There are marked differences between the north of the country (industrialised), the centre-north (where Mexico City is located), and the less well-developed south (mostly agriculture-based).

In terms of finance and access to credit, while the banking sector remains sound and well capitalised, with increases to the domestic credit to the private sector and new fiscal reforms[3] having been introduced (OECD, 2019b), some actions to improve the access of financial options still need to be implemented. For example, the general population still has limited access to finance, as the share of adults with an account at a formal financial institution decreased from 39% in 2014 to 35% in 2017, while only one in four of the poorest 40% of Mexicans have an account in a financial institution. The situation is also present for business, as Mexican SMEs in general face more difficulties than big enterprises for

[3] At the end of 2005, Mexico amended its Securities Market Law and introduced the *Sociedad Anónima Promotora de Inversion* a new form of a fiscal corporation which increases the alignment of interest among shareholders as well as control and transparency.

accessing bank credit to develop, as only a third of them have loans, thus, relying more on costly suppliers' credit (OECD, 2013a, 2019b; World Bank, 2019).

In Mexico, the National Development Plan is the key planning document that establishes the national public policy priorities. In its current edition (2019–2024), it has three main areas of policy interest: justice and rule of law, welfare policies, and economic development. STI policy is only obliquely included in the current NDP; even though the country ranks 2nd among 18 economies in Latin America and the Caribbean in terms of innovation capabilities (Cornell University, INSEAD, WIPO, 2020), it still suffers from a rather low political commitment to STI policy as a major driver of economic growth and social welfare. For example, the main political goal of increasing R&D spending to 1% of the country's GDP still is far from materialising as it has remained in similar levels for nearly 30 years, close to 0.5 of GDP (OECD, 2019b). Moreover, innovation appears disconnected from science and technology in the current policy plans as the NDP (2019, p.58) states that "[t]*he Federal Government will promote scientific and technological research; will support students and academics with scholarships and other stimuli towards knowledge. Conacyt will coordinate the National Plan for Innovation for the benefit of society and national development, with the participation of universities, the people, scientists, and businesses*" (our translation).

The policy conception above is problematic since it relegates the role of other actors to the role of participating entities, placing knowledge production as a by-product of government's promotion, and innovation coordination under its central agency (Conacyt).

11.3 Why Inclusive Development and STI Policies Need to Go Hand in Hand?

These snapshots of the two countries actually converge to Chang and Rivas' description of how the Latin American economic model has remained essentially stuck in a first-sector commodity production system. Under this model, exports cluster in few traditional low-value products that concentrate riches in a small elite and offer no prospective transition towards higher quality better-paying jobs for citizens, all of which generate frustration, discontent, and angry reactions. Ultimately, as Chang asserts, several factors behind such a situation may be related to Latin American countries having built only a minimum basis to start a transition towards knowledge-based economies where innovation may drive more modern and egalitarian economies. Such transition has been delayed and is still too slow to create new and better conditions for their citizens (Bakker et al., 2020).

In fact, there is ample evidence on how low levels of social inclusiveness and participation in innovation-related activities across the globe and the uneven distribution of innovation-related capabilities or skills (e.g., entrepreneurial, research-related, knowledge-related, access to finance, etc.,) across different social groups such as women, ethnic minorities, and immigrants impact the welfare of the population. Along that line, the problems of social inclusiveness are connected to those of territorial (or spatial) and industrial inclusiveness and impact the endowment of business capabilities across regions since "*the uneven distribution of innovation capacities across firms has contributed to widening the gap in productivity performance between the most productive and less productive firms*" (Planes-Satorra & Paunov, 2017, p. 13).

Among the different reasons found to generate this uneven participation of individuals in innovative activities are their different levels of educational attainment. It has been argued that the lower the educational attainment of an individual, the less perception of the benefits knowledge would bring to one's welfare. Other factors impacting uneven participation are discrimination in the labour markets on the grounds of gender, age, race, religion, or ethnic origin; persistence of stereotypes (e.g., women in STEM activities); barriers to access finance; weak connections to entrepreneurial networks; or even living in or belonging to deprived areas (Planes-Satorra & Paunov, 2017).

Thus, the problem of inclusiveness is one of proper allocation of resources to create capacities and, therefore, it has to be urgently confronted to modify such outcomes. Other rationales that go hand in hand when implementing inclusive innovation policies include tackling missing social, industrial, or territorial inclusiveness either by reducing discrimination or by fostering participation.

To this extent, inclusive innovation policies have explicit targets and instruments (Table 11.3) and specific challenges not usually shared and greater than those faced by general innovation policies, such as raising the target group's awareness of the policy programme and increasing their involvement and thinking inclusively and actively incorporating target groups (Bortagaray & Ordoñez-Matamoros, 2012; Planes-Satorra & Paunov, 2017). Furthermore, the transition to inclusive and sustainable

Table 11.3 Inclusive innovation policies: Aims, targets, and related instruments

Policy main objective	*Target*	*Instruments*
Fostering the integration of disadvantaged groups in innovative activities	General capacity building	• Targeted grants to fund research projects led by researchers from disadvantaged groups • Funds to research institutions to improve the research environment for women
	Entrepreneurship skills	• Entrepreneurship education in schools • Entrepreneurship courses in the context of vocational education • Entrepreneurship training provided out of the formal education system
	Strengthen the scientific literacy of the public	• Investment in high-quality science education for all • Projects for communication regarding and popularisation of science and technology
	Addressing discrimination and stereotypes	• Awareness-raising activities • Role models • Mentoring programmes
	Providing incentives to invest in (inclusive) innovation	• Grants and repayable grants
Addressing barriers to entrepreneurship faced by disadvantaged groups	Facilitating access to finance	• Microcredit (or micro-loans) • Equity financing • Financial education

(continued)

Table 11.3 (continued)

Policy main objective	*Target*	*Instruments*
	Providing business development support	• Provision of information to entrepreneurs • Coaching and mentoring • Professional business counselling or advice to entrepreneur • Assistance to access new markets • Technology transfer assistance
	Promoting networks	• Innovation vouchers • Entrepreneurial networks
	Improving access to talent by small businesses	• Grants to recruit researchers • Access to specialised online job portals
Enhancing innovation in lagging areas	Accessing global knowledge and technology	• Demonstration of new technologies and training provided by S&T specialists • Financial support to projects that use science, technology, and innovative solutions to address local challenges
	Maximising the potential of existing assets	• Design of tailor-made development • Identify areas of specific relevance for a region and train potential local entrepreneurs in those sectors • Intellectual property protection • Support to regional governments to implement science, technology, and innovation projects
	Attracting innovative firms to peripheral regions	• Technology parks • Special economic zones • Grants to promote business R&D in peripheral regions

Source Own elaboration based on Planes-Satorra and Paunov (2017) innovation systems require systemic changes that go hand in hand with changes in markets, productive and consumption practices (Bortagaray, 2016).

11.3.1 Inclusiveness Policies for STI in Latin America

As stated above, Latin America is a region full of contrasts. Both, extreme richness and poverty coexist with generalised low income, low productivity, and low competitiveness levels, relatively high job informality (Bortagaray, 2016; Casas et al., 2013; Sampedro, 2013). Also, there are great inequalities in terms of entrepreneurship capabilities, knowledge production, and STI development (Arocena & Sutz, 2014). These characteristics have shaped to a certain extent the way in which industrial and STI policy has been designed and implemented. Latin American countries were concerned as early as 1970s about the relationship between knowledge, innovation and social development acknowledgeing that both knowledge and technology play a fundamental role in social change and its related processes (Casas & Corona, 2013; Dagnino, 2012; Herrera, 1973). Although knowledge has been considered important in the region, Latin America, in general, is still a technology adapter rather than a creator (Bortagaray, 2016; Dutrénit & Sutz, 2014).

Historically, Latin American regional policy agendas have placed an important focus on scientific policies and funding scholarships for training scientists. During the 1990s, Latin American countries saw different, often non-favourable changes in their Science, Technology, and Innovation (STI) policy agendas mostly due to a greater influx of market-oriented forces that had a role in shaping the industrial and economic ideas and their consequent outcomes. Furthermore, the decisive influence of several international organisms when offering their recommendations for the formulation and design of such STI policies has led to a homogenisation of policies, which are often in direct conflict with the region's context, history, and socio-economic tradition (Bortagaray, 2016; Casas & Corona, 2013).

The rationale for Latin American STI policy formulation, during the first decade of this century, was aligned with the European, Japanese, and North American tradition, which considered such policies as the favoured public instrument to enhance national economic standards through the improvement of productivity, welfare, and business competitiveness at a national and global level (Casas & Corona, 2013). On the other hand, the transition of some Latin American countries towards politically left-oriented governments has meant that their STI policy agendas have begun incorporating objectives more explicitly related to social development.

However, as Bortagaray (2016) indicates, the transition between different policy rationalities has not been one of substitution, but rather of adding layers of complexity and generating a vast policy mix system where multiple rationalities coexist but might not work in synchronicity with each other. In this sense, Casas and Corona (2013) argue that the discussion of STI policy and social inclusion was not an explicit part of the policy agenda, both in Colombia and Mexico.

As stated above, both Colombia and Mexico exhibit ample social and economic disparities and several areas of social exclusion ranging from health to energy and drinkable water access, to living standards, hunger, and minorities' rights. Even though things are slowly improving (OECD, 2019a, 2019b), several policies implemented to tackle these exclusions have not been sufficient. Table 11.4 illustrates selected examples of inclusive innovation policies in both Colombia and Mexico along with the programme's rationale and main components.

In the case of Colombia, social development and inequity reduction have been objectives in the national STI policy agenda pushed forward from 2010 by means of the inclusion of the social innovation concept and its connection with productive and inclusive development. For example, the National Development Plan 2010–2014, Chapter 3, proposed that developing three major pillars (innovation, competitiveness, and productivity policies) and fostering key employment activities would help to achieve the goals of sustainable economic development. Similarly, Colciencias published in 2010 the National Strategy for the Social Appropriation of STI with the goal of sharing and transferring knowledge between producers and users (Salazar et al., 2013).

Nonetheless, far from helping to close the inclusiveness gap, these policy efforts have had little impact. The authors argue that some of the reasons for such meagre impact include the ambiguity on how innovation has been articulated in these policies without a clear strategy path, nor subsequent monitoring and evaluation criteria. Furthermore, the different ways in which innovation is understood and defined lead to operative confusion (Salazar et al., 2013).

Likewise, several policies to tackle poverty were introduced in Mexico (e.g., *Programa Progresa* 1997 and *Oportunidades* 2002) since 1990, but these have not contributed to generate capabilities or impacted

Table 11.4 Inclusive innovation policies in Colombia and Mexico (selected examples)

Policy	*Country*	*Rationale*	*Components*
Ideas for change programme (2012–2014)	Colombia	Engage the target group in the design and implementation of the programme/solution	Allows vulnerable communities to identify their specific needs through a virtual platform, after which the STI community can propose specific solutions to their problems Target: Poor and vulnerable local communities with unmet needs, particularly relating to the environment and energy fields
Productive territories programme (pilot phase)	Mexico		Reduce poverty through tailor-made development plans for poor rural communities. Technical expert teams elaborate and validate these plans in collaboration with the local communities, which ensures that the specific needs of the targeted community and the actual financial and technical opportunities are adequately identified. The plans count on local support for their implementation Target: Poor rural households (to be eligible, households need to be beneficiaries of the social programme "*Prospera*" and live in rural municipalities)

Policy	*Country*	*Rationale*	*Components*
Royalties for science, technology, and innovation programme (2012–present)	Colombia	Encouraging involvement and articulator of different actors within the innovation system	The scheme devotes 10% of the royalties obtained from the extraction of non-renewable natural resources to finance regional STI projects that generate long-term capacities in the region, conditional on being consistent with public policies at the national, territorial, and sectorial levels Target: Regions with weak innovation performance
Dialogo de Saberes (2005, 2012)			Develop social innovation through co-sharing local communities' knowledge (e.g., indigenous peoples) with users of knowledge Target: Research groups, universities, corporations
Special economic zones programme in targeted regions (2016–present)	Mexico	Develop and deliver inclusive innovation programmes as part of broader development strategies	The programme foresees the design and implementation of other policies improving the human capital endowment through education, the improvement of health services, the expansion of financial services, and the development of public infrastructure Target: Peripheral regions (three lagging regions in southern Mexico)

Source Own elaboration based on Salazar et al. (2013) and Planes-Satorra and Paunov (2017) the productive fabric of the country and these were not connected to other national policies (neither industrial, nor S&T-related) that tackle associated problems. Furthermore, Mexican STI policies have placed an excessive interest in the development of human resources coupled with meagre investments in other STI-related activities (Casas et al., 2013).

Finally, as Casas et al. assert, the Mexican innovation system has a "*low density of connections between its agents, reflected on the countries' low innovative capacity. Furthermore, it is characterised by a scarce propension to establish agreements between the collective interest and social objectives*" (2013, p. 54, our translation).

11.4 Critical Considerations on the Relationship Between Inclusive Development and STI in Colombia and Mexico

The economies of Colombia and Mexico can be described as mostly based on the endowment of natural resources and the consequential exploitation of comparative advantages rather than competitive advantages, under very limited international engagement. In fact, these two nations stand far away from knowledge-based economies and, furthermore, typical n-tuple helix analyses and recommendations—that is to say, a systemic view of the relations and interactions among four major actors (government, universities, enterprises, civil society) created with specific reference to knowledge-based economies—are hard to implement because the reality of the mutual commitment among such actors is quite poor. Additionally, the two countries exhibit a limited international trade engagement mostly characterised by outflows of commodities and inflows of high value-added goods as their productive sectors are made up of a huge number of SMEs grouped into traditional activities in low technology sectors.

Reality actually strikes hard when a closer look is taken at the Colombian and Mexican n-tuple helix characterisation, for instance. As a matter of fact, the usual three stakeholders appear in a statist configuration where universities and enterprises are essentially "commanded" by governments about their interactive initiatives (far away from the balanced configuration which is characteristic of knowledge-based economies), and civil society (the fourth helix) is rather weakly acknowledged or, in some cases, even marginalised by the other three.

Thus, it is not surprising that the existent national STI systems in these countries are, as stated previously, essentially top-down, State-driven, centralised, linearly conceived regarding different dimensions (national, regional, sectoral), highly inarticulate and fragmented, and poorly funded. Even under the more conventional neo-institutional approach that makes the Triple Helix converge with Innovation Systems,[4] it is difficult to visualise a relatively high degree of STI performance in Colombia and Mexico. This happens precisely because knowledge generation, diffusion, and application for innovation are rather scarce and not well articulated.

In effect, it is actually hard to find out how universities and other knowledge institutions in these countries "... *act in a partnership with industry and government and even take the lead in joint initiatives*". (Etzkowitz & Leydesdorff, 2000). Moreover, this is true in a context (Colombia and Mexico) where universities are still stuck in a backward model in which these are even now little more than a traditional source of human resources and knowledge (for companies) and their role as key innovation stakeholders is still weak and embryonic. In fact, their internal organisational mechanisms and resources allocated to this purpose are not sufficient nor mature enough to stop their dependence on mostly informal ties.

This situation takes the Colombian and Mexican STI systems farther away from more convenient arrangements such as the views which assume that the Quadruple Helix Model should aim at the creation of feasible synergies that articulate wealth creation, knowledge production, and normative control "*...whereby institutions and interinstitutional arrangements can be stimulated by local or national governments* [and] *markets and sciences operate at the global level...* [so] *the function of institutional agency involves distributed instances*" (Ranga & Etzkowitz, 2013). In fact, even under a statist helix configuration (e.g., top-down legal and policy measures), universities and enterprises in these two countries have serious difficulties to figure out a model where they can work together to formulate and implement synergic initiatives to articulate their key roles in order to transform society and the economy.

[4] Under such perspective, the Functions building block (defined as a set of competences that determine the system's performance) helps secure the Triple Helix system's main function which essentially involves the generation, diffusion, and utilisation of knowledge and innovation by making use of all available competencies embedded in the Triple Helix knowledge, innovation, and consensus spaces.

This being said, it is by no means extraordinary that development policies and programmes rarely seem clearly articulated to and supported by STI institutions, policy, and programmes in Colombia and Mexico. It is much less so when the incorporation of the civil society and their agency capacity to development initiatives has been weak, at best.

It is from this perspective that Chang and Rivas' earlier assertions resonate strongly. One could ask: *why* and *how* the governing elites in Colombia and Mexico have failed to boost STI development and implementation to create a knowledge-based socio-economic system which, in turn, demand better-qualified people (not just labour) and create and foster more knowledge-intensive, better-paid jobs and, consequently, lesser inequality in society?

Why refers to the reasons that the governing elites have had to maintain a tight control of economic and political power by restraining access to assets and activities dominated by them. But it also refers to such elites' rare attempts to modernise such activities (no matter if in primary, secondary, or tertiary sectors) so that, for instance, agricultural activities become more technologically intensive or manufacturing and services incorporate new knowledge and advance more dynamically through sustained innovation. This is reflected in an entrepreneurial mindset which focuses on rent-seeking economic activities (with low reinvestment rates), short-termism (that goes against long-term investment projects such as innovation-related initiatives), client-based politics and policies, low appreciation of eventual new competitors (several virtually monopolistic/oligopolistic sectors), and oligopolistic control of key production factors (e.g., land), among other common features.

In a way, this approach may help us understand to a certain extent why Colombia and Mexico have become the nations that they are nowadays. Of course, this may be related to a number of factors that have somehow helped drive the configuration of the socio-economic traits of these societies: for instance, the size of the internal market and the purchasing power of internal market consumers or the dynamics of subnational regional economies and the role of national/regional/local governments.

How, instead, refers to processes that were eventually started but were somehow aborted or did not reach the outcomes expected but represent some sort of advance, though. This may have happened for a number of reasons: opposition and direct action of incumbents whose interests were threatened, bad planning, and implementation, emerging circumstances that mislead the effort and doom it, among others.

A telling example is this: Colombian governments have consistently set a goal for STI spending to reach 1% of GDP and it has regularly failed over the last twenty years. Even if every single government in this century has committed to accomplish that goal over their constitutional term, twenty or so years have gone by without even getting close to the target, not once even if the concept is conveniently widened (from STI strictly to STIA). To top it all, in a rather cynical manner, the current government has proposed an even higher goal: 1.5% of GDP. How is that possible? Well, neither public (government agencies), nor private (enterprises) spending has lived up to the promise. This is related to the first question, at least partly. Short-termism and a rent-seeking mentality are still deeply embedded in public and private actors; and client-based politics and policy have got in the way of sensible initiatives to coordinate synergistic efforts to do so, among other factors. However, this failure is widely visible and marks an obligatory reference when discussing or proposing STI policies in Colombia nowadays.

11.4.1 Some Illustrative Examples

In this section, we offer several examples that help us to exemplify how and why the NSSTI are shaped as they are, and the way knowledge is created and used in Colombia and Mexico in relation to inclusiveness. Firstly, we analyse the structure of the Colombian and Mexican economies in terms of the value added of their GDP (see Graphic 11.1). For comparison purposes, the graphic includes two blocks, Latin America and the Caribbean, and the structure of OECD members (including Mexico and Colombia).

As seen in Graphic 11.1, in terms of diversification, there is no great difference among the composition of the observed economies, as all have had a similar composition over the past decade, with the services sector becoming more important over time (World Bank, 2020). For the year of comparison (2017), the greater share of economic activity was in the services sector, representing above 60% in each economy, with both Colombia and Mexico performing below the OECD average.

For Colombia, Mexico and LAC, in general, agriculture still represents an important source of value, as these are above the OECD average value of 1.5%. As expected, there is a transition of capacities from agriculture and manufacturing to services, more clearly seen in the case of the main OECD countries, but happening in the other economies as well. Despite this similarity in terms of composition, the greatest contrast among these

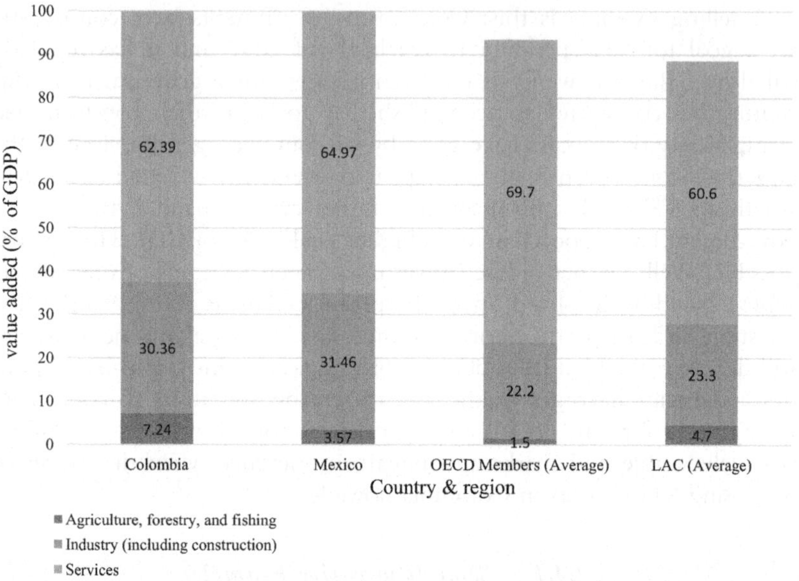

Graphic 11.1 Composition of the Colombian, Mexican, LAC, and OECD member economies (2017). *Notes* Data for OECD members (average) and LAC (average) as reported in original statistics. Differences in data correspond to either unreported values or incomplete information (*Source* Own elaboration with data from World Bank [2020a] and CIA [2020])

economies remains in terms of their sizes (Table 11.5) and the value added and performance of each of the sectors.

Table 11.5 GDP and GDP per capita at current prices (2019)—selected economies

Country	*GDP*	*GDP per capita*
Colombia	324	6421
Mexico	1259	9999
OECD Members (mean)	53,653	39,438
Latin America & Caribbean (mean)	5720	8847.4

Source Own elaboration with data from Focus-economics (2020a, 2020b) and WorldBank (2020)

Now, beyond the basic size and structure comparison, what needs to be carefully analysed regards the way in which resources in those sectors are used and other inputs (e.g., labour, knowledge) are incorporated in the productive processes, as well as the effect of such in terms of outcome (e.g., resource productivity) and impact (e.g., job quality, families' welfare).

As shown in Graphic 11.1, agriculture, forestry, and fishing represent the smaller share of the Colombian and Mexican economies. However, many of the main products both Colombia and Mexico export come from this sector and the mining activity. This is telling, since there are some prevailing problems in this sector, such as the unequal distribution of land (Oxfam, 2013; USAID, 2017a, 2017b), and the low integration of knowledge (i.e., R&D an innovation) present in such sector.

In terms of land ownership and its concentration or distribution, evidence indicates that Colombia is among the most unequal countries in the world in terms of land allocation (second only to Paraguay in Latin America). This implies that land is allocated to few, and not as productive as proclaimed, elite groups whose agricultural practices focus on large-scale industrial monoculture modes (Oxfam, 2013; USAID, 2017a). Other than that, the land distribution problem has been worsened by violence. In the case of Mexico, land ownership is distributed among large transnational agribusinesses, which control through contract farming, the entirety of the production process for large areas and *ejidal* (communal) owners, whose land is highly fragmented, and often unregulated as they lack appropriate ownership records. This has generated a situation in which there is a high concentration of owners and of products (USAID, 2017b; OECD/FAO, 2019).

A second problem, present also in the rest of LAC economies, is related to agricultural capability and its productivity. In a nutshell, the Latin American agriculture sector can be described as highly heterogeneous, where "... [a] *capital and technology intensive corporate sector that has successfully managed to integrate itself into global agri-food markets coexists alongside a broad socio-productive sector based on subsistence farming, non-farming rural activities and landless rural populations that have been unable to participate in dynamic economic circuits*" (OECD/FAO, 2019: p. 72).

For example, in the Colombian case, out of the land available for agricultural use, nearly 31% is used for pastures, which in some instances is overexploited for grazing purposes resulting in soil erosion and destruction of water and forest resources as cattle-growing farms hold 20.7% of the Colombian cattle herd (USAID, 2017a; González et al., 2020). In the Mexican case, its agricultural productivity is low when measured by international standards despite nearly 55% of Mexico's land being dedicated to agriculture (USAID, 2017b).

Finally, as for the incorporation of knowledge, qualified labour and other significant inputs, Latin American agriculture has had some improvements, but unresolved challenges remain such as infrastructure problems, poor irrigation, a great deal of unpaved rural roads, lack of logistics, and poor facility infrastructure (OECD/FAO, 2019). In terms of research, spending in agricultural R&D has increased steadily across the region, but at different paces and not always allocated to the most efficient or productive sources nor to the most needed populations.

Similarly, public investment in infrastructure (annual average growth) has increased over the past two decades (i.e., Colombia, 8.5% and Mexico, 7.0% of their respective GDPs) but, as mentioned above, rural infrastructure is still lagging. Lastly, knowledge is used sparingly to solve some agricultural problems, such as the introduction of new crops and—specifically in Mexico—for using water more efficiently (OECD/FAO, 2019), but many other challenges remain unheeded across the region.

Now we turn our attention to the manufacturing and industrial sectors. Like the agriculture sector, manufacturing in LAC is full of significant heterogeneity across countries with ample differences in terms of how volatile and exposed the economies are to external shocks, their main trade partners, and the different policy frameworks that regulate them (OECD et al., 2019).

In general, industrial production in Colombia had a sustained growth from 2000 until 2008 (when the international crisis began and when Venezuela virtually stopped being the second most important trade partner that bought most industrial exports from Colombia), registering a weak growth afterwards (Carranza et al. 2018; OECD, et al., 2019). For the latest period, Table 11.1 shows the Colombian industrial production has had an annual variation of 1.8% on average for the 2015–2019 period, while the industrial production for Mexico registered a contraction (−0.2%) for the same period.

Now, as for how efficient these countries are in terms of the use of the production factors they employ in their industrial sectors and the amount of knowledge added to such activities, recent research argues the value added of the Colombian manufacturing industry is low, even lower than that of the services sector (Carranza et al., 2018). Moreover, while the R&D OECD intensity (expenditure on R&D as a percentage of GDP) was 2.38% on average (2018), in Colombia it was 0.28% and in Mexico 0.31% for the same year (OECD, 2020).

Furthermore, in the case of Mexico, the R&D intensity of some sectors[5] is very low. For example, during 2015 the total business R&D productivity was 0.18% (OECD, 2017). This is due to some sectors which generated little to no value (i.e., the primary sector), and some more productive sectors such as the textile sector (0.22%) or the paper industry (0.33%). Finally, in terms of its total factor productivity, Mexico experienced a negative average growth (−4.0%) during 2000–2018 (CPC, 2020).

Finally, both in Colombia and Mexico, services are the most dynamic and important sectors representing 62% and 64.5% of their GDP, respectively (Graphic 11.1) (Castiblanco-Moreno et al., 2017). For Colombia, the current Annual Services Survey 2018 (EAS for its acronym in Spanish) shows that the most productive sectors from the services survey were employment activities in the building sector (21.1%) and telecommunications and health services (each producing 13.2% of value added per sector) (DANE, 2020).

The data above can be contrasted with the degree of innovation present in the services sector, which is low, with the exception of service firms belonging to the banking sector (70% claim to innovate) and R&D centres (65% innovate). Reasons for such low performance include that many firms lack in-house R&D and innovation-related skills, a lack of technology to invest in developing services, and limited financing (Castiblanco-Moreno et al., 2017; CPC, 2020).

In the Mexican case, recent research suggests that the transition of the Mexican economy to the tertiary sector has been a by-product of migration (mostly to the USA) and the globalisation process (initiated in 1994), resulting in a services sector which demands skilled labour to satisfy the needs of Mexican trade partners (Castillo et al., 2014). In terms of the evolution of the service sector GDP, Dutrénit et al. (2013) report that traditional and other services have accounted on average for 89.5% for the period 2003–2011, while knowledge-intensive business services

[5] No similar data were found on Colombia for comparison purposes.

(i.e., scientific and technical, management of corporate enterprises and waste management, and remedial services) have accounted on average for 10.5%, for the same period.

Similar to its Colombian counterpart, the Mexican service sector is not particularly innovative with a majority of firms claiming not to conduct any type of innovation, or if they do, doing so only in terms of incremental innovation (Dutrénit et al., 2013).

It is not surprising, then, given the characteristics of the productive sectors in Colombia and Mexico to observe its performance in terms of its internationalisation process. Though LAC, in general, has opened up to international trade, it has been observed that the region's low productivity seems to be associated with an export structure concentrated in primary and extractive sectors with low levels of sophistication and predominance of low-productive micro and SMEs in the region, which account for 99.5% of the LAC economic structure (OECD et al., 2019).

This is clear in the case of Colombia, for even after three decades of beginning its internationalisation process, its insertion in international markets is low, with an economy that has a heavily concentrated exporting basket (close to 61% for 2017) in low added-value products, such as coffee, bananas, flowers, coal, ferronickel, and oil. This is reflected, for example, in the Herfindahl–Hirschman export concentration index[6] in which Colombia (0.34 for 2019) ranks 16 among 17 LAC nations, only above Venezuela (0.82) (Carranza et al., 2018; CPC, 2020; García et al., 2019).

The Colombian export process is hindered by both high transit times and costs, staying behind Mexico, average Latin America, and well below other OECD nations. For example, in terms of exporting time, it took (in 2018) an average of 112 h and a cost of nearly 630 USD (average cost per container) for a Colombian export to reach its destination, whereas a Mexican one took close to 40 h and an average of 400 USD per container. These are well below other OECD members in which an export takes only 13 h and costs USD 200 on average (CPC, 2020).

Another problem associated with the under-performance of Colombia's foreign trade is the disappearance, during the 1990s, of the Colombian Institute of Foreign Commerce (Incomex, for its Spanish acronym), a regulating body and arbiter. This led to the emergence of a

[6] Index with values ranging from 0 to 1 measuring absolute diversification or concentration. Values closer to 1 mean a less diversified economy (CPC, 2020).

number of actors with the power to design and manage the trade policies of the country, mostly through lobbying and not always to the benefit of the economy (Echavarría et al., 2019).

In addition to the above, Colombia's insertion into Global Value Chains (GVCs) has been low and continues to occur mostly for the primary sector, with a very low level of adoption of international supplies, both for backward and forward operations. Recent evidence suggests some problems faced by Colombia for successfully integrating into GVCs are related to non-monetary tariffs, which are high, and trade tariff behaviours, which are protective of specific sectors and industries without clear rationality for the selection of such industries (CPC, 2020; Echavarría et al., 2019). Other problems associated with the integration dynamics are the presence of a set of incentives which prioritises linkages with low technology-intensive sectors (i.e., basic products); for example, foreign direct investment inflows to Colombia have been mostly directed to the extractive and mining industry, leaving behind other more dynamic activities (CPC, 2020).

Moreover, high non-monetary tariffs (77% in 2017) still represent the greatest cost when importing into Colombia thus impacting the supply chain of goods needed to produce other intermediate or higher intensity technology products. Additionally, trade tariffs, although diminishing, are still higher than those of trade partners and other economies in the region (CPC, 2020).

Moreover, Colombia currently has a heterogenous trade tariff ranging for certain products (e.g., egg and dairy, meat, agricultural products) from 5 to 85% on average. This, as Echavarría et al. (2019) argue, punishes exports for several reasons, either by disincentivising them or by raising production costs and reducing competitiveness. More significantly, a greater variation in tariffs tends to increase technical smuggling, a situation where products are erroneously classified either by under-invoicing or by changing its place of origin (CPC, 2020). This, in turn, raises overall customs administrative costs required, for instance, for inspection and correct labelling.

On the other hand, Mexico has managed to diversify its exporting profile over the past years (e.g., the concentration of its exporting basket in 2018 was below 25%) because of the countries' involvement in GVCs, aided mostly by NAFTA (now USMCA) (CPC, 2020). Mexico's integration to GVCs occurs in different industries (e.g., aviation, cars,[7] electric and electronics), where it undertakes lower value-added activities (e.g., *maquiladora)*, activities with a high weight to value ratio (e.g., production of cars, flat screens for televisions, and electronic appliances of large size), and activities that require strong managerial involvement in order to meet high quality standards (e.g., aerospace industry and production of medical instruments) (Watkins, 2007, in Dougherty & Reynaud, 2017).

Despite the country's integration into GVCs, there is evidence indicating that the share of Mexican value added embodied in foreign countries' exports is low, below that of peer countries, even if the country's backward participation[8] seems to be concentrated in medium–high to high technology industries (Dougherty & Reynaud, 2017; OECD, 2019). Similarly, this integration process does not seem to be linked to the development of highly innovative skills, nor require labour that is knowledge intensive, as Kuznetsov and Dahlman (2008, p. 33) highlighted that the challenge for Mexico's *maquiladoras* is to "*go beyond footloose manufacturing*".

Furthermore, an important driver for upgrading in GVCs is investment in knowledge-based capital, as the highest level of value creation in GVCs are found in upstream activities (e.g., new concept development, design, R&D) and in certain downstream activities (e.g., marketing, branding, or customer service). This process simply does not occur in Mexico, since its industries with larger technical assets have not been found to be more integrated into GVCs (Dougherty & Reynaud, 2017).

Moreover, those authors also report that the integration process into GVCs has not been inclusive since more than 60% of the domestic value added in exports has been found to be done by large firms and not by SMEs, while the share of firms engaging in GVCs is low compared with other countries (OECD, 2019).

[7] The car industry, for example, benefited since 1994 of several assembly plants moving to Mexico, thanks in part to low operative costs and easy market access to the USA and Canada. This trend helped Mexico to become (by 2015) the seventh largest manufacturer of vehicles in the world, the first of Latin America, and the fourth largest exporter in the world (Cuevas, 2016 cited by Chiquar & Tobal, 2019).

[8] Share of foreign value added in a country gross export.

Finally, the integration to GVCs has led the country to specialise in activities which use low-skilled human capital industries.[9] That is, Mexico's insertion into GVCs from 1993 to 2017 has seen three periods: First, a period beginning after NAFTA and ending in 2001, in which the country specialised in relatively skilled-labour intensive industries (e.g., computer and peripheral equipment, and electro-medical and control instruments). A second period (running from 2002 to 2006, coinciding with China's accession to the WTO), in which the country's use of human capital and its trade specialisation patterns seem to not have changed significantly. Finally, a third period (2007 onwards) in which the skill change in Mexican production seems to have reversed to intensive use of low-skilled human capital since industries such as automobiles and trucks manufacturing or fruit and vegetable preserving increased their trade balance (Chiquar & Tobal, 2019).

Another significant feature regards the technological intensity of exports as it highlights some difficulties faced by Colombia and Mexico to fully exploit their limited knowledge-related capabilities. Graphic 11.2 shows the technological intensity composition of exports of selected economies for 2018.

It is evident that, except for Mexico, all other main Latin American economies are above the average of the region in their dependence on the primary sector and below the average in what concerns high and medium intensity manufacturers. Manifestly, they are even farther from the OECD averages.

A look at the evolution of exports (Graphic 11.3) provides some interesting traits found in both countries. As a matter of fact, it shows the great dependency that both economies have on the USA as their main commercial partner. In the case of Colombia, this dependency is lessened by the fact that it has other partners rising in terms of importance (e.g., China and Panama). However, Colombia's trade was severely affected by the deterioration and subsequent breakdown of the political/economic relationship with Venezuela, once Colombia's main buyer of medium-intensity goods. Mexico, instead, does not as its remaining trade partners represent less than 10% of the country's exports.

[9] A study that analyses the six industries that contributed most to the change in the difference between the average human capital intensity of export and imports over the period 1995–2017.

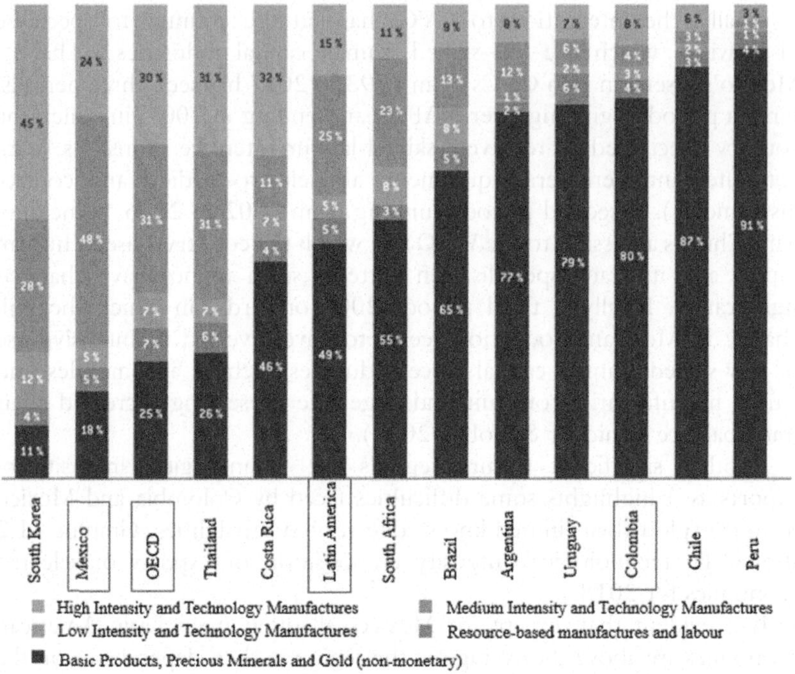

Graphic 11.2 Technological composition of exports (2018)—selected economies (*Source* CPC [2020, p. 280]. Our emphasis)

Furthermore, Table 11.6 provides information about the type of products (based on their technology intensiveness) that each country sells to their main trade partners. As can be seen, the bulk of Colombian exports belong to basic products (e.g., flowers, coffee, and minerals) and their importance (relative weight) is considerable as these represent a high volume of trade to the countries' main partners. These products require little transformation and low investment in knowledge. Only in the case of medicines (exported to Panama), there is a higher requirement of productive knowledge/expertise.

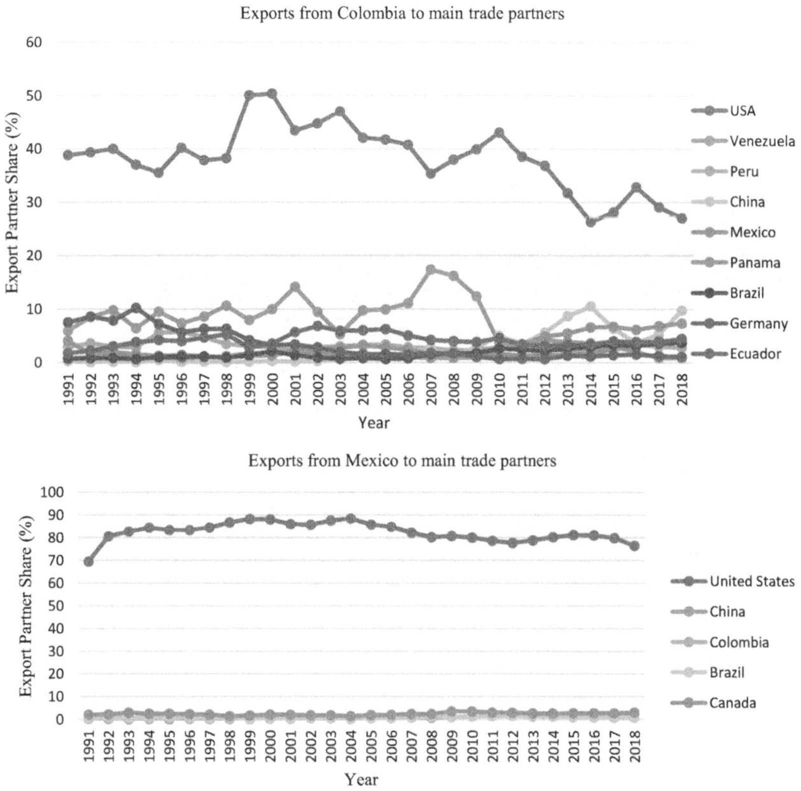

Graphic 11.3 Evolution of exports from Colombia and Mexico (1991–2018) to selected partners (*Source* Own elaboration based on WITS [2020a, 2020b])

As for Mexico, the type of products exported to its main partners are medium intensity/technology manufactures integrated into several GVCs. This supports the idea that the exporting profile of Mexico is more diversified than that of most Latin American economies and Mexican exports are relatively more intensive in knowledge, particularly in the car industry and the production of electrical components.

There is evidence on Colombian and Mexican firms having a disperse capability to produce knowledge, use it to transform it into innovations, or to connect to knowledge producers. Some of the reasons for such phenomena include: low proportion of researchers linked to the

Table 11.6 Colombian and Mexican chief exports to main trade partners (2019)

Country	USA		China		Panama		Canada	
Colombia	**Total (X)**	**12,265,652,574**		**4,564,928,828**		**2,354,487,706**		**446,193,647**
	Crude petroleum	4,898,842,865 (39.9%)	Crude petroleum	3,930,435,614 (86.1%)	Crude Petroleum	1,924,337,103 (81.7%)	Coffee	175,799,898 (39.4%)
	Flowers (ornamental & bouquets)	1,154,274,107 (9.4%)	Ferroalloys (Iron)	398,344,506 (8.7%)	Coal	45,977,312 (1.9%)	Coal	131,723,462 (29.5%)
	Coffee	1,053,044,377 (8.6%)	Coal	88,150,304 (2.0%)	Medicaments packed for retail sale	34,821,397 (1.5%)	Flowers (ornamental & bouquets)	11,982,443 (2.7%)
Mexico	**Total**	**358,870,588,964**		**6,854,364,873**		**1,237,259,291**		**14,132,557,428**
	Motor cars and other motor vehicles	37,352,575,334 (10.41%)	Copper Ores & concentrate	2,067,770,799 (30.2%)	Other commodities	384,642,439 (31.1%)	Other commodities	4,470,639,154 (31.6%)
	Automatic data processing machines	29,439,611,201 (8.20%)	Other commodities	1,426,515,566 (20.8%)	Petroleum oils and oils from bituminous minerals	275,479,752 (22.3%)	Vehicles	2,470,386,955 (17.5%)
	Motor vehicles; parts and accessories	26,107,796,552 (7.27%)	Vehicles	407,989,563 (6.0%)	Medicaments packed for retail sale	93,617,633 (7.6%)	Piston engines for vehicles	1,552,527,583 (11.0%)
	Vehicles for the transport of goods	25,368,512,067 (7.07%)						
	Insulated wire, cable, and other electric conductors	11,836,866,620 (3.30%)						
	Monitors and projectors, not incorporating television reception apparatus	11,186,614,203 (3.12%)						
	Other Commodities	9,423,679,616 (2.63%)						
	Telephone sets, including telephones for cellular networks or for other wireless networks	9,298,132,042 (2.59%)						
	Tractors	9,193,785,663 (2.56%)						
	Instruments and appliances used in medical, surgical, dental, or veterinary sciences	7,726,728,282 (2.15%)						
	Seats (different industries)	5,750,581,247 (1.60%)						

Notes All in USD current prices
Number in parenthesis is share of total exports to each market. Figures do not add to 100% as the table includes only main products per partner
Source Own elaboration with data from UN Comtrade Database (2020)

productive sector; a lack of connectedness between the agents related to knowledge creation (universities and research centres) and the productive sector, associated with not enough exploitation of these (sparse) linkages; a lack of incentives to produce or generate applied knowledge in enterprises intended to solve business and society-related problems. An associated problem identified by Malaver and Vargas (2020) relates to the insufficient use that productive sectors make of the skills of highly educated human resources. The authors found that, in some instances, much of the creative talent available in Bogota "*dilutes in the firms that employ* [them]". (CPC, 2020; Malaver & Vargas, 2020; Pietrobelli, 2012 in Wood et al., 2014).

Then again, the capability to turn knowledge into innovation is uneven in both Colombia and Mexico, as there are marked contrasts within regions and sectors. It is a situation in which the capital cities (Bogota and Mexico City), and other few and selected regions attract more talent as these have a higher concentration of universities, research centres, and productive agents actively producing and using knowledge (Cotte and Andrade, 2018; Cotte et al., 2018; Garavito & Cifuentes, 2018; Rodriguez, 2016; Torralba & Cotte, 2018). Despite this, there have been some public and private efforts, though sporadic and disconnected, towards generating better linkages between the productive sector and knowledge producers. One example of this is the creation of Technology Transfer Offices (TTOs) in many countries with the goal of improving the connection between universities/research centres and enterprises (Garrido & Rondero, 2015).

In Colombia, for example, most investments placed in STI-related activities by knowledge producers (HEIs) have been concentrated on average (for the period 2007–2018) on conducting R&D (close to 69% of total investments), while activities such as providing scientific and technological services have (for the same period) accounted only for 7.5% of their expenditures (Cotte & Andrade, 2018). This is telling as these figures describe, albeit partially, the importance placed by these actors onto generating knowledge and then diffusing it into other actors.

Moreover, many of Colombia's highly qualified human resources (close to 95.6% PhD and postdoctoral researchers) end up working for HEIs, due to the productive sector offering fewer opportunities (for example, in terms of career development and competitive salaries) and incentives for incorporating these resources (Burbano & Nubia, 2011; CPC, 2020; CNC et al., 2020). Similarly, there is a lack of connectedness between manufacturing and service companies in Colombia and knowledge producers. In fact, according to the National R&D and Innovation Survey (EDIT VIII 2015/16 and EDITS VI 2016/17), out of 7497 manufacturing companies and 8651 services companies, only 2.9 and 4.8% firms, respectively cooperated with universities or R&D centres to conduct their innovation activities (Andrade, 2018).

In terms of connectedness between knowledge producers and users in Mexico, there has been important efforts to train highly specialised human resources (national scholarship programme) and incentivise research production (national researchers' system) over the past forty-five years. Similarly, great care has been placed in creating a system of public research centres (supervised by Conacyt) and in establishing solid connections between these and HEIs. In this sense, since 2010 there is a stronger policy framework[10] (i.e., strategy 4.1 for the creation of TTOs in the Special Programme for Science, Technology, and Innovation and the creation of the FINNOVA programme) that explicitly recognises the need and advantages of transferring knowledge between actors in the innovation system. Despite these policies, the linkages between research centres, HEIs, and the productive sector remain weak and sparse (Chiapa, 2019; Ibarra et al., 2015).

This weak integration between knowledge producers and the productive sector is due in part to the low propensity of Mexican companies to invest in R&D and innovation. For 2016,[11] the expenditure on R&D as a share of the GDP of the private sector accounted for only 0.1% (INEGI, 2020). Additionally, there is evidence of lack of skills among business managers concerning their willingness to share confidential information or knowledge to effectively interact with TTOs (Ibarra et al., 2015). Another systematic problem, and somewhat paradoxical with TTOs themselves, refers to these lacking skilled labour specialised in technology transfer processes. However, some collaborating efforts have occurred between TTOs and the private sector. For example, during 2017/18, the country's TTOs signed a total of 2103 collaboration agreements, mostly with the private sector (38%), to transfer technology and do intellectual property work (Chiapa, 2019; Ibarra et al., 2015).

Additionally, there are financial constraints, lack of access to financial services to start innovation processes, and technical innovation is usually expensive (Zanello et al., 2016). Current research shows the effects of such financial constraints on innovation. Colombian innovative companies, for instance, are financially constrained and do not know well nor trust the STI ecosystem, particularly its financial actors (Sierra, 2020).

[10] One of the firsts TTOs to be established in Mexico was the Centre for Technological Innovation in 1984 in UNAM, the largest public university of the country (Ibarra et al., 2015).

[11] Latest available figure.

Moreover, innovative companies in Colombia exhibit certain financing behaviours that are worth noting. "*Colombian companies invest very little in STI, and those that do are not numerous, are mostly big, belong to sparsely populated technology-intensive sectors, and do mostly incremental innovation*" (Sierra, 2020, p. 252). Furthermore, those Colombian firms that do innovate, prefer not to resort to fresh equity and favour internal funding. Only when internal funding is not feasible, they do attempt to get loans from commercial banks. Similarly, low-liquidity companies prefer going to more costly local banks than using more convenient government subsidies or low-rate credits and they are somehow not interested in taking advantage of "*available cheaper, relatively specialised funding sources/mechanisms (e.g., Colciencias) as they feel official agencies' red tape is excessive*" (Sierra, 2020, p. 252).

As for the Colombian financial system, only a few first- and second-tier banks may eventually fund STI projects. Venture capital is not abundant (e.g., *Fondo Emprender* from SENA, and the ALDEA programme by iNNpulsa) (CPC, 2020) and faces several serious restrictions, and the stock market is small and underdeveloped. Finally, international bank leverage and bond funding are infrequent. "*So, the primary obstacles seem to regard rather poor matching environment and mechanisms and, subsequently, a very limited set of mostly generalist funders with rigid conditions (e.g. screening criteria) that make adaptive demand–supply matching difficult*" (Sierra, 2020. p. 253).

Now, for the Mexican case, recent research suggests Mexico's funding structures inhibit innovation. That is, traditional private capital is risk-averse and private funding is limited and concentrated, since Mexican private banks are reticent to fund entrepreneurial and innovation-related projects, and large investors prefer to invest in traditional sectors rather than in start-ups (León & Saveedra, 2018; Rios, 2018).

Additionally, Mexican companies invest little in R&D and innovation, and few of them undertake innovation (only 3.8% for 2016) (INEGI, 2020). Of those firms which innovate, many are unaware of the available private funding instruments and only a little proportion of innovative firms rely on public funding for their projects. In this sense, the public sector has increased the availability of programmes to support innovation and entrepreneurship (e.g., Finnova, National Entrepreneurship Fund), but it still faces many difficulties such as the presence of middlemen operating within the system—thus hampering its performance—and cumbersome administrative steps to obtain financing (León & Saveedra, 2018; Rios, 2018).

From a different perspective, a look at some regions of Colombia and Mexico unveil examples of the articulation that takes place through configurations such as the Triple Helix model. Some of these are more successful than others, but most certainly represent isolated efforts, not the norm.

In Colombia, interactions that involve Triple Helix actors (State–university–private businesses) have motivated the creation of a number of science and technology parks now operating in the country, as well as other collaborative outcomes. Though cases of success exist (e.g., project Lion[12]—Castellanos, 2013) where technology transfer did occur, the evaluation of the performance of such configurations indicates that there is a limited number of collaborations actively happening between the interested agents; this, in turn, limits the production and diffusion of innovation (Burbano & Nubia, 2011; Herrera et al., 2015). Furthermore, such configurations seem to be oblivious of the role that the civil society needs to play in n-helix configurations and the way financing needs to be articulated, especially in a context such as the Colombian one (Sierra, 2018).

The Mexican experience with the n-Helix approach finds clusters that, albeit successful, have followed a State-led Triple Helix model or more traditional approaches of connecting the relevant agents. Two prominent examples are available. In the electronics cluster in the State of Jalisco (western Mexico) the State Council of S&T has actively pushed towards the collaboration between public research centres (CINVESTAV) and private businesses (e.g., Intel) (Rivera, 2006; TBY, 2018; Xicoténcatl et al., 2020). In the Research and Technological Innovation Park in Monterrey, in the State of Nuevo Leon (north of the country), the strong presence of private universities (e.g., ITESM) and a long-established entrepreneurial base had made them a fertile ground for connecting the productive sector and knowledge producers. Evidence suggests these efforts have resulted in stronger linkages within business and academia,

[12] An IT and automation collaboration between Pontificia Universidad Javeriana (HEI) and Heinsohn Business Technologies, which is co-financed through former Colciencias (currently, Minciencias).

observed as a process of co-creation of training courses and workshops intended for the support of business activities (Olvera et al., 2020). As in the case of Colombia, the discussion of the role other actors can play within the Helix system (e.g., the financial sector and civil society) is scarce or non-existent.

Nonetheless, of course, there has been some evolution in the NSSTIs of both countries, particularly in terms of training and the development of highly qualified human resources. Graphic 11.4 shows the number of graduates from HEIs during the period 2008–2017. Over the seven-year period shown on the graphic, the number of bachelor's graduates from HEIs in both countries has almost doubled. This signals better access to education, as well as a higher degree of coverage in general (OECD, 2013b; OECD, 2019c). However, additional effort needs to be incorporated as many of these graduates do not have incentives to join postgraduate programmes. In both countries, the ratio of master graduates to bachelor's is almost one-half, and the PhD share is the vast minority.

The increased number of highly skilled labour in Colombia and Mexico represents doubtlessly an advance in terms of the strengthening of the NSSTI in both countries, as this increases the chances that these human resources have to incorporate more successfully into the labour market (OECD, 2019c). Similarly, the increase in numbers of highly skilled labour (PhD graduates) has benefited HEIs, since these have been able to grow not only in physical terms, but have as well expanded their training activities, research base, and knowledge production. However, it also implies that the lack of or imperfect integration of these highly educated human resources into the productive sector unveils the type and quality of linkages between STI actors as there are well-known asymmetries in the type of knowledge and capabilities present in both the productive and the academic sector.

An important effort is also needed to improve the regional differential conditions in both countries as regional development is highly unequal and centralised. The differences shown in Table 11.7 are striking, not only between both countries but also internally, as they show a prevailing problem in terms of access to quality education. This, in turn, is associated with the concentration of capabilities (centralisation), infrastructure problems, and generalised inequality. This situation leaves regions like Vichada (in Colombia) or Campeche (in Mexico) to lag behind their respective national capital cities. Furthermore, it is this vast regional heterogeneity

Table 11.7 Number and percentage of graduates from HEIs—Colombia and Mexico (selected regions)

Country[a]	*Bachelor's*	*Master's*	*PhDs*	*Other*[b]	*Total*
Colombia	208,917 (45.0%)	25,351 (5.5%)	770 (0.2%)	227,329 (49.3%)	462,367
Bogotá D.C	75,201	9749	330		
Guainía	15	0	0		
Vichada	14	0	0		
Mexico	465,186 (77.5%)	66,106 (11%)	8264 (1.5%)	60,460 (10%)	600,016
MexicoCity	63,274	13,890	1948		
Baja California Sur	2361	198	45		
Campeche	3716	514	17		

[a]Data for Colombia corresponds to 2017 and 2019 for Mexico
[b]Other: technical degrees, technological degrees, diplomas
Source Own elaboration based on Garavito and Cifuentes (2018) and ANUIES (2020)

that has been observed as a deadweight for national innovation indicators (Malaver & Vargas, 2020; Wood et al., 2014).

Now, the differences are not only present in terms of education but also in different indicators relevant for the use and exploitation of knowledge. Take, for example, income poverty levels. In Colombia, 12.4% of the population of Bogota live below the poverty line, while the poverty rate of Chocó is 58.7% (Ramírez & Aguas, 2015). Likewise, in Mexico, only 14.2% of the population in Nuevo Leon live under the national income poverty line, while 77.1% of the population do so in Chiapas (INEGI, 2019). With such levels of poverty, certain trends become persistent: crime, business informality and early education drop-out (OECD, 2019c).

Furthermore, the Colombian State (Departamento) of Cundinamarca (where the capital city Bogota is located) outperforms all other Colombian *Departamentos* in terms of economic strength, infrastructure, human capital formation, and STI-related indicators. Not only that, but when analysed as regions, the country shows stark differences. The Andes region performs much better in all economic and social indicators (health, education, society, etc.), followed by the Atlantic coast, with the Pacific littoral being left well behind and the South-West of the country (the Amazonas and Orinoco regions) performing the worst (Malaver &

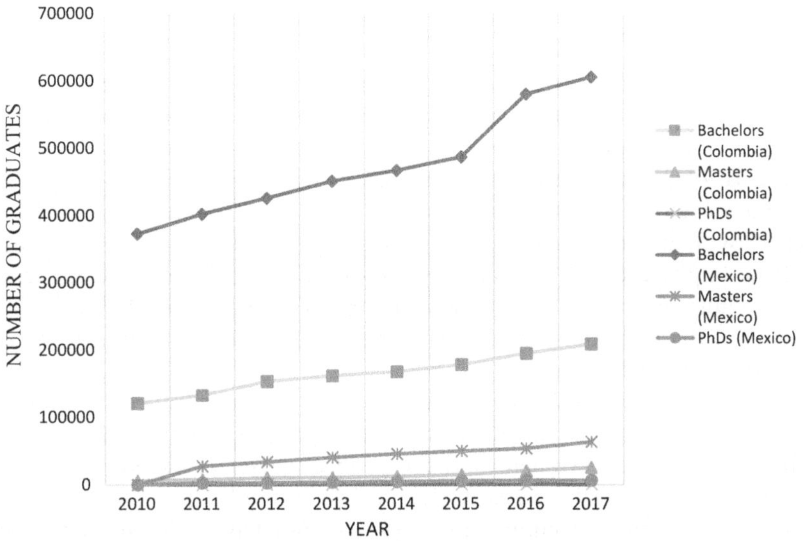

Graphic 11.4 Colombia and Mexico—graduates from HEIs at different levels (2007–2017) (*Source* Own elaboration with data from Garavito and Cifuentes [2018] and ANUIES [2020])

Vargas, 2020; Prieto et al., 2018; Ramírez & Aguas, 2015). In Mexico, a similar regional disparity has been observed with the North region (e.g., Nuevo Leon and Jalisco) outperforming the South (e.g., Chiapas or Oaxaca)—Mexico City being the only exception—in terms of educational attainment, poverty, and infrastructure (OECD, 2019b).

In addition to the progress made in the areas of specialised human resource training, there are other positive examples of capacity building in these countries. On issues related to the articulation between knowledge producers and users, the creation of agricultural technology centres (for example, Agrosavia, previously Corpoica in 1993 in Colombia, or INIA in 1960 in Mexico) has been a remarkable experience. Both Agrosavia and INIA develop applied technology, offer information services, and supply laboratory services. The products derived from this offer have been disseminated among producers in the agricultural sector through collaboration agreements between these centres and private companies, local corporations or associations, and the respective National Ministries of Agriculture (Lemarchand, 2010).

However, just as progress has been made, there have also been cases in which capacities created over time have been destroyed either by erroneous political decisions, by systemic failures or by limitations in the articulation between actors, among other factors. For example, progress in the development of the Colombian innovation system has been lessened by inadequate action about generating suitable societal recognition of the importance of STI and the lack of guidelines from State agencies and regulating bodies as to how and why STI is important for the well-being of the Colombian society, in general (Oquendo & Acevedo, 2012; Prieto et al., 2018).

On the other hand, integrating Mexico into an advanced manufacturing sector is a strategy with great potential but requires joint efforts from both the government and the productive sector as not all industries in the manufacturing sector exhibit the same level of development. For example, the automotive industry does not have enough specialised manufacturers located in Mexico, therefore the manufacturing of some components depends on imported inputs: 71% of the total demand for advanced manufacturing processes (e.g., computer-based ones such as high-level computing simulation and analysis services, fast prototyping and robotics) heavily depend on imported services and items (Dutrénit, 2015).

Now, how do these facts and trends impact job and life quality in Colombia and Mexico? One of the main problems in both economies is the high level of informality, which is estimated to correspond to about 50% of total employment in Latin America (Chacaltana, 2019; IMF, 2019). This phenomenon is problematic because "… *informality prevents access to social security benefits, hinders the application of the laws that regulate working hours and remuneration, and is associated with jobs in companies with less than 5 workers that tend to have low productivity and do not promote the development of skills*" (Fedesarrollo, 2019, p. 3).

Labour informality, especially in the context of developing economies (e.g., Latin America), is a phenomenon that presents multiple edges, which makes it difficult to generalise about its causes and effects. In this sense, the first difficulty associated with informality is an estimation problem (Loayza & Sugawara, 2009). Although, both in Colombia and in Mexico, the current levels of informality are high (48 and 56%, respectively) (Fedesarrollo, 2019; Medina and López, 2019; INEGI, 2020), it does not necessarily refer to the same concept. For example, Colombia statistics office estimates that 47.9% represents the proportion of informally employed persons for the last quarter of 2019 (DANE, 2020). On the other hand, Mexican INEGI (2020) estimates that informality reached 56.3% in 2019 (representing close to 22.5% of the country's GDP for 2018). In the Colombian case, the Large Integrated Household Survey estimates the levels of informally employed persons[13] as those who are employed (paid or not), in companies with five workers or less (DANE, 2020). While, in the Mexican case, the definition of informality includes both the informal sector and informal employment,[14] where the former includes all those market economic activities that operate from household resources but not established as companies, no matter the size of the productive unit (INEGI, 2020).

Despite these conceptual differences, a common point about the levels of informality present in both countries concerns the deficiencies pointed out by Fedesarrollo (2019) related to the difficulty of accessing social security and the regulation of working hours. For example, recent estimates value that the pension system ceases to receive about USD 6 billion per year due to the lack of contributions from informal workers in Colombia (CPC, 2017).[15]

Additionally, recent evidence shows that informality is more prevailing in populations with lower educational attainment levels. Moreover, the informal sector exhibits lower productivity levels than the formal sector and absorbs low-skilled workers in a greater proportion. For example, it is estimated that 26.2% of workers belonging to the informal economy have tertiary education in the American continent (data for 2016). Finally, current evidence indicates that populations that are integrated into the informal economy are more vulnerable in various ways (legal, economic, or social), so many of the corrective actions taken relate to generating

[13] This classification excludes independent professionals and government employees.

[14] The configuration of the informally employed population by employing economic unit reveals that about 48.9% are employed in the informal sector. Additionally, 7.5% is made up of paid domestic workers, 24.8% are those linked to companies, government, and institutions, and 18.8% are individuals in the agricultural field (INEGI, 2019).

[15] This discussion is actually much more complex as another possible reason for such high levels of informality may have to do with the fact that some informal workers obtain a higher income than many formal workers who only receive a minimum salary compensation.

policies of inclusion and generation of opportunities (OECD, 2018; OECD/ILO, 2019).

From a different perspective, that of labour skills demanded by different economies, evidence indicates that during the last decade there has been a generalised transition from the manufacturing to the service sector, which has deepened a generalised polarisation between jobs that require low-paying skill levels and those requiring high-paying skills. This adds to a trend in which the share of middle-skill occupations in total employment has declined in general for all sectors of the economy during the last decade. Thus, examples of high-skill sectors which demand increasing numbers of workers are the ICT-related industries and finance, while low-skill sectors which still are experiencing growth are the hospitality industry and restaurant services (OECD, 2018). Nonetheless, both in Colombia and in Mexico, the dynamics of insertion into the labour market follow the trends described above, observing a greater insertion of workers into the service sector (OECD, 2019). Thus, there are particularities in each case that are important to point out.

In Colombia, for example, the labour demand-side posted during 2019 a greater number of jobs (published vacancies) for workers with a baccalaureate degree (29.5% out of 1,888,992), followed by university graduates (23.6%). The least vacancies offered correspond to personnel with postgraduate education (master's and PhDs) with a combined proportion of 0.3% (Servicio de Empleo, 2020). These data are important since, as mentioned in Table 11.7, an average of 200,000 students graduate every year from undergraduate programmes. The ensuing question is obvious: where are the rest of the graduate and postgraduate professionals not absorbed by the productive sector? Arguably, a somewhat large proportion of postgraduates is absorbed by some HEIs that are transiting towards international standards (e.g., those seeking international accreditation programmes), while others probably emigrate abroad in search of better job opportunities, and finally, another group of university graduates probably transits towards some sort of informal employment. In fact, precise data about this situation is hard to obtain.

In terms of economic activity, those sectors that registered the most vacancies were administrative services (12.5%), retail trade and vehicle repair (12.3%), and professional, scientific, and technical activities (12.1%) (Servicio de Empleo, 2020). Finally, in terms of staff absorption, a total of

462,183 employed persons were reported, 0.51% held a position at directive or management level, while the majority (49%) obtained a position in qualified trades (SENA, 2019).

In Mexico, the National Survey of Occupation and Employment (INEGI, 2019) indicates that the number of employed professionals in the country is 9.2 million people, most of whom (64%) are employed in economic-administrative areas (administration, accounting, and law) and to a lesser extent (0.36%) careers such as teacher training for upper secondary education, earth and atmospheric sciences, and medical diagnosis. The majority (about 33.6 million Mexicans) insert into the service sector, followed by the secondary sector (13.6 million) and the primary sector, which employs about 6.6 million people.

Finally, both in Colombia and Mexico, the insertion of personnel into the sectors mentioned above does not necessarily translate into satisfactory salary conditions that secure adequate welfare of the population. This is reflected in the average annual income per full-time employee, which is considerably lower than the OECD average (close to USD 43,241). In fact, 2018 average income in Colombia was USD 13,073, while in Mexico it was USD 15,314 (Fedesarrollo, 2019). However, minimum salary compensation, which is actually paid to most low-skilled and many mid-skilled formal workers, is much lower. Thus, recent research data unsurprisingly indicate that many workers in these economies require two or more jobs that allow them to compensate for decent living standards (OECD/ILO, 2019).

In short, Colombia and Mexico perfectly embody what might be termed the "societal misalignment" of inclusive and responsible STI where some major open challenges include what some authors sum up as: the pending creation of public value, the effective internationalisation/operationalisation of responsibility principles in businesses, the real possibilities of bottom-up innovations/engagement/co-construction, and the achievement of sustainability and social justice (Ribeiro et al., 2018).

11.5 Challenges Ahead: What Does Colombia and Mexico Need to Do to Build up an Inclusive STI-Based Society?

As shown above, the discussion in Latin America and the Caribbean about inclusive development and its links with science, technology and innovation has traditionally been fragmented in societal terms, conceptually biased, and left to "the experts" to decide. As a result, LAC national STI systems have invariably become mostly top-down, State-driven, centralised, linearly conceived regarding their national/regional/sectoral dimensions, highly disjointed, and financially deprived. This profile has, in turn, determined the scarce articulation between STI and inclusive development which promotes the evident backwardness in terms of societal equity that is so characteristic of LAC nations.

The consequences of this standpoint have not allowed Mexico and Colombia—and the whole LAC region—to move forward at the rate needed to transition towards a knowledge-based society in which the production, diffusion, and use of knowledge be the base of an economic model where opportunities and capacities, resources and skills, ideas and achievements, efforts and compensations are conveniently paired in order to boost widespread and balanced social advance and inclusive stability.

How can that be attained? We propose that the drivers of the "societal misalignment" explained above need to be addressed as effectively as possible, here and now, to build feasible pathways forward. Initially, the progress achieved in knowledge production needs to be consolidated and enhanced. Next, the connection with and the engagement of other actors relevant for knowledge diffusion and application demands to be thought of and implemented in more effective manners.

These two issues involve some deep mid-to-long term transformations. Effective knowledge production and usage to support economic change demands that (public and private) universities and other research organisations strengthen their capacities to create, disseminate and use knowledge aimed at impacting economic activity at different levels and in different sectors. This means that universities need to widen and deepen their mission-related work and impact concerning the schooling of professional figures beyond the current relatively simple demands of potential employers (e.g., enterprises) to create higher societal value and benefits. That will need a new, more profound *vis-à-vis* interaction with economic actors, government agencies, and civil society organisations to transform the institutional framework under which such relations shall, in turn, renovate the relationship between society and knowledge. Balanced, consensual, joint efforts where bottom-up initiatives are as valued as top-down ones is a key condition.

Universities also need to include STI education/capacities as a cornerstone of long-lived learning processes that need constant updating if STI is meant to be the foundation of a new economy whose benefits reach out to all citizens. This has enormous implications in terms of the so-called three university missions. It includes not only the creation of knowledge-based spin-offs whenever that is more convenient than just transferring/selling or licensing know-how to existing commercial companies, but also the creation of life-long learning proposals that allow graduate professionals to constantly update their skills and enterprises to absorb the latest know-how they do not possess. Such initiatives are more consonant with rapidly changing knowledge and environments and mean a better way to benefit from continued systemic feedback.

Of course, that raises new challenges to a system where public education has not the capacity to produce the appropriate answers to the social problems posed and where private education has to better tune in their interests and actions with those of emerging societies that crave for inclusive and sustainable initiatives. It remains to be seen if a mostly for-profit activity can become more socially effective to compensate for public education shortages.

Furthermore, a responsible STI-based development model needs the coordinated involvement of other knowledge-related actors downstream (e.g., public and private research/technology centres), a new type of governance and innovative sociopolitical mechanisms to lead it. Public and private roles and participation need to be assessed and reconfigured to avoid excess pressure on some actors and excess return on some others. The main goal is to transform the incumbent system characterised above to counter the dominant features towards a more balanced model of systemic governance.

This change should take into account a much-needed modification of perspective concerning the inflexible and rather static view of the connections among national/regional (subnational)/sectoral STI systems. This implies a better understanding of the way in which STI actors and components articulate into and shape those dimensions in terms of concurrent overlaps/gaps, similarities/differences, closeness/distance characteristic of coexisting elements that hold varying relationships over time. This is particularly important in the case of evolving sectors whose dynamics go beyond traditional definitions and practically reconfigure entire sections of the economy of a country.

A valuable illustration here is given by bio-economy, a complex strategic concept that incorporates several activities based on the intensive production and usage of knowledge about territories and their resources to redefine the ties among these, communities and highly sustainable and equitable ways of life. Bio-economy involves multiple economic sectors, several scientific fields of knowledge, all walks of culturally defined practices, innovative ideas and applications, and numerous principles to transform economic activity in given regions according to the peculiar characteristics of such territories.

Bio-economy simultaneously involves all the known dimensions of STI systems with no pre-specified hierarchy or relationship, demands community-wide participation in intensive knowledge creation/appropriation and decision-making, extended mutual support among all actors and constantly changing roles and capacities to grant competitiveness, equity, sustainability, decentralisation, multi-sectoral coordination for a successful, rather smooth transition that secures the results expected.

It is improbable that Colombia or Mexico can successfully create and implement bio-economy applications in the framework of their current STI systems and regimes as their traits will probably represent/raise more barriers than they can embody/facilitate solutions. The prevailing view on national/regional (subnational)/sectoral STI governance is highly incompatible with any bio-economy strategy where overlooked territorial, natural, cultural, sociopolitical, and historical differences imply a meaningful undervaluation of subnational variations and, consequently, exposure to high risks and, probably, failure.

Along the same line of thought, a key governance feature—STI funding—needs to be reviewed and appropriately redesigned and implemented. Public and private investment in STI cannot simply remain a low, second-rate priority mainly embodied by State-designed incentives that lack the power to massively attract private national and international investors. But, other than bulky money, the funding problem refers to within-the-system lack of knowledge and trust among STI actors. State agencies, diverse potential investors, and assorted project owners need to get to know one another and build up the conditions for mutual successful interaction if financing is to boost relevant STI-based projects aimed at transforming Colombian and Mexican economies and nations into world-class models.

Only a decisive turn based on these considerations will allow Colombia and Mexico to move away from traditional resource-based business sectors and models with low value added and low sustainability and enter intensive knowledge-based activities/models where constant innovation and high sustainability are the norm. And this is the best way to fight some of the problems that hurt their populations and lifestyles.

So far, the recipes tested to fight poverty, inequity, lack of/missed opportunities and the consequent wide social discontent have proved partial and insufficient. Structural change has not taken place as the results of the models, strategies, and policies adopted exhibit their limitations and point the finger at other concomitant serious problems such as corruption.

Thus, we posit that the considerations sustained above may seriously help to elucidate the manifold difficulties identified by repeated diagnostic exercises that, however, have failed to lead to structural solutions so far. One common problem this approach may be successful at avoiding is the common procedure of tackling problems as independent, unrelated phenomena that invariably bring about equally inconsistent and disparate solutions.

High job informality, for instance, needs to be approached from a perspective that clearly overflows typical cost-structure or breach-of-legal-requirements views. Such perspective may be effectively complemented by the understanding of how this phenomenon relates to systemic failures about knowledge generation/diffusion and creation of better opportunities for skilled labour. If human talent is formed by an educational system tailored according to relevant societal needs such as the availability of knowledge-intensive positions in internationalised enterprises, the problem acquires a different connotation.

Thus, Colombian and Mexican societies need to urgently address issues such as quality health and education beyond individual differences in income in order to counter widespread vulnerability structurally. This is the best way to support socio-economic progress characterised by substantially higher social cohesion in the long term, a desirable response to current persistent inequity and violence.

There are signals that this approach is feasible and practicable even in the short term. If anything, the recent SARS-COVID-19 pandemic has brought up the boundaries of the current model and has pinpointed the limitations of nationalistic/individualistic responses to global crises. However, it has also surprisingly unveiled the potential of existing underlying factors in these and like countries. Colombia, for instance, did not produce any personal protection equipment (PPE), medical testing materials nor mechanical ventilators or surgical masks before the start of the health crisis (early 2020). Everything had to be imported.

In approximately four months, nonetheless, the joint effort of some universities, private and State-owned enterprises, social organisations, government agencies, and international cooperation partners allowed to set up and run the national production of brand new locally designed or adapted models of ventilators, medical bio-protection suits and high-efficiency filtering surgical masks (N98) that are destined to meet local demand and international orders. Such is a very positive signal about the potential hidden under the current state of affairs.

References

Andrade, J. (2018). Innovation in the manufacturing and services. Chapter 6 in C. Pardo, & A. Cotte (Eds.), *Science and technology indicators.* Observatorio Colombiano de Ciencia y Tecnologia (OCyT).

Arocena, R., & Sutz, J. (2014). Innovación y democratización del conocimiento como contribución al desarrollo inclusivo. Chapter 1 in G. Dutrenit, & J. Sutz (Eds.), *National innovation systems, social inclusion and development: The Latin American experience.* Cheltenham.

Asociación Nacional de Universidades e Instituciones de Educación Superior (ANUIES). (2020). *Anuarios estadísticos de educación superior.* http://www.anuies.mx/informacion-y-servicios/informacion-estadistica-de-educacion-superior/anuario-estadistico-de-educacion-superior

Bakker, B. et al. (2020). *Lack of human capital is holding back Latin America's growth.* IMF Country Focus. https://www.imf.org/en/News/Articles/2020/08/12/na081320-lack-of-human-capital-is-holding-back-latin-americas-growth

Bortagaray, I. (2016). *Políticas de ciencia, tecnología, e innovación sustentable e inclusiva en América Latina.* UNESCO.

Bortagaray, I., & Ordoñez-Matamoros, G. (2012). Introduction to the special issue of the review of policy research: Innovation, innovation policy, and social inclusion in developing countries. *Review of Policy Research*, *29*, 669–671.

Burbano, P., & Nubia, M. (2011, abril). Los cuellos de botella del desarrollo endógeno territorial, desde la perspectiva del sistema de ciencia, tecnología e innovación en Colombia. *Revista Iberoamericana de Ciencia, Tecnología y Sociedad - CTS, 6* (17), 161–177.

Carranza, J., Aria, F., Bejarano, J. A., Casas, C., González, A. X., Moreno, S. A., & Velez, J. S. (2018, November). La industria colombiana en el siglo XXI. *Revista ESPE - Ensayos Sobre Política Económica, Banco de la República - ESPE, 87*, 1–69.

Casas, R., & Corona, J. M. (2013). Políticas de ciencia, tecnología e innovación en América Latina: Entre la competitividad y la inclusión social. Conferência Internacional LALICS 2013 "Sistemas Nacionais de Inovação e Políticas de CTI para um Desenvolvimento Inclusivo e Sustentável" 11 e 12 de Novembro, 2013 – Rio de Janeiro, Brasil.

Casas, R., De Fuentes, C., Torres, A., & Vera-Cruz, A. (2013). Estrategias y gobernanza del Sistema Nacional de Innovación Mexicano: Retos para un desarrollo incluyente. In G. Dutrénit, & J. Sutz (Eds.),*Sistemas de innovación para un desarrollo inclusivo: La experiencia latinoamericana*. FCCyT.

Castellanos, Y. (2013). *Proyecto Lion: Una triple hélice que sí funciona*. Pesquisa Javeriana, Marzo/Mayo.

Castiblanco-Moreno, S., Castro, O., & Gomez, A. (2017). The services sector in Colombia: Relationship between innovation and internationalization. *Dimensión Empresarial, 15*(2), 117–139.

Castillo, R., Flores, C., & Rodriguez, M. (2014). The relative importance of the service sector in the Mexican economy: A Time series analysis. *Lecturas de economía*, 80, 133–151.

Central Intelligence Agency (CIA). (2020). *The World Factbook*. https://www.cia.gov/library/publications/the-world-factbook/fields/214.html

Centro Nacional de Consultoría (CNC) et al. (2020). *Vinculación de doctores: Formación de alto nivel*. Colombia.

Centeno, J., Ordoñez-Matamoros, G., & Montenegro, I. (2020, Julio 27). *Es hora de renovar la conversación sobre Ciencia e Innovación en Colombia*. www.razonpublica.com

Chang, H. J. (2020, Febrero 4). El fracaso de construir una economía más igualitaria e innovadora es lo que está en el corazón de las protestas latinoamericanas, Hay Festival Cartagena 2020. *BBC News*. https://www.bbc.com/mundo/noticias-america-latina-51295950.

Chacaltana, J. (2019). *Formalization policies in Latin America*. Presentation in the Seminar New and old forms of informality, ECLAC. Santiago de Chile. April 2019, CEPAL.

Chiapa, A. (2019, Marzo–Abril). Technology transfer and economic growth: A comparative framework for transfer policy making in Mexico. *Economia Informa*, 415, 41–56.

Chiquar, D., & Tobal, M. (2019). *Global value chains in Mexico: A historical perspective*. Banco de México Working Papers N° 2019–06.

Consejo Privado de Competitividad, (CPC). (2017). *Informalidad: Una nueva visión para Colombia*. https://compite.com.co/wp-content/uploads/2017/11/CPC_Informalidad-V03.pdf

CPC. (2020). *Informe Nacional de Competitividad 2019–2020*. https://compite.com.co/wp-content/uploads/2019/11/CPC_INC_2019-2020_Informe_final_subir.pdf

Cornell University, INSEAD, and World Intellectual Property Organization (WIPO). (2020). Global Innovation Index 2020: Who will finance innovation? In S. Dutta, B. Lanvin, & S. Wunsch-Vincent (Eds.), 13th edn. Ithaca, Fontainebleau, and Geneva.

Cotte, A., & Andrade, J. (2018). Investment in science, technology and innovation activities. Chapter 1 in Cotte, A., Parra, J., Torralba, D., Garavito, M., Caho, D., Jimenez, C., Cifuentes, M., Ramirez, L., Castellanos, J., Cuellar, J., & Pardo, C. (2018). Science and technology indicators, Colombia 2018. C. Pardo, & A. Cotte (Eds.), Observatorio Colombiano de Ciencia y Tecnología (OCyT).

Cotte, A., Parra, J., Torralba, D., Garavito, M., Caho, D., Jimenez, C., Cifuentes, M., Ramirez, L., Castellanos, J., Cuellar, J., & Pardo, C. (2018). Science and technology indicators, Colombia 2018. C. Pardo, & A. Cotte (Eds.), Observatorio Colombiano de Ciencia y Tecnología (OCyT).

Dagnino, R. (2012, October). Why science and technology capacity building for social development? Special Section: The Use of Knowledge for Social Inclusion. *Science and Public Policy, 39* (5), 548–556.

DANE. (2020). Boletín Técnico Gran Encuesta Integrada de Hogares (GEIH) Diciembre 2019 – febrero. https://www.dane.gov.co/files/investigaciones/boletines/ech/ech_informalidad/bol_ech_informalidad_dic19_feb20.pdf

Departamento Nacional de Planeación (DNP). (2020). Plan Nacional de Desarrollo 2018–2022: Pacto por Colombia, Pacto por la Equidad.

Dougherty, S., & Reynaud, J. (2017). *Boosting productivity in Mexico through integration into global value chains*. OECD Economics Department Working Papers No. 1376, OECD, France.

Dutrénit, G. (2015). Políticas de innovación para fortalecer las capacidades en manufactura avanzada en México. Innovación tecnológica, Santiago de Chile: CIEPLAN.

Dutrénit, G., & Sutz, J. (2014). Introduction to national innovation systems, social inclusion, and development. In G. Dutrénit, & J. Sutz (Eds.), *National innovation systems, social inclusion and development: The Latin American experience*. Edward Elgar.

Dutrénit, G., De Fuentes, C., Santiago, F., Torres, A., & Gras, N. (2013). *Innovation and productivity in the service sector the case of Mexico*. Competitiveness and Innovation Division, Institutions for Development Discussion Paper No. IDB-DP-293, Inter-American Development Bank 2013.

Echavarría, J.J., Giraldo, I., & Jaramillo, F. (2019). Cadenas globales de valor, crecimiento y protección arancelaria en Colombia, Borradores de Economía Núm. 1080 2019, Banco de la Republica.

Etzkowitz, H., & Leydesdorff, L. (2000). The dynamics of innovation: From national systems and 'Mode 2' to a triple Helix of University–industry–government relations. *Research Policy, 29*(2), 109–123.

Fedesarrollo. (2019). Informe mensual del Mercado Laboral: La calidad del empleo, Diciembre 2019, Centro de Investigación Económica y Social, Fedesarrollo, Colombia.

Focus Economics. (2020a). *Colombia economy data.* https://www.focus-economics.com/countries/colombia

Focus Economics. (2020b). *Mexico economy data.* https://www.focus-economics.com/countries/mexico

Función Pública. (2020). *Manual de Estructura del Estado Colombiano.* https://www.funcionpublica.gov.co

Garavito, M., & Cifuentes, M. (2018). Education in science and technology. Chapter 2 in Cotte, A. et al. (2018). Science and technology indicators, Colombia 2018. C. Pardo, & A. Cotte (Eds.), Observatorio Colombiano de Ciencia y Tecnologia (OCyT).

García, J., & Prado, N. (2019). Financiación pública de la innovación en Colombia: Efectos y retos en la industria manufacturera. Masters' thesis in Economics, Pontificia Universidad Javeriana (Col).

García, J., Montes, E., & Giraldo, I. (Eds.). (2019). Comercio exterior en Colombia: Política, Instituciones, costos y resultados', Banco de La República.

Garrido, C., & Rondero, N. (Coord.). (2015). *Oficinas de transferencia tecnológica.* UDUAL/REDUE ALCUE, Colección Digital Idea Latinoamericana.

González-Quintero, R., Sanchez, M., Bolivar, D., Chirinda, N., Arango, J., Pantevez, H., Correa-Londoño, G., & Barahona-Rosales, R. (2020). Technical and environmental characterization of Colombian beef cattle-fattening farms, with a focus on farm size and ways of improving production. *Outlook on Agriculture, 49*(2), 153–162. https://doi.org/10.1177/0030727019884336

Herrera, A. (1973). Los determinantes sociales de la política científica en América Latina, Desarrollo Económico, 13 (49), México.

Herrera, J. J., Salas-Navarro, L., Domínguez-Moré, G., & Torres-Saumeth, K. (2015, . Julio–Diciembre). Parques científicos-tecnológicos y modelo triple-hélice. Situación del Caribe colombiano. *En: Entramado, 11* (2), 112–130.

Ibarra, R., Solleiro, J., & Gonzales, J. (2015). Los retos de las Oficinas de Transferencia de Conocimiento en México. In C. Garrido, & N. Rondero (Coord.) (2015). *Oficinas de transferencia tecnológica.* UDUAL/REDUE ALCUE.

Instituto Nacional de Estadística y Geografía (INEGI). (2019). *Resultados de la Encuesta Nacional de Ocupación y Empleo, Cifras Durante el Primer Trimestre de 2019*. https://www.INEGI.org.mx/temas/pibmed/

INEGI. (2020). *Indicadores*. https://www.INEGI.org.mx/app/areasgeograficas/#tabMCcollapse-Indicadores

International Monetary Fund (IMF). (2019, October). Labor Dynamics and Informality, Regional Economic Outlook: Western Hemisphere, IMF.

Kuhlmann, S., & Ordoñez, G. (Eds.). (2017). *Research handbook on innovation governance for emerging economies—Towards better models*. Edward Elgar Publishing Limited.

Kuznetsov, Y., & Dahlman, C. (2008). *Mexico's transition to a knowledge-based economy challenges and opportunities*. WBI Development Studies, World Bank.

Lemarchand, G. (Ed.). (2010). *National science, technology and innovation systems in Latin America and the Caribbean, science policy studies and documents in LAC* (Vol. 1). UNESCO.

León, E., & Saavedra, M. (2018). Sources of financing for MSMEs in Mexico, UV, MX.

Loayza, N., & Sugawara, N. (2009). El sector informal en México Hechos y explicaciones fundamentales. *El Trimestre Económico, 76*(4), 887–920.

Lundvall, B. (Ed.). (1992). *National systems of innovation: Towards a theory of innovation and interactive learning*. Pinter.

Malaver, F., & Vargas, M. (2020). Bogotá-Región en el escenario OCDE. Prismas e indicadores de innovación. *Cuadernos de Economía, 39* (79), 103–138.

Medina, O., & López, O. (2019). Informalidad laboral y derecho a la salud en México, un análisis crítico. *Ciência & Saúde Coletiva, 24*(7), 2583–2592.

Mejía, S. (2020). Identifican tierras raras y metales raros en carbón colombiano. *UN Periódico Digital*. https://unperiodico.unal.edu.co/pages/detail/identifican-tierras-raras-y-metales-raros-en-carbon-colombiano/

Mondragón, F. (2020). Sobre el Sistema Nacional de Ciencia y Tecnología. Opinión in El Espectador, Monday 27th July 2020.

National Development Plan (NDP). (2019). https://observatorioplanificacion.cepal.org/sites/default/files/plan/files/Plan%20Nacional%20de%20Desarrollo%20de%20M%C3%A9xico.pdf.

Nelson, R. (1993). *National innovation systems: A comparative analysis*. Oxford University Press.

Observatory of Economic Complexity (OEC). (2020). Colombia. OEC.world.com

Organisation for Economic Co-operation and Development (OECD). (2013a). Knowledge-based start-ups in Mexico. *OECD Reviews of Innovation Policy*.

OECD. (2013b). *Education policy outlook Mexico*. OECD.

OECD. (2017). *Science, technology and industry scoreboard 2017*. OECD.

OECD. (2018). *Good jobs for all in a changing world of work: The OECD jobs strategy*. OECD.

OECD. (2019a, October). *OECD Economic Surveys Colombia OVERVIEW*. OECD. http://www.oecd.org/economy/surveys/Colombia-2019-OECD-economic-survey-overview.pdf

OECD. (2019b, May). *OECD Economic Surveys Mexico OVERVIEW*. OECD. http://www.oecd.org/economy/surveys/Mexico-2019-OECD-economic-survey-overview.pdf

OECD. (2019c, October). *Education at a glance 2019: OECD indicators*. OECD.

OECD. (2020a). Gross domestic product (GDP) (indicator).

OECD. (2020b). *MSTI database*. https://www.oecd.org/sti/msti.htm

OECD et al. (2019). *Latin American Economic Outlook 2019: Development in tansition*. OECD.

OECD/FAO. (2019). *OECD-FAO Agricultural Outlook 2019–2028*, Chapter 2. Latin American Agriculture: Prospects and Challenges.

OECD, ILO. (2019). *Tackling vulnerability in the informal economy*. OECD.

Olvera, C., Piqué, J., Cortés, U., & Nemirovsky, M. (2020). Evaluating university-business collaboration at science parks: A business perspective. *Triple Helix Journal,* 1–41. https://doi.org/10.1163/21971927-bja10007

Oquendo, A., & Acevedo, C. (2012). Colombian innovation system: Foundations, dynamics and avatars. *Trilogía Ciencia Tecnología Sociedad, 4* (6).

Oxfam. (2013).*Divide and purchase: How land ownership is being concentrated in Colombia*. Oxfam Research Reports, UK.

Planes-Satorra, S., & Paunov, C. (2017). Inclusive innovation policies: Lessons from international case studies. *OECD Science, Technology and Industry Working Papers*, No. 2017/02. OECD.

Prieto, G., Mayorga, A., & Piñeros, A. (2018). Limitaciones de la articulación de la ciencia, la tecnología y la innovación con la política nacional de desarrollo productivo, Análisis, 2/2018, Friedrich Ebert Stiftung, Colombia.

Ramírez, J., & Aguas, J. (2015). Escalafón de la competitividad de los departamentos de Colombia, 2015, Serie Estudio y Perspectivas, CEPAL.

Ranga, M., & Etzkowitz, H. (2013). Triple Helix systems: An analytical framework for innovation policy and practice in the knowledge society. *Industry and Higher Education, 27*(4), 237–262.

Ribeiro, B., Bengtsson, L., Benneworht, P., Bührer, S., Castro-Martinez, E., Hansen, M., Jarmai, K., Linder, R., Olmos-Peñuela, J., Ott, C., & Shapira, P. (2018). Introducing the dilemma of societal alignment for inclusive and responsible research and innovation. *Journal of Responsible Innovation, 5*(3), 316–331.

Rios, V. (2018). *Innovation happens in Mexico. It should and could happen more.* Wilson Center, Mexico Institute, Woodrow Wilson International Center for Scholars/Fundación Idea.

Rivas, G. (2020). La innovación: Un imperativo para crecer con inclusión social, Blog, Online, InterAmerican Development Bank. https://blogs.iadb.org/innovacion/es/innovacion-imperativo-para-crecer-con-inclusion-social/

Rivera, M. (2006). The foreign factor within the triple Helix model: Interactions of national and international innovation systems, technology transfer and implications for the region: The case of the electronics cluster in Guadalajara, Jalisco, México. *Journal of Technology Management Innovation, 1* (4).

Rodríguez, C. (2016). *El Sistema Nacional de Investigadores en Números*. Foro Consultivo Científico y Tecnológico, A.C., (FCCyT).

Salazar, M., Lozano, M., & Lucio, D. (2013). Ciencia, tecnología e innovación para un desarrollo inclusivo en Colombia: Programas piloto desarrollados por Colciencias. In G. Dutrénit, & J. Sutz (Eds.), *Sistemas de innovación para un desarrollo inclusivo: La experiencia latinoamericana*. LALICS, FCCyT.

Sampedro, J. (2013). Innovación inclusiva con instituciones inclusivas. Conferência Internacional LALICS 2013 "Sistemas Nacionais de Inovação e Políticas de CTI para um Desenvolvimiento Inclusivo e Sustentável" 11 e 12 de Novembro, 2013 – Rio de Janeiro, Brasil.

SENA. (2019). Boletín anual - Tendencia de las ocupaciones a nivel nacional y regional Observatorio Laboral y Ocupacional Año 2019.

Servicio de Empleo. (2020). *Anexo estadístico de demanda laboral (vacantes)*. https://www.serviciodeempleo.gov.co/estudios-e-investigacion/oferta-y-demanda-laboral/anexo-estadistico-de-demanda-laboral-vacantes

Sierra, J. (2018). La cuarta hélice y la financiación de la innovación. *Journal of Economics, Finance and Administrative Science, 23*(45), 128–137.

Sierra, J. (2020). How financial systems and firm strategy impact the choice of innovation funding. *European Journal of Innovation Management, 23*(2), 251–272.

The Business Year (TBY). (2018). Triple Helix model, Mexico. https://www.thebusinessyear.com/mexico-2018/triple-helix-model/interview

Torralba, D., & Cotte, A. (2018). Scientific production, Chapter 4 in Cotte, A. et al. (2018). Science and technology indicators, Colombia 2018. C. Pardo, A. Cotte (Eds.), Observatorio Colombiano de Ciencia y Tecnologia (OCyT).

United Nations Development Programme, (UNDP). (2020). *Human development reports*. http://hdr.undp.org/en/content/table-1-human-development-index-and-its-components-1

United Nations (UN) Comtrade Database. (2020). *Commercial trade data*. https://comtrade.un.org/data/

USAID Land and Urban Office (USAID). (2017a). *USAID country profile property rights and resource governance*. Colombia Report.

USAID. (2017b). *USAID country profile property rights and resource governance*. Mexico Report.

Wood, D., Wilson, C., & García, A. (2014). *Fostering innovation in Mexico: Ideas from the high-level innovation forum for policymakers*. Woodrow Wilson International Center for Scholars/Fundación Idea.

World Bank. (2019). *Systematic country diagnostic*. WB Publishing. http://documentos.bancomundial.org/curated/es/588351544812277321/pdf/Mexico-Systematic-Country-Diagnostic.pdf

World Bank. (2020a). *Indicators*. https://data.worldbank.org/indicator/NY.GDP.MKTP.KD.ZG

World Bank. (2020b). *Mexico country profile*. https://www.worldbank.org/en/country/mexico/overviewBank,2020

Villavicencio, D. (2012, October 30). Cambios Institucionales y Espacios para la Investigacion Cientifica y la Innovacion en Mexico. In G. Valalenti (Ed.), *Ciencia, tecnología e innovación: Hacia una agenda de política pública* (p. 338). FLACSO.

World Integrated Trade Solution. (WITS). (2020a). *Colombia No. of exported HS6 digit products*. https://wits.worldbank.org/CountryProfile/en/Country/COL/StartYear/1991/EndYear/2018/TradeFlow/Export/Partner/ALL/Indicator/NMBR-XPRT-HS6-PRDCT, World Bank.

World Integrated Trade Solution (WITS). (2020b). *Mexico no of exported HS6 digit products*. https://wits.worldbank.org/CountryProfile/en/Country/MEX/StartYear/1991/EndYear/2018/TradeFlow/Export/Partner/BY-COUNTRY/Indicator/XPRT-PRTNR-SHR

WorldBank. (2020). *Data bank*. https://databank.worldbank.org/reports.aspx?source=2&series=NV.AGR.TOTL.ZS&country=#

World Intellectual Property Office (WIPO). (2020). Colombia. https://www.wipo.int/edocs/pubdocs/en/wipo_pub_gii_2019/co.pdf

Xicoténcatl, R., Ríos, J., & Gómez, E. (2020). Implementación de un modelo de triple hélice (universidad-empresa-gobierno) en la región sur del estado de jalisco (México) y su impacto en la organización del centro universitario del sur, de la universidad de Guadalajara. *Revista del Salomé, II* (2).

Zanello, G., Fu, X., Mohnen, P., & Ventresca, M. (2016). The creation and diffusion of innovation in developing countries: A systematic literature review. *Journal of Economic Surveys, 30*(5), 884–912.

Index

A

B

L. A. Orozco et al. (eds.), *Science, Technology, and Higher Education*, Palgrave Studies in Democracy, Innovation, and Entrepreneurship for Growth,
https://doi.org/10.1007/978-3-030-80720-7

C

The manufacturer's authorised representative in the EU is Springer
Nature Customer Service Centre GmbH, Europaplatz 3, 69115 Heidelberg,
Germany. If you have any concerns regarding our products, please
contact ProductSafety@springernature.com

Printed and bound by CPI Group (UK) Ltd, Croydon, CR0 4YY
30/09/2026
02225455-0017

